In the Image of God

In the Image of God

Religion, Moral Values, and Our Heritage of Slavery

David Brion Davis

Yale University Press/New Haven and London

Designed by Mary Valencia.
Set in Adobe Garamond type by Binghamton Valley
Composition, Binghamton, New York.
Printed in the United States of America by Vail-Ballou Press,
Binghamton, New York.

Library of Congress Cataloging-in-Publication Data
Davis, David Brion.
    In the image of God : religion, moral values, and our heritage
of slavery / David Brion Davis.
        p. cm.
    Includes bibliographical references and index.
    ISBN 0–300–08814–0 (alk. paper)
    1. Slavery. 2. Slavery—United States. 3. Slavery—Book
reviews. 4. Slave trade. 5. Slavery and Judaism. 6. Slavery
and Islam. 7. Religion and culture. I. Title.

HT871 .D28 2001
306.3'62'0973—dc21   2001033248

A catalogue record for this book is available from the British
    Library.

The paper in this book meets the guidelines for permanence
    and durability of the Committee on Production Guidelines
    for Book Longevity of the Council on Library Resources.

10 9 8 7 6 5 4 3 2 1

To Stanley L. Engerman, Michael Kammen, David Eltis, Orlando Patterson, Philip Morgan, Ira Berlin, John Stauffer, William W. Freehling, Robert William Fogel, Lewis C. Perry, Christopher Brown, Kenneth M. Stampp, Seymour Drescher, Jon Butler, James Brewer Stewart, and Robert Forbes

*So God created man in his own image, in the
image of God created he him; male and female
created he them.*

—Genesis 2:27

*Attendu que toute créature humaine qui est for-
mée à l'image de Notre-Seigneur doit générale-
ment être franche par droit naturel.*

*—Philippe the Fair, upon
freeing the serfs in Valois*

Contents

Introduction

The connections between what a historian chooses to write about and the winding path of his or her personal life are cloudy and obscure. Yet such connections obviously do exist. On May 5, 1988, at the age of sixty-one, I converted to Judaism after a year of required study and passing an oral examination given by three rabbis (a *Bet din*, or rabbinical court). In 1993 and 1994 I wrote several essays, some of them reprinted here, on American Jewish history, on Jews and the slave trade, and in 1999 on the complicated history of Jewish–black relations. One could easily attribute my choice of these subjects to my becoming Jewish. Yet my book *Slavery and Human Progress* (1984), published before I ever thought of becoming Jewish and before I ceased calling myself an "agnostic," contains a chapter, "Jews and the Children of Strangers," which analyzes the Jews' historical involvement with slavery.[1]

No doubt my change of religious identity, coupled with my historian's anger at the Nation of Islam's (not to be confused with genuine Islam) highly deceptive, anti-Semitic, and seemingly scholarly book of 1991, *The Secret Relationship Between Blacks and Jews, Volume One*, played a part in my attempt to set the record straight regarding one aspect of a subject, slavery, I had been studying and writing about for some thirty-three years. In a much deeper and more complex way, my interest in slavery and racism had long been linked with my decision as an undergraduate to major in philosophy, and with my subsequent interest in both religion and the history of moral values. Even Thucydides began his history with a theory of human nature.

Both my parents, with whom I had as an only child an unusually close relationship, were true agnostics. They were certainly not atheists, who take God so seriously that they angrily and confidently deny His existence. They were skeptics who had rejected their strict Christian upbringings, who doubted that a reasonable and responsible God could allow the appalling evils of their century, but who worshiped in their own way the incredible mystery and grandeur of our planet, cosmos, and existential being. I shall always remember seeing my thirty-three-year-old mother, when I was eleven, standing by the rocks near Carmel, California, where we lived for a year, gazing out to sea and experiencing a moment of spirituality, of communion, which washed over me with the power and timelessness of the waves beneath us. And when my mother suddenly died of a heart attack, at age forty-six, I felt, despite my total lack of religious training, that she had somehow achieved a state of "grace," of harmony with the world, during her last months or even years of life, when she was a professional painter. Even my father, in his tribute at her burial, referred to "Whatever unknowable immortality there may be, you still will live with us you leave, to the end of our days."

I too considered myself an agnostic, though I repeated those words when my father died ten years later. Much earlier, when I was drafted at age eighteen in the spring of 1945, I chose for my dog-tags the letter "N," signifying "Nothing," as opposed to the religious identities of "P" for Protestant, "C" for Catholic, and "H" for Hebrew. After initially treating the "signifying Nothing" as a joke taken from *King Lear*, even the memory of being "Nothing" began to prey upon me in some psychological way. And when my father died I found strange truth and reassurance in the lines from Blake that a close friend and colleague sent to me: "The ruins of time build mansions in eternity." The secret of human life, I began to suspect, lies in the illusion of time—or the illusion that time destroys everything that we regard as "past." Perhaps, I speculated, the past continues to exist even as we plunge on into new eras. As Reinhold Niebuhr has written:

Eternity stands over time on the one hand and at the end of time on the other. . . . It is not a separate order of existence. For this reason the traditional connotation of the concept, "supernatural," is erroneous. The eternal is the ground and source of the temporal. The divine consciousness gives meaning to the mere succession of natural events by comprehending them simultaneously, even as human consciousness gives meaning to segments of natural sequence by comprehending them simultaneously in memory and foresight.[2]

After being rigorously trained as an armored infantryman for the planned invasion of Japan in the fall of 1945 (with the Battle of Okinawa giving us a foretaste of what to expect), I was sent after the war unexpectedly ended for a year of "occupation" in the rubble of Germany. Then in February 1947 I began my three-and-a-half years of GI-Bill-funded college education at Dartmouth, a school my non-college educated parents had selected for me after they encountered Hanover's isolated beauty on a lovely summer day. Though revolted by the dominant fraternity culture (which involved heavy drinking and a blasé attitude toward study, and thus made it much easier for me to graduate in the class of 1950 *summa cum laude*),[3] I soon made contact with knowledgeable nonfraternity seniors who recommended the outstanding courses in philosophy, Dante, political theory, and comparative literature. I had originally intended to major in history and even become an academic historian, but I found that Dartmouth's history department was surprisingly weak and old-fashioned.

The single experience, however, that shaped the basis of my entire future career was Professor Francis Gramlich's charismatic lectures on changing views of "human nature." A Princeton-trained philosopher as well as a former army psychotherapist, Gramlich devoted much time to Freud as well as to the "dualisms" that extended from Plato and Descartes to Kant. Yet the capstone of the course, as in Perry Miller's year-long course on the history of religion in America, which I took a few years later as a graduate student at Harvard, was Reinhold Niebuhr's *Nature and Destiny of Man* (1941 and 1943), later supplemented by Niebuhr's *Irony of American History* (1952).

I was by no means alone in being intellectually and spiritually transformed by Niebuhr, who also gave spellbinding lectures at Dartmouth. His influence extended from Martin Luther King, Jr., Arthur M. Schlesinger, Jr., Felix Frankfurter, Hubert Humphrey, and Perry Miller to some of the pundits who later surrounded John F. Kennedy. Especially in view of Niebuhr's passionate attacks on pride and arrogance, I have often pondered the paradox of the blustering *Realpolitik* of some of his pretended followers.

In later years I came to perceive the weakness and oversimplification of some of the intellectual history in *The Nature and Destiny of Man*. Nevertheless, Niebuhr's central paradigm, which of course he borrowed in part from predecessors, continues to govern my thinking about human nature and history. Rejecting the numerous traditional dualisms of mind and body, soul and flesh, Niebuhr was above all open to evolutionary biology and to science in general. He expressed special hostility to the Christian views that locate sin in our sexual organs or our libidinal impulses to reproduce our genes. Yet for Niebuhr such ascetic, antimaterialist visions do point to the heart of our problem as human beings.

As evolved animals, Niebuhr argued, we are above all *finite*, temporal blobs of matter: cells, molecules, atoms (and today we might add, subatomic particles and "strings" for which an atom might be as immense as the solar system is for an atom). We grow from a fertilized egg into young men and young women, and then with luck we hurtle at seemingly accelerated speed into old age. That said, Niebuhr insisted, we are also self-conscious beings who *know* that we are finite. Even the rationalists, he argued, "do not always understand that man's rational capacity involves a further ability to stand outside himself, a capacity for self-transcendence, the ability to make himself his own object."[4] We not only know we will die, but can envision such death. We can study the cells and atoms of which we are made, and to update the argument, we can analyze our galaxy, antimatter, dark matter, black holes, other galaxies, and the Big Bang. No less important, we can imagine what it would be like to be someone else. We can even imagine a totally "other" Creator somewhere behind the Big Bang, within us, or accessible to us. We are, as Niebuhr put it, self-transcendent even in our finiteness.

Niebuhr succeeds, I think, in distinguishing this existential human dilemma from the many dualisms of the past. He does contend, however, that the tension between our self-transcendence and our finite reality creates an inevitable "anxiety," which is the source of all human sin. Thus to escape such anxiety many humans deny, at least temporarily, their capacity of self-transcendence and become immersed in a "sin of sensuality," a sensuality much intensified by repressed yearnings for infinitude and immortality. All animals love to mate and reproduce, but only humans become wholly obsessed with sex. And sin, according to Niebuhr, is "both unconscious and conscious."[5]

Much worse, other humans (one thinks especially of a Hitler, Stalin, or Mao) deny their human limits and finitude and carry "the sin of pride" to the point of self-deification, so that their own ends justify the most ghastly means. And ironically, Niebuhr points out, "the attempt to maintain one's own pride and self-respect by holding others in contempt adds an uneasy conscience to the general insecurity which the attitude of contempt is meant to alleviate."[6] Various religions have nourished this idolatry and sin of pride by feeding delusions of divine sanction, holy alliances, or the arrogance symbolized by the "Gott mit uns" logo on the belt buckles of German soldiers. The archetype of this sin of pride and contempt for others, I later concluded, was human slavery, especially racial slavery. Yet for Niebuhr the proper role of religion, which can be seen in Judaism and Christianity at their best, lay in the cultivation of humility and repentance—in the maintenance of a balance between the inspirations of self-transcendence and a sober acceptance of our finitude.

This perspective led Niebuhr in his youth to the position of a radical, socialist reformer (best expressed in his landmark book, *Moral Man and Immoral Society* [1932]). A full generation before the civil rights movement, he chaired as a minister an interracial committee to study the living conditions of Detroit's black population, and also attacked Henry Ford's "moral pretensions" as well as the greed and self-indulgence of American consumer culture. With World War II and the Cold War, he moved from socialism to become a leader of the more moderate but still left-wing Americans for Democratic Action, a liberal whose analysis of the illusions and brutal cruelties of communism proved to be on target and was more than balanced by his critique of American self-righteousness and his unqualified opposition, even when long debilitated by a stroke, to the Vietnam War.

If Niebuhr has remained a major influence on my own historical work— and one could say that my studies of homicide, slavery, and major historical shifts in moral perception have been ways of examining his "rediscovery" of sin—I also need to acknowledge the importance of William James and George Santayana, who at first glance seem to be as different from each other as each figure is from Reinhold Niebuhr. As an undergraduate at Dartmouth I wrote a long but mediocre paper (according to my father) on James's two-volume *Principles of Psychology* (1890). James's description of the stream of consciousness, coupled with *The Will to Believe* (1879) and his vivid accounts of "the varieties" of religious experience, seemed to link up, in my own mind at least, with Niebuhr's notion of self-transcendence and with Santayana's *Realm of Spirit* (1940). "Spirit," for Santayana, "is not an ether or a fluid coursing through space, but a moral focus of recollection, discrimination, and judgment";[7] I also read with enthusiasm most of Santayana's other works, to say nothing of Emerson and Thoreau (the founders, one might argue, of "the genteel tradition," which Santayana later found "at bay").

Perhaps as a result of this background, I became increasingly dissatisfied as a student in Harvard's History of American Civilization program with the kind of intellectual history that traces the flow, convergence, and succession of many "isms"—such as rationalism, nominalism, neo-classicism, romanticism, and naturalism. Especially as I became more aware of the anthropologists and other social scientist of the 1950s, particularly Talcott Parsons, the Kluckhohns, John Dollard, Erich Fromm, and David Riesman, I became taken by the notion of studying concrete human *problems* as a way of tracing, within social and cultural frameworks, broad shifts in beliefs, moral values, assumptions, and ideologies. Thus after being forced at Harvard to abandon a proposed dissertation on the literary and artistic responses to the new cities of the 1890s and early 1900s (because my project seemed too close to that of another student, who then dropped out), I turned to homicide as a universal human "problem," with clear Niebuhrian dimensions. Whether one looks at a murder, duel, or official execution, there is no more dramatic way of asserting a kind of godly self-transcendence than by *proving*, through killing, the finitude of another human being. Though I originally planned an interdisciplinary study of criminal trials, changes in American state and national criminal laws, the insanity plea, literary and pamphlet treatments of homicide, and capital punishment, my personal need to begin and complete a dissertation in one year forced me to concentrate on homicide in American fiction from 1798 to 1860, with "background" sections on such subjects as legal views of insanity and responsibility.[8]

In the spring term of 1955, while completing my dissertation and before taking a full-time teaching position at Cornell in the fall, I had the immense good fortune to become acquainted with Kenneth Stampp, who was then a visiting professor at Harvard on leave from Berkeley. Stampp was finishing his groundbreaking book, *The Peculiar Institution*, the first full-scale challenge to Ulrich B. Phillips's unapologetically racist but deeply researched *American Negro Slavery* (1918).

In the early to mid-1950s Phillips's book was still the standard work on the subject and appeared on course syllabi at Harvard and other leading universities. Though his book still contains useful information gathered from a wide range of plantation records, Phillips frankly affirmed that blacks were inferior to whites and that southern slavery had been a benign civilizing force for "easy-going, amiable . . . sturdy light-hearted" savages from Africa.[9] This had been the message conveyed by popular films like *Gone with the Wind* (1939) as well as by popular books like W. E. Woodward's *New American*

History (1936), which affirmed that slavery "served as a vast training school for African savages. Though the regime of the slave plantation was strict it was, on the whole, a kindly one by comparison with what the imported slave had experienced in his own land. It taught him discipline, cleanliness and a conception of moral standards."[10] While my parents esteemed this Woodward book because of its liberal, Beard-like approach to American history, I have no idea how they responded to these pages on slavery.[11]

Only after long talks with Kenneth Stampp did I begin to realize how the crucial subject of racial slavery had been repressed and marginalized in my courses at both Dartmouth and Harvard. Indeed, in 1953–1954 I had taken a year's leave from Harvard Graduate School in order to accept a Ford Foundation teaching internship at Dartmouth. This proved to be an invaluable experience, but one of my mentors, a seasoned professor of American history, maligned Radical Reconstruction and presented the Ku Klux Klan as a harmless group that used humorous tricks and devices to "put the Negro in his proper place." In the early twenty-first century it is so difficult to recapture the consensual white views on slavery and race in the 1940s and 1950s that I have begun several public lectures with the startling and defensible affirmation that in terms of ideology regarding race, the South won the Civil War.[12]

Yet by the 1950s I could not have been more excited by the importance of Kenneth Stampp's work on slavery, based on the bedrock assumption that blacks were inherently equal to whites.[13] By 1955 I was already familiar with Gunnar Myrdal's *American Dilemma: The Negro Problem and Modern Democracy* (1944) as well as the shocking report published by President Truman's Committee on Civil Rights, *To Secure These Rights* (1947).

Far more important, the segregated army of World War II had exposed me to the kind of raw racism that had led to thousands of lynchings, repeated antiblack race riots, and continuing opposition, even during the New Deal, to effective antilynching legislation. Trained for the invasion of Japan at Ulrich Phillips's Camp Gordon, near Augusta, Georgia, I had seen the Jim Crow segregated South at its worst and had mixed with southern white soldiers who spoke of blacks with savage contempt, yet boasted that you didn't know what sex could mean unless you had "laid" a young black "wench." Then on board the S.S. *Argentina*, commandeered for transporting troops to Europe, I had been ordered while still seasick to descend with a billy club to the lowest hold in the ship, "to keep the Niggers from gambling." I had not even realized that there were black troops on board. But after winding down many circular, ladder-like stairways, I came upon a scene I have always remembered as a modern slave ship. Hundreds—it seemed like thousands—of nearly naked black men were crushed into a hot, fetid space. Many of them were seeking a bit of relief and entertainment by shooting craps. When asked, "White boy, what ya doin' down here?" I mumbled something about orders and sought a shadow in which to hide for the four hours or so of "guard duty." Once in Germany, as a member of the Security Police and then the U.S. Constabulary, I was witness to a bloody racial shootout and to a white major-general who kept assuring us that the "niggers" were a much bigger problem to deal with than the Germans.[14]

Nearly nine years later, after attending Dartmouth, working in an airplane factory for a year, and spending three years at Harvard (in addition to the one-year faculty internship at Dartmouth), I was teaching my first year at Cornell, in 1955–1956, and attempting to revise my dissertation to meet the demands of the Harvard historian Frederick Merk (the thesis had already been accepted by my major adviser, Howard Mumford Jones). Though I have never again had such a trying and difficult year, Professor Merk's proposed revisions fortunately made the manuscript publishable in the eyes of Cornell University Press, which brought me the security of tenure in 1958. So with a book quickly on the way to publication, I discovered that Cornell's library contained an immense collection of American and especially British antislavery writings. This elicited the dream of doing for antislavery what Kenneth Stampp had done for American slavery. But as matters developed, I found that to understand antislavery I needed to learn a great deal more about related reform movements to say nothing of slavery itself. I have long been firmly convinced that any serious student of the abolitionist movements must learn as much as possible about the diversities of human bondage itself.[15]

The central questions that fascinated me, in light of a Niebuhrian and Santayanan view of history, were why slavery evoked virtually no moral protest in a wide range of cultures for literally thousands of years. And what contributed to a profound shift in moral vision by the mid- to late eighteenth century, and to powerful Anglo-American abolitionist movements thereafter? The latter question acquired even more importance in view of the broad consensus that New World slavery was not declining economically, that its abolition was not the result of what Seymour Drescher has termed "econocide."[16]

The word *slavery* can mean many things. For example, we can be "enslaved" to love, alcohol, drugs, or our work. But despite the amazingly late appearance of the first attacks on the institution, the term has almost always had negative connotations. Hence the repeated use in the King James Bible of "servant" or "maidservant" when the Hebrew or Greek words clearly meant "slave," to say nothing of the desire of some Southerners to find more neutral euphemisms for slavery, such as "warranteeism." "Slave," unlike "servant," has almost always referred to the most degrading, humiliating, dehumanizing condition a human being can suffer. In the 1770s American colonial rebels repeatedly exclaimed that they were fighting a war for independence because the English were determined to "enslave" them. When a typical Englishman of 1600 thought of "slavery," he or she pictured the thousands of English sailors whom the Moors of the Mediterranean had captured and converted into galley-slaves. According to Rousseau, "Man is born free, and everywhere he is in chains." And as Frederick Douglass summed up the actual experience of being "broken in body, soul, and spirit" by the "Negro-breaker" Edward Covey: "My natural elasticity was crushed, my intellect languished, the disposition to read departed, the cheerful spark that lingered about my eye died; the dark night of slavery closed in upon me; and behold a man transformed into a brute!"[17]

Douglass's testimony shows how enslavers have sought above all to extinguish or deny a person's capacity for self-transcendence, which Niebuhr identified as the essence of being human. The *ideal* slave, as both Aristotle and Frederick Douglass affirmed, would be a wholly finite person, a mere "instrument" of his or her master's will. From Dio Chrysostom to Thomas Hobbes and John Locke, philosophers perceived enslavement as a substitute for killing prisoners of war. "The killer literally reduces a human being into a non-being," as I have written elsewhere, "removed from the flow of time. The enslaver reduces a human being to a state of 'social death,' to use Orlando Patterson's phrase, in which the captive is defined as an object, a thing without history."[18] If enslavement was originally modeled on the domestication of beasts of burden, as I suggest in "At the Heart of Slavery" in this book, and if humans had really been genetically transformed into the kind of "natural slaves" Aristotle envisioned, they would have been incapable not only of reflection and analytical thought, but also of Niebuhrian sin.

Ironically, the Hebrew (*'ebd*), Greek (*doulos*), and Latin (*servus*) words for "slave" carried no ethnic connotations, and were sometimes used for "servant" (but a great many nineteenth-century Southerners also called their slaves "servants"). Yet the Western European words *slave, esclave, sklave, esclavo* all derive from the Latin term for "Slav" (*esclavus*), since beginning in the tenth century a disproportionate number of slaves were taken from the Balkans and then from the thirteenth to the late fifteenth centuries from the Caucasus and Black Sea Region. As early as 1430, Sicilian notaries began distinguishing black slaves (*sclavi nigri*, or "black Slavs") as a category separate from "black Saracens."[19] Much as the Arabic word for slave, '*abd*, had come to mean in some regions *only* black slaves or even free blacks, the Portuguese, Spanish, French, and English words for "black" (i.e., *Negro, nègre*) came to be synonyms for "slave" as Europeans purchased increasing numbers of Africans along the west coast of Africa and then transported them to work in the New World.

I was extremely fortunate to publish the first edition of *The Problem of Slavery in Western Culture* in 1966, a time when the civil rights movement was beginning to stimulate a reexamination of the very foundations upon which New World societies and economies were built. Although Frank Tannenbaum and Stanley Elkins had written pioneering comparative works that helped to lift the subject of slavery to a more global level, most teachers of American history continued to regard "Negro slavery" as a branch of local southern history. It was only in 1969 with Philip Curtin's first serious effort to compile an accurate "census" of the entire Atlantic slave trade that an increasing number of historians began to grasp the intercontinental breadth and importance of the subject.[20]

In the 1960s, however, I had no intention of devoting my entire scholarly career to the issue of slavery. I was employed at Cornell to teach "American intellectual history" (along with the traditional American history survey course); in 1969 Yale also hired me as an "American intellectual historian," who happened to write about slavery and antislavery as examples of largely intellectual and cultural change. Thus I faced an uncomfortable gap, during much of my career, between my research and writing on topics connected with slavery and race, and my teaching about such figures as Jonathan Edwards, Emerson and the Transcendentalists, William James, and the early Progressives—mostly figures who aspired to find ways of marshaling our human capacity for self-transcendence to create a happier and fairer world.

But since I have always taken a negative view of "schools" of scholars following in the tracks of some idolized mentor, I am happy to say that very few of the sixty doctoral dissertations I have directed have had anything to do with slavery or antislavery, though a recent and outstanding festschrift, which is the most gratifying honor a teacher can receive, shows that most of my students *have* addressed moral problems of enormous diversity.[21]

As my own essays in this volume indicate, I have tried to maintain a variety of interests even as my own teaching and writing have become increasingly devoted to "the problem of slavery"—to reaching a wider public in my attempt to convey some sense of the big picture regarding the place of New World slavery in creating the modern world. For the past seven summers, thanks to the aid of Richard Gilder and Lewis Lehrman, I have taught an intensive course for New York City high-school and middle-school teachers on the origins and significance of New World slavery.[22] Since 1998 I have also served as director of Yale's Gilder Lehrman Center for the Study of Slavery, Resistance, and Abolition. Yet as I look back over the essays I have written since the early 1980s—that is, since the publication in 1986 of a collection of earlier essays in *From Homicide to Slavery*—I see that religion stands as the base or foundation, leading on to questions of moral values and then to our legacy of African-American slavery. The following essays are thus divided thematically, not chronologically.

Most but not all of the essays in this book are essay-reviews, that is, reflections and commentaries on subjects suggested by the reading of one or more books. This format, encouraged by such journals as the *New Republic*, the *New York Review of Books*, and the *Times Literary Supplement*, must be distinguished from short book reviews that summarize and evaluate a given publication. Many of my essays do summarize and evaluate books, but I also try to provide historical context and bring out new perspectives and connections. Thus in the final essay of this book, "The Other Revolution," I draw on several new works to show that early feminism, an offshoot of antislavery in the United States, was really transatlantic in character and, in terms of the grand sweep of human history, marked the beginning of "the revolution of all revolutions," the movement for full gender equality.

One of the many delights of an academic profession springs from the need to read, to "keep up" on new discoveries or new trends in at least several fields of scholarship. If one is fortunate enough to be asked to reflect on the meaning of some of these books, one has a written record of personal discovery, of changed assumptions and perspectives, and of attempts to synthesize the new with the known or thought-to-be-known. I hope that readers, especially non-academics, will find some illumination in this series of commentaries that moves from religion and slavery to race, the American Dilemma, and the feminist revolution.

Part I, "From Religion to Slavery," begins with a commentary on Richard Fox's biography of Reinhold Niebuhr, whose profound influence on me in the late 1940s and 1950s I have already discussed. I then move to David J. Garrow's Pulitzer-Prize-winning biography of Martin Luther King, Jr., who was much devoted to Niebuhr and who can be said to have put Niebuhr's more radical theology into action. After surveying certain aspects of religion in American culture, in the three-volume *Encyclopedia of American Religion*, I turn to detailed overviews of American Jewish history that raise crucial questions about ethnic-religious success, assimilation, and "the meritocratic experiment," questions which now challenge the widespread belief in proportional representation—the desire for political and professional bodies "that look like America." Should the number of Jewish doctors and law professors, for example, be limited to something like 2.5 percent—the proportion of Jews in the national population? I then move on to "The Slave Trade and the Jews" and to a historical analysis of "Jews and Blacks in America."

In Part II I consider two highly respected and influential historians who also happened to be good friends: C. Vann Woodward, who was responsible for my coming to Yale; and Eugene D. Genovese, with whom I shared a year, during his Marxist phase, at Stanford's Center for Advanced Study in the Behavioral Sciences. This was a time, 1972–1973, when we read and criticized each other's work and also organized a small discussion group on "dominance and submission."

Part III, "Origins," moves from an essay, "At the Heart of Slavery," which among other things suggests that slavery may originally have been modeled on the domestication of beasts of burden, to medieval Islamic slavery, and to the Atlantic slave trade and making of New World slavery. Then an essay on the divisive and formative 1790s, prompted by Stanley Elkins and Eric McKitrick's magnificent but highly selective book, *The Age of Federalism*, ponders the authors' seeming blindness to the impact on slavery of Alexander Hamilton's vision of a new, non-slave-based economy, to say nothing of the French and Haitian Revolutions, and the period of crucial transformation of the center of the Atlantic slave system from Brazil to the new American republic. An essay on the significance of the Northwest Ordinance of 1787, excluding slavery from the Old Northwest, is followed by discussions of the repudiation of Eric Williams's economic determinism, in explaining the early triumph of British abolitionism, and an analysis of the contrary arguments of such economists and historians as David Eltis, Stanley L. Engerman, and Seymour Drescher.

In Part IV, "The Violence of Slavery as Experienced," we turn from somewhat abstract theorizing to "The White World of Frederick Douglass" to the stunning story of Celia, a coerced slave mistress of a Missouri farmer who finally resorted to murdering her owner as the only alternative to sexual exploitation; and to the critical *Amistad* affair, long neglected or oversimplified by historians, in which a southern-dominated U.S. Supreme Court *seemed* to legitimate a slave uprising at sea, or more accurately, the right of African captives, who had been illegally enslaved and transported to Cuba, to kill their white oppressors.

The vulnerability and armed defense of New World slavery is illustrated by John Stedman's account of guerrilla warfare against the maroons, or escaped slaves, of Suriname, and also by Robin Blackburn's magisterial description of "the overthrow" of colonial slavery in the Western Hemisphere. Yet by the 1850s, as Brenda Stevenson shows in her intensive study of a Virginia county, not only had slavery flourished as the result of the sale of young slaves to the Lower Mississippi Valley, but an increasingly destructive racism had reduced the free black population to the status, to use Ira Berlin's phrase, of "slaves without masters." Part IV ends with an essay, "Terror in Mississippi," based on Winthrop Jordan's impressive detective-like research on a locally and nationally repressed slave conspiracy in Madison County, Mississippi, early in the Civil War. Jordan's discoveries point to the ability of slaveholders to destroy most of the traces of planned slave rebellions.

Finally, in Part V we turn to the construction and meaning of "race" in early modern Europe, moving from the first ambivalent and superficial depictions of Africans to the national American racism Abraham Lincoln faced when he ran in 1858 against Stephen Douglas for the U.S. Senate. These two essays on the historical construction and use of racism introduce and comment on special collections of articles in the *William and Mary Quarterly* and the *Journal of the Early Republic*. In "The American Dilemma," a phrase Gunnar Myrdal famously used as a title for his survey of American racism in 1944, I examine two modern works on the legacy of slavery: Andrew Hacker's *Two Nations: Black and White, Separate, Hostile, Unequal* and Jacqueline Jones's *Dispossessed*, a study of the black underclass. In "The Other Revolution" I turn to one of the offshoots of abolitionism in America, the movement for full gender equality, which was really transatlantic and multinational in character. Yet even in France, England, and other European countries where early feminism was often tied to various forms of socialism, married women increasingly likened their condition to that of Negro slaves.

Notes

1. (Oxford University Press, 1984), pp. 82–101.
2. Reinhold Niebuhr, *The Nature and Destiny of Man: A Christian Interpretation*, one-volume edition (Charles Scribner's Sons, 1948), part II, p. 299.
3. I was able to earn enough credits to graduate in three and a half years by attending Columbia University summer school in 1948 and by taking six courses in one semester at Dartmouth.
4. Ibid., part I, 4.
5. Ibid., part I, 250.
6. Ibid.
7. *The Realm of Spirit* (Charles Scribner's Sons, 1940), p. 9.
8. My dissertation, written in 1954–1955, was published by Cornell University Press in 1957 as *Homicide in American Fiction, 1798–1860: A Study in Social Values* (paperback edition, 1968).
9. Phillips used these terms to describe both slaves and the segregated black troops at Camp Gordon, Georgia, in World War I: "The negroes themselves show the same easy-going, amiable, serio-comic obedience and the same personal attachments to white men, as well as the same sturdy light-heartedness and the same love of laughter and of rhythm, which distinguished their forbears" (*American Negro Slavery: A Survey of the Supply Employment and Control of Negro Labor as Determined by the Plantation Régime* [Peter Smith reprint, 1959], p. viii).
10. W. E. Woodward, *A New American History* (Farrar & Rinehart, 1936), p. 412. For a fuller discussion of these matters, see my "Slavery, and the Post–World War II Historians," in Davis, *From Homicide to Slavery: Studies in American Culture* (Oxford University Press, 1986), pp. 187–206.
11. Phillips, it should be noted, was a disciple of Frederick Jackson Turner, and the "Progressive" approach of Turner, Charles Beard, and Vernon Louis Parrington was by no means incompatible with a white supremacist view of slavery, the Civil War, and Reconstruction.
12. Of course there were dissenting works by African-American historians such as W. E. B. Du Bois, and white communists, such as Herbert Aptheker. In many ways the *Journal of Negro History* provided a foundation for the major reexaminations of slavery, the Civil War, and Reconstruction in the late 1960s and 1970s. On the other hand, it is revealing that Frederick Douglass's classic *Narrative* was out of print from 1850 until 1960.
13. Ironically, Stampp evoked a barrage of criticism, especially from black nationalists, for the rather naïve way he affirmed racial equality in his preface: "I have assumed that the slaves were merely ordinary human beings, that innately Negroes *are*, after all, only white men with black skins, nothing more, nothing less." Critics ignored his related statement, which in effect set the scholarly agenda for at least the next half-century: "I

firmly believe that one must know what slavery meant to the Negro and how he reacted to it before one can comprehend his more recent tribulations" (*The Peculiar Institution: Slavery in the Ante-Bellum South* [Knopf, 1956], p. vii).

14. For a fuller account of my experiences with racism and racial conflict in the American
army, see my "World War II and Memory," *Journal of American History*, 77, no. 2
(September 1990), pp. 380–387, and "The Americanized Mannheim of 1945–1946,"
in *American Places: Encounters with History*, ed. William E. Leuchtenberg (Oxford University Press, 2000), pp. 79–91.

15. After winning a Guggenheim Fellowship for 1958–1959, I and my family moved to
England for a half-year of research. Overwhelmed by the immense range of sources and
the expansion of my project, I became deeply indebted to the late Carl Bridenbaugh,
who was also on leave, working in the old British Museum, and eager to share lunches
in a nearby pub. Relaxed and in good spirits, he kept stressing that since I'd just won
tenure at Cornell, I should not worry about taking many years for a much enlarged
research project (*The Problem of Slavery in Western Culture*). The very purpose of tenure, Carl kept reassuring me, was to liberate scholars from the pressures of "publish
(often and quickly) or perish."

16. See his book, *Econocide: British Slavery in the Era of Abolition* (University of Pittsburgh
Press, 1977), and his *Capitalism and Antislavery: British Mobilization in Comparative
Perspective* (Oxford University Press, 1987), as well as the Nobel Laureate Robert William Fogel's *Without Consent or Contract: The Rise and Fall of American Slavery* (Norton, 1989).

17. From Douglass's *Narrative of the Life of Frederick Douglass, An American Slave* (1845),
quoted in Steven Mintz, *African American Voices: The Life Cycle of Slavery* (Brandywine
Press, 1993), p. 129.

18. Davis, *From Homicide to Slavery*, p. vii.

19. *Slavery and Human Progress*, p. 56.

20. Curtin, *The Atlantic Slave Trade: A Census* (University of Wisconsin Press, 1969). Even
W. E. B. Du Bois's classic work of the 1890s, *The Suppression of the African Slave-Trade
to the United States of America, 1638–1870* (Social Science Press reprint, 1954), was
limited to the United States, a region which we now know absorbed no more than 5
or 6 percent of the African slaves brought to the New World.

21. See Karen Halttunen and Lewis Perry, eds., *Moral Problems in American Life: New Perspectives on Cultural History* (Cornell University Press, 1998). The fourteen superb essays in this volume, written by seven women and seven men, show certain surprising
continuities and common concerns despite their diversity and range from seventeenth-
century England to late twentieth-century America.

22. The summer course for teachers led me to develop a larger-scale undergraduate course
which I describe in an "AHA *Forum*: Looking at Slavery from Broader Perspectives,"
American Historical Review, 105, no. 2 (April 2000), pp. 452–466. I am now in the
process of converting the lectures from this course into a book for general readers on
the rise and fall of slavery in the New World.

Part I

From Religion to Slavery

1

Reinhold Niebuhr: An American Jeremiah

Reinhold Niebuhr: A Biography
Richard Wightman Fox (1986)

Reinhold Niebuhr, who died in 1971, is little known among the rising generation of young intellectuals. Despite the renewed interest in religion at American colleges and universities, it is difficult today to imagine a charismatic Protestant preacher electrifying students and faculty on all the major campuses, influencing statesmen and reformers, and commanding respect, even among agnostics and non-Christians, as one of the leading intellects and social critics of the century. At a time when American culture is ominously divided between fundamentalists and secular humanists, it is difficult to recapture Niebuhr's remarkable presence from the 1930s to the 1960s, decades that were supposedly dominated by science and secularization. How can one explain Niebuhr's close ties with such figures as Felix Frankfurter, W. H. Auden, Lewis Mumford, Lionel Trilling, Perry Miller, Hubert Humphrey, and Arthur Schlesinger, Jr.? Did Niebuhr, who could admire the antics of an evangelist like Billy Sunday and yet disavow supernaturalism and any belief in personal immortality, leave us clues for narrowing the cultural rift in our country as we hurtle on into the twenty-first century?

Niebuhr's father was a German immigrant, a minister of the German Evangelical Synod in Illinois. Like his father, Niebuhr prepared for the ministry at Eden Theological Seminary, but then went on to study at Yale Divinity

School, where he struggled to free himself from his provincial German-American heritage. In 1915, when he was twenty-three, he became pastor of a congregation in suburban Detroit. There he acquired increasing prominence as a dynamic preacher and social critic, attacking the moral complacency of the 1920s, the labor policies of the Ford Motor Company, and the racism of the Ku Klux Klan. Niebuhr first became involved in politics when the mayor of Detroit appointed him chairman of an interracial committee to study the living conditions of the city's black population. By 1928, when Niebuhr accepted an associate professorship at Union Theological Seminary, in New York, he was already a socialist and a leading spokesman for left-wing Protestants. As Niebuhr continued to search for an effective Christian approach to the national and international crises of the 1930s, he confirmed his position as a brilliant expounder and interpreter of the American jeremiad.

The American jeremiad, as Sacvan Bercovitch has defined it, is "a mode of public exhortation . . . designed to join social criticism to spiritual renewal."[1] This kind of preaching, largely derived from the Old Testament prophets, originated in Europe but was transformed by the New England Puritans to meet the ideological needs of a people commissioned by God to build a new Jerusalem in the wilderness. As Bercovitch demonstrates, the jeremiad sermon became a vehicle for denouncing the sins of the day while reaffirming America's historical mission. The abominations of a backsliding generation, which deserved God's severest chastisement, provided the occasion for lamentation, repentance, and renewal of purpose. The worse the crisis, the greater the assurance that Americans could withstand any trial and fulfill their "errand into the wilderness."

The jeremiad rhetoric could sustain the myth of America's special mission only by addressing specific sins and such afflictions as King Philip's War, the revocation of the Massachusetts charter, and the conspiracies of papists and savages. Judgment of the society from a transcendent point outside history served to validate or even sanctify the direction of historical change.

Niebuhr himself became an astute critic of the ways in which the Puritans' vision of "new heavens and a new earth" became secularized and nationalized. By the time of the American Revolution, to use Niebuhr's example, Ezra Stiles, the president of Yale College, could preach a sermon on "'The United States elevated to glory and honor' in which he defined the nation as 'God's American Israel.'"[2] On the surface it might appear that Niebuhr offered the long-sought antidote to traditional pretensions of American exceptionalism and national mission. He repeatedly attacked every attempt to claim divine sanction for America's goals and struggles. According to Niebuhr, every nation in history has committed the fatal sin of confusing its own partial and finite interests with the objective of God or some immanent divine force. The Hebrew prophet Amos, whom Niebuhr took as a model, showed that "Israel's special mission gives it no special security in history. On the contrary it is the assumption that is has a special security and can count upon a special divine favor, which represents the corruption of pride which must be punished."[3]

But as this passage suggests, Niebuhr did not deny the possibility of a nation's historical mission; he simply denied that any nation could expect favored treatment in history or equate its own finite interests with "the destiny of man." Niebuhr found the "natural" ground for revelation in man's capacity to transcend himself sufficiently "to know that he cannot be the center of his own existence and that his nation, culture or civilization cannot be the end of history."[4] But Niebuhr qualified this insistence on God's inscrutability and otherness when he affirmed his faith in the possibilities of unrestricted moral progress in history. When traveling in Germany in 1930 he sadly concluded that the followers of Karl Barth looked for salvation "above the area of history" because they lived in an "old nation" that had suffered repeated defeats. In effect, he purged the jeremiad of "false optimism" and "liberal illusions"; but the very fervor and urgency of his prophetic judgments reinvigorated the idea of American possibilities.

The key to Niebuhr's influence was his ability to modernize the jeremiad during the decades when a growing number of college-educated intellectuals were acquiring new power in government, the press, the universities, and religious establishments. Beginning in the 1920s, when there was increasing cynicism over the political idealism exemplified by Woodrow Wilson and the industrial paternalism exemplified by Henry Ford, Niebuhr showed how tough-minded realism could expose the hollowness of official pieties without sacrificing a belief in man's limited but godlike capacity for self-transcendence. If we look at Niebuhr's many jeremiads between 1925 and 1965, we find that he exuberantly denounced the "moral pretensions" of Henry Ford, the "paganism of pleasure" of southern California, the self-indulgence of America's consumer culture, the sentimentalism of pacifists, the arrogance of modern science, and the "strategy of hate" of the Communists.

No Puritan minister surpassed Niebuhr in devising a comprehensive taxonomy of sin, which for Niebuhr was occasioned, though not caused, by man's existential "situation" of finiteness and freedom. If sin was inevitable, it was always the result of human choice and took different forms in different societies. Greed, for example, had become "the besetting sin of a bourgeois culture"; Americans had also been prone to the spiritual pride fostered by illusions of innocence, virtue, and omnipotence. While Niebuhr's thought moved through radical and conservative phases, he always sought to tame, chasten, and purify the American liberal tradition. This effort to recover an authentic American mission appealed to Henry Luce and Whittaker Chambers as well as to Martin Luther King, Jr., and President Kennedy's New Frontiersmen.

Richard Wightman Fox encountered both the liberal and conservative legacies of Niebuhr's thought in the mid-1960s when he was an undergraduate at Stanford and took courses from two "devoted Niebuhrians," Robert McAfee Brown and Michael Novak.[5] Niebuhr's delight in irony and paradox left an enduring imprint on postwar historians who were rejecting the "progressive" approach to American history. Radical historians of Fox's generation have a special need to recover "the historical Reinhold," as Fox puts it. The dogma that "sin corrupts the highest as well as the lowest achievements of human life" may be both jarring and instructive for some of them. Niebuhr himself remained an inveterate reformer and an outspoken critic of social injustice. But his theology also sanctioned an acceptance of evil, and it could have a chilling effect on hopes for human betterment. Moreover, Fox points out the limitations of Niebuhr's social and political criticism, which created the illusion of fearless inquiry and openmindedness. Yet Niebuhr helped to forge the ideological armor that in effect shielded the prevailing official premises in America at the beginning of the cold war from criticism.

Fox finds Niebuhrian irony in some of Niebuhr's own responses to events. After the bombing of Hiroshima, Niebuhr signed with twenty-two other theologians a statement that "we have sinned grievously against the law of God and against the people of Japan." But in a letter to James B. Conant, Niebuhr wrote that "the eventual use of the bomb for the shortening of the war would have been justified. I myself consistently took the position that failing in achieving a Japanese surrender, the bomb would have had to be used to save the lives of thousands of American soldiers who would otherwise have perished on the beaches of Japan." According to Fox, Niebuhr "took for granted that only unconditional surrender was acceptable. That perceived necessity made the bomb the weapon of choice. It was the quintessential revelation of 'how much evil we must do in order to do good,' of how much guilt accrues even to those who have 'defeated tyranny.'" Still, he also wrote in a magazine article about the "moral advantage" the United States would have gained by first demonstrating the power of the bomb "without the wholesale loss of life."

Niebuhr endorsed the execution of the Rosenbergs, but later said, Fox writes, that it was a "moral" as well as a "political" mistake. During the McCarthy years, he was, Fox concludes,

> caught up in a web of contradictions, unaware of his own part in creating the atmosphere of suspicion that he bemoaned. Ironies proliferated: while one organ of the federal government ran his alarmist message on the Communist threat, another held up his wife's citizenship because of the heightened fear of subversion.

Fox's biography comes as close to being comprehensive as we are likely to see in an imperfect, Niebuhrian world. Based on meticulous research which includes numerous interviews and a declassified FBI file, the book is written with a verve, grace, and depth of understanding worthy of its subject. Fox is remarkably successful in fusing criticism with sympathetic appreciation and in relating Niebuhr's evolving thought to his public career and private self-scrutiny. He also recaptures Niebuhr's frenetic pace of life as he churned out articles and crisscrossed the country, lecturing with a packed suitcase beside the podium. Anyone who heard Niebuhr speak will confirm the accuracy of Fox's descriptions:

> One did not merely listen to Niebuhr: one watched him strut, gyrate, jerk, bend, and quake. He whirled his arms, rubbed his ears and his balding scalp, stretched his hawkish nose forward. His whole lanky frame was in motion. One did not merely listen to Niebuhr: to catch the stream-of-consciousness flow of analysis and anecdote—sometimes shouted, sometimes whispered, but always at the velocity of an undammed flood—demanded a concentration that few could sustain during an entire sermon.

Fox is fully aware that Niebuhr was addressing from two perspectives the most critical issues of his time. Believing that man cannot escape from history or social responsibility, he became an ardent advocate of causes: he wanted to make capitalism democratic, to fight racism and anti-Semitism, to support the Allies' struggle against Nazi Germany. He demanded the admission of Jewish refugees to the United States, defended Israel, wanted to protect Western Europe from communism, and opposed America's involvement in the Vietnam War. Fox shows how Niebuhr's response to such issues illuminated the intellectual history of an entire era.

But for Niebuhr the most urgent political needs could never be separated from timeless questions of freedom, guilt, divine judgment, and the meaning of history. It is extremely difficult to describe the dialectical tension Niebuhr discovered between immediate political crises and the crisis we all face when we confront eternity. Fox presents a masterly account of the continuities and disjunctions in Niebuhr's thought. He is less successful in conveying the power and profundity of Niebuhr's best work, especially *The Nature and Destiny of Man*, published in 1941 and 1943. Fox devotes more space to the criticisms of Robert Calhoun, a Yale theologian, than to Niebuhr's trenchant analysis of man's attempt to overcome his inherent insecurity by a will-to-power or an escape from freedom. It is less important that Niebuhr presented a mistaken and oversimplified view of the Renaissance than that he made a convincing case for the doctrine of original sin and suggested a way to conceive life's relation to eternity without retreating into mysticism or a belief in supernatural salvation.

But Niebuhr himself would have to admire Fox's use of a Niebuhrian method to expose Niebuhr's own internal conflict between the roles of celebrity and prophet. "Reinie," as his friends knew him, always hungered for influence and acceptance as a 100 percent American. Even before the United States entered the First World War, he was proud to repudiate his own past by writing an article for *The Atlantic* called "The Failure of German-Americanism." He courted the honors he received, which included a Medal of Freedom bestowed by President Johnson. He gladly denounced communism for *Life* and *Look* and was not averse to appearing on the cover of *Time*'s twenty-fifth anniversary issue. Late in life he confessed, "I am scared by my own lack of patriotism," when he took satisfaction in America's embarrassments in the "fantastic war" in Vietnam.

Niebuhr was also painfully conscious of the dangers of playing pundit. As Fox points out, his insights into the sin of pride and its many disguises arose from his own internal struggles. At Yale Divinity School, where he felt like "a mongrel among thoroughbreds," Niebuhr found little satisfaction in scholarship. He was too restless and impatient to become a scholar or systematic theologian, although he taught for decades at Union Theological Seminary and declined prestigious chairs at Harvard and Yale. Niebuhr was sensitive both to the inadequacies of his historical knowledge and to the ego-inflating hazards of his public role. He knew very well that he never achieved the humility and independence for which he yearned, and it was this inner tension that made him such a powerful figure.

Fox seems especially drawn to the militant Niebuhr of the early 1930s. In a brilliant paragraph he imagines how the author of *Moral Man and Immoral Society* (1932) would have reviewed *The Children of Light and the Children of Darkness* (1944). The younger Niebuhr, a prominent figure in the Socialist party and the leading spokesman of radical Christianity, "would have scoffed [at the latter book's] confidence in justice through adjustment, its belief that the debates of the 'open society' operated equally in the interests of all." Fox admits that such objections could probably have been met "by a skilled New Deal apologist," but finds it especially troubling that the older Niebuhr felt no need to consider that

> even a democratic society of apparently total openness operated ideologically: its respected intellectuals as well as its ordinary citizens ignored or dismissed potential challenges to its preferred self-images. As the younger Niebuhr had insisted, reason was always the servant of interest in a social situation.

At the depth of the Depression the younger Niebuhr scorned the sentimentality of reformers who relied on the power of reason, ideals, or goodwill. In the name of Protestantism, as Fox puts it, he totally repudiated "the historic liberal Protestant quest for the Kingdom of God." Writing in *Harper's* in 1932, Niebuhr predicted that "it will be practically impossible to secure social change in America without the use of very considerable violence." The next year he called himself a "Marxian."

At that very moment, however, Reinhold seems to have been chastened by the criticisms of his younger brother, Helmut Richard Niebuhr, who had become a professor at Yale Divinity School. Although Richard later destroyed all his correspondence, Fox has found sufficient evidence to suggest that Reinhold was vulnerable to his brother's remonstrance that *Moral Man* was still "too romantic" about human nature and the promise of controlling historical change. Prodded by Richard's perceptive criticisms and by a fear that he had nearly forsaken his father's biblical heritage, Niebuhr's interest gravitated toward theology and the goal of finding a Christian alternative to the illusory hopes of communism. At the 1937 Oxford Conference on Church, Community, and State, a gathering of over four hundred delegates from forty countries, Niebuhr set the dominant tone by attributing the world crisis to original sin—a doctrine he redefined in psychological terms and expounded two years later in his famous Gifford Lectures at the University of Edinburgh later published as *The Nature and Destiny of Man*.

Niebuhr gave comfort to conservatives; he has even been hailed as the father of neoconservatives. Yet as Fox convincingly demonstrates, he remained a liberal activist. He rejected, to be sure, many of the components of the traditional liberal creed, such as the belief that social evils are wholly the result of ignorance and environmental circumstances and the faith that human goodness, guided by scientific reason, can create a just and fraternal world. Yet for Niebuhr the very contingencies and uncertainties of history were a spur to social and political action. The "children of light" could not assume that capitalism would become more just, that communism would become more democratic, or that Nazism would be defeated. Niebuhr's "tragic view of life" opened the way for a pragmatic use of power to contain evil and achieve proximate justice.

Fox devotes considerable attention to Niebuhr's involvement in public affairs from the formation of the Union for Democratic Action in 1941 to his government-sponsored tour of Germany in 1946 and his meetings with George Kennan's Policy Planning Staff in 1949. It appears that some historians have greatly exaggerated Niebuhr's influence on foreign policy, in part because Kennan was reported to have referred to him as "the father of us all." In 1980 Kennan could not recall having made such a remark, and, according to Fox, Kennan thought that Niebuhr's political judgments and foreign-policy views were "unexceptional." Kennan was attracted by Niebuhr's philosophical perspective and Niebuhr praised Kennan's book, *American Diplomacy, 1900–1950*, for its "rigorous and searching criticism of the weaknesses in our foreign policy." Yet Niebuhr also felt that Kennan's exclusive emphasis on national self-interest "is not the proper cure for an abstract and pretentious idealism."[6]

If the State Department disregarded Niebuhr's warnings against national egotism, numerous government officials invoked his name to justify a "realistic" approach to global issues, especially in the Kennedy administration. McGeorge Bundy referred to him as "probably the most influential single mind in the development of American attitudes which combine moral purpose with a sense of political reality." As Fox sums up this influence on the Kennedy circle: "He helped them maintain faith in themselves as political actors in a troubled—what he termed a sinful—world. Stakes were high, enemies were wily, responsibility meant taking risks: Niebuhr taught that moral men had to play hardball."

Although Niebuhr was an ardent Anglophile, he was primarily concerned with the place and responsibilities of America in an unpredictable world. In the mid-twentieth century America had become "a vivid symbol of the spiritual perplexities of modern man" precisely because America exemplified the most promising and most dangerous tendencies of industrial civilization. American power generated the "illusions to which a technocratic culture is already too prone"—especially the tendency to equate "the mastery of nature with the mastery of historical destiny."[7] Yet of all political systems, only democracy could do justice to man's paradoxical nature. Only America could protect the world from the tyranny and misguided messianism of the communists. In making such judgments Niebuhr knew that he risked the "subtler form of egoistic corruption" that infected even "the highest forms of Christian prophetism."[8] But that admission revealed the subtlety of his reformed jeremiad.

In 1970, after Niebuhr had suffered for eighteen years from the effects of a debilitating stroke, the old prophet, Fox tells us, fumed as he watched the evening news and contemplated the extension of the Vietnam War. When Richard Nixon appeared on the screen, Niebuhr "pushed himself up off the mattress and spat out the words, 'That bastard!' . . . 'God told us to love our enemies, not to like them,' he would say. Having no enemies meant that one lacked strong convictions. It was one more of the human paradoxes in which he always delighted."

Notes

1. Sacvan Bercovitch, *The American Jeremiad* (University of Wisconsin Press, 1978), p. xi.
2. *The Irony of American History* (Scribner's, 1952), p. 25.
3. *The Nature and Destiny of Man: A Christian Interpretation*, Vol. II: *Human Destiny* (One-volume edition, Scribner's, 1948), p. 25.

4. *The Nature and Destiny of Man: A Christian Interpretation,* p. 26.
5. Robert McAfee Brown, who studied and taught with Niebuhr, has edited an extremely useful volume of Niebuhr's essays and addresses, *The Essential Reinhold Niebuhr: Selected Essays and Addresses* (Yale University Press, 1986).
6. *The Irony of American History,* p. 148.
7. *The Irony of American History,* p. 147.
8. *Human Destiny,* p. 18.

2

Martin Luther King, Jr.

*Bearing the Cross: Martin Luther King, Jr., and
the Southern Christian Leadership Conference*
David J. Garrow (1986)

In October 1986 several hundred guests attended a well-organized two-day
conference on Martin Luther King, Jr., sponsored by the United States Capitol Historical Society in cooperation with the United States Congress and
the Martin Luther King, Jr. Center for Nonviolent Social Change. In the
Senate Caucus Room of the Russell Building the audience listened to brief
remarks by Julian Bond, Senator Charles McC. Mathias, Jr., and Coretta
Scott King, as well as to formal papers and commentaries by a variety of
scholars and civil rights activists. This ceremony of canonization, culminating
in the installation at the Capitol of a bust of King, the first black American
to occupy a place in Statuary Hall, was much preoccupied with the meaning
of canonization. What are the implications for the cause King represented
when his name is officially bestowed on schools, a national holiday, and even
an interstate expressway in Montgomery, Alabama? Can America honor a
martyred radical without wholly co-opting him?

The conference's speakers seemed to agree on the dangers of canonization,
of making King "the Uncle Tom of the century," as Hosea Williams puts it
in his epilogue to David J. Garrow's monumental biography. Washington,
Jefferson, and Lincoln had essentially won their limited revolutions before
they were sanctified. King's revolution, at least the revolution he envisioned

after 1965, has not even begun. Moreover, for the more radical civil rights veterans it is counterrevolutionary to speak even figuratively of "King's revolution." Several speakers at the conference echoed the Student Nonviolent Coordinating Committee's long-standing complaints against the "leader worship" and "cult of personality" that surrounded King. Diane Nash, a leading SNCC activist and co-worker of King's, pointed to the misconceptions fostered by a conference on a single individual. If the young people of today fail to understand that the civil rights victories of the 1960s were won by ordinary people like themselves, they will passively wait for a charismatic father figure like the mythologized King. This pathological dependency, Nash maintained, easily leads to sexism, authoritarianism, and assassination.

But despite their anti-elitist rhetoric and their discomfort over King's charismatic power, most of the speakers celebrated King as the greatest American leader of the twentieth century. Garrow, who endorses Nash's argument at the end of his biography, spoke at the conference of King's empowering sense of religious mission that flowed from his epiphanic experience on the night of January 27, 1956. Overwhelmed by the responsibilities of leading the Montgomery bus boycott, shattered by obscene phone calls and a death threat that imperiled his wife and baby daughter, King sat alone that night in his kitchen, staring at a cup of coffee. Then he heard the voice of Jesus telling him to fight on, assuring him he would never be alone. According to Garrow, it was this "mountaintop experience" that gave King the courage to follow his calling, despite his self-confessed sins and personal shortcomings. In another conference paper Nathan I. Huggins, a Harvard historian, reaffirmed the importance of King's unique religious experience and charismatic leadership. Why was it more misguided, Huggins asked, to wait for the appearance of a leader than to wait for the "rise" of an impersonal movement? Cornel West, a young theologian and philosopher from Yale, hailed King as America's greatest "organic intellectual," a man who not only "reveled in ideas" but applied ideas in action.

West's brilliant paper raises an important question about black role models. The image of King as an intellectual was virtually obliterated by the movement he became the spokesman for, a movement that felt compelled to repudiate the supposedly bourgeois ethic of initiative, learning, and achievement. How many of King's admirers know that at Crozer Theological Seminary, where he studied Reinhold Niebuhr, Marx, Rauschenbusch, and Tawney, King was valedictorian of his class and won the school's major prize scholarship for further study? Or that he chose Boston University after being accepted into doctoral programs at Yale and Edinburgh? Or that the graduate course that influenced him the most was a two-semester seminar on Hegel? King was well-equipped to pursue a successful academic career, as well as the ministry. Yet he became popularly known as a spellbinding preacher who gripped people's emotions, not as an "organic intellectual" who fused a rich heritage of Afro-American Christianity with insights derived from Hegel, Marx, Niebuhr, and Nietzsche, to say nothing of the Declaration of Independence. It is a great misfortune that black achievement has so often been equated with Uncle Toms, that attacks on the black bourgeoisie (into which King was born) have encouraged the assumption that intellectual success endangers the blacks' single privilege, which is their status as victims of white oppression.

The tributes that have been paid to King tend to obscure the conflicting interests of his rival claimants. It is a remarkable paradox that the only American who is widely honored today in Third World countries that view the United States as their chief oppressor is also the only twentieth-century American who is honored at home with a national holiday. At the October conference Sean Govendor, a South African activist who was sent in place of Allan Boesak (who was later imprisoned for fraud and theft), drew a sharp distinction between King's "underside America" and the corporate capitalism that supports apartheid and dictates America's foreign policy. Looking ahead to a total restructuring of the social order, Govendor affirmed that King belongs to South Africa's revolutionaries, to "our tomorrow." Yet King must also belong to the American people, white as well as black, and even to the multinational corporations that helped to sponsor the October conference. It may take decades to gain perspective on this apparent anomaly. For as Lewis R. Harlan pointed out, we don't yet know how far the civil rights movement will extend in redressing the fundamental inequalities between white and black Americans.

The sources of King's eclectic appeal become clearer, however, in Garrow's exhaustive study, which should remain a basic reference well into the twenty-first century. The author of two previous books on King, Garrow draws on over seven hundred interviews of key figures, including King's enemies and closest associates; he seems to have combed all the pertinent manuscript and printed sources, including 150 dissertations and essays and the files of 191 newspapers and periodicals. Most important, thanks to the Freedom of Information Act, he has gained access to the voluminous FBI and CIA files on King and his associates. Since 1917, black intellectuals, journalists, and clergy have been favored targets for covert federal surveillance. By the 1960s, improved technology allowed the FBI to monitor every aspect of King's life, from his bedrooms to his most secret discussions of strategy. It is a supreme irony that this police state apparatus should have provided historians with more complete information than they have ever had on a major public figure.

Garrow, who focuses on King's leadership of the Southern Christian Leadership Conference, relies on skillful narrative almost devoid of overt analysis, interpretation, or moralizing. He emphasizes that the civil rights movement was already gaining momentum among Southern blacks when King, at twenty-six a rising star in the Baptist ministry, reluctantly revised his life's agenda. It was only the spiritual crisis of January 27, 1956, that prepared King to accept the fear, pain, guilt, and probable martyrdom that were the necessary price for seeing the promised land. But Garrow also shows that even as a student King found Christian faith fully compatible with the hope for a more just social order—a world free of poverty, militarism, and capitalistic greed.

King's first speech at the beginning of the Montgomery bus boycott employs the strategy he would refine through later conflicts: the coupling of Christian love with nonviolent coercion, the attempt to strike a balance between militancy and moderation—a balance that would command attention and mobilize legitimate anger without severing ties with advocates of gradual reform and well-meaning members of white power structures, especially in the North and in the federal government. In December 1955 King was content with a demand for a seating plan on buses that would prevent the humiliation of blacks while not directly challenging state segregation laws. Ten years later his objectives included not only a total eradication of racial segregation, but an assault on poverty in the Northern ghettos and a negotiated settlement of the Vietnam War. Even in 1956, however, he had seen the Montgomery boycott as part of a worldwide movement against racism, colonialism, and economic imperialism. What united King's broadening concerns was an unswerving hostility to institutions that subverted respect for "the dignity and worth of all human personality."

Garrow demonstrates that King was remarkably successful in his continuous search for a synthesis of militancy and moderation. Respected for his calmness and patience, he could mollify teenage gang leaders and orchestrate stormy meetings of quarrelsome civil rights associates. He was no less adept at manipulating the media and exploiting the blunders of Southern police commissioners such as "Bull" Connor and Clyde Sellers. Although King relied heavily on advisers, particularly Bayard Rustin, Stanley D. Levison, and Andrew J. Young, he clearly felt free to select, modify, or reject their suggestions as he saw fit. Garrow's evidence indicates that Levison, who broke with the American Communist Party only in March 1963 and who was regarded by the FBI as a probable Soviet agent, was for the most part a voice of reason and moderation.

Garrow in no way minimizes King's weaknesses. King failed miserably at delegating authority, disciplining subordinates, and keeping the SCLC house in order. While Garrow does not dwell on the seamy side of the civil rights movement, he provides glimpses of appalling sexual exploitation, financial irresponsibility, and internal feuding. Moments of heroism and communal solidarity were more than balanced, as in most military campaigns, by debauchery, self-indulgence, and confusion.

As a devout Christian who had studied Niebuhr's explorations of pride and sensuality, King understood his own personal sins, which imperiled his transcendent cause. He felt that he had been thrust by forces beyond his control into world prominence at an extremely young age. Keenly aware of the corrupting effects of publicity and acclaim, he responded to his role as celebrity by embracing a self-destructive schedule of incessant travel, speeches, meetings, and writing commitments. Always repeating himself and composing in haste, King even plagiarized parts of his book *Stride Toward Freedom*, which appeared in 1958.

King found a release from public pressures and responsibilities in private binges and sexual promiscuity. Garrow never explains why King took so few precautions to conceal these escapades, even when he suspected that his rooms were being bugged and when he knew that public exposure would devastate his cause. Apart from the considered and untaken option of abandoning sexual adventures, he seems to have made little effort to circumvent or to neutralize the FBI's listening devices. There is a Niebuhrian irony in the fact that King's most searing anguish stemmed from his public honor, which he considered undeserved, and from his private dishonor, which he regretted but could not control. Yet his acknowledgment of sin may have contributed to his moral authority, and to the precarious balance he maintained between his commitment to rebellion and his commitment to traditional Christian and American ideals. In a decade when nothing was sacred, when professional agitators mocked all standards, King remained a self-confessed sinner who knew that every dream has a price.

It is easy to forget the obstacles the SCLC faced when the organization was still engaged in such limited "reform" activities as registering voters and desegregating public facilities. Besides official and unofficial white violence, the merchants and business leaders of cities like Birmingham were intransigent. President Kennedy seemed primarily interested in keeping order and avoiding unfavorable publicity abroad. While King and Ralph Abernathy sat in the Albany, Georgia, jail the *New York Times* praised "the remarkable restraint of Albany's segregationists and the deft handling by the police of racial protests." After rebuffing King's pleas for aid in his struggle against Southern white terrorists, the FBI offered tapes, including a recorded telephone quarrel between Martin and Coretta, to Florida officials for possible use as blackmail. Along with planted news stories and other dirty tricks, the FBI sent King a fabricated threatening letter and a tape containing the juiciest highlights of his stay at Washington's Willard Hotel. It was Coretta who opened the package and summoned Martin to play the tape.

But in Birmingham the civil rights forces succeeded in precipitating a crisis that stunned the nation and provoked federal intervention. While King overestimated the number of black adults who were willing to risk their lives and jobs for the cause, the recruitment of black teenagers as targets for Bull Connor's police force dramatized the violent foundations of white supremacy. Garrow sheds interesting light on King's reliance on Washington, and on the continuing chess game between King and the Kennedys, who of course had the advantage of the FBI reports. King shrewdly played on the Kennedys' fear of SNCC. President Kennedy told Birmingham's white leaders that they should be thankful that they were dealing with King and the SCLC instead of with SNCC, which had "an investment in violence" ("They're sons of bitches," he said). After the bombing of the Birmingham Baptist church, in which four young girls were killed, King wired the president that if he failed to act meaningfully "we shall see the worst racial holocaust this nation has ever seen." On the other hand, the Kennedys and their aides were able to convert the March on Washington into what Garrow terms "a celebration and public relations bonanza for both the movement and for Kennedy's civil rights program." If SNCC chairman John Lewis had started to read his radical, unrevised text, two Kennedy aides were prepared to "pull the plug" on the public address system.

King soon showed that he was anything but a captive figure, as he directed increasing attention to the plight of America's poor, white as well as black. But as one reads Garrow's lengthy chapters on the "War on Slums," the open-housing protests in Chicago, the Vietnam protest, and the Poor People's Campaign, it becomes clear that King's goals and programs were becoming hopelessly diffuse. He struggled heroically to unite reformers and Black Power militants in a cause of nonviolent revolution. He knew that the white establishment would not voluntarily surrender its privileges and open the way to genuine economic equality. He endorsed a socialist goal of vague "structural" change and called for a "radical redistribution of economic and political power." But ultimately he sought to shame whites, not to defeat them. He grafted socialist rhetoric to a Christian vision of reconciliation and brotherhood.

King's mission revived the disturbing question, posed at the very birth of the republic, of whether America can stand for anything more than the pursuit of private gain. Clearly, having a democratic government has never exempted the nation from oppression, injustice, deception, and officially sanctioned crime. At the beginning of the Civil War, the London *Times* concluded that

> the real motives of the belligerents . . . appear to be exactly such motives as have caused wars in all times and countries. They are essentially selfish motives—that is to say, they are based upon speculations of national power, territorial aggrandizement, political advantage, and commercial gain.

Whatever the accuracy of this judgment, Lincoln insisted that the war was being fought for the American dream, that it was "a struggle for maintaining in the world, that form, and substance of government, whose leading object is, to elevate the condition of men—to lift artificial weights from all shoulders—to clear the path of laudable pursuit for all." Like Lincoln, Martin Luther King revitalized faith in the Declaration of Independence and the Bill of Rights, in what he termed the "amazing universalism" of the American dream. For all his talk of socialism and revolution, King wept in an open display of emotion when President Johnson, addressing Congress and a national television audience, compared the Selma demonstrations of 1965 to

Lexington, Concord, and Appomattox, and intoned that "we shall overcome" America's "crippling legacy of bigotry and injustice."

This very hope in America's capacity for repentance opened the way for the bitterness and disillusion of King's last years. Garrow, who tends to slight social and political context, could well have said more about the poisoning effects of the Vietnam War. But it was also in the old tradition of the American jeremiad to work for redemption by denouncing the nation as a racist, power-hungry state guilty of "psychological and spiritual genocide" against black people. King's timely warning that there is "nothing in this world more dangerous than Negro cities ringed with white suburbs" was neutralized by his agreement with the absurd charge that ghettos were the intentional result of white economic exploitation and were essential to the functioning of the capitalist system. While King drew attention to intolerable conditions that were not being alleviated by the panacea of economic growth, he devised no effective program for fighting poverty. His rhetoric encouraged images of helpless victimization and national cataclysm.

Yet King retained his commitment to nonviolence. His most important legacy is the belief that revolutionary change can be achieved without devastating violence. This was also the goal of black and white American abolitionists, but of course they were unsuccessful. Given the increasing diffusion of weapons of mass destruction, the question of violence acquires an altogether new meaning. One takes hope from the thought that King, and the movement he symbolized, *did* achieve revolutionary change, at least when measured by the goals and expectations of 1956 or even 1963. They failed only to the extent that they assumed that an end to legal segregation would eliminate racial inequalities. They also failed to recognize that Americans historically have demanded that equality be defined in a way that does not inhibit ambition, effort, and achievement. But King and his associates did prove that it is possible to overcome the inertia, self-interest, and conservatism of establishments without lapsing into anarchy. No less important, King showed that a protest movement does not lose strength when it cultivates self-criticism and a consciousness of its own fallibility.

3

Religion and American Culture

Encyclopedia of the American Religious Experience:
Studies of Traditions and Movements (3 volumes)
Edited by Charles H. Lippy and Peter W. Williams (1988)

The word "encyclopedia" is acquiring new meanings. Not long ago serious scholars were inclined to think of encyclopedias as tools for high-school papers or as sources of scientific information for the nonscientist. Although scholars might well consult such classics as *The New Schaff-Herzog Encyclopedia of Religious Knowledge, The Encyclopedia Judaica,* or *The Encyclopedia of the Social Sciences,* they would be unlikely to turn to an encyclopedia as the first step in a new research project. In recent years, however, the flood of secondary works in almost every field has complicated the perennial question, "Where to begin?" Fortunately, the same forces that have produced more books than one can possibly track have also led to the appearance of highly professional encyclopedias on every subject from American economic history and foreign policy to "the American religious experience."

In terms of scope and volume of information Scribner's *Encyclopedia of the American Religious Experience* is breathtaking. The one-hundred-and-five essays, printed on 1,740 double-columned pages, contain almost three times as many words as Sydney E. Ahlstrom's massive, prize-winning book *A Religious History of the American People.*[1] Unlike Ahlstrom and other predecessors, the editors, Charles H. Lippy of Clemson University and Peter W. Williams of Miami University, have expanded the word "American" to include all of North America. As an alternative to short, dictionary-like entries, they have assembled essays of about ten to sixteen thousand words, each with a bibliography and cross-references. Most impressive, they have included such subjects as "Buddhism," "Hinduism," "Shinto and Indigenous Chinese Religion," "Women and Religion," "Religion and Film," "Religions of Mesoamerica," and "French Catholicism in the New World."

Inevitably, such a work lacks the thematic coherence of Ahlstrom's volume, which the editors salute in their preface. Even on a single continent the varieties of religious experience have extended far beyond the conceptual categories of William James or any other writer. But one does not turn to an encyclopedia for synthesis. The editors have wisely limited their preface to a brief description of the *Encyclopedia*'s organization and structure.

This arrangement of subject matter is not only sensible, but is in many ways ingenious. Part I, intended to illustrate the cross-disciplinary approaches to the study of religion in America, begins with historiography and then exposes the reader to sociological, psychological, and geographic-demographic dimensions of American religion before concluding with essays on folklore and theological interpretations and critiques of American society and culture. Part II moves backward in time to the Preclassic, Classic, and Postclassic periods of Mesoamerican religions, and then to Native American religions in North America, before examining the Roman Catholic heritage, the African heritage, and various aspects of religion in the Spanish empire and Canada. As an antidote to the parochial Anglo-American boundaries that have traditionally circumscribed the study of American religions, the decision to include this broadened ethnic and geographic background cannot be too highly praised.

In part III we turn to denominational history, beginning with three essays on Judaism, one on Eastern Christianity, and three on Roman Catholicism, before proceeding to a full assortment of Protestant groups and completing the unit with an examination of the Mormons. Part IV is concerned with religions "outside the Jewish and Christian traditions," which include, along with Islam, Buddhism, and other ancient faiths, "Free Thought and Ethical Movements," late twentieth-century cults, and black militant and separatist movements. Parts V and VI cover the more traditional subject matter of historical movements, such as the Great Awakening, millennialism, pentecostalism, and fundamentalism; and intellectual history, including essays on the Enlightenment, Transcendentalism, Neo-Orthodoxy, and black religious thought. Part VII concerns liturgy and worship, religious music, the history of preaching, and the arts. Part VIII, "Religion and the Political and Social Orders," moves through a rather miscellaneous assortment of topics ranging from social reform in various periods to ethnicity, the South, and religious prejudice and nativism. The final unit, part IX, turns appropriately to the dissemination of American religion by means of a professional ministry, pastoral care, schools, missions, the religious press, mass communications, and popular culture.

Unevenness is the curse of all large collections or symposia, and unevenness is especially flagrant in this *Encyclopedia*, in which gems often sparkle next to cinders. While few readers can be expected to begin at the beginning, it is particularly unfortunate that the first three articles are so unremittingly dull. Henry Warner Bowden's opening piece on historiography is little more than a superficial listing of authors and titles: the kind of bibliographical essay one encounters at the end of a doctoral dissertation. This flat appetizer is followed by the thickest brands of sociological soup, a warmed over and tedious serving of pluralism, privatization, and ideal typology that fails to nourish the mind and makes one long for the prose of Max Weber, C. Wright Mills, or Anthony Giddens.

Fortunately, the patient or selective reader will soon find essays that provide masterful and accurate summaries of subjects previously mined with error and misunderstanding; essays that will encourage the revision and reorganization of lecture notes; essays that open up new fields or new ways of thinking about familiar material; essays that stimulate innovation by leaping across conventional boundaries of topic and discipline.

"Is there any continuity," Wayne Elzey asks in his article on popular culture, "between St. Augustine's *Confessions* and the free-verse poem in *Inspiration* magazine that compares conversion to opening a new can of tennis balls? ('Becoming a Christian is like being PSSCHT . . . Released! Cor. 5: 17.')." A central problem facing students of popular culture, Elzey observes, "is trying to decide whether American Christians are innocent as doves or wise as serpents." In a witty and somewhat eccentric essay that finally points to some profound truths, Elzey discusses *Uncle Tom's Cabin*; Jerry Falwell; Rex Humbard Family Life Study Bibles, and the New Media Bible, which cost subscribers, beginning in 1976, $82,500 "for the entire set"; a tract entitled "X-Pressway to Hell/Rated X/Adults Only/Coming Soon/Heaven and Hell/Starring YOU"; Elizabeth Stuart Phelps's *The Gates Ajar*; Marabel

Morgan's *The Total Woman*; and the response of millions of Americans to Joni Eareckson, the young quadriplegic who wrote an autobiography, made a film and records, and appeared frequently at Billy Graham rallies and in an interview with Barbara Walters on the *Today* show. "The images and constructs upon which popular religion relies," Elzey concludes, "are not those of the scholar and scientist who probe for invisible causes and intangible connections. Instead popular religion works by reminding believers that meaning resides in the logical affinities one dimension of sensible experience has with another." Emerging from the chaos and contradictions of modern life, popular religion insists that "reality is finally neither unpredictable nor confusing."

Jacob Neusner's "Judaism in Contemporary America," Jaroslav Pelikan's "Lutheran Heritage," and Jan Shipps's "The Latter-Day Saints" stand out as models for synthesizing imaginative interpretation with significant information. Neusner highlights the abrupt disjunction and subtle continuity between successive generations of twentieth-century American Jews: the first-generation immigrants, scarred by savage persecution, who by the 1920s sadly acknowledged that their children would not perpetuate Yiddish, strict dietary observance, or a love for Talmudic learning; the second generation, which came to maturity during the Great Depression or Second World War and which, in a climate of overt anti-Semitism, cast off the distinguishing marks of Judaism while banding together in all-Jewish bowling leagues, athletic clubs, and philanthropic societies; and the third generation, whose quest to rediscover their heritage and historical identity has created American Judaism as we know it today.

Although Neusner's essay is sometimes marred by a tone of cynicism and contempt, which alternates rather strangely with expressions of hope, it contains brilliant passages on the ambiguity of Zionism, American rabbis as "professional Jews," and the dilemma of Jews who for the first time faced the choice of whether or not to be Jewish: "What is a Jew? . . . What makes a person into a Jew? . . . Why should I be a Jew? What does it mean, if anything, that I am born of Jewish parents?" Neusner convincingly shows that the creation of the state of Israel, an awareness of the significance of the Holocaust, and the Six-Day War of June 1967 have all had a decisive impact on modern Judaizing programs and activism. After tracing the development of contradictory yearnings in a people who hate those "Jewish traits" in themselves that set them apart from everyone else, a people who "want to be Jewish but not too much," Neusner concludes that "contemporary American Judaism, for all its distance from the classic forms of the past, its unbelief and secularity, constitutes a fundamentally new and autonomous development, not merely the last stages in the demise of something decadent." If "the archaic holy people has passed from the scene," Neusner finds comfort in the "manifest and correct claim to continue as Jews, a different, separate group, and the claim that that difference is destiny."

Jaroslav Pelikan draws a parallel between the rabbinical family and "the quasi-dynastic role of the ministerial family within Lutheran and other Protestant groups," which played a similar part in transmitting and nourishing a distinctive culture. Pelikan also describes the Lutheran affirmation of "the one, holy, catholic, and apostolic church and of its continuity—not as institution, but as the people of God, among whom 'the gospel is rightly preached and the sacraments are administered in accordance with the institution of Christ.'" When these holy people, or people of God, emigrated to America, they continued to be far more oriented than most religious groups to their Old World heritage. Paradoxically, as Pelikan shrewdly observes, this meant that American Lutherans appropriated parts of their heritage in a sequence that reversed chronological history. In the eighteenth century they strove to adapt contemporary Pietism to their New World lives. In the nineteenth century they moved backward in time to recover an understanding of primal sixteenth-century Lutheran Confessions, assembled in 1580 into *The Book of Concord.* "And it was only in the twentieth century," Pelikan writes, "that American Lutheranism, in its piety, ethics, and theology, began to come to terms with Martin Luther himself, as his thought and work came to be understood and interpreted with new vigor in the 'Luther Renaissance' of Germany and Scandinavia, in which American Lutheran scholarship would also eventually play an increasing part." American Lutheranism, in other words, cannot be understood without reference to its "confessional affinities" and dialectical relationship with the lands of its origins. Only someone like Pelikan, one of the leading authorities on the history of Christianity in Europe, possesses the knowledge needed to illuminate that relationship.

After explaining the central role in Lutheranism of religious doctrine, as contrasted with the concern for structure and polity in Anglo-Saxon Protestantism, Pelikan emphasizes the supreme importance for American Lutheranism of the northern European ethnic factor and related Germanic languages:

The perpetuation in North America of patterns of worship, religious education, social life, and also of doctrine that had developed in the folk churches of northern Europe is what has given American Lutheranism much of its distinctive character. Even when a new generation in Minnesota or Pennsylvania could no longer speak the language of its immigrant grandparents, what it expressed in English was a set of cultural values still redolent of these origins.

When examining the complex interchange between Lutheranism in Europe and America, Pelikan dismantles stereotypes and points to the political diversity and cultural creativity of various Lutheran traditions. He gently questions one of the assumptions that underlies virtually all American history, including the format of this *Encyclopedia*—namely, that an Old World "heritage" serves as a springboard for New World developments and then disappears from view, usually at some time in the distant past. American Lutheranism, Pelikan observes, has produced patterns of church life which have repeatedly "found their way into the mother churches of Europe; *stewardship* has now become a German word of sorts." Since European Lutherans have had to test their faith in a society that has been far more radically secularized than the United States, "there are many ways in which America is the Old World and Europe the New World, rather than the other way around." This insight should be pondered by historians of other denominations.

Jan Shipps's article on the Mormons is probably the finest summary ever written of the history of God's most recently chosen people. No other writer has explained this tangled, fascinating, and traditionally misrepresented story with such remarkable clarity, objectivity, and succinctness. My only complaint, an extremely minor one, is my wish that Shipps had explained to readers unfamiliar with the Bible the origins of the Mormons' Aaronic and Melchizedek priesthoods as well as the "Urim and Thummim," which Joseph Smith, Jr., used to decipher the hieroglyphics on the golden plates. A knowledge of the Hebrew sources of these words reinforces Shipps's own thesis, modestly restricted to a few words in this essay but developed more fully in a pathbreaking book.[2] Shipps maintains that "Mormonism was and is related to the Christianity that existed before 1830 in much the same manner that Christianity itself was and is related to the Judaism that existed at the time of the birth of Jesus. Indeed, Mormonism was transformed from cult to religious tradition in much the same way that Christianity developed from a cultic form of Judaism into a separate and distinct religious tradition." Although many of the first Mormon converts sought to restore the original church of the Apostles, this New Testament emphasis on repentance and baptism was soon outweighed by Smith's claim of literally restoring ancient Israel—of reestablishing the temple ordinances, fulfilling Hebrew prophecy, and re-creating Israel's patriarchal age.

Like Neusner and Pelikan, Shipps is sensitive to subtle continuities and reenactments in the history of religion as well as to the innovations that always accompany attempts at restoration. Acutely aware of the persistence of anti-Mormon history and mythology, she also scrupulously avoids the trap of reductionism. She presents the cultural and socioeconomic background of Mormon history but never uses this background to cast doubt on the authenticity of religious needs and religious beliefs. Her comprehensive essay includes the little-known efforts by Mormon Saints in Missouri to invite free blacks to join the Church, a bold step that led in 1833 to the destruction of the Mormon newspaper office and a campaign to drive the Saints out of the state. Shipps discusses the antipolygamy crusade that culminated in the Edmunds Act of 1882; the great Mormon foreign missionary movement launched in the 1960s; the role of Mormons in defeating the Equal Rights Amendment; and the 1978 revelation that opened the Mormon priesthood to black male members of the Church.

Given the immense scope of the *Encyclopedia*, important subject matter omitted from one article is likely to turn up in another. For example, Lino Gómez Canedo's disappointing essay on "Religion in the Spanish Empire" simply states that in 1680 an Indian revolt in New Mexico "destroyed all that had been attained up to that point. The territory was reclaimed in 1693, and again in 1696 after another insurrection." Nothing is said about Native American religions, about syncretization of religious practices, or about the Spanish enslavement of Indians and use of forced labor to build the Salinas Pueblo Mission churches. Henry Warner Bowden's "North American Indian Missions" does, however, provide a brief sketch of Franciscan missionaries denouncing local gods, closing native worship chambers, "burning Indian ritual objects, and whipping persistent leaders." Also, Sandra Sizer Frankiel's article "California and the Southwest" discusses not only the culture of the Pueblos and Zuni but the nature of the massive 1680 uprising, which extended from Arizona to Santa Fe, where the Pueblos killed the governor as well as large numbers of Spanish friars and colonists.

Alternative articles are no solution for factual errors, which fortunately seem to be quite rare. One's confidence in Leonard E. Barrett's "The African Heritage in Caribbean and North American Religions" is almost immediately shaken by the author's discussion of the demography of the African slave trade, which shows no awareness of recent and highly sophisticated research; by his assignment of wrong dates for the publications of Edward Long and Bryan Edwards; by his reference to "Moreau de Saint Mery of Haiti" (meaning Moreau de Saint-Méry of Martinique, who later lived in France, Saint-Domingue, and Philadelphia); and "Ulrich Bonnell Phillips, 1918, of the North American colonies." The notion that Phillips was a North American colonist in 1918 is no more absurd than Barrett's assertion that "European writers of the seventeenth and eighteenth centuries all agreed that Africans were inferior to Europeans; that they were the most primitive of the human race and were therefore without a recognizable culture."

Although Stephen A. Marini should be faulted for ignoring blacks in his article on "The Great Awakening" (except for his doubtful claim that George Whitefield pleaded for the manumission of all slaves), he has written a first-rate and fascinating overview of a much disputed subject. One especially welcomes his treatment of German Pietism and the emphasis he gives to Isaac Watts and William Law. Mark A. Noll's stimulating essay on "The Bible in American Culture" also deserves special praise, in part because it proves that a very broad subject can be treated in an interesting and coherent way—despite the impression given by other articles on war and peace, social reform, and revivalism. As one might expect, E. Brooks Holifield has written a highly informative and erudite essay on "Pastoral Care and Counseling," plotting the journey from salvation to modern self-realization. Giving some attention to Catholicism as well as Protestantism, Holifield moves from the questioning, logical analysis, and argumentation of early pastoral counseling to the twentieth-century cult of the therapeutic—from Petrus Ramus to Harry Stack Sullivan and Paul Tillich.

Finally, one of the most stunning pieces in the entire collection is Daniel Walker Howe's "The Impact of Puritanism on American Culture," a tour de force that should be required reading in countless history and literature classes across the land. How, one may ask, could anyone say anything worth reading about this moldy subject, especially in eighteen pages? Howe's article is such a brilliant synthesis, such a masterpiece of wit, subtlety, and condensation, that it defies brief summary. Suffice it to say that he invokes the names of William Perkins and Hugh Hefner, Anne Hutchinson and Martin Luther King, Jr., John D. Rockefeller and Fidel Castro; he warns the reader not to exaggerate the power of Puritanism even in its prime; and his few remarks concerning postindustrial, "largely post-Puritan" America address some of the same concerns that Jacob Neusner examined with respect to Judaism in contemporary America.

Charles H. Lippy and Peter W. Williams deserve the gratitude of several academic disciplines to say nothing of the American clergy for the enormous care and effort that these volumes obviously required. Researchers may possibly grumble over a number of minor irritants. The table of contents fails to indicate where one volume ends and another begins; the list of authors' names at the end of Volume III fails to note the appropriate field or discipline; the alphabetical listing of articles, also at the end of Volume III, fails to give page numbers. The index, however, seems to be quite comprehensive and easy to use.

On the first page of Jon Butler's new book, *Awash in a Sea of Faith: Christianizing the American People*, we read that "despite complaints about 'secular humanism' and eroding religious values, over 97 percent of Americans polled on religion expressed a belief in God, and 60 percent regularly attended public worship, figures that stood in marked contrast to polls in Western Europe, where 40 percent of respondents said they did not believe in God and less than 10 percent regularly attended church."[3] When all is said and done, it must be confessed that the *Encyclopedia* does not prepare the reader for these statistics or anything approximating them. By "prepare" I do not mean by sociological analysis of various religious and cultic groups but by the way most of the articles treat spirituality and the human sense of eternity. The articles do not appear to be the products of a highly religious society, a society that may conceivably think of the fundamental dualism of life as that between humanity and God, not between self and society, the I and the me, language and speech, or the synchronic and diachronic. If among the authors there are true believers, they have repressed or censored their faith in the interest of what they conceive as objective scholarship. This may be a prerequisite for modern scholarly dialogue, but the absence of much sense of the sacred, of the mystery of life and being, should not pass without comment.

Notes

1. Sydney E. Ahlstrom, *A Religious History of the American People* (Yale University Press, 1972). Ahlstrom's book contains about 444 words a page; the *Encyclopedia*, about 832 words a page.

2. Jan Shipps, *Mormonism: The Story of a New Religious Tradition* (University of Illinois Press, 1985).
3. Jon Butler, *Awash in a Sea of Faith: Christianizing the American People* (Harvard University Press, 1990), 1.

4

The Other Zion: American Jews and the Meritocratic Experiment

A History of the Jews in America
Howard M. Sachar (1992)

What Is the Use of Jewish History?
Lucy S. Dawidowicz, edited with an
introduction by Neal Kozodoy (1980)

The Jewish People in America (5 volumes):

A Time for Planting: The First Migration, 1654–1820
Eli Faber (1992)

A Time for Gathering: The Second Migration, 1820–1880
Hasia R. Diner (1992)

A Time for Building: The Third Migration, 1880–1920
Gerald Sorin (1992)

A Time for Searching: Entering the Mainstream, 1920–1945
Henry L. Feingold (1992)

A Time for Healing: American Jewry Since World War II
Edward S. Shapiro (1992)

❋

I have been teaching American history for thirty-nine years, but I was frankly astonished by much of the information contained in Howard M. Sachar's monumental volume on the history of American Jewry, and in the uneven but generally outstanding five volumes (collectively entitled *The Jewish People in America*) sponsored by the American Jewish Historical Society in its centennial year. Both of these surveys of Jewish life in America record the extraordinary achievements of a people who overcame abysmal poverty as well as the barriers of religious and ethnic discrimination. And both works also show how the drive for material and vocational success has undermined Jewish religious observance and the communal bonds of ethnic peoplehood.

The late Lucy S. Dawidowicz, in a fascinating lecture titled "What Is the Use of Jewish History?" pointed out that early nineteenth-century German-Jewish historians, who were "alienated from Judaism and the Jewish community, undertook to use Jewish history"—that is, to celebrate the high level of past Jewish achievements—in order to win credit from gentile authorities and "to hasten Jewish assimilation." That is emphatically not the intention of Sachar or the authors in the AJHS series. They alternate between pride in what Jews have done and despair over their loss of community. But whatever the intention, these new works illuminate neglected aspects of American history. More important, they show how Jewish history has been a testing ground for American ideals, especially the ideal of apportioning rewards according to individual merit as opposed to hereditary privilege or ethnic identity.

I do not mean to suggest that standard histories of the United States have totally ignored the Jewish presence. Jews are included, of course, in accounts of the "new immigration"; they move along with other ethnic groups from Ellis Island to their enclaves in New York and other cities, arousing prejudice and increasing demands for the restriction of immigration. Students in American colleges become familiar with Samuel Gompers, Louis Brandeis, Emma Goldman, and Morris Hillquit, though such figures are seldom identified as Jews; they may even learn that Judah P. Benjamin became the first "acknowledged" Jew in the United States Senate (David Levy had earlier converted to Christianity and changed his name), before being chosen secretary of war and secretary of state of the Confederate States of America.

In textbook histories, however, there is a rough correspondence between the space devoted to Jews and the proportion of Jews in the American population—a figure that rose to 3.7 percent in 1937 and then dropped by the late 1980s to 2.5 percent. It is true that throughout American history Jews have been the only non-Christian group with any appreciable influence or visibility (excluding African and Native Americans, who were more willing than Jews to accept Christian conversion), but they appear in our national self-portraits as one of the smallest and least significant minorities.

Even well-informed Jews are likely to think that American Jewish history really begins with the massive immigration and the teeming city streets and tenements of the late nineteenth and early twentieth centuries. No doubt there is some popular, almost folkloric knowledge of the Sephardic Jews of Newport, Rhode Island, who were assured by President Washington of "the exercise of their inherent natural rights," not mere "toleration," and protection by a federal government "which gives to bigotry no sanction, to persecution no assistance." Still, I suspect that even most professional historians would be amazed to discover the ubiquity of Jews in virtually all the significant episodes of American history.

A few examples will provide the background needed for a discussion of the volatile issues of merit and success. In the mid-eighteenth century, Jewish merchants such as Daniel Gomez and Hayman Levy helped to link the interior hinterland trade, especially in furs, with a network of Atlantic commerce that extended to England, Holland, Africa, and the Caribbean. Levy became the largest fur trader in the British colonies. Daniel Boone, who has come down in legend as the antithesis of the urban Jew, was hired by Jacob Cohen and other Jewish merchants to survey land, mark out roads, and locate land claims in Kentucky. Expansion into the supposedly "regenerating" frontier depended on the expanding markets that Jewish Americans helped create.

Since ordained rabbis did not arrive in the United States until the 1840s, the hazanim or cantors led services inside the synagogue, and outside the synagogue they gave symbolic representation to the Jewish people. On July 4, 1788, when a great parade in Philadelphia celebrated Pennsylvania's ratification of the Constitution, the Jewish hazan marched arm in arm with two Christian clergymen. New York's hazan, Gershom Mendes Seixas, served on the board of trustees of Columbia College from 1784 to 1815. Known as the "minister of the Jews," he appeared with the Christian clergy on days of thanksgiving and fasting—another indication that American Jews did not have to wait until the period 1920–45 to "enter the mainstream." As it happened, Jewish merchants in the early national period had business partnerships and social ties with gentiles. European travelers were astonished to see that the clothing and hairstyles of American Jews were indistinguishable from those of American Christians. And Jewish leaders in the early nineteenth century already expressed considerable anxiety over the rate of intermarriage.

In 1860 Jews constituted only one-half of 1 percent of the American population. Still, before the Civil War Jewish newspapers reached readers in 1,250 locations, and in upstate New York alone a mohel, or ritual circumciser, could be found in Utica, Oswego, Auburn, Rochester, Syracuse, and Binghamton. Jews tended to be concentrated in a few cities along the eastern seaboard, but the remaining minority was widely dispersed. In the 1840s and 1850s, Jews served in the legislatures of Indiana, North Carolina, South Carolina, Georgia, and New York. Edward S. Shapiro, the author of the final volume in the AJHS series, is thinking of the great metropolitan centers when he asserts that "few cities had had Jewish mayors prior to the 1960s."

One seldom associates Jews with the frontier West, yet the nineteenth-century cities and towns that were governed by Jewish mayors included Dodge City and Wichita, Kansas; Butte, Montana; Boise, Idaho; Portland and Eugene, Oregon; Seattle, Washington; Albuquerque, Santa Fe, Roswell, Tuscan, Yuma, Phoenix, Prescott, and Tombstone in New Mexico Territory; El Paso, Texas; San Francisco and Sacramento, California; Denver and Trinidad, Colorado. Three Jews died in the Battle of the Alamo in 1836, and seventeen Jewish sailors sank with the *Maine* in 1898. It was Adolph Gluck, a councilman of Dodge City, who selected Wyatt Earp to be the law-enforcing sheriff later romanticized by Hollywood; and Earp, who had a common-law marriage with a Jewish woman, was buried in a Jewish cemetery.

Jews have long had a significant connection with American icons and symbols of achievement, even apart from the Jewish magnates of Hollywood. Charles Lindbergh, the "Lone Eagle" who evoked deserved public censure for his response to Nazi Germany and his infamous anti-Semitic speech in 1941, toured the country as a hero under the auspices of the Daniel Guggenheim Foundation for the Promotion of Aeronautics, which had offered the prize that led to Lindbergh's solo flight. Countless scholars and artists have looked to fellowships from another Guggenheim Foundation (or to Pulitzer Prizes, endowed by another Jew) for the honorific windfall that would change their careers. For numerous writers the same can be said of the Book-of-the-Month-Club, another institution founded by Jews. It is true that Horatio Alger, Jr., the creator of the classic rags-to-riches literature read by millions of aspiring American youth, was not a Jew; but Alger served as a tutor to the sons of Joseph Seligman, the financier and former dry-goods merchant who supplied clothing to the Union Army during the Civil War and marketed hundreds of millions of dollars' worth of government bonds in Europe. According to Sachar, who unfortunately provides no endnotes or references that can be checked, Alger "used his employer as inspiration for his subsequent rags-to-riches stories."

For many American Jews, the historians' neglect of the extraordinary disparity of Jewish achievements has not been a cause for sorrow. (Though it should be noted that Oscar Handlin and a few other historians have celebrated the consequences of what Handlin termed in 1954 the Jewish "adventure in freedom.") It is important to note that anti-Semites have long exploited the widespread but pernicious assumption that the proportion of Jews or any other group in desirable or privileged positions should roughly reflect their proportion in the general population.

For supporters of what I will call "the quota ideal," gentiles should logically voice alarm whenever Jews constitute much more than 3 percent of the nation's college graduates, lawyers, doctors, publishers, news editors, arbitrageurs, advertising executives, college professors, television producers, investment bankers, computer scientists, Nobel Prize winners, or millionaires. Since Jews are "overrepresented" in all these categories and have often exceeded their quota by a factor of ten or more, there is much room for the classic anti-Semitic strategy of imposing a collective character on stories of individual success, and of then constructing the image of a transcendent Jewish conspiracy to control Wall Street investment, money and banking, the medical establishment, higher education, the media and entertainment, and other industries and professions. Recent efforts to portray the Jews as the power behind the African slave trade and as the inveterate enemies of the African race suggest the risks of even an accurate historical account: since Jews were deeply involved in Atlantic commerce and in the interior expansion of the American economy, it is easy enough to identify a few Jews among the tens of thousands of Protestant and Catholic slave traders and promoters of the South's cotton kingdom.

Despite these potential dangers, Shapiro presents impressive evidence that American Jews now have little to fear from public knowledge of their disproportionate role in the modern history of merchandising, investment banking, real estate, science, medicine, philanthropy, journalism, labor organization, and other areas. (I must add that Shapiro has a pronounced bias. He is an Orthodox Jew who scorns Reform and Conservative Judaism and their "outreach" programs to incorporate the children of mixed marriages into the community and to convert non-Jewish spouses. Shapiro is extraordinarily pessimistic when he discusses the supposedly rapid erosion of Judaism and the loss of a separate Jewish identity. And his definition of a Jew is hardly consistent: in his lists of prominent Jewish intellectuals, for example, he includes the offspring of Jewish fathers and non-Jewish mothers, even though he later warns that Reform's 1983 decision to recognize such people as Jews "meant that non-Reform Jews could never be sure that potential spouses were in fact Jewish." Shapiro's despondency could have been avoided by a less rigid definition of religious observance and a more open-minded interpretation of Jewish history.) Shapiro observes that the period from 1945 to the present, a time of unparalleled Jewish advance and achievement in secular spheres, has also witnessed a dramatic decline in anti-Semitism among American whites. In fact, it was the sudden collapse of anti-Semitic barriers, such as quotas on college admissions, that opened virtually unlimited frontiers for achievement.

Shapiro stresses that Jews have found it difficult to admit "that American anti-Semitism had dwindled to the point of insignificance," in part because anti-Semitic responses to public opinion polls had peaked as recently as 1944. As late as 1945, when Bess Myerson became Miss America and Hank Greenberg's ninth-inning home run won the American League pennant for the Detroit Tigers, a large proportion of advertisements for jobs printed in the Jewish-owned *New York Times* used code words that told Jews not to apply.

Discrimination against Jews, which was particularly intense from the First World War to the mid-1940s, provides an indispensable context in which to consider the quota ideal and the spectacle of Jewish achievement. Jews were never welcome in such enterprises as iron and steel manufacturing, machine tools production, the petroleum and automotive industries, commercial banking, chain stores, and newspaper chains. In the interwar period Jewish scholars were systematically denied appointments in most colleges and universities. Few Jews sat on the boards of large corporations, banks, railroads, or insurance companies—even those firms founded or directed by Jews, such as Kennicott Copper, American Smelting and Refining, Sears Roebuck, NBC, and CBS.

Throughout the United States restrictive covenants or "gentlemen's agreements" excluded Jews from attractive residential housing and suburban towns. In cities like Minneapolis, Jews were barred by 1920 from all social, fraternal, and service clubs, including the local branch of the American Automobile Association. At a time when four out of five of New York's Regents scholarship winners were Jewish, as well as some 70 percent of the student body at CCNY, medical schools began applying the quota ideal to curb the stream of Jewish applicants, which in the 1920s ran as high as 50 percent. By 1939 Dean William Rappleye of Columbia's College of Physicians and Surgeons could take comfort from the fact that the proportion of Jewish students had fallen to 6 percent: "The racial and religious makeup in medicine ought to be kept fairly parallel with the population makeup." In 1922 Harvard's President Abbott Lawrence Lowell took a similar stand and contended that a quota would actually help Jews by reducing anti-Semitic resentment. In less than a decade new admissions policies enforcing a "silent quota" lowered the number of Jews at Harvard from nearly 22 percent to 10 percent of the student body.

The most revealing sign of Jewish weakness in American society—and therefore the most irrefutable answer to anti-Semitic fantasies of Jewish power—was the failure to modify discriminatory immigration and refugee policy from 1921 through the years of the Holocaust. This time the issue of quotas involved not college admissions, but the life or death of many European Jews; and the issue was closely related to the most controversial question in American Jewish history, the response of the American Jews themselves to the Holocaust. Both Sachar and Henry L. Feingold give considerable space to these matters. Feingold takes the position that "history" (a substitute for God?) "assigned" American Jewry a providential role "as advocate for world Jewry," but that American Jews failed in that role, largely because their obsession with individual achievement and private self-realization had led to secularization, assimilation, and an inability "to act collectively."

Yet Feingold also admits that it is difficult to imagine how even a unified American Jewry, "a group not winning medals for popularity," could have "persuade[d] the American people to change their restrictive immigration policy in the midst of a severe depression and then, during a bloody war for survival, to alter wartime priorities and permit the rescue of European Jews." Whatever the grounds for retrospective guilt, it is clear that a group that made up less than 4 percent of the population and still faced barriers in higher education and most employments had little chance of altering the anti-Semitic policies of the State Department, which refused to issue even the number of visas allowed by the quota system, and thereby to save at least some tens of thousands of lives. It is because of such cumulative memories that American Jews have found it difficult to think of themselves as an elite.

Shapiro's summary of the sociological surveys adds substance to an almost incredible story of upward mobility and achievement. According to a 1974 study of America's "intellectual elite," half of the nation's 200 leading intellectuals were Jews; 76 percent of "the most influential intellectuals had at least one Jewish parent." Stressing that Jews in the media have always appeared "along the entire political spectrum" from right to left, Shapiro claims that in 1982 "one-quarter of those employed by *The New York Times, The Wall Street Journal, The Washington Post, Time, Newsweek* and the major television networks were Jews." Similarly, by the 1980s Jews made up one-quarter of the faculties of the Ivy League colleges and universities, and an even higher percentage of elite law and medical school faculties (at Yale Law School, 35 percent by 1970 and now around 50 percent). Even the discreet distaste for Jews that had long characterized the boardrooms of corporate America was beginning to evaporate by 1973, when Irving Shapiro, the son of a Lithuanian-born pants-presser, became chairman and CEO of Du Pont. As Jews moved into the highest ranks of such firms as Chrysler, Ford, Disney, and United Airlines, *Forbes* magazine reported that of the richest Americans, more than one out of four was a Jew. And unlike many of the gentiles on *Forbes*'s list, few of the Jews had inherited their money.

Even more significant, however, were the statistics pertaining to the Jewish "masses," who once toiled in sweatshops or hawked goods from street stalls or pushcarts (in part, as Gerald Sorin points out, in order to avoid anti-Semitic bosses and to be free to observe the Sabbath). By 1970 some 60 percent of all employed Jews were professionals, technical managers, or administrators. By 1988, according to the sociologist Steven M. Cohen, Jews were twice as likely as non-Jewish whites to report annual household incomes of more than $50,000. Although some poverty persisted, mainly among elderly Jews, the vast majority had become what Shapiro terms "the richest ethnic group in the richest country in history"; and the Jewish working class in America had "virtually disappeared." (For Shapiro, unfortunately, this astonishing upward mobility does not evoke humility or a sense of concern for less favored ethnicities.)

None of the books under review provides an explanation for the range and the diversity of Jewish accomplishment. Centuries of mercantile and cosmopolitan experience in Europe no doubt helped even nineteenth-century German-Jewish peddlers to found high-risk department stores that came to dominate retail trade in such inland cities as Atlanta, New Orleans, Little Rock, Memphis, Columbus, and Jacksonville. By the time Hart, Schaffner and Marx emerged as the largest manufacturer of men's clothing in the world, such Jewish names as Isaac Magnin, Filene's, Gimbel's, Macy's, Abraham and Straus, Bloomingdale's, and Neiman-Marcus had become synonymous with consumer culture from San Francisco to Boston, from New York to Dallas.

But while the great Jewish merchants endowed symphony orchestras and other cultural institutions, merchandising talent can hardly explain the achievements of such Jewish composers and performers as Gershwin, Copland, Koussevitzky, Ormandy, Monteux, Reiner, Bernstein, Heifetz, Rubenstein, Irving Berlin, and Jerome Kern. What did the great Jewish real estate magnates or the founders of Inland Steel, Consolidated Foods, and Hyatt Hotels have in common with such writers as Malamud, Bellow, or Roth, or with such scientists as Jonas Salk, Einstein, and Oppenheimer, who transformed the world in which we live? For that matter, what did any of these figures share with the Jewish pimps and vice lords who dominated the white-slave traffic and "sex industry" in the early twentieth century, or with the founders of "Murder, Inc." and such famous gangsters as Arnold Rothstein and "Big Jack" Zelig?

Jewish subcultures and religious traditions—particularly the laws of *tze-dakah*, which taught that philanthropy to the poor is a matter not of charity, but of religious obligation and legal right—played a crucial part in extending opportunities to the poor and in linking successive generations of Jewish immigrants. Writers of eastern European Jewish background have long denounced the German Jews who arrived in America before the 1880s as condescending and pretentious snobs who were far more concerned with winning gentile approval than with making common cause with their brethren. There is some truth to this stereotype, but Hasia R. Diner succeeds in modifying and humanizing the image of mid-nineteenth-century Jewish immigrants, many of whom were not really German Jews. Unlike Sachar, however, she almost totally ignores towering figures such as Jacob Schiff, who, for all his elitism, spent vast fortunes to aid the victims of Russian pogroms and to create organizations and institutions that would empower Jews while ensuring the degree of assimilation needed for survival.

As Sachar, Diner, and most of the other writers indicate, one can hardly overemphasize the importance of the small organizations that pooled savings and provided Jews with credit, at a time when "Hebrews" or "Israelites" were excluded from borrowing start-up capital by R. G. Dun and other credit-rating firms. Nor should one forget the fraternal societies, the *landsmanschaften* and the organizations like B'nai B'rith, which helped Jews adapt to the conditions of American life while providing both a sense of self-worth and models of achievement. For all their humiliation and hardship, the millions of eastern European Jews entered an America in which a small number of Jews from central Europe had already created an elaborate institutional framework, as well as precedents for spectacular success.

✳

I have suggested that American Jewish history provides a test case for the values of a meritocracy, as opposed to what I call the quota ideal. The word "merit" has become extremely unfashionable, partly because it has been used to legitimate colossal inequalities, and partly because it implies moral virtue in addition to deserved reward, honor, and esteem. But I wish to use "merit" in a limited pragmatic or operational way. If I develop heart disease, I want to be treated by the very best cardiologist available—a doctor who has met the highest standards of medical education and of a demanding practice, but who may in his or her private life be far less admirable than a less professionally competent partner.

No doubt such standards are easier to agree upon in medicine, science, engineering, and mathematics than in many other fields. No sensible person would contend that American society even approximates an ideal meritocracy, or that our gross inequalities, which often stem from childhood environment or random chance, are mostly "deserved." But educational systems and market forces do tend to reward skill and to penalize incompetence. I am not referring to a utopia in which the most creative potentialities of every individual are nurtured and given a place, though many Jewish and non-Jewish educators have aimed at that goal. What I have in mind is the widespread ideal that all Americans, as consumers, have a right to insist on high-quality products and on constantly improving professional services.

Unfortunately, this commitment to excellence is totally subverted by the quota ideal. Although Americans have overwhelmingly rejected the socialist vision of distributive wealth (once embraced and championed by large numbers of Jews), multiculturalism has encouraged the assumption that rewards and inequalities should roughly mirror the proportion of each ethnic group in the population as a whole. Such a correlation would presumably obtain (1) if all cultural traditions prepared people equally well for the demands of a market economy and a technological society; or (2) if admissions in higher education and all occupational appointments were decided by lottery. Lotteries eliminate the fear that any particular group has an advantage or a handicap. And indeed many Americans are more comfortable with huge prizes won in a lottery than with prizes achieved by merit in a competitive contest (with the exception of beauty contests for women). They are also more comfortable with merit displayed in sports, or even in popular art and entertainment, than with merit demonstrated in scholastic competition or business enterprise. (Thus it was that the celebrated Jewish boxers and baseball players, such as Benny Leonard, Barney Ross, Max Benny, and Hank Greenberg, reinforced by a sparkling galaxy of Jewish actors, comedians, and entertainers, made it easier for the public to accept the mounting number of Jewish business leaders, doctors, lawyers, intellectuals, and government officials.)

The history of anti-Semitic quotas shows that it has been difficult to accept the inescapable fact that, for a variety of historical and cultural reasons, members of certain groups will be over-represented as students in the most prestigious colleges, law schools, medical schools, and business schools, as well as in philanthropic and social protest movements, assuming there are no discriminatory barriers. In the modern secular world, a high proportion of Jews have shown a flair for test-taking, academic analysis, debate, and hermeneutics. Unlike Feingold and Shapiro, who present unconvincing arguments for separating Jewish religious and secular spheres, I find it highly probable that these secular talents are related to centuries of talmudic study and disputation, which led eventually to a print-oriented culture preoccupied with inquiry, argument, and systematic thought. The administrators at Harvard, Yale, Princeton, and other universities complained that Jewish students were too bookish and academic when the institutions adopted what amounted to an "affirmative action" policy to recruit "well-rounded" WASPs.

By the 1980s, however, Jewish students at Ivy League and other elite schools were overrepresented by a factor of ten. And one of the results of such meritocracy in action was to raise concerns about the inequitable allocation of resources in accordance with factors defined at birth: it could be argued, in other words, that being a Jew at birth gives a child a statistical advantage with respect to education, career, and income. Yet one must distinguish here between correlation and causation. Children were receiving good grades and awards in school and college not because they were Jews: as Shapiro laments, a diminishing number of "Jewish" students could claim a meaningful Jewish identity, especially with a recent intermarriage rate of 52 percent. Large numbers of Jews, however defined, were reaping scholastic rewards because they studied hard, did well on tests, and seemed to excel at juggling abstract concepts, perceiving relationships, and mastering detail without losing sight of the main point.

The ideal of selection and advancement according to merit, though corrupted in practice by racial and ethnic prejudice, had long been a keystone of America's republican ideology. By the 1960s this standard appeared at last to be vindicated by the collapse of the quota ideal and the spectacular upward mobility of America's Jews. The consumer orientation that flowered after World War II encouraged a new respect for cosmopolitan diversity as well as quality; as consumers sampled foreign foods, furniture, films, and fashions, the ethnicity of a doctor or lawyer became increasingly irrelevant, as long as he or she appeared to be an expert who had an assured mastery of his or her field. It was ironic, then, that just as Americans were beginning to assume that many of their doctors, dentists, lawyers, and accountants would be Jews, the whole framework of objective standards fell under attack, first by the New Left and then by postmodernist literary and philosophical critics—an attack in which Jews, of course, played a prominent part.

Yet a solution to the problem of disparities need not involve the denigration of standards or a subtle reimposition of the quota ideal. A defense of the merit ideal is perfectly compatible with the extension of special remedial measures to groups who have always been exploited and shut out from genuine opportunity. After all, the barriers that Jews faced in America were in no way comparable to the systematic degradation and deprivation suffered by African Americans as they endured centuries of slavery, segregation, and racial hate. While blacks in the nineteenth and early twentieth centuries were exhorted even by their own leaders to behave more like Jews, one could hardly expect former slaves and sharecroppers to draw on generations of experience with merchandising, credit, cooperative enterprise, and intellectual discussion.

The comparison between Jews and blacks served for a time to enlist extraordinary Jewish support for civil rights, but it has probably contributed in the long run to black anti-Semitism. Shapiro, whose brief discussion of this subject amounts to little more than reproaching blacks for ingratitude, is blind to the fact that virtually every immigrant group has forged ahead and won white acceptance in America by climbing over the African Americans. (Neither Sachar nor Diner gives nearly enough attention to Jewish complicity in America's system of racial oppression. Even apart from Jewish slaveholders, Jewish merchants, land speculators, entrepreneurs, and bankers profited from a developing economy in which blacks served the function of a surrogate proletariat or undercaste.)

I do not mean to suggest that special programs for education and job training should be allowed to undermine standards of merit. It is true, alas, that some types of affirmative action have been justified by the quota ideal, and have implied the revival of informal quotas that would drastically reduce Jewish representation in positions of power, expertise, and influence. Such a course would be extremely harmful in two ways. From an instrumental perspective, particularly in medicine, the entire population would suffer from a lowering of standards of competence and excellence. Even more disastrous, however, would be the dissipation of every group's aspiration for improvement. Although modern Americans seem to understand such striving better in the world of sports than in science, business, or education, it is this drive for limitless achievement and improvement in all spheres, including social betterment, that remains the most valuable legacy that its Jewish citizens have given the United States.

＊

In many parts of the world Jews have been in the vanguard of modernization—inventing and discovering scientific and mathematical paradigms, spearheading movements for social justice, anticipating and promoting changes in consumer needs and tastes. Yet Judaism has also represented an unbroken tradition that has required resistance to certain kinds of threatening change, and certainly to the threat best typified, perhaps, by the centuries of missionary efforts to persuade or coerce Jews into accepting Jesus as the Messiah. The tension and the balance generated by this paradox of innovation and continuity may help to explain Jewish creativity. But it also produces constant anxiety and controversy over the validity of diverse forms of Jewish expression and the future fate of a Jewish identity.

In view of the debates that have divided the American Jewish community since the 1960s, it is hardly surprising that both Sachar and the final two volumes of the AJHS series link spectacular Jewish achievement with "assimilation," leaving the reader with the sense that American Jews now face an unprecedented and perhaps hopeless crisis. This message of gloom and doom may mitigate the alarm of some gentiles, who might otherwise find it impossible to repress jealous resentment over Sachar's and Shapiro's tales of limitless success. When reading Shapiro especially, it almost seems as if the disintegration of *Yiddishkayt* and any meaningful Jewish identity is God's retribution for the hubris of American Jews, who have deserted the "world of our fathers" for the false and suburbanite gods of the American Dream.

Sachar concludes his massive volume on a more ambiguous note. With admirable artistry he returns in the afterword to the Myers family of Springfield, Illinois, whose chronicle he salutes in the prologue as "a palimpsest of the United States itself." From their founding of a men's clothing store in the 1860s to the military service of three brothers in World War II, the Myers clan provides Sachar with a lens for a succession of snapshots of middle-class American Jews taking part in American history. Turning to the present, we find that three of the four grown children of James and Edith Myers have married non-Jews. This reflects the soaring rate of intermarriage that Shapiro and numerous other commentators interpret as the death sentence of Jewish "peoplehood." Yet all of the grandchildren of these three mixed marriages are being reared as Jews! One of the gentile wives has converted to Judaism, and her three children "are among the Temple's best Hebrew students." Sachar refrains from speculation about the future of such Judaism by choice. He closes with the story of Jamie, the eldest of James and Edith's children, who traveled to Israel, married a sabra, fathered a son, Adam, and then returned with his family to the United States. With memories of his natal land, the 11-year-old Adam can affirm, "Israel is my home . . . There I know where I am," while his father and grandfather "listen thoughtfully, saying nothing."

Sachar knows, of course, that Israel is never likely to become a meaningful option for American Jews. If we take the history of the Myers family as a weather vane, that means confronting what Shapiro terms the threatening "friendliness of American society" and the "insoluble dilemma" of intermarriage, which he portrays as a symptom of a much larger and irreversible "disease." The disease, quite simply, is apathy, secularism, and a willingness to assimilate in order to succeed. Although Shapiro is deliberately provocative in his scorn for non-Orthodox Jewry and for the "cultural lag" of Jews' political liberalism, he does raise a central question that cannot be evaded:

The major question facing American Jewry throughout the postwar years was whether their valiant efforts to fill the cultural vacuum created by the Holocaust would prove to be sufficient: would Jewish culture and religion be sufficiently attractive so that Jews would voluntarily identify with the Jewish community and reject acculturation and assimilation?

Shapiro's pessimistic answer must be put within the context of the annihilation, in the Nazi genocide, of one-third of the world's Jewish population, to say nothing of the wellsprings of Jewish cultural and intellectual life; and the cutting off thereby of the kind of immigration and trans-Atlantic influence that had traditionally reinvigorated American Judaism and counterbalanced the seductive forces of acculturation. Prospects for the future appear even bleaker when one adds to this picture the aging of the American Jewish population and its negative population growth, which has already brought a startling drop in absolute as well as relative numbers. And one could also mention the recalcitrance and self-insulation of most Orthodox communities and of "survivalists" like Shapiro, who asserts that "Jewish survival" is justified only if "the quality of that life"—as defined by a small minority of Orthodox Jews—"was worth preserving."

No one can deny that American Jewry faces a demographic and spiritual crisis that will only deepen as memories of the Holocaust and of Israeli triumphs continue to fade. I cannot begin to address this momentous and complex issue here, but it is important to point to certain omissions and blind spots in all the books under review. Although several non-Jewish historians have persuasively challenged the long-held dogma that modern history moves in an irreversibly secular direction, these new works on American Jewish history take "secularization" uncritically, as a self-evident proposition.

More specifically, they give virtually no attention, for example, to changes in Jewish liturgy, ritual, and theology. Sachar is a doctrinaire secularist who seemed wholly unaware that college campuses in 1993, including Hillel and other Jewish organizations, were far more preoccupied with prayer, religious experience, and religious issues than they were in previous times. Although synagogue affiliation has increased dramatically since the 1930s (a threefold growth from 1930 to 1960), Shapiro dismisses this transformation as a purely social and secular phenomenon. It is all too easy to caricature suburban bar mitzvahs and bat mitzvahs while ignoring the adult classes in Talmud, Hebrew, biblical interpretation, and Jewish history, especially those drawing large numbers of women, who were long excluded from such intellectual excitement.

The proliferation of adult study groups is related to the issue of intermarriage and conversion. The Myers family is unusual in having all their grandchildren brought up as Jews, but even Shapiro admits, albeit in negative language, that by the 1980s 20 percent of the gentile spouses in intermarriages were converting to Judaism and 25 percent of the children of non-converted spouses in mixed marriages were being raised as Jews. While he uses the examples of Marilyn Monroe and Elizabeth Taylor to ridicule the seriousness of spousal conversion, he refrains from mentioning that even in Reform congregations many converts devote a year or more to the study of Hebrew and Judaism. I myself know converts expert in Hebrew, halakah, and Jewish history who belong to Orthodox congregations and would take considerable offense at Shapiro's statement that even the "small minority of converts [who] were attracted to Judaism," as opposed to the "vast majority" who simply desired to please a prospective Jewish spouse, "[lacked] any feeling for the ethnic or historical dimensions of Jewishness." The saddest thing about this essentially racial view of Jewishness is that it shuts off the only possible path for adaptation and survival—vigorous outreach programs to the children of Jews, to the 1.35 million gentile adults who live with Jews, and to the estimated 3.5 million "core Jews" who are not affiliated with synagogues or other Jewish institutions.

In the midst of the Jewish debate over outreach and conversion, together with the guilt and the anguish over a waning sense of ethnicity, it is easy to lose sight of the extraordinary popularity of college courses in Judaic studies and of books on virtually every aspect of Judaica. Indeed, American Jewish history, a subject often ignored or marginalized in the past (as in the widely read, Israel-originated, 1,096-page *A History of the Jewish People*, edited by the late H. H. Ben-Sasson), is itself a great resource for study and contemplation, an incredible narrative of struggle, loss, adaptation, triumph, and anxiety. The experience of the Jews in America provides an alternative to the Old World narrative of "ghetto-to-genocide" persecution. It has often been pointed out that American Jews, for all their masterful achievements in organization and philanthropy, have produced no Bubers, Heschels, or Rosenzweigs; but perhaps the contrast between the two modes of historical experience will someday inspire profound theological reflection. Secularization, too, requires a spiritual understanding.

5

The Slave Trade and the Jews

The ghastly slave trade from Africa to the Atlantic sugar islands such as Madeira and São Tomé and then to the Western Hemisphere began in the mid-1400s and flourished for over four centuries. Though historians continue to debate the numbers, it now seems probable that from eleven to twelve million Africans were forcibly shipped out from their continent by sea. Millions more perished in African wars or raids for enslavement and in the deadly transport of captives from the interior to slave markets on the coast.

The participants in the Atlantic slave system included Arabs, Berbers, scores of African ethnic groups, Italians, Portuguese, Spaniards, Dutch, Jews, Germans, Swedes, French, English, Danes, white Americans, Native Americans, and even thousands of New World blacks who had been emancipated or were descended from freed slaves but who then became slaveholding farmers or planters themselves. Responsibility, in short, radiated outward to peoples of every sort who had access to the immense profits generated from the world's first system of multinational production for a mass market—production of sugar, tobacco, coffee, chocolate, rum, dye-stuffs, rice, spices, hemp, and cotton.

Today it is both remarkable and deeply disturbing to discover that this Atlantic slave system evoked little meaningful protest until the late eighteenth century. When it did finally appear, the Anglo-American antislavery movements were overwhelmingly religious in character, and drew on developments in sectarian and evangelical Protestantism.[1] Yet the world's religions had long given slavery its ultimate sanction. Catholic popes enthusiastically blessed and authorized the first Portuguese slave traders in West Africa. For centuries Muslim *jihads* justified the enslavement of untold numbers of sub-Saharan infidels. In eighteenth-century Barbados the Church of England acquired possession of hundreds of slaves whose chests were branded with the letters "SOCIETY" to signify ownership by the Society for the Propagation of the Gospel. As late as the 1750s many devout British and American Quakers were actively involved in the slave trade. The small number of Jews who lived in the Atlantic community took black slavery as much for granted as did the Catholics, Muslims, Lutherans, Huguenots, Calvinists, and Anglicans. And while at least one Jewish merchant joined New York's first antislavery society in the 1790s, Judaism was as resistant as other tradition-oriented religions to such intellectual and moral innovations.

For four centuries the African slave trade was an integral and indispensable part of European expansion and settlement of the New World. Until the 1820s the flow of coerced African labor exceeded all the smaller streams of indentured white servants and voluntary white immigrants willing to endure the risks of life in the Western Hemisphere. The demand for labor was especially acute in the tropical and semitropical zones that produced the staples and thus the wealth most desired by Europeans. In the mid-1700s the value of exports to Britain from the British West Indies was more than ten times that of exports from colonies north of the Chesapeake. And the economy of the northern colonies depended in large measure on trade with Caribbean markets, which depended in turn on the continuing importation of African labor to replenish a population that never came close to sustaining itself by natural increase.

Fortunately for the planters, merchants, consumers, and other beneficiaries of this lethal system, West Africa offered a cheap and seemingly unlimited supply of slave labor, and the efforts of African kings to stop the ruinous sale of subjects were few and ineffective. Long before the Portuguese African voyages of the fifteenth century, Arab and Berber merchants had perfected the trans-Saharan slave trade and had delivered hundreds of thousands of black slaves to regions extending from the Persian Gulf (via a seaborne trade from East Africa) to Egypt, Sicily, Morocco, and Spain. Sharply divided by tribal rivalries, black Africans never looked upon one another as a homogeneous African "race." Most tribes and kingdoms were accustomed to a variety of forms of servitude, and developed highly sophisticated methods for recruiting captives and bartering slaves for coveted commodities, eventually including firearms, which Arabs or the Portuguese could bring from distant lands. The political power and commercial networks of the Sokoto caliphate, the Asante, and the Yoruba states, to name only three examples, were wholly at odds with the popular picture of "primitive" peoples overawed and dominated by European military might.

Though first monopolized by the Portuguese, the Atlantic slave trade attracted ships from the Netherlands, France, Britain, Denmark, Spain, Sweden, and the English mainland colonies. Even the northern German ports sought to cash in on the lucrative traffic. How did Jews fit into this picture? To keep matters in perspective, we should keep in mind that in 1290 England expelled its entire Jewish population; only a scattering of migrants began to return in the latter half of the seventeenth century. In France a series of expulsions and massacres in the fourteenth century virtually demolished the medieval Jewish communities. In Spain, beginning in the mid-fourteenth century, a much larger Jewish population was subjected to periodic massacres, forced conversion, mob attacks, and final expulsion in 1492. Most of the refugees fled to Turkey and other Muslim lands. The estimated 100,000 Jews who escaped into Portugal were soon compelled to accept Christianity. Large numbers of these "New Christians" intermixed with the "Old Christian" population and lost any Jewish identity, although the Inquisition continued to search for the signs of secret Jewish rituals that could bring arrest, torture, and death.

By the 1570s, during the beginning of Brazil's sugar boom, which depended on African slave labor, Judaism as a religion had been virtually wiped out in England, France, the Germanies, Spain, Portugal, the Low Countries, and most of Italy; the great mass of Jewish survivors had emigrated to Poland, Lithuania, and Ottoman lands in the Balkans and Turkey. No professing Jews were allowed to contaminate the Spanish or Portuguese colonies of the New World; in the 1680s they were also banned from the French West Indies and restricted in British Barbados. These sustained anti-Semitic measures clearly reduced the opportunity Jews might have had for participating in the Atlantic slave system and certainly precluded any Jewish "initiation," "domination," or "control" of the slave trade. Yet the continuing persecution and exclusion, especially of the "New Christians" or Marranos, did lead to a desperate search for new commercial opportunities in the New World, where there was less surveillance by the Inquisition, and in the rebellious Spanish province of the Netherlands, which struggled from 1568 to 1648 to win independence.[2]

At this point one must emphasize that Jews, partly because of their remarkable success in a variety of hostile environments, have long been feared as the power behind otherwise inexplicable evils. For many centuries they were the only non-Christian minority in nations dedicated to the Christianization and thus the salvation of the world. Signifying an antithetical Other, individual Jews were homogenized and reified as a "race"—a race responsible for crucifying the Savior, for resisting the dissemination of God's word, for manipulating kings and world markets, for drinking the blood of Christian children, and, in modern times, for spreading the evils of both capitalism and communistic revolution. Responsibility for the African slave trade (and even for creating and spreading AIDS) has recently been added to this long list of crimes.[3]

Such fantasies were long nourished by the achievements of a very small number of Jews who, barred from landholding, the army, and traditional crafts and professions, took advantage of their cosmopolitan knowledge and personal connections that favored access to markets, credit, and such highly desired commodities as diamonds, spices, wool, and sugar. Much of the historical evidence regarding alleged Jewish or New Christian involvement in the slave system was biased by deliberate Spanish efforts to blame Jewish refugees for fostering Dutch commercial expansion at the expense of Spain. Given this long history of conspiratorial fantasy and collective scapegoating, a selective search for Jewish slave traders becomes inherently anti-Semitic unless one keeps in view the larger context and the very marginal place of Jews in the history of the overall system. It is easy enough to point to a few Jewish slave traders in Amsterdam, Bordeaux, or Newport, Rhode Island. But far from suggesting that Jews constituted a major force behind the exploitation of Africa, closer investigation shows that these were highly exceptional merchants, far outnumbered by thousands of Catholics and Protestants who flocked to share in the great bonanza.

I should add that in trying to determine who was or was not a covert Jew, the historian comes perilously close to acting like the Inquisition. In the early eighteenth century a large number of Brazilian planters, said to be Marranos, were arrested by the Inquisition, extradited, and taken to Lisbon for trial. By any modern definition, excluding the racial definition of the Nazis, these planters were not Jews. Yet various historians have counted such Marranos as Jews and have assumed that an earlier Brazilian planter, Jorge Homen Pinto, who owned six sugar mills, 370 slaves, and a thousand oxen, was a Jew. More careful investigation, however, reveals that Pinto passed the most stringent racial tests as an Old Christian.

Jews and Jewish names are virtually absent from the texts and indexes of all the scholarly works on the Atlantic slave trade and from recent monographs on the British, French, Dutch, and Portuguese branches of the commerce in slaves. To expose the supposedly "secret relationship" between Jews and slavery, anti-Semites have therefore turned to histories of the Jews in such regions as Amsterdam, Brazil, and Curaçao. These works provide material that can easily be misquoted, distorted, and put in totally misleading contexts.

To give only two examples, *The Secret Relationship* asserts that "Dr. Wiznitzer claims that Jews 'dominated the slave trade,' then the most profitable enterprise in that part of the world." The footnote refers to a book review by Herbert I. Bloom which in no way supports this statement. The Nation of Islam authors never acknowledge that Arnold Wiznitzer, whose *Jews in Colonial Brazil* is frequently cited, writes that "[I]t cannot be said that Jews played a dominant role in Dutch Brazil as 'senhores de engenho,'" or sugar planters—he estimates that Jews made up about 6 percent of the planters—or that he adds that historians have tended to exaggerate the number of Jews in colonial Dutch Brazil from 1630 to 1654.

From Columbus to Jean Lafitte, the slave-dealing New Orleans pirate, the authors pounce on the most farfetched claims of "crypto-Jewish" identity. Florida's Senator David Yulee renounced his Jewish origins, converted to Christianity, and even claimed he was descended from a Moroccan prince. But since Yulee took a strongly pro-slavery position in the Senate, the Nation of Islam authors count him as a Jew. Such techniques hardly conform to the standards of fairness, justice, and "great sensitivity" set forth at the beginning of the book in a remarkably hypocritical "Editor's Note." But more insidious than the misquotations and slipshod documentation is the total lack of historical context. Even if every purported "fact" presented in *The Secret Relationship* were true, the uninformed reader would never suspect that for every Jew involved in the Atlantic slave system there were scores or even hundreds of Catholics and Protestants.

In actuality, Jews had no important role in the British Royal African Company or in the British slave trade of the eighteenth century, which transported by far the largest share of Africans to the New World. According to the Dutch historians Pieter C. Emmer and Johanes Menne Postma, Jews had a very limited and subordinate role even at the height of the Dutch slave trade in the seventeenth century: "They did not serve on the *Heren X*, the directorate of the Dutch West India Company. Their investment share amounted to only 0.5 percent (or one two-hundredth) of the company's capital."[4] I should add that between 1658 and 1674 the Jewish investment in the slave-trading West India Company seems to have risen to 6 or even 10 percent. Keeping in mind that the Dutch share of the trade accounted for only 16 percent of the total, one sees how small the involvement was, and it is as close as Jews ever came to "dominating" the nefarious Atlantic traffic.

If we expand the issue beyond the slave trade itself, small numbers of Sephardi Jews and Marranos were crucial to the process of refining and marketing sugar and then in shifting transatlantic commerce, including the slave trade, from Portugal to Northern Europe. Throughout the Mediterranean, Jews had acquired expertise in refining and marketing sugar, which until the eighteenth century was a much-desired luxury only the well-to-do could afford. Marranos and Italians were prominent in the international sugar trade of the fifteenth and sixteenth centuries. Some of them helped to establish sugar plantations in Madeira and São Tomé, in the Gulf of Guinea. Indeed, in 1493, when Portugal was flooded with Jewish refugees from Spain, the government forcibly baptized their children, large numbers of whom were separated from their parents, and shipped off to São Tomé as colonists. Most of these Marrano children died, but some survived to become sugar planters, an occupation that was hardly a matter of choice.

The Marranos who moved to Brazil took with them the technical skills of artisans, foremen, and merchants, and took a leading part in developing the sugar export industry. Other Marranos, who sailed with Portuguese expeditions to the Kongo Kingdom and Angola, became expert at contracting for cargoes of slave labor. There can be no doubt that these New Christians contributed much to transform Portugal into Europe's first major supplier of slave-grown sugar. Yet given the extent of intermarriage and loss of Jewish identity, most Marranos were "Jewish" only in their vulnerability to suspicion, persecution, and anti-Semitic fantasies of conspiracy. Ironically, the Inquisition's anti-Semitic crusade, which "fabricated Jews like the mint coined money," as one cynical Inquisitor observed, convinced other Europeans that "Portugal was a nation of crypto-Jews, as exemplified by the coarse Castilian proverb: 'A Portuguese was born of a Jew's fart.'"[5]

Fears of Jewish power were greatly stimulated by the leadership Marranos and professing Jews took in marketing Portuguese East Indian spices and then sugar throughout northern Europe, especially after they became allied with the rebellious Dutch and heretical Protestants. Although the Dutch barred professing Jews from many trades and occupations—it was apparently not until 1655 that two Jewish merchants received permission from the Amsterdam government to establish a sugar refinery—the Netherlands presented a climate of relative religious toleration that encouraged the founding of synagogues and the revival of a small Jewish religious community. The Twelve Years' Truce with the then united Spain and Portugal, from 1609 to 1621, helped the Dutch Sephardi merchants expand various branches of trade with the Iberian Peninsula, Brazil, and Africa. Their knowledge of Spanish and Portuguese, as well as the intricacies of international finance, gave them a particular advantage in procuring and marketing sugar.

Even though Jewish merchants suffered from the resumption of the war with Spain and from Europe's Thirty Years' War, they retained temporary control of sugar and its distribution, which should not be confused with control of the Dutch slave trade. This involvement with sugar was largely the result of the Dutch conquest of northeastern Brazil in the early 1630s. By 1645 some 1,450 Jews made up about one-half of the white civilian population of Dutch Brazil and owned about 6 percent of its sugar mills. Jewish merchants bought a large share of the slaves transported by the Dutch West India Company (WIC) and then retailed them to Portuguese planters on credit, arousing complaints of high prices and interest rates. A few Amsterdam Jews, such as Diego Dias Querido, originally a native of Portugal, challenged the WIC monopoly and chartered their own ships to transport slaves from Africa to Brazil or the Spanish Caribbean. But the Jewish presence in Brazil was short-lived. In the early 1650s, with the collapse of the Dutch occupation and the impending return of the Portuguese, Jews faced the choice of emigration or death.

Some of the émigrés from Brazil moved northwestward to the Caribbean, where they were soon joined by Jewish and Marrano entrepreneurs from Holland. There were a number of reasons for the upsurge of interest in the Caribbean. By the 1650s the British island of Barbados had made a decisive conversion from tobacco to sugar, as African slaves and a new class of large planters replaced a population of white indentured servants. In 1662 Spain awarded an *asiento* (monopoly contract) to the Dutch West India Company, seeking a non-Portuguese source of African slaves for the Spanish Caribbean colonies. The main *asientista*, or monopoly contractor, was the Protestant banker Balthazar Coymans, and Jews had little to do with the WIC shipments of slaves from Africa. Still, in 1664 the king of Spain appointed don Manuel de Belmonte, a Jew of Spanish origin, his Agent-General in Amsterdam for the procurement of slaves. And it was in Curaçao, which Marranos had helped to establish in 1651, that Jews found their main outlet for selling slaves and Dutch manufactured goods along the Spanish Main.

For a time Curaçao became the great entrepôt of the Caribbean, trading legally and illegally with Barbados and other rising British and French colonies as well as with the Spanish mainland. In the eighteenth century Jews made up about half the population of Curaçao—as opposed to one percent of the population of New York City—and seem to have been involved mainly in the transshipment of commodities other than slaves to the Spanish colonies. The mainland Spanish colonies never developed true plantation systems; their demand for slaves declined abruptly in the eighteenth century, since they could not begin to compete with colonies like Jamaica, St. Domingue, and Brazil, which constituted the heart of the Atlantic slave system and which imported their labor directly from Africa.

The one colony where a significant number of Jews took up plantation agriculture was Suriname, or what later became Dutch Guiana. The religious freedom of the Dutch colonies allowed Jews to establish their own self-governing town, Joden Savanne (Jewish Savannah), in the interior jungle. There in the late seventeenth and early eighteenth centuries the Sephardim lived the life of sugar planters, extracting labor from African slaves in one of the most deadly and oppressive environments in the New World. Suriname, however, never became a major sugar-producing region.

The significant point is not that a few Jewish slave dealers changed the course of history, which would have been the same without Jewish slave traders and planters. The significant point is that Jews found the threshold of liberation from second-class status or worse, in a region dependent on black slavery. Before turning to the sobering and depressing part of this message, I should stress that even with regard to the Dutch Sephardi sugar trade, we're dealing with a few hundred families. By the 1670s the Dutch sugar boom had ended and Britain would soon emerge as the world's greatest sugar importer and slave-trading nation. In Barbados, to be sure, there were fifty-four Jewish households in 1680. But these were not great slave traders or planters; they were mostly the managers of retail shops and moneylending firms who owned fewer slaves per household (three) than the non-Jewish residents of Bridgetown.

To keep matters in perspective, we should note that in the American South, in 1830, there were only 120 Jews among the 45,000 slaveholders owning twenty or more slaves and only twenty Jews among the 12,000 slaveholders owning fifty or more slaves. Even if each member of this Jewish slaveholding elite had owned 714 slaves—a ridiculously high figure in the American South—the total number would only equal the 100,000 slaves owned by black and colored planters in St. Domingue in 1789, on the eve of the Haitian Revolution.

In actuality, so far as ownership of slaves is concerned, the free people of color in the Caribbean greatly surpassed the much smaller number of Jews. Even in Charleston, South Carolina, the percentage of free African Americans who owned slaves increased from one half to three quarters as one moved up the socioeconomic scale as indicated by the ownership of real estate. The thousands of Southern black slave owners included freedpeople who had simply purchased family members or relatives. But there were also colored planters, especially in Louisiana, who owned more than fifty or even one hundred slaves. The allure of profits and power transcended all distinctions of race, ethnicity, and religion.

No one should defend the small number of Jews who bought and sold slaves, or who forced slaves to cut cane on the estates of Joden Savanne. No one should defend the infinitely larger number of Catholics and Protestants who built the Atlantic slave system, or defend the Muslims who initiated the process of shipping black African slaves to distant markets, or defend the Africans who captured and enslaved perhaps fifteen million other Africans in order to sell them to European traders for valuable and empowering goods. But while posterity has the right and even duty to judge the past, we must emphatically renounce the dangerous though often seductive belief in a collective guilt that descends through time to every present and future generation.

While insisting that no group is responsible for the sins of its ancestors, I find it deeply disturbing that many Jews, including those who established the first synagogue in Curaçao, found a path to their own liberation and affluence by participating in a system of commerce that subjected another people to contempt, dishonor, coerced labor, and degradation. It has even been said that the more enlightened rulers of eighteenth-century Europe were much swayed by the early achievements of enfranchised Jews in Dutch Brazil, the Caribbean, and North America.[6] This is one side or aspect of the dismal truth that our New World—conceived as a land of limitless opportunity, breaking the crust of old restraints, traditions, and prejudices—was made possible only by the near extinction of indigenous populations and by the dehumanizing subjugation of the so-called African race.

Notes

1. I have analyzed the origins of antislavery thought in two books: *The Problem of Slavery in Western Culture* (Oxford University Press, 1988) and *The Problem of Slavery in the Age of Revolution, 1775–1823* (Oxford University Press, 1999).

2. For some of this information I am much indebted to Seymour Drescher, "The Role of Jews in the Transatlantic Slave Trade," in *Strangers and Neighbors: Relations Between Blacks and Jews in the United States*, ed. Maurianne Adams and John Bracey (University of Massachusetts Press, 1999), pp. 105–115.

3. For the extreme example of anti-Semitic accusations masquerading as a documented history of Jewish involvement in the slave trade and American slavery, see *The Secret Relationship Between Blacks and Jews*, Volume One (The Nation of Islam, 1991). This book begins by suggesting that the expulsion of Jews from forty-six specified European cities and states was the result of the Jews' "economic exploitation, monopolizing, or 'sharp practice,'" which "incited the moral indignation of Europe's Gentile population" (p. 10). As the Jews escaped "with considerable sums of money," "they would reunite later in an unholy coalition of kidnappers and slave makers" (pp. 12–13). The Atlantic slave system was essentially the creation of these roving refugees and "secret Jews" (Marranos), who "procured Black Africans by the tens of thousands and funnelled them to the plantations of South America and throughout the Caribbean" (p. 19). Displaying 1,275 footnotes, most of them citing respectable works by Jewish historians, *The Secret Relationship* moves on to the American South and Civil War, to a section on "Jews and the Rape of Black Women," and to a final lengthy rogues' gallery of Jews, or "Chosen People," who participated in "the Black Holocaust." Any reader who accepts this work as legitimate and accurate history—and the volume has been widely distributed in black communities— would have to conclude that Jews were mainly responsible for New World slavery and its tragic legacy, and have long been the worst enemy of the African race. The deceptive and malicious nature of the Nation of Islam's volume has been exposed by the booklets *Jew-Hatred as History: An Analysis of the Nation of Islam's "The Secret Relationship Between Blacks and Jews"* (Anti-Defamation League, 1993), and Harold Brackman, *Farrakhan's Reign of Historical Error: The Truth Behind The Secret Relationship Between Blacks and Jews* (The Simon Wiesenthal Center, 1992). Since my essay was written, Eli Faber has shown in a deeply researched work that Jews played an extremely minor part in the British slave trade and British slave colonies. See *Jews, Slaves, and the Slave Trade: Setting the Record Straight* (New York University Press, 1998).

4. Drescher, "The Role of Jews in the Transatlantic Slave Trade," p. 111.

5. C. R. Boxer, *The Portuguese Seaborne Empire, 1415–1825* (Knopf, 1969), p. 271.

6. See my *Slavery and Human Progress* (Oxford University Press, 1984), p. 101.

Jews and Blacks in America

In the Almost Promised Land:
American Jews and Blacks, 1915–1935
Hasia Diner (1977 and 1995)

Struggles in the Promised Land: Toward a History
of Black–Jewish Relations in the United States
Edited by Jack Salzman and Cornel West (1997)

Blacks in the Jewish Mind: A Crisis of Liberalism
Seth Forman (1998)

What Went Wrong? The Creation and Collapse
of the Black–Jewish Alliance
Murray Friedman (1995)

African Americans and Jews in the Twentieth Century:
Studies in Convergence and Conflict
Edited by V. P. Franklin, Nancy L. Grant,
Harold M. Kletnick, and Genna Rae McNeil (1998)

killing rage: ending racism
bell hooks (1995)

✳

In 1963, at the time of Martin Luther King, Jr.'s, March on Washington, it
was assumed by many American liberals that Jews and African-Americans

were natural allies, a belief seemingly confirmed when a disproportionate number of Jewish students participated in the Freedom Summer of the following year. Yet by 1995, when Louis Farrakhan led his Million Man March, the conventional view held that Jewish and black communities were divided by deeply rooted conflicts. In the spring of 1996 Howard University and the American Jewish Committee, in a desperate attempt to promote "mutual understanding and a just society," launched the admirable *CommonQuest: The Magazine of Black–Jewish Relations*. The first issue reviewed Murray Friedman's book *What Went Wrong? The Creation and Collapse of the Black–Jewish Alliance.*[1]

During the past decade numerous books and academic conferences have addressed the issue of conflicting or incompatible interests between blacks and Jews. The first important survey of black–Jewish relations, by Robert G. Weisbord and Arthur Stein, was published soon after New York's Ocean Hill–Brownsville school crisis of 1968 and was revealingly entitled *Bittersweet Encounter: The Afro-American and the American Jew.*[2] Since 1970 little sweetness has remained. After bitter divisions over Israel, affirmative action, and the Black Power movement, some African-American academics have dismissed the contributions of Jewish philanthropists to black causes as paternalism and have argued that it was secular radicalism, not Jewish ancestry or religion, that distinguished the white civil rights workers in the South. In the history of black–Jewish relations, according to this view, the Jewishness of an eighteenth-century slave trader or a later Harlem merchant or landlord was far more meaningful than the Jewishness of Michael Schwerner and Andrew Goodman, who served in 1964 as voting-registration volunteers in Meridian, Mississippi, before being murdered by the Ku Klux Klan.

Such second thoughts about black–Jewish relations have by no means been limited to African-American historians. In *Struggles in the Promised Land*, an anthology edited by Jack Salzman and Cornel West, a number of Jewish writers stress the great caution and self-interest of Jewish organizations that worked for civil rights. In another anthology, *African Americans and Jews in the Twentieth Century: Studies in Convergence and Conflict*, Michael Rogin draws on his book *Blackface, White Noise: Jewish Immigrants in the Hollywood Melting Pot*[3] to describe the racist "stain of shame" incurred by Jewish performers who wore burnt cork on stage and screen early in the twentieth century. A few Jewish radicals joined black nationalists in arguing that Jews had been mainly interested in using and exploiting blacks for their own advancement as Jews. Many other Jews were deeply troubled that only a fairly small number of prominent blacks, such as Henry Louis Gates, Jr., were willing to denounce black anti-Semitism, and that such publications as the Nation of Islam's 1991 *The Secret Relationship between Blacks and Jews, Volume One*, were being circulated in American colleges.[4] By the middle and late 1990s, diverse Jewish historians, among them Murray Friedman, Jack Salzman, and Seth Forman, concluded that little common ground remained and that the black–Jewish alliance was ready for last rites.

No one has equaled the American historian Hasia Diner in richly documenting the strong support given to African-American legal, economic, and educational rights, between 1880 and 1935, by Jewish newspapers, religious leaders, lawyers, labor leaders, social workers, and philanthropists.[5] These were the decades when black migration from the South to Northern cities coincided with large-scale Jewish immigration from Eastern Europe. Yet even Diner shows great unease in accepting that Jews were motivated by "empathy" and "altruism"; she has consistently put emphasis on motives of Jewish self-interest—essentially endorsing the view of the historian David Levering Lewis, author of a biography of W. E. B. Du Bois, that Jews helped African-Americans as a means of fighting anti-Semitism "by remote control."[6] While there is doubtless some truth to this argument (what would be wrong about one persecuted group helping another if they faced a common peril of racist prejudice?), it fails to address the probability that twentieth-century Jews, like the earlier nineteenth-century Jewish and Irish immigrants, would have won more rapid acceptance as genuine and patriotic "whites" if they had adopted the prevailing and insidious antiblack prejudices of white Anglo-Americans.[7]

While the term "self-interest" has many meanings and can obviously lead to a recognition of mutual interests, it cannot easily be harmonized with empathy, compassion, or benevolent goodwill—all of which appear in Jewish editorials about blacks, as quoted and described by Diner, from the *Jewish Daily Forward*, which was then left-wing, to the conservative and religious *Tageblatt* and *Morgen Journal*. Unlike individual philanthropists and editors, Jewish agencies and organizations were explicitly devoted to the principle of Jewish self-interest. Yet in her essay in the collection *Struggles in the Promised Land*, Cheryl Greenberg shows that in the mid-twentieth century "Jewish organizations also spent much of their time furthering the cause of Black civil rights even when Jewish interests were not at stake." Indeed, Greenberg even finds examples of collaboration with black causes that "went far beyond direct or even indirect self-interest, as both communities moved toward a sense of the indissoluble nature of equality."[8] In fact, self-interest often appeared in a more negative form, inhibiting Jewish support for some of the more radical black protests, especially during World War II when most Jews were intent on proving their own patriotism and allegiance to the white majority and the power elite.

Whether examining the motives and behavior of early abolitionists or the antiracist position of most early twentieth-century American Jews, ranging from rich philanthropists to urban radicals, we should use great care in resorting to the simplistic and often cynical formula of "self-interest," which inevitably suggests a degree of selfishness and limited commitment. The students I knew who went to Mississippi in 1964, sometimes risking their lives for a full year, were not thinking, "This will help the Jews," or "This will look good on my transcript." Of course the thought of doing good made them feel good about themselves. Yet it is also true that the relative purity of their motives can hardly impose an eternal moral debt on African-Americans. As bell hooks remarks in *killing rage: ending racism*, solidarity between blacks and Jews

> must be mutual. It cannot be based on a notion of black people as needy victims that white Jews "help." It cannot be based on gratitude extended by blacks to white Jews for those historical moments when they have been steadfast comrades in struggle furthering black liberation.

The vast recent literature on blacks and Jews, even that written by historians, suffers from a foreshortened perspective.[9] Perhaps if we had a clearer vision of how far both blacks and Jews have come, and how much they have overcome, we would be less skeptical about the recent past and less pessimistic about the future. It should never be forgotten that during the past millennium no other ethnic groups have suffered such prolonged persecution, oppression, and dehumanization as have blacks and Jews. Whether defined as the slayers of Christ, the cursed children of Ham, vermin to be exterminated, or apelike savages, Jews and sub-Saharan Africans were for Europeans the archetypal outsiders—outsiders who were frequently likened to pigs and maggots whose genes supposedly threatened what fifteenth-century Spaniards began calling "purity of blood."

According to Voltaire, "One regards the Jews the same way as one regards the Negroes, as a species of inferior humanity." As the medieval historian

William Chester Jordan demonstrates, this theme pervaded the Middle Ages, when "allegorically the words 'Jew' and 'Blackness' conjured up the Devil; morally they denoted evil; and mystically they evoked the Day of Judgment."[10] Beginning in 1290 Jews were expelled from dozens of European states and regions, a policy that late Elizabethan England attempted to impose on black Africans. In 1777, after decades of legal dispute over the status of black slaves brought in from the colonies, the French government tried to prohibit all blacks from entering the country. Beginning in the 1790s, U.S. immigration laws were more successful in barring the influx of free blacks. Despite dramatic differences between black and Jewish occupations and ways of life, the Eastern European pogroms of the late nineteenth and early twentieth centuries bore a haunting resemblance to the roughly contemporary antiblack race riots, lynchings, and autos-da-fé in the United States.[11]

It was doubtless this similarity, along with a new eruption of pseudo-scientific racism and anti-Semitism, that led some Jewish immigrants to identify with blacks in a way that would have been unthinkable for Jews before the Civil War except for a handful of radical abolitionists like August Bondi and Jacob Benjamin. Modern writers have also drawn comparisons—some insightful, some absurd—between the four-year Nazi Holocaust and the four centuries of the Atlantic slave trade, now often termed "the Black Holocaust."[12]

Because the Jewish response to oppression goes back in time to the biblical Exodus narrative and to early modern quests for religious toleration, African-Americans began at least two centuries ago to look to the history of Jews for models of liberation. By the mid-nineteenth century the spectacular success of small numbers of Jews in Western Europe persuaded some African-American leaders that even the deepest forms of prejudice and bigotry could be overcome—though in the longer run, Jewish achievement fostered anti-Semitism, especially in Europe, and doubtless stimulated black–Jewish rivalry in the U.S. as well as pointless debates over which group has suffered the most. (If the Nazi Holocaust means that Jews have won what might be called the "global victimization prize," as well as an extraordinary number of Nobel Prizes, even the lynching of Leo Frank in 1915 can hardly be compared, on the American front, with the centuries of African-American agony and persecution.)[13]

One can invert the question of emulation and ask whether the blacks' long struggle for liberation has furnished useful models for Jews. In the early twentieth century, when most Jewish immigrants were poor and when their status as "whites" was challenged by anti-Semitic restrictions on residence, education, and employment, many Jewish writers and intellectuals found a kind of spiritual liberation in African-American culture. From Al Jolson to Irving Berlin and George Gershwin, and from Norman Mailer's *The White Negro* to the comedian Sandra Bernhardt's revival of blackface, one can compile an impressive list of Jews who eagerly embraced black motifs and identities as a way of breaking free from coercions of the past. One can also point to Jewish performers such as Jack Benny, whose dim friend Rochester was obviously intended to make fun of blacks and to patronize them.

Still, after analyzing the image of African-Americans in the Yiddish press, Hasia Diner writes that the underlying assumption in the published discussions of black art was that "blacks reacted more sensitively, felt pain and suffering more sharply, and expressed themselves with greater depth and with more poignancy." Though the subject is complex and controversial, blackface performance ultimately helped in some ways to subvert the racist conventions that gave it birth. It was part of a broader Jewish identification with blacks that became a twentieth-century version of the "romantic racialism" that the historian George Fredrickson has found among earlier abolitionists and such popular writers as Harriet Beecher Stowe.[14]

Whatever one might mean by "Jewish liberation," Jewish history and religion present it as an unfolding process that is far from complete. This point is underscored for observant Jews by the fasting and mourning of Tisha B'av, which commemorates the historical disasters and catastrophes that began with the destruction of the First and then the Second Temple in Jerusalem. The Shoah is conceived of in a similar way in some of the literature recalling the Holocaust. That said, we can speak of three instances of Jewish liberation that have served as models for black leaders and occasionally, as with Marcus Garvey's followers, for a mass movement.

The first instance is the deliverance of the ancient Hebrews from bondage in Egypt and their agonizing exodus toward the Promised Land. The second liberation comes with the Zionist or nationalist vision of a final refuge and homeland where Jews (or African-Americans) may achieve physical security while living in accordance with their own laws and traditions. The Zionist ideal is to create a national center that will radiate pride, dignity, and standards of conduct for those Jews (or African-Americans) who remain in the

Diaspora (and it should be stressed that many Jews and peoples of African descent have long believed that they live in a Diaspora).[15]

The third model, deriving from the Enlightenment and the ideals of the American and French Revolutions, envisions a liberation from all legal disabilities, the acceptance of a common citizenship, and an opening of equal opportunity for upward mobility based on individual merit. It is significant that the Abbé Grégoire, who during the French Revolution was one of the most eloquent in demanding the emancipation of both Jews and blacks, also called for the elimination of all ethnic dialects so that all French citizens could share a common "republican" language. Today such a call for extinguishing cultural and religious differences has little appeal.[16]

✳

The first theme, that of Exodus, was exemplified on January 1, 1808, when the Reverend Absalom Jones preached a thanksgiving sermon in Philadelphia celebrating the abolition of the African slave trade by the U.S. and Britain. A former slave himself and a founder of the African Episcopal Church, Jones hailed the American and British laws as the providential prologue to slave emancipation, building his vision on the biblical "circumstances which preceded the deliverance of the children of Israel from their captivity and bondage in Egypt." After comparing the misery, grief, and despair of the ancient Hebrews with the horrors of the Atlantic slave system, Jones told his black congregation that God had commanded the Jews as part of their worship "never to forget their humble origin" and their "historic deliverance from slavery." Accordingly, "it becomes us, publickly and privately, to acknowledge, that an African slave, ready to perish, was our father or our grandfather":

> Let the first of January, the day of the abolition of the slave trade in our country, be set apart in every year, as a day of publick thanksgiving for that mercy. Let the history of the sufferings of our brethren, and of their deliverance, descend by this means to our children, to the remotest generations.

In effect, Jones was calling for a day like Passover, when Jews are asked to "relive" their historical liberation from bondage.[17]

Everyone has heard the Exodus theme in slave spirituals—"Way down in Egypt's land. . . . Let my people go"—but few whites are aware that Moses, Joseph, Joshua, Daniel, David, Solomon, Zipporah (Moses' black Cushite wife), and the Queen of Sheba all had a deep meaning for American slaves and their descendants. As late as 1960 Michael Walzer, then a young graduate student who was writing about black sit-ins as well as the centrality of the Book of Exodus in the English Puritan Revolution, described a powerful sermon in a black church in Montgomery, Alabama, in which the preacher "cringed," he wrote, "under the lash, challenged the pharaoh, hesitated fearfully at the sea, accepted the covenant and the law at the foot of the mountain."[18] Whereas white Christian hymns tended to spiritualize "Egyptian bondage" and "the Promised Land," American slaves, more attracted to the Old Testament, concentrated on the fact that God had presented an alternative to slavery and had punished oppressors in *this* world. And in the words of one spiritual: "And the God dat lived in Moses' time is jus' de same today."[19]

Again and again the songs and sermons by black preachers repeated the hopeful theme of the Red Sea opening, of the enemy's army being destroyed, and of a Promised Land that was not heaven, as whites maintained, but a physical place. As General Sherman's troops marched through Georgia they heard slaves sing: "I fasted an' I prayed till I came through / Thank God A'mighty, I's free at las!" "Shout the glad tidings o'er Egypt's dark sea, / Jehovah has triumphed, his people are free!" A Union army chaplain, W. G. Kiphant, was deeply troubled by the discovery that

> Moses is their *ideal* of all that is high, and noble, and perfect, in man. I think they have been accustomed to regard Christ not so much in the light of a *spiritual* Deliverer, as that of a second Moses who would eventually lead *them* out of their prison-house of bondage.[20]

One can conclude that the first, or biblical, liberation of the Jews was exceptionally meaningful for African-Americans because it conveyed, as Walzer points out, a "sense of possibility" and genuine escape from oppression combined with a realistic message that freedom is not a clear-cut condition instantly achieved but a goal requiring self-discipline and arduous collective effort. It is also worth noting the continuity of the theme in African-American literature from Frances Harper's allegorical poem of 1869, *Moses: A Story of the Nile*, to the novels of James Baldwin, who used the journey out of Egypt as a symbol for overcoming the corruptions of the dominant white world.[21]

If we turn to the model of Zionism, or the Return—and it is worth recalling that a few Sephardic Jews did return to Turkish Palestine in the mid-sixteenth century after their expulsion from Spain and Italy—we find that some slaves and free blacks in New England petitioned to be returned to Africa as early as the American Revolution. Paul Cuffe, the black shipowner and captain who transported thirty-eight African-Americans to Sierra Leone in 1816 and thus initiated the "colonization movement," said he was following the Jewish example of the ancient Exodus narrative.[22] In 1820, when the American Colonization Society and the U.S. government sent the first group of free black colonists to Africa, the Society's white agent, while dying of disease, transferred his commission as leader to Daniel Coker, a mulatto minister. Coker prayed that "He that was with Moses in the wilderness, be with us," and that "He that divided the waters for Israel will open our way, I know not how." By May 1821, as increasing numbers died, Coker confided in his journal that "Moses was I think permitted to see the promised land but not to enter in. I think it likely that I shall not be permitted to see our expected earthly Canaan. But this will be of but small moment so that some thousand of African children are safely landed."[23]

During the 1820s and the years that immediately followed, free American blacks overwhelmingly opposed the colonization movement, sensing that it was largely motivated by white racist desires to "cleanse" the continent of a people who had been among the first to arrive, clear, and plow the land, and had even helped fight for American independence. Yet by the 1850s many Northern black leaders, deeply disillusioned by the series of events from the Fugitive Slave Law to the Dred Scott decision, began to advocate or plan large-scale emigration to Africa or Haiti. Thus when many white clergymen, including some rabbis, were citing Noah's curse to justify black bondage, various Northern black clergymen—"pioneer black nationalists," in George Fredrickson's phrase—"put forth a prophetic view of black redemption that would inspire African-American emigrationists, the first Pan-Africanists, and leaders of the 'Ethiopian' movement among black Christians in South Africa."[24]

In the 1890s this back-to-Africa campaign was revived by Henry McNeal Turner, a prominent African Methodist Episcopal church bishop, and Henry Sylvester Williams, the Trinidadian architect of the first Pan-African Conference, who may have been inspired by Theodor Herzl's speeches to workingmen in London.[25] In 1902 Theodor Herzl, the "father" of Zionism, envisioned in his utopian novel *Altneuland* a double stream of migrations that would restore Negroes to Africa as well as Jews to Palestine. Herzl maintained that only a Jew could fully comprehend what it meant for blacks to grow up "in alien surroundings despised and hated because their skin is differently pigmented." For their part, some prominent blacks, though highly ambivalent about Jews in general, were horrified by the Russian pogroms of the 1880s. "My heart goes out," Booker T. Washington wrote, "to our Hebrew fellow-sufferers across the sea."[26] Black editors and writers publicized the persecution of Jews in Russia and began to draw parallels between black nationalism and Zionism. Whatever elements of self-interest lay in these acts of identification, both Jews and blacks were searching for pride, dignity, and self-respect at a time of increasing persecution, debasement, and caricature.

Black emigrationists repeatedly drew parallels with what the black leader Edward Blyden hailed as "that marvellous movement called Zionism." Blyden, who had learned Arabic and had visited what he called "Jerusalem and Mount Zion, the joy of the whole earth," wrote in 1898, in *The Jewish Question*, that the entire civilized world recognized the claims and the right of the Jews to the Holy Land. "There are few," he wrote, "who, if the conditions were favourable, would not be glad to see them return in a body and take their place in the land of their fathers as a great—a leading—secular power."[27]

Two decades later Marcus Garvey and his followers found somewhat similar inspiration in both the biblical and Zionist sense of mission, though by Garvey's time anti-Semitism had become more rampant and relations between Jews and blacks were becoming more strained and complex. Garvey, in the words of Martin Luther King, Jr.,

> was the first man of color in the history of the United States to lead and develop a mass movement. He was the first man on a mass scale and level to give millions of Negroes a sense of dignity and destiny and make the Negro feel he was somebody.[28]

And in a speech of 1921 Garvey informed his listeners that for centuries Jews had been a despised race in Europe, "buffeted worse than the Southern Negro today." Even in the U.S., "it was a disgrace to be a Jew."

What did the Jews do? Garvey asked. They were too few in number to carry out any physical conquest. Therefore, they had devised a master plan for the financial conquest of the world. Jewish financiers had brought on the First World War, presumably as a profit-making venture, and had then abruptly stopped the war when they were promised the possession of Palestine. "The Jew has gone back to Palestine," Garvey concluded, "and the Jew it is that has the world in the palm of his hand." While much of this sounded like Henry Ford and other contemporary anti-Semites, Garvey conveyed no sense of outrage. On the contrary, he was exhorting his followers to learn from the Jewish example. Since Jews in Palestine had already enhanced the prestige and opportunities of Jews in England and America, he said, one could be assured that self-governing blacks in Africa would help to liberate blacks in the entire Diaspora.[29]

*

The "Zionist" model of black liberation proved to be a disastrous failure. Since Liberia was founded in 1822 very few blacks have chosen to emigrate from the U.S.; like the present world's largest population of Jews, they have viewed the U.S., or at least "the American dream," as the closest approximation to a promised land. Moreover, even apart from Garvey's financial collapse and imprisonment, Garveyism easily fostered a kind of anti-Semitism mixed with envy and admiration, as in Malcolm X's statement in a 1963 *Playboy* magazine interview:

> The Jew never went sitting-in and crawling-in and sliding-in and freedom-riding, like he teaches and helps Negroes to do. The Jew stood up and stood together, and they used their ultimate power, the economic weapon. That's exactly what the Honorable Elijah Muhammad is trying to teach black men to do. The Jews pooled their money and bought the hotels that barred them.[30]

As with Zionism, various forms of black nationalism helped to overcome racist stereotypes of weakness and animality, conveying instead a sense of dignity and power. Yet despite the early hints of common interest, voiced by such figures as Herzl, Blyden, and Garvey, divisions between blacks and Jews were deepened in the late 1960s by Israel's relations with white South Africa, by sympathy among African-Americans with Arabs and Palestinians, and by the Six-Day War of 1967, which evoked a sharp attack on Israel from SNCC. The B'nai B'rith's Anti-Defamation League labeled SNCC as racist and anti-Semitic, while many black leaders, for their part, supported the UN's equation of Zionism with racism.

Fortunately, the third and major model of Jewish liberation had been the struggle against legal discrimination and disabilities, and the attempt to erode prejudice, coupled with the use of education to encourage upward mobility. Of course, traditional Christian thought had sharply separated the "Chosen People" of the Old Testament from their grasping, "stiff-necked" descendants.

Nevertheless, in the second half of the nineteenth century African-American leaders increasingly cited the contemporary Jews of Western Europe to prove that the effects of racial prejudice, especially what Frederick Douglass termed a "consciousness of inferiority," could be overcome.

In a speech celebrating Lincoln's Emancipation Proclamation, Douglass pointed out:

> At one time to hate and despise a Jew, simply for being a Jew, was almost a Christian virtue. The Jews were treated with every species of indignity, and not allowed to learn trades, nor to live in the same part of the city with other people. Now kings cannot go to war without the consent of a Jew. The Jew has come up, and the negro will come up by and by.

As Waldo E. Martin, Jr., explains, in *The Mind of Frederick Douglass:*

> The lessons of the historical saga of the Jews—he [Douglass] and many others, white and black, agreed—were worthy of emulation. In spite of racial and religious proscription, Jews strove for knowledge, achievement, and socioeconomic mobility. They also prized and fought for human rights, dignity, and their identity as a people.[31]

In 1899 Booker T. Washington took up the same theme: "There is, perhaps, no race that has suffered so much. . . . But these people have clung together. They have had a certain amount of unity, pride, and love of race. . . . Unless the Negro learns more and more to imitate the Jew in these matters, to have faith in himself, he cannot expect to have any high degree of success."[32] Four years earlier a black lawyer in Cleveland had enlarged on the point:

> We feel and think our lot in this so-called "white man's country," is a hard one; and in very truth it is . . . but when we scan the bloodstained recitals of what the Jews have passed through since the destruction of Jerusalem . . . , and then note how conspicuous they are in all civilized communities for their real attainments along the lines of science, art, literature and finance, we may well cheer up and persevere along the same lines until victory crowns our efforts.[33]

James Weldon Johnson similarly called on his fellow blacks to emulate Jews in measuring up "brain for brain" with white America.

Unfortunately, this kind of rhetoric was bound to backfire, especially as the disparities in education, wealth, and power between the two groups continued to widen. By the late 1980s the per capita income of American Jews, who made up less than 3 percent of America's population, was almost double that of all non-Jews; and *Forbes* magazine reported that Jews made up 40 percent of the richest Americans. According to Seymour Martin Lipset and Earl Raab,

> During the last three decades Jews have made up 50 percent of the top two hundred intellectuals, 40 percent of American Nobel Prize winners in science and economics, 20 percent of professors at the leading universities . . . , 40 percent of partners in the leading law firms in New York and Washington, 26 percent of the reporters, editors, and executives of the major print and broadcast media, 59 percent of the directors, writers, and producers of the fifty top-grossing motion pictures from 1965 to 1982, and 58 percent of directors, writers, and producers in two or more primetime television series.[34]

Moreover, at a time when more young black men were in jail or prison than in college, nearly 90 percent of college-age Jews were attending college, and a disproportionate number of them winning Phi Beta Kappa keys and other honors at the nation's most prestigious colleges and universities.

These Jewish achievements mostly took place after World War II. That Jews often had to overcome prejudice in order to succeed became significant for African-Americans only when more blacks themselves began to attend the same colleges and enter the professions and the business world. In the mid-1920s, in view of the virtual absence of blacks in America's best colleges, one could hardly expect African-Americans to be horrified by the news that Yale restricted the admission of Jewish students to 13 percent, when Jews made up 5.5 percent of Connecticut's population. Because Jews long struggled against such quotas and considered it normal for the number of Jewish students to rise to one quarter or one third of the student body in some of the nation's best universities, law schools, and medical schools, they were often fearful of affirmative action programs that might substitute ethnic quotas for supposedly objective standards of merit. As the historian Jerome Chanes put it, "For Jews, quotas were a way of keeping people out; for African Americans, quotas were a way of letting people in."[35]

For Jews, eighty years or so of upward mobility have come close to eliminating all but a few pockets of genuine Jewish poverty. Few Jews, one suspects, tried to imagine during those years what it must be like for African-Americans to face a group of whites who, while claiming a large debt of gratitude for past aid to blacks, achieved great material and professional success and could also point to the greatest victimization in history as part of their past. What were African-Americans to make of people who, although they would sometimes admit they were by no means free of racism, kept extending an imploring hand and asking, "What went wrong?"

Thus today it is a shock to read in books like *Struggles in the Promised Land* the often quoted words of Louis Marshall, the great Jewish jurist and strong supporter of African-American causes, spoken before the 1926 annual convention of the NAACP: "We were subjected to indignities in comparison with which to sit in a Jim Crow car is to occupy a palace." It happens that Marshall, often quoted out of context, was referring to the wholesale massacres and explusions of Jews in late medieval and early modern Europe.[36] Yet the insensitivity of such comparative victimization remains, especially when one thinks of the thousands of Jim Crow lynchings and the failure of the federal government to stop them. Marshall's remark was not far in spirit from an all-too-common view privately expressed by some Jews and other descendants of recent immigrants: "Our people arrived penniless, and they made it. Why can't the Negroes be more like us? Our people aren't living in drug- and crime-infested ghettos."

In fact, we do not have to minimize the obstacles and prejudices that Jews overcame in America to observe that there was nothing in American Jewish history remotely comparable to the social, economic, and psychological effects of centuries of African-American slavery and racial persecution, including the period from the 1870s to the 1960s. Competition over which group suffered most can only encourage Jewish racism and black anti-Semitism; but knowledge of the larger historical picture, including millenniums of violent anti-Semitism and the lethal, destructive legacy of racial slavery and the Atlantic slave system, could serve as a basis for mutual understanding in dealing with the stark realities of human evil.

For the first third of the twentieth century such shared knowledge was promoted by the Yiddish press, which, unlike the publications of other immigrant groups, was filled with accounts of lynchings and racial injustice, together with informative essays on the achievements of African-Americans and their struggles for racial equality. Well-to-do and powerful German Jews contributed millions of dollars to such organizations as the National Urban

League, the NAACP, the Tuskegee Institute, and other black schools and colleges, while Jewish-led unions like the ILGWU were the first to admit black workers and fight for racial equality. It is also true that for many blacks, Jewish landlords and merchants became the symbol of exploitation in a market-driven society—in part because Jews were often the only whites who would lend money to blacks, locate their shops in black districts, and cater to black tastes.

In 2001 one can cautiously conclude that the third model of liberation, that of upward mobility and assimilation, as envisioned by Douglass, Booker T. Washington, and James Weldon Johnson, has begun to work. If the black–Jewish "alliance" has mostly crumbled, there has been a spectacular increase in the size of the black middle class, in levels of black employment, in the skills and preparation of black students at the best colleges, and in the numbers of top-level black administrators and law firm partners (often promoted by Jewish employers).[37] For decades the nation has admired black actors, athletes, models, and other black celebrities of various kinds. Clearly such admiration has its limits; but only one Jew has come close to matching Colin Powell as a leader with a plausible chance of becoming president. And as African-Americans have begun to acquire a prouder sense of their own history and cultural continuity, they increasingly face a dilemma that has long plagued Jews—assimilation.

It is true that while intermarriage with whites has begun to increase, it is still far from the 52 percent rate of Jewish intermarriage with gentiles; and the choices of blacks are circumscribed by the rigid American definition of "race." But many African-Americans are still troubled by the thought of dilution of their identity and by increasing divisions among them according to shades of skin color. Furthermore, as upwardly mobile blacks follow Jews and other whites to the suburbs, their behavior may reinforce the conviction of many inner-city youth that education and success come from "acting white." The problems raised by upward mobility and assimilation—and the question of the social responsibilities of those who are more successful than others—could provide new ground for dialogue between Jews and blacks.

Finally, Jewish history provides another note of caution. Countless times, in various kinds of societies from Moorish Spain to Weimar Germany, Jews have "succeeded" and won "acceptance," only to encounter a sudden pogrom or outburst of ancient anti-Semitic canards. Like Jews (to say nothing of Kosovars, Serbs, or Tutsis), African-Americans might seem more accepted and then, sometime in the future, face a revival of the kind of antiblack racism that had supposedly disappeared. When we look at other parts of the post–cold war world, we see how often nationalism is based on a hatred and mistrust of others.[38] We have no reason for complacency about having conquered such feelings here.

Notes

1. This essay makes no pretense of summarizing the extremely complex history of African-American and Jewish relations. As several writers have recently pointed out, we still lack a detailed and comprehensive history of this subject, although some of the books listed above provide indispensable insights and information.
2. Negro Universities Press, 1970.
3. University of California Press, 1996. As both Harold Brackman and Hasia Diner point out, Al Jolson's *The Jazz Singer* was enthusiastically applauded in 1927 by both blacks and Jews (one black newspaper proclaimed that "every colored performer is proud of [Jolson]"; the Jewish *Forward* interpreted the performance of Jews in blackface "as a sign of intense cultural bonding"). Brackman's observations appear in *Modern Judaism* in his essay "The Attack on 'Jewish Hollywood': A Chapter in the History of Modern American Antisemitism"; Diner, *In the Almost Promised Land*, pp. 68–69. I'm much indebted to Harold Brackman for sending me a prepublication copy of his study as well as some valuable editorial advice.
4. See "The Slave Trade and the Jews" in this volume.
5. In addition to her excellent book, *In the Almost Promised Land*, Diner has written important essays for the anthologies edited by Salzman and West, and V. P. Franklin, et al.
6. In her essay in *African Americans and Jews in the Twentieth Century*, Diner attempts to expand the definition of self-interest to include friendship and empathy, as well as a Jewish "special mission," based on Jewish persecution in Europe, to make white Americans live up to their own ideals as embodied in the Declaration of Independence. Yet she undercuts the moral value of this mission by affirming that "the issues of Black exclusion and oppression provided a stalking horse for American Jewish writers who constantly fretted over the power of anti-Semitism in America and Europe" (p. 37).
7. Much recent research confirms Bertram Wallace Korn's conclusion that many American Jews in the pre–Civil War period accepted slavery and the prevailing belief in Negro inferiority as a way of gaining "status and security from the very presence of this large

mass of defenceless victims who were compelled to absorb all of the prejudices which might otherwise have been expressed more frequently in anti-Jewish sentiment" (Korn, *Jews and Negro Slavery in the Old South, 1789–1865*, Reform Congregation Keneseth Israel, 1961, p. 67, quoted in Weisbord and Stein, *Bittersweet Encounter*, p. 22). In 1860 there were only about 150,000 Jews in the U.S., a nation of 31,443,321 people, including nearly four million slaves. However one should note that by the late nineteenth century, Lillian Wald was organizing settlement houses for African-Americans in New York City and Jacob Schiff was agitating for racially integrated public schools.

8. Greenberg, "Negotiating Coalition: Black and Jewish Civil Rights Agencies in the Twentieth Century," in *Struggles in the Promised Land*, p. 163.

9. Along with the extensive verbal arguments and analyses of various books, one should not overlook the pictorial dimension as portrayed in Milly Heyd's remarkable book, *Mutual Reflections: Jews and Blacks in American Art* (Rutgers University Press, 1999).

10. Jordan, "Medieval Background," in *Struggles in the Promised Land*, p. 53.

11. For vivid, unforgettable accounts of American whites torturing and lynching blacks, see Leon F. Litwack, *Trouble in Mind: Black Southerners in the Age of Jim Crow* (Knopf, 1998) and Orlando Patterson, *Rituals of Blood: Consequences of Slavery in Two American Centuries* (Civitas/Counterpoint, 1998), pp. 171–232.

12. For a fair-minded, well-informed, and rational comparison, see Seymour Drescher, "The Atlantic Slave Trade and the Holocaust: A Comparative Analysis," in *From Slavery to Freedom: Comparative Studies in the Rise and Fall of Atlantic Slavery* (New York University Press, 1999), pp. 312–338.

13. By "global victimization prize" I refer to a modernized and systematic effort to exterminate an entire people from the earth, a program that succeeded in killing about one third of all Jews.

14. According to Fredrickson, romantic racism "resembled Herder's relativism more than Gobineau's hierarchical racism, and was widely espoused by Northern humanitarians who were more or less antislavery. Although romantic racialists acknowledged that blacks were different from whites and probably always would be, they projected an image of the Negro that could be construed as flattering or laudatory in the context of some currently accepted ideals of human behavior and sensibility." Stressing the supposedly childlike, affectionate, docile, and noncompetitive traits of Negroes, the "logical extreme was to argue, as Methodist Bishop Gilbert Haven did during the Civil War, that the Negro was the superior race—'the choice blood of America'—because his docility constituted the ultimate in Christian virtue" (*The Black Image in the White Mind: The Debate on Afro-American Character and Destiny, 1817–1914*, Wesleyan University Press, 1971, pp. 101–102). Since the 1960s African-Americans have succeeded in demolishing the once-prevalent stereotype of docility.

15. In America, Africa, and Israel there are, of course, an increasing number of black Jews. This is not the place to discuss the definition and variety of black Jews; the black Jews I have known, students and academics, have been unquestioning Americans.

16. For a new English translation of Grégoire's extraordinary attack in 1808 on arguments

for racial inferiority, see Henri Grégoire, *On the Cultural Achievements of Negroes*, translated with notes and an introduction by Thomas Cassirer and Jean-François Brière (University of Massachusetts Press, 1996).

Some black writers have accused Jews of working for black assimilation and loss of identity while finding ways to preserve and magnify their own Jewish power. This is a distortion which, as Wilson Jeremiah Moses points out in *Afrotopia: The Roots of African American Popular History* (Cambridge University Press, 1999), ignores the contribution of such Jewish anthropologists as Franz Boas and Melville Herskovitz to the development not only of cultural pluralism but of contemporary Afrocentrism.

17. Absalom Jones, *Thanksgiving Sermon, Preached January 1, 1808, in St. Thomas's, or the African Episcopal Church Philadelphia; On Account of the Abolition of the African Slave Trade, on that Day, by the Congress of the United States* (Philadelphia, 1808), pp. 5, 10–11, 13, 19–20.

18. Walzer, *Exodus and Revolution* (Basic Books, 1985), p. 3.

19. For biblical themes in slaves' spirituals, see Lawrence W. Levine, *Black Culture and Black Consciousness: Afro-American Folk Thought from Slavery to Freedom* (Oxford University Press, 1977), pp. 11–80.

20. Albert J. Raboteau, *Slave Religion: The "Invisible Institution" in the Antebellum South* (Oxford University Press, 1978), pp. 311–312.

21. One should note the importance of a different version of history disseminated as early as the 1820s by *Freedom's Journal*, America's first black newspaper, and David Walker's *Appeal to the Colored Citizens of the World*. According to this view, the Pharaoh and Egyptians had been the black ancestors of African-Americans and the Jews had benefited from a mild form of servitude in no way comparable with slavery in the New World. See Peter P. Hinks, *To Awaken My Afflicted Brethren: David Walker and the Problem of Antebellum Slave Resistance* (Pennsylvania State University Press, 1997), pp. 186–201. While this argument has persisted to the present, it would appear that most Christian slaves identified with Moses and the Israelites even if they were taught that Jews were later "Christ killers."

22. Of course Jews in the Diaspora had always prayed for the messianic time when they or their descendants would return to Jerusalem.

23. Daniel Coker, *Journal of Daniel Coker* (Baltimore, 1820), pp. 15–17, 27, 31; Tom W. Shick, *Behold the Promised Land: A History of the Afro-American Settler Society in Nineteenth-Century Liberia* (Johns Hopkins University Press, 1980), p. 22.

24. George M. Fredrickson, *Black Liberation: A Comparative History of Black Ideologies in the United States and South Africa* (Oxford University Press, 1995), p. 61.

25. Robert A. Hill, "Black Zionism: Marcus Garvey and the Jewish Question," in *African Americans and Jews in the Twentieth Century*, p. 45. Henry McNeal Turner had advocated colonization since the Civil War.

26. Louis R. Harlan, "Booker T. Washington's Discovery of Jews," in *Religion, Race, and Reconstruction: Essays in Honor of C. Vann Woodward*, edited by J. Morgan Kousser and James M. McPherson (Oxford University Press, 1982), p. 270.

27. Hollis R. Lynch, *Edward Wilmot Blyden: Pan-Negro Patriot, 1832–1912* (Oxford University Press, 1967), pp. 64–65. Some powerful African-Americans gave strong support to the founding of Israel. In 1947 Walter White won much applause from Jews by persuading Haiti and Liberia to vote in the UN for the partition of Palestine.

28. David J. Garrow, *Bearing the Cross: Martin Luther King, Jr., and the Southern Christian Leadership Conference* (Morrow, 1986), p. 428.

29. *The Marcus Garvey and Universal Negro Improvement Association Papers,* edited by Robert A. Hill (University of California Press, 1983–1984), Vol. 2, pp. 245, 317, 466; Vol. 3, pp. 215–216; Vol. 5, pp. 127–128. Though Garvey cursed "the Jews" (and then a Jewish judge) when a jury found him guilty of mail fraud, he had earlier posed as a black Moses and had repeatedly stressed that "we have been as much enslaved mentally, spiritually and physically as any other race and a fair comparison is the race that Moses led out of Egyptian bondage."

30. Quoted in Weisbord and Stein, *Bittersweet Encounter*, p. 97. While in the 1870s Jews launched a collective boycott of the A. T. Stewart department store, which owned a luxurious hotel that began barring Jews, beginning with the eminent and wealthy Joseph Seligman, Malcolm X's mythology of Jewish power concealed the fact that for nearly a century Jews were systematically excluded from gentile hotels, resorts, and country clubs, to say nothing of law firms, medical schools, and corporate administrative positions; indeed, in the 1890s Southern whites sacked and burned many Jewish stores and farmhouses.

31. University of North Carolina Press, 1984, p. 123. One should note that Douglass and other black abolitionists were part of a movement that included such Jewish abolitionists as August Bondi, Jacob Benjamin, Michael Heilprin, David Einhorn, Moritz Pinner, and Ernestine Rose. Bondi and Benjamin fought in John Brown's guerrilla band in Kansas; Einhorn and Heilprin played an important role in refuting the biblical justifications for Negro slavery put forth by Orthodox rabbis and conservative Christian ministers and theologians.

32. Harlan, "Booker T. Washington's Discovery of Jews," p. 270.

33. Harlan, "Booker T. Washington's Discovery of Jews," p. 277, note 10.

34. *Jews and the New American Scene* (Harvard University Press, 1995), pp. 26–27.

35. See Jack Salzman, "Introduction," in *Struggles in the Promised Land,* p. 14.

36. Nancy J. Weiss gives the short version of the quotation in her essay in *Struggles in the Promised Land.* Hasia Diner provides the full quotation in context. To be fair to Marshall, one should note that in his lectures to Jewish immigrants in 1907, he exhorted the East Side Educational Alliance to avoid the racism of Jim Crow.

37. "Inside Outsiders: As Blacks Rise High in the Executive Suite, CEO Is Often Jewish," *The Wall Street Journal,* April 22, 1998.

38. While nations like Ivory Coast in Africa are the products of arbitrary agreements among European colonial powers, *The New York Times* of August 8, 1999, carried a distressing story about the rising xenophobia of "pure Ivoirian Pride," which has driven many fishermen of Malian ancestry back to the deserts of Mali.

Part II

Historians of Two Generations

7

The Rebel: C. Vann Woodward

The Future of the Past
C. Vann Woodward (1990)

Historians sometimes forget that history is continually being made and experienced before it is studied, interpreted, and read. The latter activities have their own history, of course, which may impinge in unexpected ways on public events. It is difficult to predict when new pasts will erupt through the surface of established understandings and change the landscape of the future.

In the fall of 1954, for example, C. Vann Woodward delivered a lecture series at the University of Virginia that challenged the prevailing dogma concerning the history, continuity, and uniformity of racial segregation in the South. He argued that the Jim Crow laws of the late nineteenth and early twentieth centuries, far from codifying traditional practice, were a determined effort to wipe out the considerable progress made by blacks during and after Reconstruction. This revisionist view of the history of Jim Crow legislation grew in part from the research that Woodward and John Hope Franklin had done for Thurgood Marshall and the NAACP legal campaign during their preparation for *Brown* v. *Board of Education.* A few months before Woodward lectured at Charlottesville to a nonsegregated audience, the Supreme Court had issued its ruling in this epochal desegregation case.

The lectures were soon published as a book, *The Strange Career of Jim Crow.* Ten years later, in a preface to the second revised edition, Woodward confessed with ironic modesty that the first edition "had begun to suffer under some of the handicaps that might be expected in a history of the American Revolution published in 1776." That was a bit like hearing Thomas Paine apologize for the timing of his pamphlet *Common Sense*, which had a comparable impact. Although *Common Sense* also had a mass readership, Paine had intended to reach and inspire: he was not a historian concerned with accuracy, and with the danger of historical anachronism. Yet, like Paine, Woodward had an unerring sense of the revolutionary moment, and of the way historical evidence could undermine a mythological tradition that was crushing the dreams of new social possibilities. It was for this reason that Martin Luther King, Jr., hailed *The Strange Career of Jim Crow* as "the Bible of the civil rights movement."[1]

As Woodward conceives the "craft" or "guild" of professional historians, terms that recur throughout his collection of twenty-two essays and reviews, its apprentices must continually be admonished to address and hold the interest of the laity, to resist the pressures of most academic disciplines in which specialists speak in increasingly esoteric jargon only to other specialists. This public mission, which Woodward sharply distinguishes from popularization or demagoguery, has acquired special urgency from the accelerating pace of change during his own eighty-one years of life, which have witnessed such profound global transformations.

Every generation, as Woodward remarks, "has a unique experience of history." But for young people in the early 1990s, the pre-atomic, precomputer, pretelevision age is almost inconceivable, whereas for youthful Southerners of Woodward's generation, the Civil War and its consequences were still a living, and omnipresent, past. Woodward himself remembers not only the First World War as seen from the small Arkansas village in which he grew up but the look and feel of rural Arkansas in the age of mules, sharecroppers, and chain gangs, long before the advent of paved roads, rural electrification, plumbing, or tractors. During the fifty-two years in which Woodward has continued to publish books, lectures, essays, and reviews, including many notable pieces in *The New York Review of Books*, he has carried memories of visiting the Soviet Union in 1927, after crossing the Atlantic as a seaman on a Dutch freighter; of confronting Atlanta and the urban boosterism of the New South in the late 1920s; of witnessing clashes in 1932 between Nazis and Communists while he was living with a Jewish family in Berlin; of becoming chairman in Atlanta of the Angelo Herndon Defense Committee, working to prevent the execution of a young black Communist who had been charged with "insurrection," under an antiquated statute, for speaking out against the Southern system of racial control.

"I've been an academic all my life," Woodward is quoted as saying in an interview, "and never knew any other life except four years in the navy."[2] This self-effacing, hyperbolic statement apparently refers to his good fortune, as the bookish son of a school administrator, in having an academic uncle and other intellectual mentors who provided models while also encouraging his questioning spirit and desire for knowledge. But Woodward got a personal taste of the Great Depression when, as a result of budgetary cuts, he was fired in 1934 from Georgia Tech, where he had been teaching English, and had been admonished for his defense of Herndon's freedom of speech: it was then he encountered ghastly rural destitution in central Georgia as an interviewer for a WPA sociological survey. Earlier, his friendship with the poet, actor, and essayist J. Saunders Redding, "the first black man," Woodward has written, "with whom I ever broke bread and exchanged views as an equal," prepared him to win the trust of Langston Hughes and other blacks in New York who introduced him to the Harlem Renaissance and allowed him to perform in a play with a Harlem theatrical group.

Woodward was in the Soviet Union, on a second trip to Europe in 1932, when he experienced firsthand the international outrage over the sham trial and conviction for rape of the teen-age Scottsboro boys. Over a decade later, when serving in India as a U.S. naval officer, Woodward sought an audience with Dr. Bhimrao Ramji Ambedkar, the great leader of India's untouchables, who politely interrogated the white Southerner about the condition of the black "untouchables" of the United States.[3]

Few, if any, American historians have achieved Woodward's imaginative ability to view the South, or the United States, from the other side of the globe; to see whites from a nonwhite perspective; to get to the soul and inner tensions of Tom Watson or Mary Chesnut; and above all, to recapture the contingent quality of events that then come to be seen as sacrosanct or foreordained, or are mythologized as evidence of superior heroism or virtue. Woodward clearly deepened his understanding of human error, of human blunder, ambition, luck, and irony, when he worked for the Office of Naval Intelligence and the Naval Office of Public Information, writing restricted and anonymous studies of World War II battles—*Kolombangara and Vella Lavella* and *The Bougainville Landing and the Battle of Empress Augusta Bay*.[4]

These themes of contingency and fallibility added power and suspense to his masterful book *The Battle for Leyte Gulf,* "the largest engagement ever fought on the high seas," which was actually composed of four interrelated battles, "separated by as much as 500 miles," yet "fought between dawn of one day and dusk of the next" as the Americans sank thirty-two Japanese ships and finally defeated Japan's "supreme naval effort of the war." As Woodward makes clear, however, in the battle's closing phase the American "pursuer had now become the pursued, the decoy the aggressor, and though they did not make the assumption, it was the Japanese and not the Americans who had the superior gun power in the end." Is there a subliminal question here, one wonders when rereading this book, whether the South could have won the Civil War?[5]

At various times Woodward has suggested that his taste for irony and indeterminism, like his lifelong campaign against complacency, self-congratulation, and self-righteousness, arises from his Southern identity—from a legacy that includes devastating military defeat and occupation, the imposition of alien values and folkways, and the downfall and perversion of a second "lost cause," Tom Watson's anticapitalist Populism of the 1890s. This mood of chastened rebellion lies near the surface of the great books that initially made Woodward's reputation: *Tom Watson: Agrarian Rebel* (1938); *Origins of the New South, 1877–1913* (1951); and *Reunion and Reaction: The Compromise of 1877 and the End of Reconstruction* (1951).

Like his close friend Richard Hofstadter, Woodward was fortunate in being an exceptionally clear writer whose original work appeared at the very threshold of the great expansion of historical studies that accompanied the unprecedented growth of liberal arts colleges and universities after World War II. In his 1969 presidential address to the American Historical Association, reprinted in the volume under review, Woodward noted that the association's membership had more than tripled in the previous twelve years; that between 1953 and 1969, among all graduate and undergraduate degrees granted, history's percentage had nearly doubled; and that "the total number of history titles published in the United States in 1968 was three times the total for 1950." Although Woodward warned that all booms come to an end and predicted the dramatic decline in history degrees that actually began after the peak academic year of 1970–1971, this plunge did not seem to affect his own national stature or the quality of his graduate students at Yale, one of the few institutions in which the number of undergraduates who take history as their major subject continued during the 1970s and 1980s to exceed by far the number of students majoring in any other subject.

Never an animated or expressive public speaker, Woodward delivered his 1969 American Historical Association address to an impatient and seething throng of sixteen hundred academicians who were preparing to struggle over resolutions on Vietnam and black rights at the business meeting that was to follow. Under such circumstances, it is doubtful whether many listeners reflected on Woodward's witty prediction that "the current vogue of combining Cavalier hairstyles with Roundhead earnestness may well revert once more to tonsorial roundheadedness and attitudinal cavalierness"; or heeded his warning that "a fatal betrayal of the craft would be to permit the profession of history to become inextricably entangled with the future of the past, the purposeful past of the rationalizers, the justifiers, and the propagandists."

As a maverick, Woodward had always repudiated two of the leading characteristics of much postwar historical work: the "nostalgic affection for the American past, reconciliation with the present, and optimism about the future" that could be found in the works of such historians as Samuel Eliot Morison, Arthur M. Schlesinger, Sr., and Dexter Perkins; and the newer emphasis on "consensus rather than conflict . . . stability and homogeneity rather than change and contrast," an outlook popularized especially by Louis Hartz and Richard Hofstadter. As a critic of conservatism and self-satisfaction, Woodward was unavoidably "entangled with the future of the past." In 1969 he was even more disturbed by the "anti-history animus" that increasingly pervaded the arts and humanities, and that descended by various paths from Emerson, Thoreau, Nietzsche, Gide, Camus, and Sartre (he didn't mention Heidegger or the budding Deconstructionists). Each "Now Generation," Woodward implied, would become enslaved to false history precisely because they refused to consider what one of William Faulkner's characters meant when he said, "The past is never dead. It is not even past."

The supreme irony of the profession's greatest ironist is that Woodward, the central figure in desegregating the field of Southern history and in making race, slave emancipation, and Reconstruction major issues of national history, is at heart an idiomatic but unreconstructed Southern Rebel. Like a small number of fellow Confederates, past and present, he is a radical who has no apologies or rationalizations for slavery, debt peonage, Jim Crow, or racial inequality. In a 1987 lecture, "Southerners Versus the Southern Establishment," one of the most recent pieces in *The Future of the Past*, he dismisses traditional Southern liberalism with its tolerance of "separate but equal" doctrines as "conservatism under another name" and clearly directs his own sympathies to the causes of black and white Southern "subversives" ranging from Thomas Jefferson to George Fitzhugh, John Rankin, Moncure Conway, the Grimké sisters, George W. Cable, Mary McLeod Bethune, and the aristocratic Confederate veteran Lewis H. Blair, who in 1889 published "an uncompromising attack on racial segregation, discrimination, and injustice of all kinds, and a demand for full civil and political rights for the Negro, especially voting rights, which were 'as absolutely essential for freedom as is the atmosphere for life.'"

Though he has always been unyielding on the issue of racial equality, Woodward shares his ancestors' distaste for Northern abolitionists, with their "Roundhead earnestness" and uncritical worship of fanatics like John Brown. He has the deepest contempt for Reconstructionists like Edward Philbrick, depicted by one of Woodward's most brilliant students as "a brisk young engineer from Boston" who insisted that land grants would corrupt the freedmen while he himself increased his own fortune toward the end of the Civil War by buying South Carolina land for one dollar an acre, and then paying black laborers twenty-five cents a day to produce cotton and thereby prove that "free labor" could be profitable.[6]

An expert fencer, Woodward partly disguises his most lethal thrusts by agility and grace. To be sure, only the most obtuse reader could miss the blood he has drawn from the Southern "Bourbons" or "Redeemers," who promoted Yankee values and institutions while advertising themselves as preservers of the Confederate lost cause. Closer concentration is required, however, when in his essay "The Future of Southern History" he offers a brief historiographical parody of emancipation and Reconstruction, picturing the traditionally maligned South (or Southern intellectuals) as the slave, "crippled by generations of bondage," perhaps not prepared for freedom and equality. At this moment a group of dubious allies, the cliometricians of the early 1970s, come to the rescue by vindicating the pre–Civil War economy and throwing the neo-abolitionists on the defensive. Similar layers of irony unfold in a previously unpublished essay, "Reconstruction: A Counterfactual Playback," a response to the conventional leftist wisdom that "Radical" Reconstruction was not radical enough. Woodward notes that "it is becoming a bit tiresome (and it is entirely unnecessary) to be flanked on the left in speculative audacity. Armchair bloodbaths can be conducted with impunity by anyone, even a professor emeritus." Following out the lines of this logic, he considers the probable consequences of a Cromwellian or Stalinist policy of liquidating all white Southern resistance "down to the last unregenerate lord of the lash and the last bed-sheeted Ku Kluxer":

> Let no true revolutionary blanch at the implications. Remember that we must be cruel in order to be kind, that we are the social engineers of the future, that we are forestalling future bloodbaths, race riots, and relieving our Northern metropolitan friends of problems that trouble their thoughts and for a time threatened to destroy their cities. If our work is bloody our conscience is clear, and we do all that we do— compassionately.

Having "'controlled the variable' (as the quantifiers say) of Confederate slave owners' resistance in the South," Woodward turns in the same essay of comparison to the way Union army officers, reformers, missionaries, and educators treated Indians in the West, unencumbered "by die-hard Confederate reactionaries, former owners and masters of the red people," concluding that the deception, degradation, exploitation, and segregation of the western Indians, during the very period of Reconstruction, suggests what Northerners would have done to blacks even in a South purged of Confederate evil.

This is not to say that Woodward has cynically rejected belief in historical progress; he simply rebels against the claim that any group or region is blessed with collective innocence or cursed with collective guilt. As a sensitive native of H. L. Mencken's "Sahara of the Bozart," Woodward grew up in an era when it became increasingly fashionable for Northern historians to portray the South as the nation's seedbed of bigotry, mobism, fundamentalism, and prohibition. "Whatever appeared retrograde in national history," Woodward told an audience at Vanderbilt University in the mid-1970s, "whether among the Founding Fathers, the Jacksonians, the Populists, the Bryanites, or the Progressives, was somehow attributable to Southern votes or influence."

As a Southern exile who has long lived among the Yankees and who has experienced how it feels to be mugged on a New Haven street, Woodward became uncharacteristically bitter when he exposed Northern hypocrisy to a Southern audience:

> To explain or account for any and all of the ills that beset the black people in the Northern ghettos—deterioration of the black family, de-

sertion of black fathers, mounting welfare rolls, soaring crime rates, increasing drug addiction, multiplying dropouts, and declining school performance—the answer was always the same: "Look away! look away! look away! Dixie land!" It was all due to evils of long ago and far away—slavery, racism, peonage, or whatnot, way down South in the land of cotton—which, of course, could not possibly be remedied by further strains on the city budget of Boston or New York, and which could not in any reasonable way be attributed to the shortcomings of the free enterprise system and the deterioration of industrial capitalism.

Consider the way the above passage arouses expectations of racial blame and then shifts abruptly to a neo-Beardian attack on the whole system and ideology that triumphed in what Charles and Mary Beard called "the Second American Revolution," namely the Civil War. Woodward, almost as if he himself were a victim of Sherman's march through Georgia, has at times expressed a certain quiet glee at the spectacle of moralistic and "antiracist" Northerners fleeing to escape cities and public schools that become filled with Southern immigrants of a different color. Unlike the many Marxist scholars he has encouraged, disagreed with, and trained, Woodward has shown no more faith in panaceas or optimistic visions than in "the national myths of affluence, innocence, and invincibility"—"the normal enthusiasm," as he puts it, "for such perennial historical themes as progress in urbanization and industrialization, technological advance, the westward movement, immigration, ethnic voting, social mobility, and the rise of the middle class."

The subversiveness of this unreconstructed Rebel has largely been concealed by Woodward's Southern courtesy and judicial bearing, to say nothing of his richly deserved but somewhat astonishing worldly success. Throughout his career he was won the nation's most prestigious prizes and awards, countless honorary degrees, and such distinctions as the Jefferson Lecture in the Humanities (1978) and the inauguration, in February 1989, of a lecture series sponsored by the New York Public Library and Oxford University Press. He has been elected president of the three major historical associations in the United States, an honor now shared by one of his former students, Louis Harlan, who along with a number of other of Woodward's students has also won a Pulitzer prize.

No other American historian, it seems safe to say, has ever trained a group of such loyal and distinguished Ph.D.s.[7] Male and female, black and white,

Woodward's students have written much of the best work on nineteenth- and early twentieth-century Southern history and race relations. While they are by no means members of a doctrinaire or even identifiable "school," their dominance of the field has no doubt shielded their teacher from some of the challenging criticism he has always called for but seldom received. It would be a serious distortion if this emphasis on unbroken public success were not qualified by one somber note. *The Future of the Past* ends, appropriately, with memorial tributes to Richard Hofstadter and David Potter, two of Woodward's most revered friends, who were cut off in the prime of their careers. As a man all too familiar with private tragedy, Woodward could easily have expanded his concluding obituaries and expressions of grief. When he records in an essay on Francis Parkman that the great historian lost his only son and then his wife, Woodward does not tell the reader that he has shared the same fate himself.

Woodward's two previous books of collected essays, *The Burden of Southern History*[8] and *American Counterpoint: Slavery and Racism in the North-South Dialogue*, dealt almost exclusively with the issues of Southern history, race, and the legacy of slave emancipation.[9] *The Future of the Past* breaks from this tradition and reminds us that for the past thirty years Woodward has been much more than a regional historian or a historian limited by any "field" or even national boundary. If Woodward has avoided technical debates over method and philosophies of history, he has thought deeply about similarities and differences, continuities and innovations, and the links between literature (especially the work of Faulkner and his intimate friend, the late Robert Penn Warren) and the social sciences. He has been influenced by Marc Bloch and David Lowenthal, but he also knows how much Elvis Presley owed to W. C. Handy, Jelly Roll Morton, and Leadbelly.[10]

In graduate schools today there is a tendency to assign and discuss only the more recent historical literature, in part because the sheer volume of publications soon obscures the memory of earlier work. Woodward's own insistence on the constant need for "reinterpretation" would seem to validate this trend. His willingness to republish addresses he gave two or three decades ago can therefore be taken as a test of "the future of the past" in a quite different sense—an illustration of the presumed obsolescence of a voice speaking to us from the era of Kennedy, Johnson, or Nixon. Strangely enough, several of Woodward's older pieces have acquired new force and significance as a result of the global changes of 1989–1990.

In "The Age of Reinterpretation," for example, an essay published in 1960 at the height of the Cold War, Woodward deliberately downplayed the long-term significance of "the ideological war between the communist and the non-communist worlds." He mentions the topic at the end of his reassessment of fundamental changes in the modern world, and then only briefly. Looking at the United States from a comparative perspective, in a conscious effort to avoid narrow vision, he was much more impressed by the long age of "free security" that the nation had enjoyed until World War II, a security from enemy attack or invasion which had exempted young men from military training and discipline and which had lowered military expenditures to a small fraction of those of other nations. Thanks in part to the British navy, American military spending after 1815 seldom rose to as much as 1 percent of the gross national product. "In the decade preceding Pearl Harbor," Woodward pointed out, "the percentage of federal expenditures devoted to military purposes fell lower than ever before in our history."

Taking a cue from Frederick Jackson Turner's famous theory of the frontier, Woodward raises fascinating questions about the effects of "free and easy security" on both social and economic behavior, on the pervasive spirit of optimism, and on "the national myth that America is an innocent nation in a wicked world." Is it possible, Woodward asks, that this unique security allowed Americans to indulge in "the doubtful luxury of a full-scale civil war of four years without incurring the evils of foreign intervention and occupation"? Did the same immunity account for the Americans' "peculiar national attitudes toward power," enabling them to separate, check, and divide power, or entrust it to unregulated private business?

David Potter thought that this essay was "widely regarded as [Woodward's] most significant single piece of work and as one of the major contributions to the interpretation of American history."[11] Yet few historians have explored the implications of Woodward's discussion of free security, military expenditures, the anachronism of mass warfare in a nuclear age, or even his final theme regarding the end of a "Europocentric view" of world history. In some ways, the essay seems more daring and brilliant today than it did thirty years ago, since we are now better prepared to understand the linkages between drastic cuts in military spending and the compelling need to avoid the dangers of nuclear war and to see the world in less parochial, anachronistic ways. Much the same can be said of his pleas for comparative history, especially his forays into the comparative study of slave emancipations and periods of reconstruction, which, unfortunately, he never felt able to expand.

During the next decade an entire generation of post–World War II historians will be replaced. Although their successors will have no direct memories of mules, chain gangs, legal segregation, the struggle for civil rights, or even the Vietnam War, they may well be freed from the poisonous influences of the Cold War era and may perceive a much clearer panorama of the previous century, much as one catches a fuller view of entire mountain ranges as a train leaves the foothills and begins to speed away across the plain. As Woodward continues to emphasize, history is never more needed than in such moments of apparent liberation from the past. For it is in moments of *kairos*, of abrupt discontinuity, that anachronisms become especially perilous—and "anachronisms are pre-eminently the business of historians."

Long after Woodward's specific "theses" have been revised or forgotten, one wishes that the following statement from him could be as frequently framed and displayed as the Hippocratic oath:

> The historian is peculiarly fitted also to serve as mediator between man's limitations and his aspirations, between his dreams of what ought to be and the limits of what, in the light of what has been, can be. There is no other branch of learning better qualified to mediate between man's daydream of the future and his nightmare of the past, or, for that matter, between his nightmare of the future and his daydream of the past. So long as man remains recognizably human, he will remain a creature with both a past and a future. A creature so long described as earthbound and so newly transcending those bounds, so giddy over his spectacular innovations, so guilt-ridden about his past, and so anxiety-ridden about the present and the future is not a creature who can safely turn away from history.[12]

Notes

1. C. Vann Woodward, *The Strange Career of Jim Crow* (Oxford University Press, 1966), p. v; John Herbert Roper, *C. Vann Woodward, Southerner* (University of Georgia Press, 1987), p. 198. Woodward himself, who renders the King quote as "historical Bible," notes that sales of the book in hard cover were "unexceptional . . . for a couple of

years," and recalls that as "a member of the great throng of Selma marchers who listened to Martin King's eloquent speech in front of the Alabama state capitol, I heard him read and endorse passages from the book as support for his crusade. I say my feelings were 'mixed' only because I knew perfectly well what those Montgomery white people who silently lined the streets were thinking and saying about a certain Yale professor of Southern origins being quoted by Martin King in those circumstances." Woodward credits the remarkable use and misuse of passages from his book, "in editorials, articles, congressional debates, even judicial opinions," to the South's violent defiance in the late 1950s and to "the great Civil Rights movement" that arose from the Montgomery bus boycott and the black sit-in demonstrations in Greensboro, North Carolina (C. Vann Woodward, *Thinking Back: The Perils of Writing History* [Louisiana State University Press, 1986], pp. 90–93).

2. Roper, *C. Vann Woodward*, p. 20.

3. Woodward, *Thinking Back*, pp. 85, 87–88; Roper, *C. Vann Woodward*, p. 54.

4. Roper, *C. Vann Woodward*, pp. 130–131.

5. C. Vann Woodward, *The Battle for Leyte Gulf* (Norton, 1965, originally published by Macmillan, 1947), pp. 1, 4, 161–162. My question draws some force from Woodward's review of Richard E. Beringer, Herman Hattaway, Archer Jones, and William N. Still, Jr., *Why the South Lost the Civil War*, in *The New York Review of Books*, July 17, 1986, pp. 3–6, and from his description, in *The Future of the Past*, of "the first historical problem I confronted as a boy. . . . If Marse Robert was all that noble and intrepid, if Stonewall was all that indomitable and fast on his feet, if Jeb Stuart was all that gallant and dashing, and if God was on our side, then why the hell did we lose that war?"

6. Willie Lee Rose, *Rehearsal for Reconstruction: The Port Royal Experiment* (Bobbs-Merrill, 1964), pp. 46, 217–229, 300–313. This pioneering work by another southerner, originally a Johns Hopkins Ph.D. dissertation directed by Woodward, also gave credit to Philbrick's philanthropic gifts and sincere belief in free-market values. Woodward's continuing aversion to northern abolitionists can be seen in his 1962 review essay, "The Antislavery Myth," which he has chosen to include in *The Future of the Past*, as well as in "The Northern Crusade Against Slavery," in C. Vann Woodward, *American Counterpoint: Slavery and Racism in the North-South Dialogue* (Little, Brown, 1971; reprinted by Oxford University Press, 1983, pp. 140–162).

7. Roper, *C. Vann Woodward*, contains an incomplete list of Woodward's Ph.D. students from Johns Hopkins and Yale Universities (Appendix, A and B), as well as a comprehensive bibliography of Woodward's writings to the mid-1980s (pp. 345–362). In addition to Louis R. Harlan, some of Woodward's better-known students include James M. McPherson, Bertram Wyatt-Brown, Willie Lee Rose, Daniel H. Calhoun, Charles B. Dew, John Blassingame, Robert F. Engs, Barbara J. Fields, Francis Sheldon Hackney, J. Morgan Kousser, Richard L. McCormick, Lawrence N. Powell, Vincent P. De Santis, Daniel T. Rodgers, J. Mills Thornton III, Thomas C. Holt, William S. McFeely, and Steven Hahn.

8. Louisiana State University Press, 1960.

9. This is also true of the superb Festschrift assembled by some of his students, J. Morgan Kousser and James M. McPherson, eds., *Religion, Race, and Reconstruction: Essays in Honor of C. Vann Woodward* (Oxford University Press, 1982).

10. C. Vann Woodward, "The Narcissistic South," *The New York Review*, October 26, 1989, p. 13.

11. Kousser and McPherson, eds., introduction to *Religion, Race, and Reconstruction*, p. xxxii.

12. While this paragraph sums up much that I learned from Reinhold Niebuhr, I unfortunately never asked Vann about his views or knowledge of Niebuhr.

8

A Tribute to Woodward

C. Vann Woodward, who died on December 17, 1999, at age ninety-one, was the most respected, honored, and influential American historian of the post–World War II era. He led the way in desegregating the history of his native South and in demolishing a deeply rooted mythology that dominated white Americans' views of race relations from the end of Reconstruction in 1877 until the 1950s and 1960s—a mythology endorsed by many leading historians and popularized by novelists and filmmakers in, for example, *Birth of a Nation* and *Gone with the Wind*.

Negro slavery, according to this mythological tradition, had been a mild and benign means of civilizing African savages. Slavery would have evolved into a more productive and less authoritarian system of peasantry had there been no Civil War, a wholly "repressible conflict" ignited by extremists on both sides. The subsequent Reconstruction, with carpetbaggers and clownish blacks running corrupt state legislatures, had been a grotesque circus, moderately and often humorously checked by the Ku Klux Klan, until "the Redeemers" restored white supremacy and a reasonable system of "separate but equal" Jim Crow.

This was essentially the story I and other GI-Bill veterans were taught even in an Ivy League college in 1947, the year Macmillan published Vann Woodward's masterful book *The Battle for Leyte Gulf,* "the largest engagement ever fought on the high seas." By 1954, after doing research for Thurgood Marshall and the NAACP legal campaign that led to *Brown* v. *Board of Education,*

Vann initiated his own major battle by delivering at the University of Virginia, to a racially mixed audience, a lecture series that was later published as a book, *The Strange Career of Jim Crow* (1955), which Martin Luther King, Jr., hailed as "the Bible of the civil rights movement."

Woodward argued that the disfranchising and segregating laws of the late nineteenth and early twentieth centuries were a determined effort to wipe out the considerable progress made by blacks during and even after Reconstruction. In his first book, *Tom Watson: Agrarian Rebel* (1938), Woodward had dramatically demonstrated a temporary alliance between African-Americans and Southern white Populists in the 1890s. This emphasis on discontinuity, contingency, and alternative possibilities was reinforced by Woodward's landmark works, *Origins of the New South, 1877–1913* (1951) and *Reunion and Reaction: The Compromise of 1877 and the End of Reconstruction* (1951), books that prepared the way for Kenneth Stampp's pathbreaking reexamination of Southern slavery (*The Peculiar Institution* [1956]). While John Hope Franklin and other African-American scholars had long attacked the dominant Southern mythology, the impact of such important books as W. E. B. Du Bois's *Black Reconstruction* (1935) was limited in a highly racist society. It was Woodward's scholarly stature, coupled with his prose, that undermined the strategic foundations of the racists' historical fortress and helped to reveal and reverse the fact that the South, despite its military defeat, had long been winning the ideological Civil War.[1]

Yet ironically—and Woodward himself loved irony—Vann was a Southern Rebel living in exile in a cold capitalist world he could never love. He felt more at home in Mary Chesnut's complex world of the Civil War than in a self-righteous North that blamed its racial problems on a demonized Dixie. And this sense of a heritage of sin and defeat gave him the freedom to criticize the ideology of an "innocent nation in a wicked world." He could exhort his many distinguished graduate students and fellow historians to mediate "between man's limitations and his aspirations, between his dreams of what ought to be and the limits of what, in the light of what has been, can be."

Notes

1. See David Blight, *Race and Reunion: The Civil War in American Memory* (Harvard University Press, 2001).

9

Southern Comfort: Eugene D. Genovese

*The Southern Tradition: The Achievement and
Limitations of an American Conservatism*
Eugene D. Genovese (1994)

*The Slaveholders' Dilemma: Freedom and Progress
in Southern Conservative Thought, 1820–1860*
Eugene D. Genovese (1992)

The Southern Front: History and Politics in the Cultural War
Eugene D. Genovese (1995)

The easiest way to approach Eugene D. Genovese's fascinating work on
Southern conservatism is to compare the two lost causes that he has long
admired. For in his view the slaveholders' ideology, theology, and political
theory, which culminated in the Southern Confederacy of 1861–1865, and
the Marxist-Leninist ideology, which culminated in the Soviet Union and
Maoist China, represented the only serious challenges in modern history to
the domination of bourgeois values and finance capitalism. "The fall of the
Confederacy," Genovese points out, "drowned the hopes of southern conservatives for the construction of a viable noncapitalist social order, much as
the disintegration of the Soviet Union—all pretenses and wishful thinking
aside—has drowned the hopes of socialists."

Genovese has been drawn to this analogy since the late 1940s, when he
was a teen-age Stalinist at Brooklyn College. His tolerant anti-Communist

professors encouraged him to develop his unusual interest in Southern slave-holders, who must have seemed rather remote to an Italian-American young man of the working class. An older generation of Marxist historians, led by Herbert Aptheker (to whom Genovese now pays appropriate tribute), served as bold pioneers in the reassessment of Southern slavery and slave resistance at a time when an earlier form of "political correctness" prohibited major deviations from the official view of Happy Darkies, as they were portrayed, for example, in *Gone with the Wind.* But Aptheker and the other innovators, who were blacklisted and seldom read, saw no parallels between communism and the anticapitalism of the Southern slavocracy. In fact, in the eyes of some orthodox Marxists, as one reviewer put it in the late 1960s, "Genovese's work is to Marxism as masturbation is to sexual love."

However one wishes to classify a self-professed Marxist who rejected eco-nomic determinism and who reserved the highest respect for religion and even theology, there is much truth to Genovese's claim that the depth and strength of his work emerged from his Marxism, not in spite of it. Indeed, Genovese's Marxist sensitivity to the nuances of class interactions among both slaves and masters enabled him to convey the appalling oppression and horror of slavery without sounding like a latter-day abolitionist. This was one of his major achievements.

Beginning in 1965 with *The Political Economy of Slavery* and in 1969 with *The World the Slaveholders Made,* Genovese brilliantly explored the social, psychological, and cultural consequences of a ruling class's ownership of other human beings. More than any previous historian he seemed to recapture the mentality of a master faced with the need to command, exhort, care for, and win some respect from slaves, as distinct from a merchant capitalist who could buy and sell slaves as a commodity. Five years later, in his masterpiece of 1974, *Roll, Jordan, Roll: The World the Slaves Made,* Genovese created what is still the most vivid, imaginative, and comprehensive picture we have of slave life in the South. But it is a picture that rests, significantly, on a complex and often misunderstood theory of paternalism and on a sympa-thetic understanding of the figures, such as the Negro driver, the preacher, and the "Mammy," who served as intermediaries between the ruling class and their own people.

While some historians and economists still picture the antebellum South as a specimen of unadulterated capitalism, and while Genovese long ago abandoned the Marxian notion of a precapitalist "slave mode of production," he and his historian wife, Elizabeth Fox-Genovese, have presented a convincing case that the "social relations" engendered by slavery in the South supported a moral and intellectual world increasingly at odds with the capitalism that spawned the Atlantic slave system and then consumed its products. Anyone who doubts that Genovese and Fox-Genovese have long been the most influential and imaginative historians of the antebellum South needs only to examine the central themes of the work of such excellent younger scholars as Peter Kolchin, Drew Gilpin Faust, Robert L. Paquette, and even James Oakes, who began his career with an unqualified attack on Eugene Genovese's basic premises.[1]

The parallels between socialism and a Southern conservatism originally rooted in slaveholding do not end with their common hostility to rampant, irresponsible individualism and the dominance of marketplace values. Those responsible for both forms of dissent from the capitalist system have been portrayed as the Great American Enemy. The Southern conservatives were seen as making up a cohesive clique of immensely rich slaveholders, "the Slave Power" as it was known, who dominated the presidency, the Senate, and the Supreme Court through the 1840s and 1850s. They supposedly presided over a cultural and intellectual wasteland governed by the need to defend the oppression of black slaves and poor whites; and they also allegedly conspired to provoke the Mexican War, to cripple and enclose the free Northern economy, and to open up a vast empire for slavery from the Caribbean to California.

A century later, the international Communist movement was charged with recruiting an army of secret agents who blindly obeyed the dictates of Soviet authorities and tried to exploit the Great Depression and especially the brief wartime alliance with "Uncle Joe" Stalin. Their alleged aim was to subvert democracy by infiltrating the government, labor unions, the universities, Hollywood, and the press and broadcasting.

Genovese of course knew that the Southern cause was irretrievably lost during the decades when he still looked to the Soviet Union as the potential redeemer of all mankind.[2] Nothing inhibited him from exposing in vivid detail the dark realities of American bondage that Southern pro-slavery ideology sought to conceal. It was only after the collapse of the Soviet Union, however, that he confronted the unprecedented human costs of the movement to create a socialist utopia. While in the past Genovese could warn against the "totalitarian tendencies inherent in our own program," he could also proclaim, in July 1983, that "the great Soviet, Chinese, and Cuban revolutions, among others, have transformed the world and ushered in, however painfully, the social system of the near future."[3]

Now, however, in *The Southern Front*, he astringently confesses that

> Having substituted what may fairly be called a gnostic vision for Christianity and scoffed at the moral baseline of the Ten Commandments and the Sermon on the Mount, we [i.e., Genovese and his fellow Communists] ended a seventy-year experiment with socialism with little more to our credit than tens of millions of corpses.

Even the atrocities of all the European and American slave-traders and slave-holders, Genovese concludes, might not match those "of our own blood-drenched romance with the utopia of a man-made heaven here on earth."

Throughout his professional life Genovese has sought to combine the roles of social critic and objective historian. In his remarkable early essay, "On Being a Socialist and a Historian,"[4] he denounced all ideologically motivated history as bad history, which could only serve the oppressive purposes of new elites and deny people knowledge of their own heritage. Acknowledging that all writing and teaching are unavoidably political, Genovese exhorted socialists "to struggle for maximum objectivity" and affirmed that "all good (true, valid, competent) history serves our interest." He also dismissed the faddish calls for "relevance," defended the "rational and critical tradition" of Western civilization, and underscored the responsibility of intellectuals to "present some chapter of the infinite grandeur of the human spirit—a grandeur no less for the inescapable frailty and evil that must forever go into the making of everything human."

These were precisely the standards of the most distinguished postwar historians—among them Richard Hofstadter, David Potter, Perry Miller, and C. Vann Woodward—and they are standards that have long been under attack in the so-called culture wars. A cleavage thus emerged between the Genovese honored for his academic work and the combative militant who could praise Stalin's tough leadership, who boasted of his own "Sicilian temper," and who sometimes wrote as if the world were divided between "comrades" and decadent "bourgeois" foes. Ironically, the bourgeois academy tended to dismiss Genovese's Marxist rhetoric as a harmless eccentricity, particularly in a scholar who could have been expected to be embittered by Richard Nixon's personal campaign in the 1960s to get him fired from Rutgers University.

For three decades after the mid-1960s Genovese's most vehement and outraged critics were identified with the left, especially the new left. In the eyes of some academic radicals and liberals he had followed the classic route of the apostate: to the far right. Others, noting Genovese's constant and open-minded willingness to listen to conservatives, concluded that he was never an authentic radical and had only recently shown his true colors. Since he is still centrally concerned with the ravages and injustices of unbridled capitalism, Genovese has tried to speak for the left and has repeatedly maintained that what remains of it must reexamine its basic principles, in light of the economic collapse and moral bankruptcy of socialism, and consider new alliances with groups of different tendencies if it hopes to confront the appalling social problems that the nation now faces. Since he has also come to question the "series of gigantic illusions" on which "our whole project of 'human liberation' has rested," and has bitterly concluded that "only the radical Left practices character assassination and mendacity as a matter of course," he has increasingly found an audience among more traditional conservatives.

Despite this transformation, one can see a continuity in Genovese's choice of enemies, a continuity that helps to illuminate his historical contributions and the cogent as well as dubious arguments he makes about political issues and the future of American society. Reared as a Roman Catholic, he then proclaimed his atheism so defiantly he did not always sound entirely convincing. He has always expressed contempt (mixed with some pity) for the liberal sects of Protestantism. He is equally contemptuous of the Pelagian heretics who denied original sin; of the Socinian heretics (and their Unitarian descendants) who denied the Holy Trinity; of Emersonian Yankees and Transcendentalists; of self-righteous abolitionists; and of the contemporary cultural and intellectual progeny of all these groups.

In particular, he has attacked bourgeois hippies and the drug-taking new left and anti-elitist academic elites, some of whom celebrated individual self-expression without paying much attention to the obligation to take responsibility for one's acts. He has been particularly critical of radical deconstructionists who have tried anachronistically to discredit the main works of Western culture as racist or sexist or imperialist. He has charged that there is a closer relation than might appear to be the case between, on the one hand, campus radicals and, on the other, professedly liberal capitalists, bureaucrats who embrace egalitarian principles and affirmative action but who turn a blind eye to the commercialization of all aspects of human life and to the creation of an ever-growing pool of unemployable citizens who can neither compete nor consume.

For Genovese the unexpected triumph of capitalism has simply underscored Marx's accurate description of capitalism as

> permanently revolutionary, tearing down all obstacles that impede the development of productive forces, the expansion of needs, the diversity of production and the exploitation and exchange of natural and intellectual forces.[5]

Genovese writes that he now recognizes the inherent economic superiority of the free-market system, which has proved to be a prerequisite for raising the living standard of the world's working classes. But he insists that we must recognize the market and "cash-nexus" as "a revolutionary solvent of social relations," a ubiquitous acid that has eaten away the bonds of family, church, community, and nation. As market values have intruded into all spheres of life and have come to govern even moral and political decisions, Americans have become captivated by dreams of autonomy, equality, and infinite self-liberation, as if they could all become Emerson's "transparent eyeball." The result is that the Judeo-Christian respect for "the irreducible element of divinity" in all human beings—a belief whose value has been heightened, according to Genovese, by "the terrible human cost of the socialist experiments"—has been gradually perverted. It has become, he writes, "an ignoble dream of personal liberation," and whether it is "in its radical-democratic, communist, or free-market form, has proven the most dangerous illusion of our time."

These convictions and prejudices are clearly open to objections, not least for their broad use of such phrases as "personal liberation." But they have also helped Genovese surmount the ideological barriers that have long denied scholars an appreciative understanding of the intellectual history of the antebellum South. Even today an American historian influenced by texts reflecting Northern views, by the neo-abolitionist exposés of the racist South, and by the travel descriptions of Frederick Law Olmsted in *The Cotton Kingdom* is likely to ask, "What intellectual history?"[6] It has been known for many years, however, that Genovese and his wife have been working together on what promises to be a detailed, multivolume history of the mind of the planter class.

The three books under review, one consisting of twenty-three miscellaneous essays and the others presenting two sets of three lectures each, delivered at Harvard and Georgia Southern University, give tantalizing foretastes of the major project. These preliminary works combine some fresh and much-needed intellectual history with more cloudy pleas for a new American coalition that can build on the insights of antebellum and twentieth-century Southern conservatives while shedding their noxious racism. It is the latter theme that has attracted the mostly hostile attention of reviewers. One hopes that Genovese and Fox-Genovese will limit their magnum opus to the non-ideological scholarship that both have defended.

Contrary to prevailing stereotypes, Genovese claims, Southern slaveholders were a remarkably well-educated class by the standards of their time. The sons of planters commonly attended college—if not Princeton or Yale, then one of the proliferating Southern state universities and private colleges. Many entered the ministry or other professions, and some of them quickly "matched and sometimes overmatched Northerners in one discipline after another":

> St. George Tucker, T. R. R. Cobb, Thomas Ruffin in legal theory and jurisprudence; George Tucker and Jacob N. Cardozo in political economy; James Henley Thornwell and Robert L. Dabney in theology and ecclesiology; Thomas Roderick Dew and William H. Trescot in historical studies; John C. Calhoun and Albert Taylor Bledsoe in political theory—the list could be extended—deserve to rank among America's ablest thinkers. . . . But most of these southerners defended slavery, and even St. George Tucker and George Tucker, who did not, staunchly defended "southern rights" and the political principles and policies of the slaveholders' regime. The slaveholders lost the war; slavery has properly been condemned as an enormity; and, not surprisingly, the southern intellectuals have virtually been expunged from memory.

In their confused search for an alternate route to modern society, the Southerners had much in common with English and Continental conservatives, with whom they had more contact than one might think. For all their supposed medievalism, Southern intellectuals accepted science and the many benefits and conveniences of technology and economic growth. Even the South as a whole, Genovese points out, was far more tolerant of Catholics and especially Jews than was the Northeast, notwithstanding later stereotypes of Southern prejudice and bigotry. Genovese especially admires the Southern conservatives' understanding of human depravity and historical limits; their rejection of radical individualism; their respect for family, community, and other "organic" social connections; and their advocacy of broad-based prop-

erty ownership coupled with a recognition of the inevitability of social strat-
ification.

But unlike conservatives elsewhere, such Southern spokesmen as George
Fitzhugh and John C. Calhoun identified the system of free wage labor as
the source of social disintegration and related moral evils in the North and
Western Europe. While they argued that slavery could be the only safe, secure, and Christian foundation for freedom, they increasingly sought to
achieve what now seems an absurd contradiction: the reform of human bondage. The theologians, in particular, sought to legalize slave marriages, prevent
the breakup of slave families, and repeal laws against teaching slaves to read.
James Henley Thornwell, a towering figure who charged that the abolitionist
argument "fully and legitimately carried out, would condemn every arrangement of society, which did not secure to its members an absolute equality of
position," had even drafted a plan for gradual emancipation shortly before
his native South Carolina seceded from the Union.

Although the Civil War destroyed the material foundation of Southern
conservativism, Genovese sees a straight line—"a tradition that has resisted
bourgeois society, its atomistic culture, and its marketplace morality"—running from figures like Thornwell to the Southern Agrarians of the 1930s and
1940s—including the writers Allen Tate, John Crowe Ransom, and Cleanth
Brooks—and on to the conservative postwar writers Richard M. Weaver,
M. E. Bradford, and John Shelton Reed. Genovese claims that the postwar
conservatives, unlike the Agrarians, have been valiantly struggling to purge
themselves of racism; that despite their bleak pronouncements about modern
man becoming "a moral idiot," they have not repudiated progress, science,
or modernity, only "the cult of progress, scientism, and the moral and political decadence of a modernity run wild." Genovese, who won the Weaver
Award in 1993, was a close friend of Bradford, who, with such books as *A
Better Guide than Reason*, had "assumed the mantle of Weaver" before his
own death. And Genovese warns that the left will fail, even in some historically unprecedented coalition, "unless it comes to terms with the positive
side of the Southern tradition," exemplified not least in the ability of men
like John Shelton Reed "to laugh at themselves."

It is no doubt true that much remains to be said on the deeper meanings of
socialism's collapse. (In his now well-known essay "The Question," which
concludes *The Southern Front*, he never confronts this question: Would Gen-

ovese have denounced the appalling crimes and dangerous illusions of socialism if the economy of the Soviet Union had grown and prospered into
the twenty-first century?) No doubt many liberals could profit from reading
such Southern conservatives as James Henley Thornwell and John Crowe
Ransom. And Genovese can be telling when he describes the contradictions
between socially destructive individualism and the pretensions of multinational corporate culture. The embarrassed attempt of Time Warner—an
alliance of the moralizing Luce publications with the entertainment conglom-
erate—to defend its investment in some of the more vicious gangsta rap
lyrics provides a case in point.

Genovese is at his best when he exposes the hypocrisy of liberals and
radicals and when he analyzes the work of Southern theologians against a
historical background of Christian doctrine, reminding us of the dangers of
believing in human perfectibility and of the need for social restraints on our
capacity for depravity. He seems to forget, however, that Reinhold Niebuhr
taught a generation of American liberals that a sophisticated understanding
of original sin could be combined with advancing social progress and "proximate" justice.[7] Nor does he seem to have taken account of the moral complexity of the thought of such liberals as Isaiah Berlin, Charles Taylor, and
Michael Walzer, all of whom are skeptical about ideologies of human perfectibility.

Although Genovese has sometimes posed as a tough, streetwise Sicilian-
American fighter who has mastered the mysteries of power, he may well be
as isolated from current realities as some of the academics he criticizes. From
his recent books on Southern conservatism one would never suspect that the
Republican Party and much of our national politics itself have been dominated by Southern conservatives and a Southern-led Christian Coalition.
Genovese's Agrarians and such quietly ironic writers as Richard Weaver seem
to come from quite another world from that of Phil Gramm, Strom Thur-
mond, Jerry Falwell, Jesse Helms, and Ollie North. To be sure, Genovese on
occasion draws a distinction between the conservatives who blindly embrace
all aspects of free-market corporate capitalism and those few who see the
damage it can cause. But it is hardly reassuring to learn that M. E. Bradford
"took dead aim at rightwingers for whom conservatism means little more
than market economics and pro-business economic policies, describing them
as 'centralizers' and as 'egalitarians on every subject but money.'" Genovese,
in an essay written in 1990, warned that racists like David Duke might
succeed in stealing the conservatives' thunder and inheriting their power in

U.S. politics. But he says he agrees on some topics with William Bennett, Pat Robertson, "and a few other unmentionables." Robertson's belief in theories of a world conspiracy by Jewish bankers seems to have escaped him.

While the fall of socialism has given Genovese an admirable sense of his own fallibility, he does not seem to sense that his lifelong hostility to Emersonian liberalism and market values might drive him into a camp that uses the language of communalism and family values to justify the dismantling of the only agencies of power that can check corporate crime and corruption; regulate the excesses of the market; protect the environment; provide some physical assistance and decent treatment for the unemployed and unemployables; and sustain the kind of culture and scholarship that transcends the marketplace in highly diverse communities. In short, by joining the current highly deceptive campaign of big business to demonize the national government, Genovese renounces not only the abolitionist-liberal tradition but the equally hard-won tradition of the Progressives and New Dealers who knew that sinful private bigness can only be checked by sinful public bigness.

Notes

1. While James Oakes's *The Ruling Race: A History of American Slaveholders* (Knopf, 1982) stressed the thoroughly capitalist behavior and orientation of Southern slaveholders, his second book, *Slavery and Freedom: An Interpretation of the Old South* (Knopf, 1990), builds on the work of Genovese and others and takes a far more subtle and convincing view of the divided and dialectical nature of slaveholding society.

2. As an adopted Southerner, living in Atlanta, Genovese is acutely aware that the secessionist movements in Canada, southern Brazil, Italy, and, of course, the former Yugoslavia and Soviet Union have encouraged a new secessionist movement in the South, led by the Southern League. Founded in Alabama in 1994, the League endorses the same Southern conservative principles that Genovese now admires, and honors the same historical figures, such as John Randolph of Roanoke, John Taylor of Caroline, Albert Taylor Bledsoe, and John C. Calhoun. The board of the Southern League includes a clergyman, a magazine editor, and such academics as Michael Hill, a professor of European history at the University of Alabama and president of the League; Grady McWhiney, a well-known professor of history at Texas Christian University; and Clyde Wilson, editor of the John C. Calhoun papers. In an interview Professor Hill claims that the League

welcomes members of all races as long as they support "limited government, states' rights, and the right to local self rule." Not satisfied by the political triumph of Southern Republicans, who according to Hill will inevitably compromise with Yankees and "The New World Order," League members talk openly of achieving their ancestors' dream of "secession and Southern independence" (*Southern Partisan*, Fourth Quarter 1994, pp. 34–37).

3. Genovese, "Introduction to the New Edition," *In Red and Black: Marxian Explorations in Southern and Afro-American History* (University of Tennessee Press, 1984), pp. xx, xxii.

4. Included in *In Red and Black*, pp. 3–22.

5. Karl Marx, *The Grundrisse*, edited and translated by David McLellan (Harper and Row, 1971), pp. 94–95; Marx and Friedrich Engels, "Manifesto of the Communist Party," *The Marx-Engels Reader*, edited by Robert C. Tucker, second edition (Norton, 1972), pp. 475–477.

6. Several historians, however, in particular Michael O'Brien and Drew Gilpin Faust, have produced outstanding work that should modify this kind of reaction; significantly, both O'Brien and Faust have paid tribute to Genovese's recent work.

7. In *The Nature and Destiny of Man* (Scribner, 1948) and *The Irony of American History* (Scribner, 1952) Niebuhr also exposed all the illusions and dangers of Marxism that Genovese now discusses.

Part III

Origins

10

At the Heart of Slavery

*

As even Aristotle acknowledged, natural slavery—the bondage of people who are born to be slaves—is different from other varieties of servitude, which Aristotle admitted might sometimes be unjust, such as slavery forced upon the conquered by the conqueror. Yet the condition of slavery itself has not always been the most abject form of servitude, and is not necessarily so today. Some contract labor, though technically free, is more oppressive than many types of conventional bondage. One thinks, for example, of the Chinese "coolies" who were transported in the mid-nineteenth century across the Pacific to the coast of Peru, where they died in appalling numbers from the lethal effects of shoveling sea-bird excrement for the world's fertilizer market.

The same point applies to much convict labor, which as "involuntary servitude" is specifically made legitimate by the Thirteenth Amendment of the U.S. Constitution as an exception to its national abolition of slavery. While the twentieth century witnessed the slow eradication of most chattel slavery in Africa, Asia, and the Middle East, it also set wholly new records for cruelty and atrocity to the tens of millions of men, women, and children who were subjected to state servitude by Nazi Germany, Communist Russia, Communist China, and smaller totalitarian nations. Even in the southern United States, for instance at the notorious Parchman Farm in Mississippi, those sentenced to prison—most of them African American, and many of them convicted unjustly or for very minor crimes—were subjected to chain gangs and other forms of penal servitude that approximated the Soviet and Chinese gulags.

In contrast to traditional chattel slaves, who usually represented a valuable investment, these political or ethnic prisoners were by definition expendable. As late as the 1990s, testimony from former political prisoners in China has proved once again how torture, constant surveillance, and a near-starvation diet can transform human behavior. Students of slavery should at least be aware that strong-minded men and women admit that in the Chinese camps they fawningly tried to ingratiate themselves with guards, stole food from one another, informed on friends, and finally became convinced that it was their own fault that they were dying from starvation.[1]

More than thirteen hundred years before Aristotle, the Hammurabi Code in Babylonia defined a concept of chattel slavery that served as a way of classifying the lowliest and most dependent workers in society. Among the salient features of this legal status were that once they were owned slaves could be sold or inherited; the same features would reappear through the ages in scores of cultures. Yet in the ancient Near East, as in Asia, Europe, Africa, and the pre-conquest Americas, slavery almost certainly existed long before it was systematized by legal codes. Their effect was to encourage the holders of power to make servitude conform as much as possible to a debased condition of hereditary dishonor and powerlessness that existed before legal codes had been elaborated—much as the holders of power promoted, for themselves, the opposite ideal of hereditary kingship.

The difficulties of appraising slave systems, which vary greatly in the way they treat their subjects, have been underscored by Orlando Patterson's great comparative study, *Slavery and Social Death.*[2] In some primitive societies, such as the Tupinambá of Brazil, slaves were spared from heavy labor but were destined to be eaten, like sacrificial animals, following a ceremonial killing. In more advanced societies, such as that of the Aztecs, some "slaves" (captured enemy warriors) were in fact held in much honor before they were ritually dispatched. Other societies that achieved high rates of manumission by allowing slaves to purchase their freedom were extraordinarily brutal and oppressive in other ways, such as by sanctioning torture and mass executions.

As historians have carefully examined specific systems of slavery, they have often expressed surprise over the privileges and even freedom enjoyed by certain individual slaves. In ancient Babylonia and Rome, as in the medieval Islamic world and sub-Saharan Africa, chosen slaves served as soldiers, business agents, and high administrators. In seventeenth-century Virginia a black slave named Francis Payne harvested enough tobacco to buy his owner two indentured servants and then purchase freedom for himself, his wife, and his children. In the interior of Britain's Cape Colony in southwestern Africa, black slave herdsmen in the 1820s were allowed to tend livestock in regions so remote that they would travel many weeks without supervision or without even sighting a white figure of authority. In the 1850s, an American slave named Simon Gray served as the captain of a flatboat on the Mississippi River, supervising and paying wages to a crew that included white men. Entrusted with large sums of money for business purposes, Gray carried firearms, drew a regular salary, rented his own house, and took a vacation to Hot Springs, Arkansas, when his health declined.

Some decades earlier, a South Carolina slave named April Ellison won his freedom after learning how to build and repair cotton gins. After changing his first name to William, buying the freedom of his wife and daughter, and winning a legal suit against a white man who had failed to pay a debt, Ellison became a wealthy planter and owner of sixty-three slaves, a number which by 1860 placed him among the upper 3 percent of slaveholders in South Carolina.

Such examples show that, regardless of law or theory, a slave's actual status could historically vary along a broad spectrum of rights, powers, and protections. They could include, as Moses Finley suggested, claims to property or power over things; power over one's own and others' labor and movement; power to punish or be exempt from punishment; privileges or liabilities within the judicial process; rights and privileges associated with the family; privileges of social mobility; and privileges and duties in religious, political, and military spheres.[3]

Historically, however, it is clear that impressive-sounding laws to protect slaves have seldom been enforced. As Jean Bodin suggested in the sixteenth century, only an absolutist state can override the absolute authority of slaveholders. Yet, as in the nineteenth-century American South, this principle of slaveholder autonomy also meant that slaveholders might strongly encourage slave marriages and slave families, even though such marriages had no legal standing.

While Orlando Patterson has been especially interested in pre-modern slavery and its social and psychological attributes—the "natal alienation" that resulted from being deprived of stable and legitimated family ties and the "generalized dishonor" to which societies subject bondsmen—we should remember that the central quality of most forms of slavery has been defined by the nature of the work performed. Comparatively speaking, for example, one can observe an ascending order of status, starting with the slaves who cut sugar cane or sweat in the boiler room of a sugar mill in the tropical West Indies, going on to the slaves who serve as sex objects in a Persian harem, or wear fine linens and drive rich white people in a coach in Virginia, or have a still higher status, performing as acrobats, dancers, soldiers, doctors, or bureaucrats in ancient Rome.

But when we think of highly privileged slaves—the well-to-do farm agent in Babylon, the Greek poet or teacher in Rome, the black silversmith, musician, or boat captain in the American South—we must also remember another central point. Being slaves, they could at any moment be stripped of their privileges and property. They could be sold, whipped, or even killed at the whim of an owner. Such radical uncertainty and unpredictability was characteristic of all slave systems. The Mumluk army officer or powerful eunuch who issued orders in the emperor's name had no outside protection in the form of family, clan, or lineage. Whatever rights or privileges a slave might have gained could be revoked without warning. This utter vulnerability may be the essence of dehumanization.

Though historians have long recognized dehumanization as central to slavery, they have not—despite the significant clue Aristotle provided when he called the ox "the poor man's slave"—explored its *bestializing* aspects. This neglected point seems to me central. Drawing on comparisons of slaves with domestic animals that have been made throughout history, Karl Jacoby has argued convincingly that the domestication of sheep, goats, pigs, cattle, horses, and other animals during the Neolithic revolution served as a model for enslaving humans.[4] Whether used for food, clothing, transport, or heavy labor, these domesticated animals underwent an evolutionary process of neoteny, or progressive "juvenilization." That is, they became more submissive than their wild counterparts, less fearful of strangers, and less aggressive (which in physical terms was reflected in a shortening of the jawbone and a decrease in the size of the teeth). Far from being chance occurrences, these changes in anatomy and behavior were closely geared to human needs, especially in farming.

To control domesticated beasts, human beings devised collars, chains, prods, whips, and branding irons. They also castrated males and subjected animals to selective breeding. More positive incentives arose from a kind of paternalism in which human beings replaced the dominant male animal that had exercised some control over the social group. As Jacoby astutely observes, once the harvests and livestock accumulated by agricultural societies had revolutionized the objectives of warfare, similar means of control were applied to human captives.

No doubt the archetypal slave, as Gerda Lerner has maintained, was a woman.[5] And in patriarchal societies, women were treated like domesticated or petlike animals in order to ensure their dependence and submission; they not only worked in the fields but reproduced, augmenting the size and wealth of tribes and lineages. In the Hebrew Bible, as in Homer and other early sources, male captives were typically killed on the spot; otherwise they might have escaped or risen in revolt. Women, one gathers, were customarily enslaved as workers or concubines.

But with the rise of great urban and agricultural states the need for servants and labor for public works coincided with improved techniques for controlling male prisoners (whose inability to understand their captors' language might have made them seem more like animals than men). As the laws governing chattel property evolved in the earliest civilizations, it was almost universally agreed that a slave, like an animal, could be bought, sold, traded, leased, mortgaged, bequeathed, presented as a gift, pledged for a debt, included in a dowry, or seized in a bankruptcy. This treatment as a commodity applied even to the most privileged slaves in Babylonia and other ancient civilizations; for the Western world, it was eventually codified in Roman law.

Despite the many attempts to equate human captives with domestic animals—the first African slaves shipped to Lisbon in the mid-1400s were stripped naked and marketed and priced exactly like livestock—slaves have fortunately never been held long enough in distinct, isolated groups to undergo significant hereditary change. Yet neoteny, the development of childlike characteristics in slaves, was clearly the goal of many slaveholders, despite their lack of any scientific understanding of how domestication had changed the nature and behavior of animals.

In ancient Mesopotamia slaves were not only named and branded as if they were domestic animals but were actually priced according to the equivalent in cows, horses, pigs, and chickens. As Orlando Patterson has pointed out, the key to the "Sambo" stereotype of the typical slave, "an ideological imperative of all systems of slavery," is the total absence of "any hint of 'manhood.'" Patterson quotes the famous description by the historian Stanley Elkins:

> Sambo, the typical plantation slave, was docile but irresponsible, loyal but lazy, humble but chronically given to lying and stealing; his behavior was full of infantile silliness and his talk inflated with childish exaggeration. His relationship with his master was one of utter dependence and childlike attachment: it was indeed this childlike quality that was the very key to his being.[6]

This stereotype describes precisely what a human male slave would be like if slaves had been subjected to the same process as that of domesticated animals. While ancient Greeks saw such slavelike traits in the people they called "barbarians" and the stereotype was much later associated with so-called Slavs—the root of the word *slave* in Western European languages—it was only in the fifteenth century, when slavery increasingly became linked with various peoples from sub-Saharan Africa, that the stereotype began to acquire specific racial connotations.[7] As slavery in the Western world became more and more restricted to Africans, the arbitrarily defined black "race" took on all the qualities, in the eyes of many white people, of the infantilized and animalized slave.

✳

Since human beings have always had a remarkable ability to imagine abstract states of perfection, they also succeeded at an early stage in imagining a perfect form of subordination. Plato compared the slave to the human body, and the master to the body's rational soul. Slaves incarnated the irrationality and chaos of the material universe, as distinct from the rationality of the masterlike Demiurge. There was thus a cosmic justification for Aristotle's dictum that "from the hour of their birth, some men are marked out for subjection, others for rule." Aristotle's idea of the natural slave, which would help shape virtually all subsequent proslavery thought, also in effect pictured what a human being would be like if "tamed" by neoteny. He began by stressing the parallel between slaves and domesticated beasts:

> Tame animals are naturally better than wild animals, yet for all tame animals there is an advantage in being under human control, as this secures their survival. And as regards the relationship between male and

female, the former is naturally superior, the latter inferior, the former rules and the latter is subject. By analogy, the same must necessarily apply to mankind as a whole. Therefore all men who differ from one another by as much as the soul differs from the body or man from a wild beast (and that is the state of those who work by using their bodies, and for whom that is the best they can do)—these people are slaves by nature, and it is better for them to be subject to this kind of control, as it is better for the other creatures I have mentioned.

Aristotle then proceeded to distinguish the natural slave as having a different body and soul from other men:

> For a man who is able to belong to another person is by nature a slave (for that is why he belongs to someone else), as is a man who participates in reason only so far as to realize that it exists, but not so far as to have it himself—other animals do not recognize reason, but follow their passions. The way we use slaves isn't very different; assistance regarding the necessities of life is provided by both groups, by slaves and by domestic animals. Nature must therefore have intended to make the bodies of free men and of slaves different also; slaves' bodies strong for the services they have to do, those of free men upright and not much use for that kind of work, but instead useful for community life.[8]

Aristotle did recognize that on occasion "slaves can have the bodies of free men, free men only the souls and not the bodies of free men." Even more troubling, he observed, was the fact that some people "of the most respected family" sometimes became slaves "simply because they happened to be captured and sold." Yet such instances of injustice could not weaken Aristotle's conviction that "it is clear that there are certain people who are free and certain people who are slaves by nature, and it is both to their advantage, and just, for them to be slaves."

This tactic of "animalization" may well be universal; enslavement is simply its most extreme and institutionalized manifestation. Yet, as Aristotle noted, the slave was not a completely dehumanized being and was not to be seen as only an animal or *nothing but* an animal. Various Greek philosophers, especially the Cynics and Stoics, saw a fundamental contradiction in trying to reduce any human being to such a subordinate status. "It would be absurd," Diogenes of Sinope reportedly said, when his own slave had run away, "if Manes [the slave] can live without Diogenes, but Diogenes cannot get on without Manes." When pirates captured Diogenes and took him to a slave market in Crete, he pointed to a customer wearing rich purple robes, and said, "Sell me to this man; he needs a master." Externally, according to the Stoics, the servant might be the instrument of his master's will, but internally, in his own self-consciousness, he remained a free soul.

In other words, the master's identity depended on having a slave who recognized him as master, and this in turn required an independent consciousness. Contrary to Aristotle and in contrast to the relationship between a man and his dog, the roles of master and slave could be reversed: Diogenes could become the slave and Manes, who even as a slave might have had a freer soul and been less enslaved to his passions, could become the master.[9]

This is the basic "problem of slavery," and it arises from the irreducible humanness of the slave. Although slaves were supposed to be treated in many respects like dogs, horses, or oxen, as reflected in all the laws that defined slaves as chattel, the same laws had to recognize that throughout history slaves have run away, outwitted their masters, or rebelled, murdered, raped, and stolen. No masters or lawmakers, whether in ancient Rome, medieval Tuscany, or seventeenth-century Brazil, could forget that the obsequious servant might also be a "domestic enemy" bent on theft, poisoning, or arson. Throughout history it has been said that slaves, although occasionally as loyal and faithful as good dogs, were for the most part lazy, irresponsible, cunning, rebellious, untrustworthy, and sexually promiscuous. This central contradiction was underscored in Roman law (the Code of Justinian), which ruled that slavery was the single institution contrary to the law of nature but sanctioned by the law of nations. That is to say, slavery would not be permitted in an ideal world of perfect justice, but was simply a fact of life that symbolized the compromises that must be made in the sinful world of reality. This was the official view of Christian churches from the late Roman Empire to the eighteenth, or even the nineteenth, century.[10]

The institution of slavery, then, has always given rise to conflict, fear, and accommodation. The settlement of the New World magnified these liabilities, since the slaves now came from an alien and unfamiliar culture and they often outnumbered their European rulers. Many colonial settlements were vulnerable to military attack or close to wilderness areas that offered easy refuge. Accordingly, the introduction of black slavery to the Americas brought spasmodic reactions of warning, anxiety, and racial repugnance. But the grandiose visions of New World wealth—once the Spanish had plundered the Aztecs and Incas—seemed always to require slave labor. Largely because many experiments in enslaving Indians failed, African slaves became an intrinsic part of the American experience.

All the European colonizers—from the Spanish and Portuguese to the English, Dutch, and French—turned to the purchase of slaves in Africa as the cheapest and most expedient way to meet the immediate demands for labor in mining and tropical agriculture. The institution of slavery in the Americas took on a variety of forms. Some were the result of cultural differences, for example between Catholics and English Protestants; some depended on the differences between the work performed—mining as distinguished from agricultural labor. But slavery in the Americas was not unique in treating human beings as animals—or in defining the bondsman as chattel property that happened to be endowed with elements of human personality. In the mid-eighteenth century, when black slaves could be found from French Canada to Chile, there was nothing unprecedented about New World chattel slavery, or even the enslavement of one ethnic group by another. What was unprecedented by the 1760s and early 1770s was the emergence of a widespread conviction that New World slavery was deeply evil and embodied all the forces that threatened the true destiny of the human race.

This eruption of antislavery thought cannot be explained by economic interest. The Atlantic slave system, far from being in decay, had never appeared so prosperous, so secure, or so full of promise. Among the first groups to denounce the principle of slavery, and all that it implied, were the seventeenth-century perfectionist and millennialist Christian sects—Diggers and Ranters among them—who challenged all traditional authorities and sought to live their lives free from sin. In essence, their ideal involved a form of mutual love and recognition that precluded treating men in any way as objects or animals. Since the more radical sectarian groups that emerged in the English civil wars of the mid-seventeenth century also threatened all forms of private property and patriarchal rule, they exceeded the bounds of even Cromwell's tolerance and never survived the Stuart Restoration.

The notable exception was the Society of Friends, which early found a way to compromise with the society around it, and thus to survive. The Quakers not only undertook their quest for a purified life more pragmatically but they institutionalized methods for bearing witness to their faith. They did not, in their religious zeal, call for the faithful to reject the conventional trappings of church and state, as many other millennialist sects did. In other

words, the Quakers tried to achieve a balance between the impulse to perfection and the necessity of living in an imperfect world. They also acquired
considerable economic and political power, and were the only sect to become
deeply involved with the Atlantic slave system. By the early eighteenth century there were Quaker planters in the West Indies and Quaker slave merchants in London, Philadelphia, and Newport, Rhode Island.

Yet very soon slaveholding came to attract more moral censure among
Quakers than it did among other denominations. This was partly because of
the Friends' ethical opposition to war, which some philosophers were then
using as an apology for human bondage; John Locke, for instance, justified
slavery as "the state of War continued, between a lawful Conquerour, and a
Captive." The Seven Years' War (1756–1763) brought about a spiritual crisis
within the Society of Friends over the acceptability of war itself, resulting in
much soul-searching, attempts at self-purification, and, finally, commitment
to withdraw entirely from slaveholding as well as slave trading.

The Quakers' growing anguish coincided with other reformist developments
in Western culture, particularly in British Protestantism. First, the rise of
secular social philosophy, from Thomas Hobbes onward, necessitated a re-
definition of the place of human bondage in the rational order of being. Yet
in the language of humanist philosophy, slavery was extremely difficult to
justify. Because John Locke made natural liberty the center of his philosophy,
he had to place slavery outside the social compact, whose purpose was to
protect all men's inalienable rights. By the 1730s, arguments in favor of
slavery, including the one that equated it with war, were beginning to appear
absurd to a generation of English and French writers who had learned from
Locke and others to take an irreverent view of past authority and to subject
all questions to the test of reason.

It was Montesquieu, more than any other thinker, who put the subject of
black slavery on the agenda of the European Enlightenment in his *Pensées*
and *L'Esprit des lois*. He weighed the institution against the general laws or
principles that promoted human happiness and encouraged his readers to
imagine the response of a defender of slavery to a national lottery that would
make nine-tenths of the population the absolute slaves of the remaining
tenth.[11] By the 1760s the antislavery arguments of Montesquieu and the
Scottish philosopher Francis Hutcheson were being repeated, developed, and
propagated by many of the intellectuals of the enlightened world, including
such different thinkers as Burke and Diderot. John Locke, the great enemy

of all absolute and arbitrary power, had been the last major philosopher to seek a justification for absolute and perpetual slavery.

A second and closely related transformation was the increasing popularity of the ethic of benevolence as personified by the "man of feeling." The insistence on man's inner goodness, on his capacity for sympathy, became part of a gradual secularizing tendency in British Protestantism. Ultimately, this liberal spirit led in two directions, each described by the titles of Adam Smith's two books: *The Theory of Moral Sentiments* and *The Wealth of Nations*. Smith's theory of sympathetic benevolence toward other persons as the source of moral judgment and his theory of individual enterprise both condemned slavery as an intolerable obstacle to human progress. The man of sensibility needed to act on his virtuous feelings by relieving the sufferings of innocent victims; the economic man required a social order that allowed, and morally vindicated, the free play of individual self-interest. By definition, the slave was both innocent and a victim, since he could not be held responsible for his own condition.

For Smith, the African's enslavement, unlike the legitimate restraints imposed upon the members of society by rational laws, seemed wholly undeserved. He represented innocent nature, and hence his actions corresponded, psychologically, to the natural and spontaneous impulses of the man of feeling. Accordingly, for Smith the key to progress lay in recognizing the innocent nature that was objectively characteristic of the slave and that was also the source of the subjective affections of the reformer. The slave would be lifted to a level of independent action and social obligation; the reformer would be assured of the beneficence of his own self-interest by his participation in a transcendent cause. These, at least, were the expectations of the philanthropists, who, as the eighteenth century wore on, increasingly transformed the quest for salvation from a sinful world into a mission to cleanse the world of sin.

By the eve of the American Revolution there was a remarkable convergence of culture and intellectual developments which at once undercut traditional rationalizations for slavery and offered new ways of identifying with its victims. Thus the African's cultural difference acquired a positive image at the hands of eighteenth-century students of the primitive, such as Rousseau, and evangelical Christians, such as John Wesley, who searched through travel accounts and description of exotic lands for examples of man's inherent virtue and creativity. In some ways the "noble savage" was little more than a literary convention that conflated the Iroquois and South Sea islander with sable Venuses and tear-bedewed daughters of "injur'd Afric."

The convention did, however, partially weaken Europe's arrogant ethnocentrism and create at least a momentary ambivalence about the human costs of modern civilization. It also tended to counteract the many fears and prejudices that had long cut Africans off from the normal mechanisms of sympathy and identification. Ultimately, literary primitivism was no match for the pseudo-scientific racism which drew on the Enlightenment and reduced the African to a "link" or even a separate species between man and the apes. But for many Europeans, as diverse as John Wesley and the Abbé Raynal, the African was not a human animal but an innocent child of nature whose enslavement in America betrayed the very notion of the New World as a land of natural innocence and new hope for mankind. By the early 1770s such writers portrayed the black slave as a man of natural virtue and sensitivity who was at once oppressed by the worst vices of civilization and yet capable of receiving its greatest benefits.

This complex change in moral vision was a precondition for antislavery movements and for the eventual abolition of New World slavery from 1777, when Vermont's constitution outlawed the institution, to 1888, when, in a state of almost revolutionary turmoil, Brazil finally freed some half-million remaining slaves. But the diffusion of religious and secular antislavery arguments in no way guaranteed such an outcome. If Washington, Jefferson, Madison, and other slaveholding founders could view human bondage as an embarrassing and even dangerous social evil, they also respected the rights of private property and expressed deep fear of the consequences of any general and unrestricted act of emancipation. The U.S. Constitution was designed to protect the rights and security of slaveholders, and between 1792 and 1845 the American political system encouraged and rewarded the expansion of slavery into nine new states.

As the American slave system became increasingly profitable, the moral doubts of the Revolutionary generation gave way in the South to strong religious, economic, and racial arguments that defended slavery as a "positive good." Historians are still sharply divided over the fundamental reasons for slave emancipation, which ultimately required an imposition of power even in the regions that were spared a Haitian Revolution or an American Civil War. Yet whatever weight one gives the contending economic and political interests that were involved in the abolition of slavery, it was the inherent contradiction of chattel slavery—the impossible effort to bestialize human beings—that eventually evoked a revolution in moral perception. What finally emerged was a recognition that slaves could become masters or masters slaves, and that human beings are therefore not required to resign themselves to the world that has always been.

Notes

1. Jonathan Spence, "In China's Gulag," *The New York Review*, August 10, 1995, pp. 15–18.
2. Orlando Patterson, *Slavery and Social Death: A Comparative Study* (Harvard University Press, 1982).
3. M. I. Finley, "Between Slavery and Freedom," *Comparative Studies in Society and History*, April 1964, pp. 247–248.
4. Karl Jacoby, "Slaves by Nature? Domestic Animals and Human Slaves," *Slavery & Abolition: A Journal of Slave and Post-Slave Studies*, April 1994, pp. 89–97.
5. Gerda Lerner, *The Creation of Patriarchy* (Oxford University Press, 1986), pp. 76–100.
6. Patterson, *Slavery and Social Death*, p. 96. The quotation describing the Sambo stereotype comes from Stanley M. Elkins, *Slavery: A Problem in American Institutional and Intellectual Life* (University of Chicago Press, 1959). Without implying any biological or hereditary change, Elkins argued that slavery in the United States was so distinctively harsh that it produced a psychological transformation in slaves and created many Sambos.
7. The Slavic root for slave, *rab*, as in *rabotat*, to work, made its way into "robot" (actually the old Czech word for serf). The likening of a slave to a robot or inhuman machine parallels the comparison of the slave to an animal or a permanent child.
8. Thomas Wiedemann, *Greek and Roman Slavery* (Johns Hopkins University Press, 1981), pp. 18–20. I have found Wiedemann's translation of this part of the *Politics* clearer than that of Richard McKeon and others.
9. Robert W. Harms describes cases in the Zaire Basin in Africa in which a slaveholder lost his wealth in gambling and then became enslaved to one of his own former slaves. *River of Wealth, River of Sorrow: The Central Zaire Basin in the Era of the Slave and Ivory Trade, 1500–1891* (Yale University Press, 1981). This interchangeability of power and status is one of the characteristics that differentiates the oppression of human slaves from the oppression of animals. This point is overlooked in Marjorie Spiegel's fascinating and disturbing book, *The Dreaded Comparison: Human and Animal Slavery* (Mirror Books, 1996), which I discovered only after writing this essay. While some of my own

earlier work has touched on the connections between slavery, racism, and animalization, I hope to explore this theme far more systematically in *The Problem of Slavery in the Age of Emancipation: Dilemmas of Race and Nation*.

10. The meaning and desirability of baptizing slaves became a contentious issue at the Synod of Dort in 1618, the last international meeting of Protestant leaders and theologians from Great Britain and the Continent. While the delegates could not agree on a single policy regarding the baptism of pagans, their written opinions narrowed the gap between Christian masters and baptized slaves and either ended or limited the marketability of Christian slaves. Giovanni Deodatus, a Swiss professor of theology, even ruled that masters should "use them [baptized slaves] as hired servants clearly according to the customs of other Christians." Robert C.-H. Shell shows that these principles had some limited and temporary effect at the Cape of Good Hope but were specifically counteracted by colonial legislation in North America (*Children of Bondage: A Social History of the Slave Society at the Cape of Good Hope, 1652–1838*, Wesleyan University Press, 1994, pp. 332–370).

11. It should be noted that defenders of slavery drew some comfort from Montesquieu's emphasis on the importance of environment and climate; he even surmised that slavery might be founded on natural reason in tropical countries, where coercion might be a needed inducement to labor.

Slaves in Islam

Race and Slavery in the Middle East: An Historical Enquiry
Bernard Lewis (1990)

In 1855, five years before South Carolina defied all United States authority and seceded from the federal union, fearing that Lincoln's election would inevitably imperil the South's "peculiar institution," the Ottoman Empire ordered the governors of its far-flung districts to ban the commerce in slaves. For rebellious Arabs in the Hijāz, the province in western Arabia that contains the holy cities of Mecca and Medina, this was exactly the kind of anti-Islamic, Western-influenced measure they had been waiting for as a cause for throwing off Turkish rule. Assured by the ruler of Mecca that Ottoman power could never survive the Crimean War, which was then raging far to the north, Shaykh Jamāl issued a legal ruling, Bernard Lewis informs us, "denouncing the ban on the slave trade as contrary to the holy law of Islam. Because of this anti-Islamic act, he said, together with such other anti-Islamic actions as allowing women to initiate divorce proceedings and to move around unveiled, the Turks had become apostates and heathens. It was lawful to kill them without incurring criminal penalties or bloodwit, and to enslave their children."

One wonders whether Abraham Lincoln would have found it easier to rally Northerners around the flag if Jefferson Davis had proclaimed a holy war that justified not only the killing of any Northerner and the seizure of Northern property but the enslavement of Northern children.[1] In any event, the Ottoman Turks succeeded in suppressing their southern rebels in mid-1856, after less than a year of armed struggle. But as a conciliatory measure to prevent further secessionist movements, the Turkish government granted a major concession to the slave traders who had long made the Red Sea and the Hijāz a central route for transporting African slaves to the Middle East. Despite long-standing pressure from their British ally to end the slave trade, and despite sweeping domestic reforms in 1856 that eased Turkey's admission to the concert of Europe, the sultan's government exempted the Hijāz from its 1857 decree outlawing the trade in black slaves throughout the rest of the Ottoman Empire. As late as 1960, Lord Shackleton reported to the House of Lords that African Muslims on pilgrimages to Mecca still sold slaves upon arrival, "using them as living traveller's cheques."[2]

It has long been considered a mark of ethnocentric ignorance to equate servitude in Islamic societies with the brutal racial slavery that seemed to curse the New World with unending guilt. Ironically, the very "orientalism" that enabled nineteenth-century Europeans to project their own fears and longings upon an unchanging, exotic, and antipodal "East" also led many anti-Western Westerners to romanticize or defend black slavery in the Islamic world.[3] In 1887, for example, the Dutch orientalist C. Snouck Hurgronje ridiculed the "fantasies" that propelled what he concluded to be Britain's wholly inappropriate efforts to stop the slave trade from Africa to the Middle East. As a seasoned eyewitness who repeatedly stressed the "otherness" of Islam, Hurgronje affirmed that "public opinion in Europe has been misled concerning Muslim slavery by a confusion between American and Oriental conditions. . . . As things are now, for most of the slaves their abduction was a blessing. . . . They themselves are convinced, that it was slavery that first made human beings of them."

Self-critical Westerners have been unique in human history not only in their attempts to monopolize historical guilt, but also in their laudable efforts to imagine how they must appear to Persians, Lilliputians, Chinese, and Eskimos. As Bernard Lewis reminds us in his brilliant Jefferson Lecture in the Humanities, "Western Civilization: A View from the East": "In having practiced sexism, racism, and imperialism, the West was merely following the common practice of mankind through the millennia of recorded history. Where it is unique and distinct from all others is in having recognized, named, and tried, not entirely without success, to remedy these historic diseases."[4]

He might have added that the very discovery and naming of ethnocentrism, like racism, sexism, and imperialism, is a Western achievement that was originally intended to promote tolerance and social justice, not to destroy the cultural heritage that began to nourish the self-transcendent heresies among the great European writers of the seventeenth and eighteenth centuries that led to the world's first organized movements to abolish slavery, emancipate women, and extend equal rights to subject races and dissident or alien religions.

Whatever differences may have distinguished Islamic slavery from Christian slavery in the American South, the arguments of European orientalists who defended slavery in Islam in the 1880s could easily have been lifted word for word from standard American proslavery writing of the 1840s and 1850s. Bernard Lewis does not explicitly make this point, but he quotes British and Austrian "experts" who had traveled in Arabia and who assured their readers that "the liberated Negroes will not work even for money. For them freedom means their native idleness. . . . I would rather compare the Negroes with children, who must be made to do their stint." Or as one British traveler wrote, in words that would have brought at least a wry smile to the grim face of John C. Calhoun:

> the Negro is to be found here [in Arabia] in his proper place, an easily-managed, useful worker. The Negroes are the porters, water-carriers, and performers of most of the real labour in Meccah. Happy, healthy, well-fed, well-clothed (as such things go in Meccah), they are slaves, proud of their masters. . . . Slavery in the East has an elevating influence over thousands of human beings, and but for it hundreds of thousands of souls must pass their existence in this world as wild savages, little better than animals; it, at least, makes *men* of them, *useful men* too, sometimes even *superior men*. . . . That there are evils in Arab slavery I do not pretend to deny, though not affecting the Negro, once a slave. The exacting slave-driver is a character wholly unknown in the East, and the slave is protected from the caprice of any cruel master in that he is transferable and of money value. The man who would abuse or injure his slave would maim and willfully deteriorate the value of his horse. Whatever the Arab may not know, he most assuredly knows what is to his own immediate interest better than that. And the Negro himself . . . may through this medium be raised from a savage, existing only

for the moment . . . to a profitable member of society, a strong tractable worker, the position Nature seems to have made him to occupy.

Because writers of such orientalist literature were eager to draw the sharpest possible contrast between the allegedly benign Islamic world and the brutally exploitive American world portrayed in *Uncle Tom's Cabin*, the one book about the American South that most Europeans knew, they seemed unaware that they were simply repeating the specious arguments and clichés that had been propagated in the eighteenth century by West Indian proslavery apologists and finally anthologized in 1860 in E. N. Elliott's *Cotton Is King and Pro-Slavery Arguments*. Unfortunately, the myth that Muslims, as Arnold Toynbee asserted, "had always been free from colour prejudice vis à vis the non-White races," further shielded Islamic slavery from serious examination. The whole subject became increasingly explosive as the black nationalist and pan-Africanist movements found in Islam an antidote to the Christian hypocrisy that had been so closely linked with both New World slavery and Europe's subsequent colonization and exploitation of Africa.

Bernard Lewis, the eminent Dodge Professor of Near Eastern Studies Emeritus at Princeton, by writing a brief and highly readable "historical enquiry" into race and slavery in the Middle East, treads carefully on mine fields as perilous in their own way as those at the Battle of El Alamein. He is so extremely cautious, indeed, that his readers must usually take the risk of making comparisons and drawing conclusions on their own.

Lewis's wariness would seem to arise from two considerations: his conviction that Islam, as one of the world's great religions,

> has given dignity and meaning to drab and impoverished lives. It has taught men of different races to live in brotherhood and people of different creeds to live side by side in reasonable tolerance. It inspired a great civilization in which others besides Muslims lived creative and useful lives and which, by its achievements, enriched the whole world.[5]

But as Lewis's Jefferson Lecture also warns, certain centers of Islamic fundamentalism now see Western civilization, especially as exemplified in the United States, as the fount of pure evil. When such catchall terms as imperialism, racism, and consumerism are appropriated from Western critics and made synonymous with secular Western culture, the most objective comparisons of Islamic and Western slavery or racial beliefs will almost certainly be dismissed by some writers as ideological warfare.

Fruitful comparisons in history require certain fundamental patterns of similarity even if, as in Peter Kolchin's comparative analysis of American slavery and Russian serfdom and in George M. Fredrickson's and John W. Cell's studies of race relations in the United States and South Africa, it is the delineation of differences that eventually does the most to enhance our understanding.[6] Lewis, drawing on his vast knowledge of Arabic sources as well as on the pioneering work of Gernot Rotter and other scholars, points to the overwhelming evidence that racial slavery, as the modern world has come to know it, originated in medieval Islamic societies. Light-skinned Arabs, Berbers, and Persians invented the long-distance slave trade that transported millions of sub-Saharan captives either by camel caravans across the deserts or by slave ships from East Africa to the Persian Gulf.[7]

Arabs led the way in classifying the diverse peoples who lived from the Horn of Africa on the east to the states of Ghana and Songhay in the west as "blacks"—a single lowly group especially submissive to slavery because, as the famous fourteenth-century Arab historian Ibn Khaldūn put it, they "have little [that is essentially] human and have attributes that are quite similar to those of dumb animals." Some Muslim writers ranked the Nubians and especially the Ethiopians somewhat higher than the despised Zanj, a vague term applied to the Bantu-speaking laborers imported from East Africa and more generally to what Maqdisī described as "people of black color, flat noses, kinky hair, and little understanding or intelligence." But regardless of such minor distinctions and regardless of their continuing enslavement of white pagans and infidels from Eurasia, medieval Muslims came to associate the most degrading forms of labor with black slaves. In fact, the Arabic word for slave, ʿabd, came to mean only a black slave and, in some regions, referred to any black, whether slave or free.

If there is a sound basis for comparing Muslim with Christian slavery and even for seeing the early Arab and Berber exploitation of black laborers as a precursor to the racial slavery of the New World—a claim that Lewis's book never makes—it is crucially important to keep one fundamental distinction in mind. In some ways the speed and geographic extent of the Arab conquests, beginning in the 630s and 640s, were even more breathtaking than the expansion of the European maritime powers nine centuries later. As Lewis writes:

Islam for the first time created a truly universal civilization, extending from Southern Europe to Central Africa, from the Atlantic Ocean to India and China. By conquest and by conversion, the Muslims brought within the bounds of a single imperial system and a common religious culture peoples as diverse as the Chinese, the Indians, the peoples of the Middle East and North Africa, black Africans and white Europeans.

But in contrast to Europe's later imperial system, this explosive expansion of Islam did not lead to capitalist markets and investment, to dramatic economic growth, or to a widespread system of colonial plantation production. Therefore, slavery in the Muslim imperial system had purposes very different from the profit-making "mode of production" that developed in European plantation economies.

As Lewis points out, this distinction should not be too sharply drawn since we still know so little about life outside the Muslim towns, except for a few rare glimpses of black slaves working in mines, on construction and irrigation projects, or in huge gangs draining the tidal marshes of southern Iraq. The written records, in other words, which bustle with town slaves, military slaves, household servants, and eunuchs guarding slave harems, may convey a distorted picture. Moreover, Lewis's brief and abstract discussion of slavery, though not strictly limited to the Middle East, barely touches on the nonurban economies of Muslim Spain, Africa, India, or the later Ottoman Empire. All this said, one may safely assume that slave production in Islamic lands never approached the regimented efficiency of plantation agriculture in the West Indies and southern United States.[8]

This fundamental difference in economies did not mean that Arabs, Persians, Berbers, or Turks were immune to the lure of profits that could be obtained only by violating Muslim religious and ethical norms. There is evidence, for example, that in nineteenth-century Dār Fūr, in modern Sudan, there were farms that specialized in breeding black slaves for sale like cattle or sheep. Other enterprising merchants in upper Egypt reaped large capital gains by purchasing prepubescent boys at a price of about three hundred piastres apiece, having them castrated by Coptic monks, and then selling them as eunuchs for one thousand piastres each.

Lewis is scrupulous in distinguishing Islam as a religion from the various practices, institutions, and prejudices that eventually arose within Islamic societies. Like Judaism and Christianity, Islamic religion emerged at a time when chattel slavery was as universally accepted as human warfare. If all three religions sought to regulate and ameliorate slavery, Islam was most explicit in its conviction that freedom is the natural and presumed status of mankind; in its encouragement of private manumissions; and in its legal requirements that masters provide adequate maintenance and medical care for all slaves, and assistance for the elderly, or risk being compelled to sell or free a mistreated slave. The Shari'a, the great corpus of Islamic holy law, also flatly prohibited the enslavement of free fellow Muslims—as distinct from continuing to keep a slave who had converted to Islam. Hebrew and Christian laws were more ambiguous and for a considerable time allowed the enslavement of coreligionists.

Ironically, the very network of laws that were intended to protect both free Muslims and their slaves endowed the institution with supreme religious sanction:

> The emergence of the holy men and the holy places as the last-ditch defenders of slavery against reform is only an apparent paradox. They were upholding an institution sanctified by scripture, law, and tradition and one which in their eyes was necessary to the maintenance of the social structure of Muslim life.

If Protestant Christianity freed slaveholders from the legal duties and constraints of ancient religion, it also opened the way to abolitionism and other forms of modernization. It is not surprising that abolitionism first emerged and flourished within the Anglo-American dissenting sects or that it encountered continuing theological resistance from Lutherans, Roman Catholics, Orthodox Jews, and Muslims. The mid-nineteenth-century debates among American Jews and among Swedish and American Lutherans over the biblical support of slavery were largely academic; by the time Brazil abolished slavery in 1888, Cardinal Lavigerie, the archbishop of Algiers, with the support of Pope Leo III, was leading a Christian antislavery crusade in Africa. Muslim leaders were well aware that this new imperialist venture was directed, like earlier crusades, at "the Islamic infidel." During the so-called scramble for Africa, the tendencies of European orientalism were thus opposed by visions of "Christian knights" freeing Muslim slaves and civilizing the Dark Continent.

Racial distinctions played no appreciable part in the slave economies of antiquity, despite the Greeks' preference for enslaving "barbarians" and despite the discriminatory biblical laws that applied to relations between Hebrew and "Canaanite" bondsmen and their masters. During the centuries of Roman domination, slave populations contained a fortuitous mixture of captives. Bondage was a condition from which no one was exempt: including Greek scholars and poets, Turks, Scandinavians, Arabs, Gauls, Jews, Persians, Ethiopians. As late as the fourteenth and fifteenth centuries, continuing shipments of white slaves, some of them Christians, flowed from the booming slave markets on the northern Black Sea coast into Italy, Spain, Egypt, and the Mediterranean islands. The vulnerability of the "wild Irish" enabled predatory Englishmen to acquire the mental attitudes and basic training they would soon need to exterminate or enslave North American Indians from New England to South Carolina.

From Barbados to Virginia, colonists long preferred English or Irish indentured servants as their main source of field labor; during most of the seventeenth century they showed few scruples about reducing their less fortunate countrymen to a status little different from that of chattel slaves—a degradation that was being carried out in a more extreme and far more extensive way with respect to the peasantry in contemporary Russia. The prevalence and suffering of white slaves, serfs, and indentured servants in the early modern period suggests that there was nothing inevitable about limiting plantation slavery to people of African origin.

Like the Hebrew and Christian Bibles, the Qur'ān and Sharīʿa show no trace or even awareness of racial or color prejudice. In the seventh century, as in the earlier centuries of antiquity, neither slavery nor bitter ethnic and national rivalries seemed to generate what the modern world would define as genuine racism. When in the Hebrew Bible Moses marries an Ethiopian woman (Numbers 12:10), his sister is stricken with leprosy and becomes "*white* as snow" for objecting to the union. In the Song of Songs the bride affirms, in the Hebrew and earliest Greek translations, "I am black and comely, / O ye daughters of Jerusalem," implying that darkness of skin is itself a mark of beauty.[9] Saint Matthew's baptism of the Ethiopian Eunuch, a popular subject in Western iconography, depicted the first non-Jew converted to Christianity. Arabs long showed similar respect for Ethiopians; they accepted concubinage and even marriage with black women from Nubia and the upper Nile. Moreover, even after racial prejudice began to fuse with a more traditional contempt for lowly status, Muslim theologians and jurists continued to reject the popular idea that black Africans were designed by nature or condemned by providence to be slaves.[10] There were no Dred Scott decisions that undermined the theological egalitarianism of Muslim law.

By the late seventh century, however, blackness of skin was becoming a symbol that evoked distaste and contempt. In popular manuals of behavior affirmations of theoretical equality were soon reduced to formulas suggesting tolerance was desirable "even though" there were obvious reasons not to be tolerant. "Obey whoever is put in authority over you, even if he be a crop-nosed Ethiopian slave"; to prove your religious humility, marry someone who is pious and who will lower rather than exalt you, even though she is "a slit-nosed black slave-woman." As Lewis aptly notes, the message conveyed by countless maxims saying "that piety outweighs blackness and impiety outweighs whiteness . . . [is] not the same as saying that whiteness and blackness do not matter."

This stage of color consciousness coincided with the even more revealing complaints, apologies, and outcries from poets of African or mixed African and Arabic parentage. "If my color were pink, women would love me / But the Lord has marred me with blackness," Suhaym lamented in the seventh century. A colorblind society would hardly have produced the kind of verses and outbursts that Lewis quotes in profusion: "Though my hair is woolly and my skin coal-black, / My hand is open and my honor bright." "My color is pitch-black, my hair is woolly, my appearance repulsive." "I am a black man," a famous singer and musician wrote after seeking lodging in Damascus: "Some of you may find me offensive. I shall therefore sit and eat apart."

From the tenth century onward, a growing body of literature defended Ethiopians and other blacks from prejudice by explaining the environmental origins of their physical difference, by describing the good and pious deeds of particular blacks, and by condemning racial prejudice as contrary to the teachings of the prophet. This defensive writing bore a remarkable resemblance to such later Christian works as the Abbé Grégoire's *An Enquiry concerning the intellectual & moral faculties, & literature of Negroes; with an account of the life & works of 15 Negroes & Mulattoes, distinguished in science, literature & the arts* (1810, original French edition 1808), and the same author's *De la noblesse de la peau ou du préjugé des blancs contre la couleur des Africains et celle de leurs descendants noirs et sang-mêlés* (1826). Like Grégoire, the medieval Muslim writers were clearly responding to what Lewis calls "a new and sometimes vicious pattern of racial hostility and discrimination."

Drawing on Middle Eastern stereotypes of slaves from the eighth to the fifteenth century, Lewis quotes depictions of the Zanj by Muslim writers as ugly, stupid, dishonest, frivolous and lighthearted, foul-smelling, gifted with a sense of musical rhythm, often inclined toward simple piety, but dominated by unbridled sexual lust. According to Ibn Butlān, for example, the "bad qualities" of the Zanj women were many:

> and the blacker they are the uglier their faces and the more pointed their teeth. . . . Dancing and rhythm are instinctive and ingrained in them. Since their utterance is uncouth, they are compensated with song and dance. . . . They can endure hard work . . . but there is no pleasure to be got from them, because of the smell of their armpits and the coarseness of their bodies.

Such quotations are barely distinguishable from Thomas Jefferson's well-known passages in *Notes on the State of Virginia*:

> They [the blacks] secrete less by the kidneys, and more by the glands of the skin, which gives them a very strong and disagreeable odor. . . . They seem to require less sleep. A black after hard labor through the day, will be induced by the slightest amusements to sit up till midnight, or later, though knowing he must be out with the first dawn of the morning. They are at least as brave, and more adventuresome. But this may perhaps proceed from a want of forethought, which prevents their seeing a danger till it be present. . . . They are more ardent after their female; but love seems with them to be more an eager desire, than a tender delicate mixture of sentiment and sensation. Their griefs are transient. . . . In general, their existence appears to participate more of sensation than reflection. To this must be ascribed their disposition to sleep when abstracted from their diversions, and unemployed in labor. . . . Comparing them by their faculties of memory, reason, and imagination, it appears to me that in memory they are equal to the whites; in reason much inferior. . . . In music they are more generally gifted than the whites with accurate ears for tune and time.[11]

How are we to account for the striking similarity in the racist stereotypes and proslavery arguments that appeared in the medieval Middle East and in eighteenth- and nineteenth-century America? Lewis never explicitly raises this question, but his short book opens the way for more systematic comparisons that may eventually explain the complex connections between enslavement and racial prejudice.

Lewis does offer a number of specific clues and conclusions about the sources of racism that pertain to the Middle East. The initial Arab conquests soon led to prolonged debates and struggles over the equal status of non-Arab converts to Islam, to say nothing of the part-Arab offspring of concubines or non-Arab wives. The resulting sensitivity to ethnic privilege and lineage was heightened by the development of a long-distance slave trade that brought an influx of captives purchased from previously unknown regions in Africa, Asia, and Europe. Whereas Arabs had long been acquainted with Ethiopia, "a country," Lewis notes, "with a level of moral and material civilization significantly higher than their own," after the conquests they "encountered fairer-skinned peoples who were more developed and darker-skinned peoples who were less so. No doubt as a result of this they began to equate the two facts."

For whatever reasons, as the Islamic slave populations became more specialized, the Eurasian captives were generally assigned to positions of higher status and privilege while Africans were reduced to the most menial and arduous labor. The Ottoman capture of Constantinople in 1453 gradually diverted the immense flow of slaves from the Crimea, the Balkans, and the steppes of western Asia to Islamic markets. As a result, Christian slave merchants turned increasingly to Moorish captives or to blacks transported across the Sahara to the Mediterranean or purchased by the Portuguese along the coast of West Africa. Later on, the southward expansion of Russia, culminating in the annexation of Crimea in 1783, gradually shut off the supply of white slaves to even the Islamic markets. Except for the decreasing numbers of Europeans taken hostage by corsairs, the Islamic lands also became dependent on the slave merchants of sub-Saharan Africa. As Africa became almost synonymous with slavery, the world forgot the eagerness with which Tatars and other Black Sea peoples had sold millions of Ukrainians, Georgians, Circassians, Armenians, Bulgarians, Slavs, and Turks.

In 1441 Portugal's Prince Henry the Navigator contemplated a group of black slaves seized on the Mauritanian coast and paraded before him in Lisbon. As the grand master of the Order of Christ, he "reflected with great pleasure upon the salvation of those souls that before were lost."[12] No doubt Henry was unaware that for many centuries slave-buying Muslims had taken comfort in precisely the same thought. Lewis comments on the unquestioned reiteration of "the notion that slavery is a divine boon to mankind, by means of which pagan and barbarous peoples are brought to Islam and civilization." Yet despite this emphasis on the slave's own benefit, Lewis concludes that even emancipated blacks were "rarely able to rise above the lowest levels" and that in the Islamic Middle East "the black is almost entirely missing from the positions of wealth, power, and privilege."

If Lewis tends to omit the crucially important Africanization of Islam as the religion spread westward and south of the Sahara, he describes the pleas and protests of African Muslims, such as the black king of Bornu (now in northern Nigeria), who in the late fourteenth century futilely appealed to the sultan of Egypt to stop the Arab tribesmen who had raided his people, devastated his land, and "carried off free women, children, and infirm men. Some they kept as slaves for their own use; the rest they sold to slave dealers in Egypt, Syria, and elsewhere."

While correcting the errors of the orientalists, Lewis warns against the opposing error of concluding that the peoples of the Middle East ever practiced "the kind of racial oppression which exists in South Africa at the present time or which existed until recently in the United States." This is surely a sound judgment and admonition, even if Lewis seems unaware of the critical importance of black slave soldiers in the Caribbean, of the open acceptance of concubinage with black women in various parts of the New World, and of the privileges and power enjoyed by a few favored slaves in the United States, all of which point to closer parallels with Islamic slavery than he detects, despite the fundamental differences in economic and social systems.

The most striking point, however, is that Christianity and Islam both arose in relatively colorblind environments. Both adhered theologically to a belief in the unity of mankind, and yet both gave birth to slaveholding societies permeated with racial prejudice. In the fifteenth century, when Europe was ready for spectacular geographic expansion and colonization, a slave system based on African labor, including sugar plantations and a fully developed slave trade from East, Northcentral, and West Africa, was already in place in the Muslim world. Like algebra and knowledge of the Greek classics, racial slavery appears to have been one of the Arabs' contributions to Western civilization.

To recognize this tragic transmission and adaptation of slaveholding culture in no way lessens the guilt of Western maritime nations, which might eventually have found ways to exploit African labor without the aid and example of Arab and Berber intermediaries. Far more study is needed regarding the precise ways in which the practices of slavery were transmitted and adapted in Sicily, the Iberian Peninsula, and North Africa. But such knowledge can be gained only by abandoning the search for historical villains, by seeking a mutual understanding of Islamic and Judeo-Christian traditions, and by acknowledging the shared guilt and moral blindness that led to centuries of immeasurable suffering for African peoples, as well as to bloody race riots in fifteenth-century Cairo and large-scale insurrections by black slaves from Iraq to Brazil, Jamaica, and South Carolina.

Notes

1. The Confederate government did in fact sanction the summary execution or sale into slavery of captured black Union soldiers, and there were occasions when these threats were carried out. See James M. McPherson, *The Negro's Civil War* (Pantheon, 1965), p. 174; and his *Battle Cry of Freedom: The Civil War Era* (Oxford University Press, 1988), pp. 565–567.

2. For documentation regarding Lord Shackleton and the situation in 1960, see my *Slavery and Human Progress* (Oxford University Press, 1984), pp. 317, 362. The most thorough study of Britain's efforts to encourage the manumission of slaves in the Hijāz is Suzanne Miers, "Diplomacy Versus Humanitarianism: Britian and Consular Manumission in the Hijaz, 1921–1936," *Slavery and Abolition: A Journal of Comparative Studies*, 10 (December 1989), pp. 102–128.

3. As William R. Taylor showed long ago with respect to pre–Civil War America, many northern writers and travelers did much the same thing by creating or contributing to the "plantation legend" of a nonpecuniary, paternalistic South. See *Cavalier and Yankee: The Old South and American National Character* (Braziller, 1961).

4. Delivered in Washington on May 2, 1990, p. 15 of the text released by the National Endowment for the Humanities.

5. National Endowment for the Humanities text, pp. 2–3.

6. Peter Kolchin, *Unfree Labor: American Slavery and Russian Serfdom* (Harvard University Press, 1987); George M. Fredrickson, *White Supremacy: A Comparative Study in American and South African History* (Oxford University Press, 1981); John W. Cell, *The Highest Stage of White Supremacy: The Origins of Segregation in South Africa and the American South* (Cambridge University Press, 1982).

7. In *Slavery and Human Progress*, I discuss some of the attempts, based on extremely fragmentary evidence, to estimate the magnitude of the Islamic slave trade from the seventh to the twentieth century. Drawing particularly on the work of Ralph Austen, I conclude that "the key point is that the importation of black slaves into Islamic lands from Spain to India constituted a continuous, large-scale migration that in total numbers may well have surpassed, over a period of twelve centuries, the African diaspora to the New World" (pp. 45–56). The absence of a large population of black survivors can

be explained by the high mortality rate (except in North America, black slave populations suffered a rapid decline and virtually disappeared, as in colonial Mexico, unless replenished by the slave trade); by assimilation with other peoples; and by the fact that many male slaves had been castrated. Even in central India, however, there are communities of blacks who are the descendants of African slaves.

8. However, when Muslim economies in East Africa became absorbed into the global commercial system of the nineteenth century, slave plantations and agricultural conditions acquired something of a "New World" character, as Frederick Cooper has shown in two brilliant books, *Plantation Slavery on the East Coast of Africa* (Yale University Press, 1977) and *From Slaves to Squatters: Plantation Labor and Agriculture in Zanzibar and Coastal Kenya, 1890–1925* (Yale University Press, 1980).

9. Lewis suspects that the Latin rendering of the passage (Song of Solomon 1:5) "I *am* black, but comely," is the contribution of Saint Jerome (p. 123, note 9). For some reason, the recent Jewish Publication Society translation follows the Vulgate and the authorized Christian version: "I am dark, but comely, / O daughters of Jerusalem" (see *Tanakh: A New Translation of the Holy Scriptures According to the Traditional Hebrew Text* [Jewish Publication Society, 1985], p. 1405).

10. Although some Muslim writers were influenced by Aristotle's belief that a certain class of men were slaves by nature, Islamic jurists continued to insist that mankind was divided only by faith: all unbelievers, regardless of skin color or ethnic origin, could lawfully be enslaved in a jihad, or holy war. In a long and scholarly endnote (pp. 123–125), Lewis discusses some of the confusion and mythology connected with Noah's biblical curse of Canaan, who was conflated with Ham and blackness by an early Syrian church father, Saint Ephrem of Nisibis. Some medieval Muslims, like still later Christians, made use of the alleged curse of Ham as an excuse for enslaving blacks. But this legend was emphatically rejected by Muslim jurists, such as the African Ahmad Bābā of Timbuktu, who wrote that "even assuming that Ham was the ancestor of the blacks, God is too merciful to punish millions of people for the sin of a single individual" (pp. 57–58).

11. Query XIV (Harper Torchbook ed., 1964), pp. 133–135.

12. David Brion Davis, *Slavery and Human Progress*, p. 60.

A Big Business

The Slave Trade: The Story of the Atlantic Slave Trade, 1440–1870
Hugh Thomas (1997)

*The Making of New World Slavery: From
the Baroque to the Modern, 1492–1800*
Robin Blackburn (1997)

By limiting their attention to nation-states, especially the United States, historians have usually fragmented and obscured our understanding of the multinational Atlantic slave system. When most Americans hear the words "African-American slavery," they immediately think of the South and the Civil War. The story supposedly begins in Virginia, in 1619, when a colonist named John Rolfe casually noted that "a dutch man of warre . . . sold us twenty Negars."[1] At best, the standard texts make only passing reference to the flow of African labor to the Caribbean, Spanish America, and Portuguese Brazil. Even in U.S. history, the subject of slavery has traditionally been given a marginal place—a chapter, as it were, in the history of the South (or recently a more prominent position in African-American studies).[2] Even most American college graduates would probably be astonished to learn that Portugal began importing slaves from sub-Saharan Africa in the 1440s; that well before Columbus's famous voyages the Portuguese were exploiting black slave labor on sugar plantations in Madeira and São Tomé, off the coast of West Africa; and that enslaved African migrants to the New World greatly outnumbered European immigrants in the first three hundred and twenty years of settlement.

An understanding of the phenomenon of racial slavery, even in a specific locale such as Virginia or Texas, requires some knowledge of what Robin Blackburn terms "The Old World Background of New World Slavery," as well as some knowledge of the *multinational* character of the Atlantic slave trade, the slave colonies, and the growing markets that absorbed the latter's produce.

Why did "white slavery" flourish in the early Middle Ages and then disappear and become morally repugnant in the very Northern European nations that became leaders in establishing plantation colonies and transporting millions of African workers to the New World? Why was it that African kings and merchants from the Senegambia region on down to the Niger delta, the Congo, and on south and eastward to Madagascar and Mozambique, continued to sell such staggering numbers of slaves, with only rare and brief protests, to Portuguese, Spanish, Italian, Dutch, English, French, Swedish, Danish, German, American, Cuban, and Brazilian traders?

Why did the representatives of so many different religions—Muslims, Catholics, Protestants, Jews, New Christians, even Moravians and for a time Quakers—express so few scruples about buying and selling human beings? How can we explain the diffusion of racial slavery into non-plantation regions, such as New England and French Canada, so that black slaves could be found by 1750 from the St. Lawrence to the Rio de la Plata, from Québec and Boston to Santiago? If American colonists like young John Adams could angrily claim in 1765 that the mother country was treating them like "Negroes," what does this say about the psychological influence of African-American slaves on the construction of white Creole, or American, identities?[3] Finally, what was the relationship between New World slavery, traditionally interpreted as a backward or regressive institution, and the much-debated industrial revolution and emergence of "modernity"?

Many thousands of scholarly works on New World slavery have appeared since the pioneering books in the 1940s and 1950s by Eric Williams, Frank Tannenbaum, Kenneth M. Stampp, and Stanley Elkins. Nevertheless, very few historians have succeeded in conveying the global dimensions of a ghastly system that first united five continents as Europeans traded Asian textiles, among other commodities, for African slaves who, after surviving the horrors of the Middle Passage to North or South America, were forced to produce the sugar, coffee, tobacco, rice, indigo, and cotton that helped to stimulate and sustain modern consumer economies. There are various reasons for this historical neglect, even apart from the racial myopia of white scholars and the parochial focus of histories limited to a particular nation-state. We are only beginning to discover the immense quantity and relative inaccessibility of many relevant records and sources. This problem is matched by the complexity and contentiousness of many issues, such as the effects within Africa of exporting millions of slaves for some twelve centuries to *Asia* (between 869 and 883 C.E. black slaves rebelled and fought Arab armies in the Tigris-Euphrates delta), and millions more for over four centuries to Portugal, Spain, and then the entire Western Hemisphere. Moreover, few historians today have a command of the nine or more languages needed to study the most important surviving records concerning the Atlantic slave trade.

Future scholars will fortunately have access to the records of at least 27,233 Atlantic slave trading voyages in a "data set" gathered, organized, and put on CD-ROM by the Du Bois Institute at Harvard.[4] This collection is said to cover some 90 percent of all British, French, and Dutch slave trading voyages, and more than two thirds of the estimated grand total. By pressing a few keys on their computers, historians and students will soon be able to track particular voyages on the Middle Passage and assemble information on captains, ship owners, ship size, crew, mortality, the number and sex of slaves, slave revolts, and changing patterns of the trade from 1562 to the late nineteenth century. Moreover, the UNESCO Slave Route Project has sponsored international conferences and teams of researchers in an attempt to gather and preserve records in five continents regarding the greatest involuntary human migration in history. While the UNESCO scholars have searched for materials from Haiti and Jamaica to the Vatican, their most original and significant findings may well be indigenous African records, many of them in Arabic, which need to be saved from various environmental hazards.[5] It may be evidence of the speed of the information revolution that neither Hugh Thomas nor Robin Blackburn mentions the Du Bois Institute data set, the UNESCO materials, or the flow of information and continuing discussions on the Internet Slavery List.

There is a pressing need at the moment, however, for accurate and comprehensive syntheses of the specialized studies usually known only to specialists. It is remarkable that the two long and immensely ambitious books under review were both published in the same year, 1997, that both are the product of many years of extensive research (mostly in secondary sources), and that both are written by Englishmen. Perhaps Britons, drawing on their own traditions of imperial history, find it easier to take on such immense subjects as the making of New World slavery and 430 years of the Atlantic slave trade. As an unapologetic Marxist, editor of *The New Left Review,* and author of the outstanding book *The Overthrow of Colonial Slavery, 1776–1848,*[6] Robin Blackburn writes in the great tradition of E. P. Thompson, Christopher Hill, and Eric Hobsbawm. Hugh Thomas, who was made a life peer in the House of Lords in 1981, has written more popular works on a variety of subjects including the Spanish Civil War and the conquest of Mexico, as well as *World History: The Story of Mankind from Prehistory to the Present.*

Thomas provides a straightforward narrative account of Muslim and Christian slave-making and how it was succeeded by the fifteenth-century Portuguese naval expeditions that first captured and then began purchasing slaves along Africa's western coast. Thomas is especially knowledgeable about Iberian history and presents much new personal detail regarding the early Portuguese and Spanish slave traders and the families who profited from the traffic. After moving on to the Dutch, English, and French internationalization of the Atlantic slave trade in the seventeenth century, Thomas devotes eight chapters to the ways Africans were enslaved by other Africans and the stages of lethal transport from the interior of the continent to the putrid barracoons on the coast and on the tightly packed, stifling slave ships to their ultimate destinations in the New World. The last part of the book deals with the abolition movement, the nature of the slave trade in the nineteenth century, and Britain's aggressive measures to suppress it. One senses that Thomas would like to be regarded as a pure empiricist and storyteller. He shuns theories and theorizing, but deluges the reader with torrents of facts— facts which are often fascinating but which, as we shall see below, include a disturbing number of mistakes.

Although *The Making of New World Slavery* is less well-written than Thomas's book, it will have far greater appeal to scholars. Blackburn's introduction is dense and disjointed, and it contains obligatory quotations from Foucault and Baudrillard, and addresses such fashionable themes as "modernity," "identity," and "the dynamics of civil society."

It was long reassuring, as Blackburn rightly suggests, "to identify slavery with traditionalism, patrimonialism and backwardness." This was the lesson of classical social science from the time of Adam Smith (Blackburn also mentions in this connection Auguste Comte, Max Weber, and Ludwig von

Mises, but not Karl Marx). While Robert William Fogel, Stanley L. Engerman, Claudia Dale Goldin, and other "econometricians" have won much acclaim for documenting the productivity, profitability, and capitalist character of slavery in the American South, Blackburn is the first historian to explore at some length the role of the larger New World slave system in "the advent of modernity," by which he means the arrival of the modern industrial economy. After making tantalizing but undeveloped references to a kind of Darwinian "'natural selection' of social institutions and practices" that favored plantation slavery, he sensibly concludes that "slavery in the New World was above all a hybrid mixing ancient and modern, European business and African husbandry, American and Eastern plants and processes, elements of traditional patrimonialism with up-to-date bookkeeping and individual ownership." Blackburn's long chapters move from the Old World background and the uses of racial slavery in Portugal, Africa, and the various New World colonies to the eighteenth-century economic boom and British industrialization.

With respect to the Africans' part in selling as many as eleven or twelve million slaves to Europeans, nothing in either book rivals a succinct quotation from the late African-American scholar Nathan Huggins, which Blackburn uses as one of his first epigrams:

The twentieth-century Western mind is frozen by the horror of men selling and buying others as slaves and even more stunned at the irony of black men serving as agents for the enslavement of blacks by whites. ... The racial wrong was lost on African merchants, who saw themselves as selling people other than their own. The distinctions of tribe were more real to them than race, a concept that was yet to be refined by nineteenth and twentieth-century Western rationalists.

Despite inevitable overlap and repetition when discussing slavery or the slave trade in the centuries from the 1440s to the 1770s, the new books by Thomas and Blackburn could hardly be more different. Thomas affirms at the outset that "historians should not look for villains," but 784 pages later he praises "the heroes"—the French, British, American, and Spanish writers and abolitionists who "achieved the abolition of the Atlantic slave trade and of slavery in the Americas." Very little is said in either book about slave heroes and slave resistance, though Blackburn discussed some slave resistance and especially the impact of the Haitian Revolution in his 1989 book.

Blackburn succeeds in conveying a deep sense of the "superexploitation" of millions of black slaves working millions of uncompensated hours to produce wealth that flowed into white industrial investment and conspicuous display. He shows no hesitation in identifying the historical villains: not the Baroque governments and popes that first authorized the African slave trade so much as the "civil society" that broke with the traditional "moral economy" and unleashed "rampant capitalism and the free market." While Blackburn's arguments regarding civil society and the transition "from baroque to modern" are difficult to follow, he reinforces the often forgotten point made by Robert William Fogel (and many others) that market forces and economic self-interest can produce the most immoral and humanly destructive institutions, epitomized historically by racial slavery in the New World.[7] I should emphasize that Blackburn does not see the New World slave system as the necessary or optimum path to a modern society. But once chosen, because of its absolute centrality to the history of the past four hundred years it left a profound taint on the Western world we know.

Whereas Thomas totally rejects Eric Williams's "shocking argument" that profits from the slave trade financed the Industrial Revolution (Williams had not confined his argument to the slave trade, but had spoken of the larger and more ambiguous "triangular trade," which would presumably include the total profits from New World slavery),[8] Blackburn carefully considers the diverse views of various economic historians and concludes that while New World slavery did not produce capitalism, profits from the New World slave system made a significant contribution to British economic growth and investment in manufacturing.

In fact, Thomas provides telling examples that support this view, such as John Ashton, a Liverpool slave trader who helped finance the canal to Manchester; John Kennion and Brian Blundell, also of Liverpool, who turned to cotton manufacture and coal mining; and the great eighteenth-century French slave trader, René Montaudoin, who founded in Nantes "a factory in the modern sense of the word which made the first dyed cottons." And quite apart from the disputed question of profits and investment, Blackburn points to the slave system's neglected contribution to "the evolution of industrial discipline and principles of capitalist rationalization."

One thinks, for example, of Joseph J. Ellis's portrait of Thomas Jefferson as an efficiency expert, a kind of proto–Frederick Winslow Taylor, personally enforcing "a rigid regimen" on the dozen or so young slave boys, "from 10 to 16 years of age," who worked long hours producing nails at the small factory at Monticello.[9] Blackburn goes on to note the seeming paradox that "not by chance were prominent Abolitionists in the forefront of prison reform, factory legislation and the promotion of public education." He might have added that English and American Quakers, who were in the vanguard of the abolition movement, also led the way in devising and imposing new forms of labor discipline. There is a profound historical irony in the fact that "Speedy Fred" Taylor, the twentieth century's exponent of efficiency and the first to dispossess workers of all control of the workplace, was born of Quaker parents in Germantown, Pennsyslvania, the site in 1688 of the world's first great petition against human bondage.[10]

British and American abolitionists initiated a tradition of sharply differentiating New World and especially Anglo-American slavery from all previous forms of servitude. They were particularly intent on showing that modern plantation slavery was more inhumane and oppressive than the bondage recognized and sanctioned in the Bible or the servitude found in contemporary Africa. This line of argument later appealed to Marxists and other critics who were eager to demonize capitalism and market forces as the sources of the world's worst example of human exploitation. Blackburn is surely right when he insists that "the novelty of New World slavery resided in the scale and intensity of the slave traffic and the plantation trades." But because Blackburn desperately wants to see New World slavery as a unique aberration, as a tragic choice dictated by capitalist greed when other choices were available, he tends to romanticize earlier forms of human bondage. He forgets that slaves in premodern societies have often been subject to cannibalism, torture, ritual sacrifice, sexual exploitation, and arbitrary death at the whim of an owner.

When Blackburn asserts that "the slavery of the Ancient World had not denied the basic humanity of the slave," he also forgets the appalling descriptions of slaves in the mine shafts at Laurium in ancient Attica and in Ptolemaic Egypt. One need not dwell on the laws that sanctioned the Romans' pouring molten lead down the throats of slaves convicted of raping a virgin or crucifying four hundred household slaves after the murder of Pedanius Secundas, in 61 c.e., in order to agree with the Quaker John Woolman that no human being is saintly enough to be entrusted with the power of owning a slave as a piece of property, a power which has always involved some degree of dehumanization.[11] As Orlando Patterson and other scholars have demonstrated, while small numbers of highly privileged slaves can be found throughout history, even in nineteenth-century Mississippi, the institution of slavery has always depended on violent domination, dishonor, and a kind of "social death."

Hugh Thomas adopts an extremely effective literary device to convey the continuities between slavery in medieval Europe and the New World. His book begins with what seems to be a dramatic turning point in world history: Gomes Eannes de Zurara's vivid description of the sale, on August 8, 1444, in southwest Portugal, of 235 African slaves, "some white enough," some "like mulattoes," others "as black as Ethiops." This document has often been cited or reprinted to mark the beginning of Europe's exploitation of Africa. But Thomas proceeds to show that this sale of African slaves was part of a long sequence of events that included centuries of warfare and mutual enslavement between Christians and Muslims; the Christian reconquest of Portugal and Spain and the Portuguese capture of Ceuta, in North Africa, in 1415; the development of the Arab and Berber caravan trade in gold and slaves, which brought increasing numbers of black slaves (classified as *sclavi negri*) to Christian Sicily after the mid-1400s; and the westward shift in slave trading and sugar cultivation, which was hastened in 1453 by the Turkish conquest of Constantinople and the decline of the Venetian and Genoese trade in "Slavic slaves" from the Black Sea.[12]

Neither Thomas nor Blackburn gives sufficient attention to the precedents set by Italian slave traders in the Black Sea and Mediterranean. As Stephen P. Bensch has pointed out, "Mediterranean slavery has frequently been brushed aside in synthetic treatments of Western servitude as a curious holdover, a peripheral phenomenon, . . . an unexpected detour on the road leading from servitude to freedom, all the more unsettling because it appeared in the sophisticated urban societies of Italy, Southern France, and Eastern Iberia."[13] But Thomas does emphasize the direct continuities between medieval multiracial servitude and the kind of black bondage that first emerged on the sugar-producing Atlantic islands such as Madeira and São Tomé and then spread in the early sixteenth century to the New World. Blackburn provides much similar information, but by placing his brief discussion of the Atlantic islands *after* his chapter on "The Old World Background to New World Slavery," he reinforces his theme of discontinuity and distracts attention from the fact that when Columbus first entered the Caribbean, thousands of black slaves in the Old World were already producing sugar for a European market.[14]

The most striking evidence of continuity can be seen in the great mercantile and banking families of the Italian Renaissance. The Marchionnis of Florence, for example, had long engaged in the Black Sea slave trade (Kaffa, their base in the Crimea, resembled in many respects the forts and trading posts Europeans would later establish along the West African coast). In 1470, after the Ottoman Turks had endangered the Italian colonies in the eastern Mediterranean and had diminished Europe's supply of both sugar and slaves, young Bartolommeo Marchionni moved to Lisbon, where he joined a growing community of Florentines. Bartolommeo soon owned sugar plantations in Madeira and purchased from the Portuguese king the right to trade in slaves from Guinea.

According to Thomas, Bartolommeo had ships in Vasco da Gama's expedition to India in 1498 and in Cabral's expedition of 1500 that discovered Brazil; he became "a monopoly trader in slaves from the Benin River in the 1490s, carrying captives not only to Portugal and Madeira but also to Elmina, on the Gold Coast, where he sold them to African merchants for gold." One might add that this friend of the Medicis and Amerigo Vespucci also sent African slaves back to Pisa and Tuscany.[15] There were many other Florentines and Genoese who provided links from slave trading in the Mediterranean, which most people took for granted except when Muslim raiders enslaved Europeans, to the new social orders in Madeira, the Canary Islands, São Tomé, the Caribbean, and Brazil.

Judging whether enslavement was a continuous historical process or whether its American form was a historical exception is partly a matter of what historians choose to emphasize, and both Thomas and Blackburn recognize the multinational sponsorship of the early slave trade to the New World. In 1518 Spain's young King Charles, soon to be the Holy Roman Emperor Charles V, received fervent pleas from various Spanish colonists who were alarmed by the mortality and "weakness" of the Indians and who argued that only African slaves, like those in the Atlantic islands, could provide the labor needed to fulfill the New World's promise. King Charles agreed, and as Thomas puts it, the Flemish-born king awarded the coveted grant for supplying slaves to a Savoyard friend, the governor of Bresse in Burgundy. He in turn sold his rights, through a Castilian, to Genoese merchants— "who, in turn, would, of course, have to arrange for the Portuguese to deliver the slaves. For no Spanish ship could legally go to Guinea [according to the papal Treaty of Tordesillas], the monarchs of the two countries were then allies, and anyway, only the Portuguese could supply slaves in that quantity."

Perhaps the most startling point that Hugh Thomas makes about the early Portuguese slave trade is the way it became dominated by New Christian or *converso* merchants. Fernão de Loronha, for example, an associate and successor of Marchionni, gained a temporary monopoly of trade in the Bight of Benin and supplied slaves and wine to Elmina (Africans in the Gold Coast region continued to buy slaves from the Portuguese in exchange for gold). José Rodrigues Mascarenhas and Fernando Jiménez were other sixteenth-century merchants of Jewish ancestry who gained control over large segments of the slave trade to the Americas. King Philip II of Spain awarded Portuguese New Christians with *asiento* contracts to supply the Spanish colonies with African slaves. Some of these merchants had relatives or close friends in Italy, Brazil, or Antwerp, long the major center for refining and marketing sugar.

Thomas, unlike Blackburn, avoids the error of thinking of these *converso* merchants as Jews.[16] Since there has been recent controversy over the Jewish role in the Atlantic slave trade,[17] it is important to be on guard against the Inquisition's or the Nazis' definition of Jewishness: that is, having the taint of Jewish ancestry. In 1492 many of the Jews expelled from Spain settled in Portugal, and in 1497 the Portuguese king banished all the Jews who refused to convert to Christianity. Given the frequency of intermarriage between New Christians and Old Christians, many of these New Christian families would have lost their *converso* identity and been assimilated if there had been no doctrine of "purity of blood" and if the Inquisition had not become obsessed with secret "judaizing" practices. Even so, with the passage of time, the great majority of New Christians became absorbed in the Iberian Catholic culture. As Seymour Drescher has pointed out, most of the New Christians who made their fortunes in Africa, Asia, or the Americas returned to Iberia and "were disinclined to resettle where they could openly practice Judaism or even syncretic brands of family religiosity."[18]

But with respect to their participation in the slave trade, the genuineness of the *conversos'* Christian faith should be irrelevant. Neither Blackburn nor Thomas fully grasps the central point. The Church and the Catholic crowns prohibited Jews from owning baptized slaves or even traveling to the New World. What qualified men like Antônio Fernandes Elvas and Manuel Rodrigues Lamego to transport thousands of African slaves to the Spanish New World was their *convincing* Christian identity. According to Thomas, Pope Sixtus V thought so highly of Fernando Jiménez, despite his Jewish ancestry, that "he gave him the right to use his own surname, Peretti." When doubts arose that a *converso* merchant or planter was not a genuine Christian, he was often burned at the stake.

On an entirely different note, it would be irresponsible not to mention a problem of accuracy. Factual errors are inevitable in all historical writing and are likely to increase in number as a historian takes on a global subject spanning many centuries. Nevertheless, the frequency and character of Thomas's mistakes shake the reader's confidence in his book as a whole. Thus, contrary to Thomas, Massachusetts and New Hampshire did not adopt gradual emancipation acts in the late eighteenth century, and New Jersey's law came in 1804, not before 1800. The article on the slave trade in Diderot's *Encyclopédie* was not written by Louis de Jaucourt, but was plagiarized by him from a work Thomas mentions, George Wallace's *System of the Principles of the Laws of Scotland.*[19] Cotton Mather was anything but a Unitarian; indeed, his interest in Yale College (not yet "University") arose from his fear that Harvard was becoming too liberal. The great slave revolt in St. Domingue (Haiti) began in August 1791, not 1792.

The American Whig party, moreover, did not yet exist in 1824, and Charles Fenton Mercer was not an abolitionist. Thomas confuses Jonathan Edwards and James Stephen with their sons. It is simply wrong to assert that "slave movements from Eastern to Western states numbered only about 127,000 between 1810 and 1860, and was worth only $3 million." (In that period the slave population in the Western states Thomas refers to increased by over 1,821,000.) The most reliable recent studies estimate interregional movements of some 200,000 slaves each decade between 1820 and 1860. The United States acquired Texas in 1845, not "in the wake of the Mexican War." According to Thomas, there were around six million slaves in Brazil in 1851, an absurdly high figure. Nineteen years later, he writes, without the benefit of any emancipation act, there were only one and a half million. Most embarrassing of all, it is the Declaration of Independence, not the U.S. Constitution, that contains a "passage . . . where all men were declared free and equal, with inalienable rights."

To be scrupulously fair, one should stress that *The Slave Trade* contains over eight hundred pages and that Thomas typically conveys dozens of "facts," most of them accurate or convincing, on each page. Given the immense amount of work devoted to this volume, it is simply unfortunate that he and his editor were not more careful.

Taking all the more substantial points into account, the new books by Thomas and Blackburn complement each other. Thomas provides much detail of the experiences of slaves and their owners that balances Blackburn's rather arid but thought-provoking arguments on the place of New World slavery in the cauldron of forces that created the modern world. Thomas's *Slave Trade* will help many general readers grasp the magnitude and profound evil of the greatest forced migration in human history. In spite of its shortcomings, *The Making of New World Slavery* should long be regarded, along with Blackburn's *Overthrow of Colonial Slavery*, as a landmark in twentieth-century historiography.

Notes

1. It now seems highly probable that Africans arrived in Virginia before 1619. See Karen Ordahl Kupperman, "The Founding Years of Virginia—and the United States," *The Virginia Magazine of History and Biography*, Vol. 104, No. 1 (Winter 1996), and William Thorndale, "The Virginia Census of 1619," *Magazine of Virginia Genealogy*, Vol. 33 (1995), pp. 155–170 (I am indebted for this information to a communication on the Internet Slavery List by J. Douglas Deal). One should also note the earlier arrival of numerous black slaves and freed-people in Spanish Florida. For an excellent brief survey of the beginnings of slavery north of Florida, see Betty Wood, *The Origins of American Slavery: Freedom and Bondage in the English Colonies* (Hill and Wang, 1997).

   Gordon Wood, writing in *The New York Review*, has noted the encouraging trend toward comparative history and interest in transatlantic connections ("Doing the Continental," *The New York Review*, November 20, 1997, pp. 51–55). But if one looks at the way most academic jobs are defined and at the courses offered by most history departments, it becomes clear that the teaching of history is still sharply categorized by nation-states and such geographic regions as colonial North America, early modern Europe, and East Asia.

2. From the time of World War I, a succession of black historians, including Carter G. Woodson, William M. Brewer, Charles H. Wesley, Benjamin Quarles, and Eric Williams, published significant work on African-American slavery, much of it in *The Journal of Negro History*. But even the many editions of John Hope Franklin's now classic work, *From Slavery to Freedom*, beginning in 1947, had little effect on the marginal treatment of slavery in most high school and college texts.

3. While historians have long been familiar with the American colonists' frequently expressed fear of being "enslaved" by the activist British government, T. H. Breen has recently shown that Adams was more specific: "'We won't be their Negroes,' snarled a young John Adams in 1765, writing as 'Humphry Ploughjogger' in the *Boston Gazette*. Adams crudely insisted that Providence had never intended the American colonists 'for Negroes . . . and therefore never intended us for slaves . . . I say we are as handsome as old English folks, and so should be as free.'" (Breen, "Ideology and Nationalism on the Eve of the American Revolution: Revisions *Once More* in Need of Revising," *The Journal of American History*, Vol. 84, No. 1 [June 1997], p. 29.)

4. David Eltis, Stephen Behrendt, David Richardson, and Herbert Klein, *The Trans-Atlantic Slave Trade: A Database on CD-ROM* (Cambridge University Press, 1999). I am indebted to Professor David Eltis, of Queens University, Ontario, for this information, which was given at a conference, "New Perspectives on Slavery and the Slave Trade," November 20–21, 1997, at the Rutgers Center for Historical Analysis.

5. I am indebted for this information to Howard Dodson, of the Schomburg Center for Research in Black Culture, New York Public Library, who presented a report at the November 20–21, 1997, Rutgers conference on slavery and the slave trade.

6. Verso, 1988. Reviewed by me in "The Ends of Slavery," in this volume.

7. Fogel, *Without Consent or Contract: The Rise and Fall of American Slavery* (Norton, 1989). In 1993 Fogel won the Nobel Prize in Economic Science.

8. Some reviewers have confused this first "Williams thesis" with a second thesis that Williams makes: namely, that Britain abolished the slave trade and then emancipated colonial slaves because the systems were in economic decline. This second line of argument has been discredited by numerous studies. See, for example, "The Benefit of Slavery," in this volume.

9. *American Sphinx: The Character of Thomas Jefferson* (Knopf, 1997), p. 141.

10. See David Brion Davis, *The Problem of Slavery in the Age of Revolution, 1770–1823* (Cornell University Press, 1975), pp. 233–254; Sean Wilentz, "Speedy Fred's Revolution," *The New York Review*, November 20, 1997, pp. 32–37. The fact that Quakers were pacificists may lend support to Blackburn's view that "unrestrained commercial calculation," not "the military revolution," was the decisive factor in leading to the "modern rational practices" described by Foucault and Weber.

11. See my essay "At the Heart of Slavery" in this volume.

12. The word for "slave" in Western European languages was derived from the Latin *sclavus*, meaning a person of Slavic origin. While most of the words for "slave" in ancient languages had no ethnic connotations, the association with Slavs began in the early Middle Ages when captives from the Balkan region were often transported overland to Muslim Spain. Later, Italian merchants extended the Slavic term to Armenians, Circassians, Georgians, Mingrelians, Bulgarians, Turks, and Tatars who were purchased along the coasts of the Black Sea and Sea of Azov. Though various terms for Africans, such as the French *nègre*, sometimes became synonymous with "slave," it is significant that the Slavic linkage (*esclave, sklave, esclavo*) has persisted for a millennium even though

chattel slavery became almost wholly identified with people of sub-Saharan African descent.

13. "From Prizes of War to Domestic Merchandise: The Changing Face of Slavery in Catalonia and Aragon, 1000–1300," *Viator*, Vol. 25 (1994), pp. 63–64.

14. Unlike Stuart B. Schwartz's *Sugar Plantations in the Formation of Brazilian Society, Bahia, 1550–1835* (Cambridge University Press, 1985), which Blackburn closely follows in other respects, Blackburn minimizes the importance of São Tomé and what he calls its "Afro-Jewish, Luso-Catholic planter class." He fails to note that 70 percent of the Jewish children (he calls them "Jewish New Christian children") who were abducted from their parents, baptized, and then deported from Portugal to São Tomé soon died; that the survivors who often mated with Africans had few if any ties with Judaism; and that the island served as a crucial bridge between what Schwartz terms "the Mediterranean sugar complex" and American plantation slavery.

15. Charles Verlinden, *L'esclavage dans l'Europe médiévale, Tome deux: Italie–Colonies italiennes du Levant—Levant latin—Empire byzantin* (Rijksuniversiteit te Gent, 1977), pp. 235, 377.

16. Blackburn actually uses the term "Jewish 'New Christians.'" In his Introduction Thomas notes that virtually no Jews were involved in the Anglo-Saxon slave trade and that whether a Portuguese New Christian "is to be seen as a Jew is not something on which I should wish to pronounce: several of the traders concerned proclaimed their or their forefathers' Christian conversion as genuine to the very last torture afforded by the Inquisition, even if the Holy Office caused to be burned to death in Mexico and in Lima several prominent slave merchants, whom they accused of 'judaizing.'"

Unfortunately, some Jewish historians, identifying with the *conversos* who were persecuted and burned at the stake, or wanting to expand the extent of Jewish population, have accepted the Inquisitors' definition of "Jew," a position decisively rejected by Benzion Netanyahu's *The Marranos of Spain* (American Academy of Jewish Research, 1966) and *The Origins of the Inquisition in Fifteenth-Century Spain* (Random House, 1995). Of course a few *conversos* (the word "*marrano*" meant "swine") did revert to Judaism when they had the opportunity. For a review of the literature and the difficulties of classifying most New Christians as Jews, see Saul S. Friedman, *Jews and the American Slave Trade* (Transaction Publishers, 1998), pp. 50–62, and the essay by Seymour Drescher cited below.

17. See my article "The Slave Trade and the Jews" in this volume.

18. See Seymour Drescher, "Jews and New Christians in the Atlantic Slave Trade," in *The Jews and the Expansion of Europe to the West, 1450–1825*, edited by Paolo Bernardini (Berghahn Books, 2000).

19. See my article "New Sidelights on Early Antislavery Radicalism," *William and Mary Quarterly*, Third Series, Vol. 28 (October 1971), reprinted in Davis, *From Homicide to Slavery: Studies in American Culture* (Oxford University Press, 1986), pp. 228–237.

13

The Triumph of the Country

The Age of Federalism
Stanley Elkins and Eric McKitrick (1993)

✳

Except for the 1860s, no decade in American history has been as dangerous, as divisive, and as formative as the 1790s, which Stanley Elkins and Eric McKitrick have aptly termed "The Age of Federalism." Beginning in 1789, American leaders implemented and began to interpret the new Constitution. They enacted most of Alexander Hamilton's financial program, which shored up the nation's credit and helped inaugurate an era of breathtaking prosperity. They agreed to build a new capital city "on a stretch of uninhabited wasteland on the Potomac." They preserved a precarious neutrality during a global war that provoked serious hostilities with England and then during an undeclared naval war with France. They suppressed the Whiskey and Fries rebellions in Pennsylvania. They passed the notorious Alien and Sedition Acts. They concluded treaties with England, Spain, and France which removed British forts and troops from American territory, opened the Mississippi to American navigation, and freed American merchant ships from the constant peril of capture by French privateers.

Elkins and McKitrick examine all these developments with thoughtfulness and care. Despite 754 pages of text, however, their monumental synthesis omits many subjects that have captivated social historians for the past thirty years. After decades of "history from the bottom up," we now have a huge volume on the 1790s which tells us nothing about sailors, artisans, midwives, farmers, indentured servants, the family, or Mary Wollstonecraft (whose *Vindication of the Rights of Woman* was partly reprinted in 1792 in the American *Ladies Magazine*). Whatever one makes of this defiant selectivity, Elkins and McKitrick have written a masterpiece that deserves to be understood and appreciated on its own terms before being compared to any hypothetical better book. Up to a point, at least, the authors' refusal to give "equal attention" to all segments of society has enabled them to present a sharper and more convincing picture of their chosen subject: the complex development and demise of a political outlook or world view called federalism (epitomized in political theory by the classic *Federalist* essays written by Hamilton, Madison, and Jay).

I shall later question the significance of divorcing the issues Elkins and McKitrick do pursue from the omnipresent setting of racial slavery and an economy dependent on the Atlantic slave system. But I must first applaud their extraordinary gift, reminiscent of Madison and Hamilton themselves, for defining and elaborating key issues, premises, principles, and dilemmas; and then shifting clearly and gracefully from this concern with abstract ideas to living personalities and actual choices, consequences, accidents, and problems of infinite complexity. No other living historians have written with greater skill and elegance to illuminate the contingency and interrelatedness of events. Even apart from the memorable portraits of Madison, Hamilton, Jefferson, Washington, Jay, John Adams, Genet, Monroe, Talleyrand, and John Marshall, sentences of *The Age of Federalism* sparkle with such playful intelligence that I never felt a trace of boredom, despite the time it took to read, and often reread, every page.

Awaited for decades, *The Age of Federalism* is dedicated to the memory of Richard Hofstadter, one of the greatest American historians of the twentieth century, who served in the 1950s as the dissertation adviser for both Elkins and McKitrick at Columbia University. In 1974, four years after he died, the two former students co-edited a distinguished Festschrift, *The Hofstadter Aegis: A Memorial*. Although McKitrick is somewhat older than Elkins and both are now retired as professors at Columbia and Smith College, respectively, they began graduate school at the same time, after military service in World War II, and taught together at the University of Chicago while working on their dissertations.[1] In 1959, when both men received their Ph.D.s at Columbia, publishers were extremely reluctant to accept any manuscript that still carried the "smell," as one university press editor put it, of a doctoral dissertation. But Elkins's *Slavery* (1959) and McKitrick's *Andrew Johnson and Reconstruction* (1960) had so much authority that they were published almost immediately, and they soon helped to revolutionize the entire interpretation of nineteenth-century American history.

As Elkins and McKitrick point out in the introductions to their first books, the South, having lost an ideological as well as a military struggle in the Civil War, achieved a decisive historiographical victory in the early years of the twentieth century. From the era of Theodore Roosevelt to the early 1950s, the most authoritative works on slavery and Reconstruction rested on a simple, bedrock assumption: "Negroes" were inherently inferior to whites, and were wholly unprepared at the end of the Civil War to look out for themselves or take on the responsibilities of equal citizenship. As W. E. B. DuBois observed in 1935, in his radical and long neglected book *Black Reconstruction*, even the most scholarly white historians "cannot conceive of Negroes as men." The writings of Ulrich B. Phillips on slavery and of William A. Dunning on Reconstruction were so rich in scholarly documentation and so closely tuned to the nation's ideological needs—exemplified by popular films from *Birth of a Nation* to *Gone with the Wind*—that their influence on textbooks, fiction, journalism, and other historians would be difficult to exaggerate.

By the time Elkins and McKitrick published their first books, a reaction against the Phillips and Dunning "schools" was already under way. For a time this historiographical groundwork for the future civil rights movement remained on the margins of academic history. In 1944 Richard Hofstadter, who had been active in the radical student movement of the 1930s, wrote the first manifesto attacking Phillips's racial bias and methodology. Significantly, his essay appeared in *The Journal of Negro History*, long known as an organ for such dissenting white Marxist historians as Herbert Aptheker and such black radical scholars as DuBois and Eric Williams.[2] Nineteen forty-four was also the year of Gunnar Myrdal's *An American Dilemma*, which drew on the advice and works of Du Bois, E. Franklin Frazier, Charles S. Johnson, and other black intellectuals as well as on the anti-racist arguments of white social scientists such as Franz Boas and Melville Herskovits. In historical writing, as Elkins pointed out, "the culmination and quintessence of the entire anti-Phillips reaction" came with the publication in 1956 of

Kenneth Stampp's *The Peculiar Institution*, sometimes called the historians' counterpart to *Brown* v. *Board of Education*. Stampp's book presented the antipode to Phillips's portrait of southern slavery as a benign and paternalistic institution, "a training school" and "civilizing agency" "for the untutored savage." Stampp's description of black oppression, dignity, and resistance soon superseded Phillips's account and became a standard work of mainstream liberal ideology.

While fully accepting Stampp's overdue and triumphant victory, Elkins wished to move beyond "the coercions of a century-old debate" regarding the physical harshness and moral evil of American slavery. He suggested an analogy between slavery and the way Nazi concentration camps supposedly infantilized many of their inmates and put forward what came to be called the "Sambo-thesis" to describe black submission to whites. Long after the years of uproar, caricature, and publicity over these ideas, it is easy to forget what this doctoral dissertation, intended merely as a "proposal" of new lines of inquiry, actually achieved. Elkins prepared the way for future comparative studies of slavery in different societies, for debates over the psychological effects of bondage on the personality of slaves, for related debates over the continuity and relative autonomy of African American culture, and for countless studies of the ways in which social conditions—such as the presence or absence of what Elkins termed "the dynamics of unopposed capitalism"—have shaped movements for slave emancipation and other reforms.

Meanwhile, McKitrick's biography of Andrew Johnson reversed a long tradition in "Progressive" historiography that had vindicated Lincoln's successor as a misunderstood populist martyr who fought bravely to defend Lincoln's rational and forgiving plans for reunion against Radical Republican fanatics. By portraying Johnson as an astonishingly stubborn and self-righteous racist, and his opponents as reformers struggling with a social problem of unprecedented magnitude and complexity, McKitrick suggested an approach that affected scores of later books reassessing the meaning and tragedy of Reconstruction.

Although Elkins and McKitrick have usually been identified as historians of slavery, emancipation, and Reconstruction, *The Age of Federalism* makes it clear that they have never been part of a tradition that sees racial slavery and its consequences as the basic reality, the grim and irrepressible theme governing both the settlement of the Western hemisphere and the emergence of a government and society in the United States that white people have regarded as "free." This view of slavery as America's haunting original sin was eloquently expressed at times by Jefferson, Madison, and Lincoln, and has been taken up by such diverse historians as Ulrich B. Phillips, Eric Williams, Eugene Genovese, Edmund Morgan, and this reviewer. But even in his first book, Elkins showed far more interest in highlighting the peculiar American social conditions that exacerbated the psychological effects of American slavery than in the slave system itself. According to McKitrick, the same social conditions—rampant individualism, demagoguery, stunted institutional development, and a glorification of self-interest—doomed the outcome of slave emancipation and Reconstruction.

This diagnosis of the central malady in American history and culture owes much to Richard Hofstadter, whose work provides a means for understanding the achievement and bias of *The Age of Federalism*. Having grown up in Buffalo, which he considered provincial and culturally impoverished, Hofstadter was drawn to the intellectual excitement and cultural ferment of cosmopolitan centers like New York. He would have applauded Elkins and McKitrick when they describe the egregious consequences of moving the national capital to a new and artificial town, long notorious for its mud, isolation, oppressive climate, and boarding-house living. He would have approved of their "counterfactual projection" in which the capital in 1790 is allowed to remain in New York City, enabling the national political culture to interact with a strong urban and commercial culture. Like London and Paris, such a nucleus of power and creativity would have attracted talent from all directions, providing encouragement and community to isolated genius and converting Columbia into the National University. Yet Hofstadter, who was also acutely sensitive to American populist traditions of anti-intellectualism, nativism, and what he termed a "paranoid style" of political rhetoric, would probably also have pointed to the long-term fatal dangers of combining in one image all the diabolical powers of Washington with all the evils of Wall Street and all the conniving un-Americanism symbolized by "Jew York City."[3]

If New York had remained the national capital and presidents had continued to enjoy the theater and other cultural amenities as Washington did (watching a New York play in 1789 was said to have been "the only public occasion at which George Washington was observed to laugh"), the already strong assaults against central government, bankers, big business, intellectuals, urbanites, and foreign influence would have become more intense. They were already driven by the forces of what Elkins and McKitrick call the "Country persuasion." This idea, which in its application owes much to Hofstadter, provides a central theme in *The Age of Federalism.*

✳

The book begins with a review of the historical literature on the evolution of "Court" and "Country" traditions in England and the North American colonies. Following the triumph of the "Court party" in England's "Glorious Revolution" of 1689 and the later regime of Robert Walpole, discontent deepened among a diverse group of "disaffected Tory squires, 'independent Whigs,' habitués of the London coffee-houses," and other outsiders, who denounced the Court's "corruption, its luxury, its rotten boroughs, and its armies of placemen, relatives, and parasites." This Country mentality, often merged with a long intellectual tradition of civic humanism and republican theory, became deeply rooted in the North American colonies and eventually unfolded as the ideology of the American Revolution.

But the Country mentality, with its constant suspicion of central power and obsession with urban conspiracies, is better suited for revolution than for instituting a stable government. The Federalists who framed and defended the U.S. Constitution could agree with their opponents that human history reveals a universal and "irreconcilable antinomy of liberty and power." The conviction that liberty is always fragile and vulnerable, that power is always aggressive, encroaching, and corrupting, was the one governing assumption, according to Elkins and McKitrick, "a kind of substructural given," that undergirded eighteenth-century political thought and the the institutions we have inherited from that era.[4] The history of the twentieth century, one might add, has hardly contradicted those elemental premises.

Still, the freedom and independence won in the Revolution could also be imperiled by a government too weak to deal with runaway inflation, debt, trade barriers between states, and internal division accelerated by national impotence in the face of Indian resistance and foreign belligerence. By the spring of 1789, when the public cheered Washington as he traveled from Mount Vernon to New York for his inauguration, the Federalists had convinced most Americans that a stronger government was desirable as long as it embodied checks and balances, and included, in a last-minute pledge, a Bill of Rights. After Washington had served two terms, as Elkins and McKitrick point out,

> the Federalists had not only established a government but had disposed of every outstanding problem that had afflicted the Confederation: pac-

ifying the Indians, opening the Mississippi, and achieving a stable national credit. Whatever the difficulties with England and France, the
country had preserved an honorable neutrality, was at peace with the
world, and enjoyed a material prosperity the extent of which could
scarcely have been imagined in 1789.

Yet despite these remarkable accomplishments, which enabled John Adams
to sustain Federalist leadership by the narrowest electoral margin until 1801,
the nation had become bitterly divided. The Country mentality, now institutionalized in the Republican Party, was on the rise. The Republicans

> had succeeded in preempting the main elements of the American idea.
> It was the core of a world-view born of the Revolution, a parochial but
> far-flung anglophobia, a rural suspicion of taxes, of manipulators of
> money, of great military and naval establishments, and of "energetic"
> government.

Although radical historians have often celebrated the Republicans' anticapitalist rhetoric, the party actually attracted many of the richest men in
America, including large slaveholders, who favored the strictest limits on
government intervention in a market economy. It is thus the Country mentality, as I read the work of Elkins and McKitrick as a whole, that prepared
the way for "the dynamics of unopposed capitalism"—for the individualism
of Tocquevillean America that would create a form of slavery far more dam-
aging to its victims than the slavery found in Latin America. The same
hostility to institutions that would have limited absolute power over private
property, including human property, combined with a strange Jeffersonian
and transcendentalist detachment from reality, precluded a peaceful and reasonable solution to the problems of slavery and racial degradation.

I am not suggesting that Elkins and McKitrick see the Country mentality
as the source of all evil in American history. Undeniably, they are partial to
the youthful Hamilton and the Federalist Madison, whose cosmopolitan realism and "projections" for civic progress owed much to the writings of David
Hume and the modernizing example of eighteenth-century Scotland. When
Elkins and McKitrick come to Hamilton's vision of industrializing an undeveloped continent, they echo, with significant and unintended irony, the
rhetoric used by Frederick Jackson Turner to describe the regenerating effects
of the American frontier. "The appearance of substantial manufacturing enterprises," they write,

would not only function as salutary examples; they would summon into being enterprises yet more highly differentiated, call upon unused resources, create hitherto unsuspected demands, and give new directions to old pursuits. Thus, Hamilton declared, "the bowels as well as the surface of the earth are ransacked for articles which were before neglected. Animals, Plants and Minerals acquire an utility and value, which were before unexplored."

Elkins and McKitrick present such a glowing picture of Hamilton's economic program and related foreign policy (at a time when Jefferson, his enemy, was secretary of state) that we are quite unprepared for their sudden conclusion that the great secretary of the treasury, "in his impatience and pride, may be said to have created the conditions for the failure of his own vision." For all his personal integrity, the authors now concede, Hamilton was blind to the corruption inherent in rampant and unrestrained speculation, the mania for "quick killings" in the market. Moreover, when no longer disciplined by his close ties with President Washington, Hamilton became almost maniacal in his hatred for President Adams and his determination to lead an immense permanent army that could enforce domestic obedience and be used in wild imperialistic ventures to the south and west. After re-creating in a convincing and sympathetic way Federalism's vitality, coherence, and sense of "firstness" in building enduring institutions, Elkins and McKitrick seem to welcome the self-demolition of the Federalist Party. They even recognize that the Jeffersonian opposition took on a corrective historical mission to check "the demonic side, the speculative side, of capitalism."

There can be no doubt, however, that the villain of *The Age of Federalism* is the man who defeated the party in 1801, and who in the last words of the book vows to "sink federalism into an abyss from which there shall be no resurrection for it." Elkins and McKitrick present a devastating if sometimes ambiguous picture of Thomas Jefferson—a shy and fastidious "cold fish" who "would have been all but ideal as a professor."[5] In situations involving power, Jefferson comes across as appallingly deceitful, cunning, manipulative, vindictive, and hypocritical. As secretary of state, for example, he not only seriously misled Edmond Charles Genet, the young minister sent to the U.S. in 1793 by the French Republic, when he assured Genet he had more support from the American administration than was the case; he also passed on to Genet confidential views expressed within Washington's cabinet and then skillfully dissociated himself from Genet's headstrong actions, as when Genet tried to raise troops to march on Spanish Florida and wanted to commission privateers to attack British ships.

Despite his disillusion over the course of the French Revolution, Jefferson as vice-president (1797–1801) remained so rigidly Anglophobic—always hoping that France would invade and conquer England—that he played into the hands of the French government during the undeclared naval war between France and the U.S. and the frustrated American efforts to negotiate with the French (the "XYZ affair"). He actually advised the French consul general on the best tactics to use against President Adams. Even if we allow for the peculiar nature of the vice-presidency before the Twelfth Amendment and for the earlier indiscretions of Hamilton and other officials, it is difficult to understand how the Jefferson we encounter in this book could aid an enemy nation and undercut his own president's peace negotiations. By emphasizing this behavior, Elkins and McKitrick evidently want to make it clear that he does not deserve to be hallowed as our preeminent Founding Father, our secular American saint.

They acknowledge, of course, that Jefferson was a "liberal idealist" who has always been associated with the tradition of American liberalism. They also see him as the ideological source of the agrarian democratic myth that has long permeated both popular and intellectual culture. As the leading proponent of the Country mentality (and the man most responsible for the compromise that moved the national capital to the Potomac), Jefferson personified everything that Federalism struggled to overcome, including an almost willful ignorance of the economics of money, banking, and credit. We may be puzzled by Jefferson's contradictory positions on cities (he actually loved the intellectual discourse of Williamsburg, Paris, and Philadelphia); on elites (for all his talk about yeoman farmers, he always belonged to Virginia's top circle and favored a "natural" aristocracy); and on local rule (he strongly favored westward expansion and the acquisition of Florida, Texas, and even Cuba). Such contradictions may be explained in part by the visceral abhorrence Jefferson felt when confronted by the specter of an aggrandizing, urbanizing, commercializing force—similar to the force that had emerged in the changed civilization of eighteenth-century England—which threatened to annihilate the balanced cosmos of Virginia's plantation society.

If Jefferson is the central enemy and destroyer of the "Age of Federalism," he is also the weakest link in Elkins's and McKitrick's book. Unlike other characters, including such unlikely figures as the arch-Federalist Timothy Pickering, Jefferson remains a flat, even one-dimensional character, and is usually seen through the eyes of opponents. For all their imaginative flair, the authors seem incapable of conveying the magic appeal of Jefferson's ideal of a more egalitarian society, a society always dedicated to the "living generation." Elkins and McKitrick might well reply that they do in the end pay tribute to Jefferson's eloquent commitment to political and religious liberty, in his 1801 inaugural address, and that little more is needed in view of the continuing popular and scholarly hagiography.[6] And I must agree that it is salutary to see the "Apostle of Liberty" through Federalist eyes, especially on the rare occasions when Elkins and McKitrick turn to matters of race.

In 1801, for example, when Napoleon was planning to send a huge expeditionary force to St. Domingue to conquer the rebellious Toussaint Louverture and reclaim what had recently been the most valuable colony in the New World, President Jefferson assured the French that he would be happy to supply a fleet and help "reduce Toussaint to starvation." Five years later, after the former slaves had defeated and expelled Napoleon's army and had proclaimed Haiti's independence, Jefferson had a law passed imposing a total embargo on the black republic. This action infuriated Senator Timothy Pickering, who as secretary of state in 1799 had supplied Toussaint's forces with desperately needed provisions and had even supported the rebellious blacks with warships and a bombardment of André Rigaud's harbor forts.

In a devastating letter of 1806, which Elkins and McKitrick have found in the Jefferson Papers at the Library of Congress, Pickering accuses Jefferson of siding with despots in an effort to deprive the free Haitians "'guilty,' indeed, 'of a skin not coloured like our own' but . . . *emancipated*, and by a great National Act declared Free . . . of those necessary supplies which . . . they have been accustomed to receive from the UStates, and without which they cannot subsist." Jefferson, having long been an apologist for the crimes of the French Revolution, was now joining Napoleon in a campaign "to reduce [the Haitian people] to submission by *starving them!*" Sometimes history does seem to move in peculiar circles.

Jefferson's reversal of Federalist policy on Haiti would appear even more significant if Elkins and McKitrick had explained the meaning of the Haitian Revolution for the slave societies of the New World. They do not even mention the momentous French emancipation decree of 1794, which legally freed some 700,000 slaves; or Napoleon's efforts to reinstitute slavery as well as the African slave trade (both Africa and the slave trade, which reached its peak in the 1790s, are missing from the index); or the independent rebellion led by the slave Gabriel in Virginia, an event, inspired by the example of Haiti, which terrified Jefferson along with such leaders as Virginia's Governor James Monroe.[7] In view of Elkins's invaluable contributions to the historiographical debates over slavery and antislavery, I find it astonishing that *The Age of Federalism* is virtually silent on the nature of the Atlantic slave system, its effects on American and British politics, and the rise of an amazingly popular antislavery movement in Britain. They have nothing to say about the narrowing of options for leaders of slaveholding regions as the northern states moved to eradicate the institution and as Britain moved to outlaw the African slave trade and to limit the expansion of the plantation system in such newly acquired colonies as Trinidad.

This is not a matter of calling for more detail of at least arguable relevance in a book already swollen with information. Before the American Revolution, the economy of the British colonies from the Chesapeake to Barbados was very largely dependent on African slave labor. Moreover, the colonies north of Maryland, where per capita wealth was strikingly lower than in the colonies that produced tobacco, rice, and indigo, found their best markets for exports in the sugar colonies of the West Indies. While Elkins and McKitrick repeatedly stress the political importance of this West India trade and its central role in America's naval conflicts with Britain and France, they never explain why the world's two leading powers were waging war in the Caribbean or why Hamilton's vision of northern investment, factories, and Anglo-American trade was, in effect, an alternative to continuing dependence on the slave plantation system.

After mastering the principles of capitalism as a teen-age clerk in the merchant houses of St. Croix, Hamilton had been personally liberated from the Atlantic slave system when Nicholas Cruger and other generous benefactors sent him to New Jersey and New York for a college education. The move can be almost seen as a parable for the economic transformation that would gradually liberate the northern states from dependence on slave systems—a liberation made considerably less complete in the 1790s by the innovations of Eli Whitney and Samuel Slater, two other names that are absent from *The Age of Federalism*'s index.[8] If Hamilton was not quite a militant abolitionist, he did propose, as Elkins and McKitrick note without adequately explaining the background, a plan at the beginning of the Revolution for enlisting South

Carolina slaves into the army with the reward of emancipation. He was also a member of the first antislavery society in New York.

The uninformed reader would never suspect that "the Age of Federalism" was also a period of crucial transition for the Atlantic slave system from Brazil to the new American republic. The interrelationships of the period—among countries, economies, cultures—are what one misses. Britain and the northern states began slowly to disengage themselves from the old colonial order, while in France's largest and richest colony slaves unbelievably took matters into their own hands. It was in this larger setting that Jefferson's Country persuasion finally triumphed and Federalism collapsed, virtually guaranteeing that for three score years the South's increasingly "peculiar" institution would be exempt from government control.[9]

Notes

1. The dissertations seem to have been virtually co-written. In his acknowledgments in *Andrew Johnson and Reconstruction* (University of Chicago Press, 1960), McKitrick notes: "The special role of Stanley Elkins, who gave both time and ideas to the project, partook of the conspiratorial." In *Slavery: A Problem in American Institutional and Intellectual Life* (University of Chicago Press, 1959), Elkins writes: "I am deeply grateful to Eric McKitrick for his unstinted assistance at every stage of the book's evolution."

2. Richard Hofstadter, "U. B. Phillips and the Plantation Legend," *Journal of Negro History*, Vol. 29 (April 1944), pp. 109–124. In a remarkably prescient passage, Hofstadter looked forward to scholars "who will realize that any history of slavery must be written in large part from the standpoint of the slave," a recommendation quoted by Elkins but not taken seriously by historians until the 1970s and 1980s. Hofstadter's own interests took quite different paths.

3. Curiously, Elkins and McKitrick never seem to sense this danger even though they clearly draw on Hofstadter in their account of the Jeffersonian "Country" tradition. Their otherwise brilliant discussion of the capital's location also ignores the significance and political necessity of selecting slaveholding territory for the site of the new capital, where slaves would in fact soon be sold in open markets. Nor do they mention the fact that when the capital was moved from New York to Philadelphia, the Pennsylvania legislature, which had already enacted a law for gradual emancipation, gave special immunity

to congressmen, who were authorized to hold and keep slaves in Philadelphia during their tenure at the nation's capital.

4. I find it astonishing, especially in view of Elkins's and McKitrick's previous work, that they seem to forget that in the classical as well as Judeo-Christian traditions slavery had been the central paradigm for understanding the nature of liberty and power.

5. This stroke of self-deprecating humor should not mislead nonacademics; I'm confident that the remark, while no doubt based on a recognition of Jefferson's scientific curiosity and astonishing range of knowledge, is not intended as a compliment.

6. For an insightful review of an October 1992 scholarly conference and collection of essays reevaluating Jefferson, see Gordon S. Wood's "Jefferson at Home," *The New York Review*, May 13, 1993, pp. 6–9.

7. Though many historians have used the name Gabriel Prosser to refer to the leader of this slave revolt, Douglas R. Egerton has recently pointed out, in the most careful and informative study of the subject, that no contemporary documents identify the slave Gabriel with the surname of his owner, Thomas Henry Prosser. See Egerton, *Gabriel's Rebellion: The Virginia Slave Conspiracies of 1800 and 1802* (University of North Carolina Press, 1993), p. ix.

8. To be fair, I should add that Elkins and McKitrick mention the cotton gin once.

9. I do not mean to imply that Federalism was implicitly antislavery. While William Lloyd Garrison and many other abolitionists had Federalist backgrounds, the Federalist Party included some of South Carolina's most ardent defenders of the institution. Still, the ideological alignments of the 1790s enabled Jefferson and other Republicans to portray the move in 1820 to exclude slavery from the new state of Missouri as a diabolical plot of desperate Federalists; similarly, the tradition of Republican Anglophobia fed the later successful strategy of picturing American abolitionism as an instrument of English imperialism and anti-republican aggression.

14

The Labyrinth of Slavery

African Slavery in Latin America and the Caribbean
Herbert S. Klein (1986)

Mutiny on the Amistad: *The Saga of a Slave Revolt and
Its Impact on American Abolition, Law, and Diplomacy*
Howard Jones (1987)

In the Age of Reason, when philosophy celebrated the natural rights of man, there was nothing peculiar about the South's "peculiar institution," a term later applied to black slavery in the United States. In the eighteenth century, exports of Africans in the Atlantic slave trade exceeded 6 million, nearly three times the number shipped out from 1450 to 1700.[1] Some 2.7 million of these eighteenth-century slaves were transported by Englishmen or Anglo-Americans, members of the supposedly freest and most progressive societies on earth. Although Brazil and the West Indies were the major markets for African slaves, accounting for 85 percent of the century's total imports, approximately 16,000 landed in Buenos Aires. In the late eighteenth century there were 89,000 black slaves in Peru and 12,000 in Chile. In New York City the number of black slaves increased so rapidly that by the 1740s they constituted 21 percent of the city's total population. In King's County the proportion reached 34 percent. Even in Boston in the 1740s about one-fifth of the white families owned slaves.

In French Canada, shortly before the British conquest, there were well over 1,000 black slaves, to say nothing of several thousand Indian slaves. Under British rule, the number of Canadian blacks increased considerably, especially following the influx of American loyalists and their slaves during the War of Independence. Black slaves appeared in British Nova Scotia in the 1750s; in 1760 an auction at the Halifax beach advertised "two hogsheads of rum, three of sugar and two well-grown negro girls, aged fourteen and twelve."[2]

Ironically, the only New World colony that barred the importation of slaves was Georgia, whose founders sought a refuge for England's deserving poor as well as a secure buffer between South Carolina's menacing black majority and the hostile Spaniards in Florida, who were accused of inciting slave rebellions and encouraging runaways by offering freedom to those who escaped into Spanish territory. By 1749, however, Georgia's trustees realized that it was impossible to exclude slaves from the colony and agreed to end their fourteen-year experiment with "free soil."

Why did Spanish, Portuguese, Dutch, French, British, and Danish colonists, in settlements extending from the tropics to the more frigid temperate zones, choose a form of labor that many colonists found dangerous if not morally distasteful, and that had long ceased to be indigenous in Western Europe? The very ubiquity of black slavery in the New World suggests the presence of some irresistible and inevitable force, though a temporary one, if we are to believe the historians who see the decline and fall of New World slavery as no less irresistible and inevitable. But when we examine the way in which black slavery took root in particular societies, as Herbert S. Klein does in his remarkably concise and informative synthesis of recent scholarship on Latin America and the Caribbean, the process seems haphazard and subject to such random variables as the density of the native Indian population and its mortality from European diseases, the availability of white indentured servants, the supply and cost of black slaves on the African coasts, the crops or precious metals obtainable from a particular region, the state of sugar-mill or mining technology, and access to the expanding consumer markets of Europe.

In the early sixteenth century, for example, the Portuguese showed little interest in colonizing Brazil, which long remained a source for dyewood and a way station for the lucrative East India trade, until Britain and France established their own Brazilian bases. This strategic threat to Portugal's Asian trade encouraged the Portuguese to develop Pernambuco and Bahia as major sugar-producing economies, modeled on the slave plantation system they had earlier perfected in Madeira and São Tomé. But even though Portugal initially dominated the Atlantic slave trade and transported Africans to Brazil and Spanish America as well as to the Atlantic islands, until 1570 most of the Brazilian sugar was grown by Indian slaves. According to Klein, it was not until the first years of the seventeenth century, after tens of thousands of Brazilian Indians had been killed by a smallpox epidemic and after three decades of large slave importations from Africa, that the number of black slaves equaled and then surpassed the number of Indian slaves.

No less fortuitous, it would appear, was the Brazilian sugar industry's original dependence on Dutch shipping and commercial networks radiating from the great sugar-refining center, Antwerp. After the Spanish and Portuguese crowns united in 1580 and after Holland began winning its long struggle for independence from Spanish rule, the Dutch conquered the Portuguese not only in the Spice Islands of Asia but in the slave-trading stations of Africa and the rich sugar-producing regions of northeastern Brazil. It was Dutch naval and commercial power that opened the Caribbean to British and French colonization and to successful plantation agriculture. In 1619 a Dutch ship unloaded what were long thought to be the first blacks in Virginia. The Dutch later supplied capital, slaves, and sugar technology to the British and French colonies from Barbados to Martinique and St. Kitts. When in 1654 the Portuguese expelled the Dutch from Brazil, the refugees helped to ensure that the Caribbean would become the world's major source of sugar.

Klein does not really explain the failure of the much earlier Spanish efforts to cultivate sugar cane in Saint Domingue, Cuba, Jamaica, and other Caribbean colonies. The Spaniards owned black slaves and they knew how to build sugar mills and how to grind, boil, and manufacture sugar and molasses. Yet Spanish colonists did not become major producers of sugar (in Cuba and to a lesser degree in Puerto Rico) until the late eighteenth and nineteenth centuries. To complicate matters, the British never anticipated that Virginia, Maryland, and even Barbados would become dependent on black slave labor. For plantation agriculture they relied with considerable success on white indentured servants—in the Chesapeake colonies for a period of some seventy years.

Klein offers no theory or thesis to account for the intermittent spread of black slavery through the New World. He takes no note of the fears and prejudices that were often aroused by the unrestricted importation of blacks and that led in the Caribbean to ineffective laws designed to ensure a minimal ratio between blacks and whites. But his book is especially useful in providing a wealth of detail on the African slave trade, the extraordinary adaptability of black slave labor, and the tensions within Afro-American cultures.

Here, for example, are some of the conclusions that may surprise readers unfamiliar with the specialized studies on which Klein has drawn. Asian textiles, followed by bar iron manufactured in Europe, were the leading commodities that Europeans exchanged for African slaves. African traders controlled the supply of slaves and conditions of sale, and were responsible for the preponderance of male slaves sold to Europeans, since for a variety of reasons Africans were reluctant to sell women and "women had a higher price in local internal African markets than men."

European merchants knew that in the Americas black women performed the heaviest plantation labor and often outnumbered men in the field gangs cultivating sugar, coffee, and cotton. But male slaves monopolized the skilled crafts and trades (except for the work of seamstresses), and in Brazil worked on cattle ranches, whalers, and even as deckhands on slave ships. In Brazil's first national census, in 1872, slaves made up 19 percent of the nation's construction workers and 11 percent of the total industrial work force. As Klein and other scholars have demonstrated, black slave labor could be applied successfully to a variety of urban and industrial tasks. Black slavery flourished economically even when mixed with other forms of labor and even after the majority of a nation's blacks had won their freedom, as in nineteenth-century Brazil.

Although Klein discusses many aspects of slavery from religion and resistance to manumission, he conveys little sense of New World bondage as part of a larger world economy. He makes no effort to clarify or even comment on the historical relationship between slavery and capitalism. As Sidney W. Mintz has reminded us, the New World's slave plantations transformed exotic luxuries, such as tobacco and sugar, into "proletarian necessities." By 1750 it was said that the poorest English farm laborer's wife took sugar in her tea. According to Mintz, the consumption of slave-grown sucrose, coffee, cocoa, and other products "was the direct consequence of deep alterations in the lives of working people, which made new forms of foods and eating conceivable and 'natural,' like new schedules of work, new sorts of labor, and new conditions of daily life."[3]

Klein is by no means the only historian who limits our understanding of the New World slave systems by considering them apart from the emerging free labor societies that consumed their produce and supplied the ships, slaves, investment capital, and manufactured goods that were parts of a larger Atlantic commercial system. For several decades historians have been so intent on exposing the serious errors and weaknesses of Eric Williams's *Capitalism and Slavery*, published in 1944, that they have usually lost sight of Williams's vision of an interdependent Atlantic economy that was fueled by the labor of African slaves. Since Klein has written a useful survey that will probably be assigned in many college courses, it is unfortunate that his readers will never suspect that Caribbean sugar plantations linked Pennsylvania farmers and New England fishermen with the iron manufacturers of Birmingham and the textile workers of Nantes.

It is clear that Klein hopes his book will evoke comparisons with slavery in the United States, though by treating Latin America and the Caribbean as a single unit he obscures the distinctive and important economic and ideological ties between the Caribbean and North America. Any reader interested in drawing comparisons must also be wary of erroneous or misleading statements. For example, Klein asserts that "in 1787 the United States Congress abolished the slave trade as of 1808." But in fact the United States Constitution prohibited Congress from ending the slave trade until 1808 and even excluded this provision from constitutional amendment. The French National Assembly did not grant citizenship in 1789 to colonial free blacks and mulattoes; the measure was passed in 1792, after much vacillation, debate, and violence. In 1794 the Assembly did not apprentice the colonial slaves it emancipated, as Klein maintains.

Denmark Vesey's failed conspiracy to mount a slave insurrection did not coincide in 1831 with Nat Turner's slave revolt, but occurred nine years earlier. It is not true that positive natural growth rates among the native-born or Creole slaves were achieved "only in those regions where the slave trade died out before the end of slavery." In Virginia, as Klein surely knows, the slave population reached a high rate of natural growth by the 1720s, at a time of reasonably heavy imports from Africa and fifty years before importations ceased.[4] While it is true that slave manumission received far more encouragement in Latin America than in North America, Klein presents a misleading picture when he talks of the effective curtailment of the numbers of North American freedmen by the end of the eighteenth century. In actuality, the free black population in the United States increased by 82 percent between 1790 and 1800 and by 72 percent between 1800 and 1810. Until the 1830s, when restrictions against manumission began taking effect, free blacks were the fastest-growing segment of the Southern population.

We still have much to learn about the connections and interactions between various New World slave regimes. As Klein makes clear, the Atlantic maritime states long participated in the common venture of transporting millions of Africans to American colonies. For an Angolan or Mende captive there was little difference between a Dutch or Portuguese ship or between the work to be done on a Jamaican or Brazilian sugar estate. While each colony followed its own path of cultural and political development, slaves throughout the Americas heard reports of the great Haitian Revolution; their masters were attuned not only to prices on the world's sugar, coffee, and cotton markets but to news of slave insurrections and abolitionist agitation.

This interrelationship of slave regimes is brought into sharp focus by Howard Jones's well-documented study of the *Amistad* affair, arising from a slave revolt aboard a Spanish slave ship in 1839. To understand the import of Jones's lively but somewhat confined narrative, it is essential to glimpse the wider setting. In the 1830s, as Britain pursued the risky experiment of emancipating 800,000 colonial blacks, slavery was expanding and flourishing in Cuba and the southern United States. Cuba's prospects as the world's leading producer of sugar were enhanced by the triumph of British abolitionism and the subsequent economic decline of Jamaica and other competitive British colonies. But unlike the United States, which could afford to express official outrage over the nefarious and illicit Atlantic slave trade, Cuba still relied on large imports of Africans, many of whom were purchased with British goods and British credit and transported on ships built and outfitted in the United States. During the 1830s Cuba illegally imported approximately 181,600 slaves from Africa.[5]

For some twenty years the British navy had been engaged in a vigorous and expensive campaign to suppress the entire slave trade by enforcing treaties that Spain and other countries had been bribed or coerced into accepting. Having already lost most of its New World empire, Spain sought to placate the British without angering the Cuban and Puerto Rican colonists who devised various subterfuges to ensure a continuing supply of African labor. From 1834 to 1845, however, Spain was shaken by civil war and continuing uprisings that raised the threat of British and French intervention. American interest in Cuba was heightened by the fear that Britain might seize the colony on the pretext of slave-trade treaty violations or undermine the slave regime, as part of a quest for global domination, by less direct means. Washington viewed this prospect much as recent administrations have viewed Soviet aid to "liberations" in Cuba and Central America.

In late August 1839 a United States revenue cutter seized a mysterious schooner, the *Amistad*, off the coast of Long Island. Equipped to transport slaves along the Cuban coast, the *Amistad* contained four African children and thirty-nine adult males including Joseph Cinqué, the de facto commander, who had ordered Pedro Montes, one of the two surviving whites on the vessel, to sail from Cuban waters to Africa. On the night of July 1 Cinqué had led his compatriots in a sudden revolt that resulted in the slaying of the captain and cook and in the unexplained disappearance of two sailors. Montes, a former skipper, had been able to deceive Cinqué by steering northward at night, hoping to encounter another ship or friendly port.

Four months earlier the Africans, mostly Mendes from the Sierra Leone region, had been forcibly enslaved and shipped to Cuba, smuggled ashore at night, and then brought to the notorious barracoons in Havana. There they had been purchased by Montes and José Ruiz, who routinely secured fraudulent papers affirming that the blacks were *Ladinos*, or assimilated and legitimate slaves who had not been imported from Africa after 1820, when the prohibition went into effect. After assigning the Africans fake Spanish names, Ruiz and Montes had chartered the *Amistad* and set out for a Cuban plantation district some three hundred miles from Havana. But the Africans, suffering from short rations and physical brutality, had struck for freedom.

President Van Buren was determined to maintain control of the affair as soon as news arrived that the *Amistad* had been captured and towed to New London, Connecticut. Already weakened politically by a disastrous economic depression, Van Buren faced an uphill struggle for reelection in 1840. Any prolonged controversy involving slavery could bring acute embarrassment to the reigning Democratic party, whose power depended on appeasing the increasingly volatile South. For nearly twenty years Van Buren had been almost obsessed with the need to suppress sectional discord; in New York State his supporters had taken the lead in anti-abolitionist riots and demonstrations intended to reassure the South that the Northern public would not tolerate antislavery "fanatics." Van Buren and his proslavery secretary of state, John Forsyth, were prepared to bypass the judicial system if necessary to prevent abolitionists from exploiting the *Amistad* affair.

The White House and Spanish ministry had legal grounds for confidence even though the federal district judge in Connecticut, Andrew T. Judson, refused to surrender the Africans to the Spanish consul in Boston. Treaties concluded with Spain in 1795 and 1819 contained detailed provisions for the return of ships and other property rescued from pirates or robbers. American courts had no jurisdiction over Spanish subjects or crimes (aside from piracy) committed on Spanish ships. Unlike Britain, the United States had never signed a treaty with Spain for suppressing the slave trade; in 1825 the United States Supreme Court had even ruled that the slave trade, though outlawed by most nations, was sanctioned by the law of nations. Since slavery was legal in both Cuba and the United States, it appeared to the Van Buren administration that American courts had no right to question the *Amistad*'s papers, which affirmed that the blacks were bona fide slaves, or to interfere with the president's prerogative to comply with Spain's demands.

As the White House soon discovered, however, a number of circumstances made the *Amistad* case a crucial test of the American judicial system. The blacks had clearly been free and in command of the ship when they anchored off Long Island and sent a party ashore in search of food and water. By what authority, then, were they seized and held in custody in a New Haven jail? American law prohibited the enslavement of imported Africans and provided for the return to Africa of blacks illegally brought in for the purpose of sale. It should have been evident that these regulations did not apply to the *Amistad* captives; but it was also clear that they would not have been held in jail if they had been whites who had forcibly freed themselves from kidnappers or pirates.

Spanish law, like American and British law, defined the African slave trade as piracy, a crime punishable by death. Witnesses testified that when José Ruiz was first rescued from the blacks, he had admitted that they were not *Ladinos* but Africans who had been recently enslaved and illegally transported to Cuba. The captives could speak only African languages, not Spanish. Later, abolitionists found Africans who could translate the captives' testimony (in time, some of the captives learned English). Expert witnesses described how Cuban officials openly defied the antislave trade laws and how they evaded British cruisers and the mixed commission court at Havana. Even at the initial trial before the United States Circuit Court in Hartford, the district attorney admitted, to everyone's surprise, that the *Amistad* captives were not legal slaves. But this maneuver, according to Jones, was intended to keep the blacks within the control of the White House.

By 1839 American abolitionists had largely failed in their efforts at "moral suasion," and they were desperately searching for ways to challenge any national authorization of slavery, such as the government's allowance of the interstate slave trade, slave markets in the nation's capital, and the settling of slaves in the common territories. Once the circuit court determined that the *Amistad* captives fell under the jurisdiction of the federal judiciary, abolitionists saw the coming trial before the United States district court as a providential opportunity to dramatize the illegal violence in which all slaveholding had originated. The central issue, as Jones repeatedly emphasizes, was the glaring discrepancy between American positive law and natural rights.

In Ronald Dworkin's terms, justice could not be approximated without violating the "integrity" or internal consistency of American laws and customs, which depended on communal understanding between free and slave states. Yet as Jones fails to realize, that integrity of legal practice had already been seriously compromised when Congress outlawed the slave trade and declared it piracy. If it was a capital crime to transport an African captive to the New World, why was it legitimate to buy or sell a captive or her descendants who by chance had arrived in Cuba before 1820 or in the United States before 1808? The Spanish were at least consistent in thumbing their noses at an externally imposed law. In the United States, as the *Amistad* case demonstrated, slavery had indeed become a peculiar institution.

While the trials evoked grotesque outbursts of racism, they also confirmed, after a half century, the strength of revolutionary ideals. As the aging John Quincy Adams explained to William Jay, the abolitionist son of the first chief justice, the blacks had "vindicated their own right of liberty" by "executing the justice of Heaven" upon a "pirate murderer, their tyrant and oppressor." Adams's view that the Africans had freed themselves by "self-emancipation" won surprising support from the Northern press.

Even Andrew T. Judson, the racist and violently anti-abolitionist district court judge, affirmed that the blacks had revolted against illegal bondage only out of "desire of winning their liberty and returning to their families and kindred." And after Van Buren had succeeded in appealing Judson's decision to Roger Taney's Southern-dominated Supreme Court, where the captives' case was strongly argued by John Quincy Adams and Roger Baldwin, Justice Joseph Story ruled for the Court that the captives had exercised their right of self-defense since they had been kidnapped in Africa and unlawfully transported to Cuba. They were not legally slaves and therefore could be allowed to go free.

Both Judson and Story, however, scrupulously upheld the positive law that sanctioned black slavery and restricted the application of natural law to situations in which no positive law applied. Indeed, Jones goes so far as to rebuke the abolitionists for ignoring "the central meaning" of the Supreme Court's final decision: "that positive law had triumphed over natural law." But his is an excessively narrow interpretation. If the abolitionists failed to win judicial approval for their higher-law doctrines, the arguments of Baldwin and Adams before the Court exposed the irreconcilable contradictions between American slavery and American conceptions of law and justice. It was Adams, the seventy-four-year-old congressman and former president, who exemplified the noblest meaning of the revolutionary heritage.

Jones is understandably disturbed by the efforts of the Van Buren administration to subvert the judicial system and deprive the blacks of their right of due process. At the time of the district court trial, the president diverted a naval vessel to New Haven Harbor and issued secret orders to the district attorney to have the captives smuggled to the ship in the event of an unfavorable decision. Because of lack of space below, the blacks would then be chained to the deck in the icy winter and shipped back to Cuba. Later, the administration obstructed every effort of the defense to obtain copies of official documents and was probably responsible for what Adams called a "scandalous mistranslation" of Spanish words that, if undetected, would have destroyed the entire case of the defense.

Van Buren's precise motives remain hidden, but Jones is too charitable when he excuses the president of "illegal intentions" and emphasizes his political anxieties over the coming election. Executive interference in the case persisted long after Van Buren had lost the election. Jones seems harsher in censuring the abolitionists' own illegal intentions to rescue the captives if the Court or the president tried to surrender them to the Spanish. While he ends with a tribute to "America's legal system [which] had performed its function of securing justice," he makes no judgment on a system that denied the captives bail. For some eighteen months, while their case was argued, the thirty-six men were imprisoned in a thirty-by-twenty-foot room, subject like animals in a zoo to the gaze of thousands of visitors who paid twelve-and-a-half cents for the sight of African "savages."

Without the aid of Lewis Tappan, Joshua Leavitt, and other abolitionists, whose "extreme positions" did not preclude skillful organization, fund raising, and tactful cooperation with nonabolitionist attorneys like Baldwin and Adams, Joseph Cinqué and his compatriots would surely have been shipped back to Cuba and executed. That outcome might well have provoked a British blockade of Cuba and American military intervention, which the Van Buren administration had in fact threatened. As things turned out, private donations and funds raised from public exhibitions paid the cost of returning the thirty-five surviving Africans to Sierra Leone.

Jones should have provided much more information about the captives themselves and the efforts to aid them by white abolitionists and American free blacks. He mentions in an endnote that some of the *Amistad* captives, including three girls, stayed in Sierra Leone and worked with Christian missionaries. Most of the blacks returned to their Mende homeland, and Cinqué eventually worked as an interpreter for the American Missionary Association.

Notes

1. Paul E. Lovejoy, "The Volume of the Atlantic Slave Trade: A Synthesis," *Journal of African History*, Vol. 23, No. 4 (1982), pp. 473–502. These numbers require some adjustment in view of the recalculations made in the 1990s.
2. Robin W. Winks, *The Blacks in Canada: A History* (Yale University Press, 1971), p. 28.
3. Sidney W. Mintz, *Sweetness and Power: The Place of Sugar in Modern History* (Viking, 1985), pp. 180–181.
4. Allan Kulikoff, *Tobacco and Slaves: The Development of Southern Cultures in the Chesapeake, 1680–1800* (University of North Carolina Press, 1986), pp. 320–324, 358.
5. The most careful and informed estimate can be found in David Eltis, "The Nineteenth-Century Transatlantic Slave Trade: An Annual Time Series of Imports into the Americas Broken Down by Region," *Hispanic American Historical Review*, Vol. 67, No. 1 (1987), pp. 120–130.

15

The Significance of the
Northwest Ordinance of 1787

Fifty-two years before Congress enacted the Northwest Ordinance, the British government excluded slaves from the colony of Georgia.[1] Although this precedent has been conspicuously ignored in debates over the meaning of Article VI of the Northwest Ordinance, the parallels are intriguing. In both cases the prohibition of slavery was adopted as part of a separate legislative act and not incorporated in a founding charter or national Constitution. While the intentions of the Confederation Congress are more obscure than those of James Oglethorpe and the trustees of Georgia, it is clear that neither measure was expected to endanger slavery in adjacent territories or challenge the legitimacy of slaveholding in general. The 1735 prohibition allowed Carolinians to reclaim blacks who escaped into Georgia, just as Article VI provided for the return of fugitives "to the person claiming his or her labor or service."

The advocates of a free-soil Georgia were anything but abolitionists. Oglethorpe was deputy governor of the slave-trading Royal African Company and also owned slaves on a Carolina plantation. The prohibition act provided for the sale of any unclaimed blacks found in the colony. The trustees were to receive the proceeds. In 1787, as far as is known, no southern members of the Congress of the Confederation voiced the slightest disapproval of Article VI, which a committee of five, including a South Carolinian and two Virginians, suddenly added at the last minute to the finished text of the Northwest Ordinance.

Staughton Lynd and Paul Finkelman, in their masterly studies of Article

VI, have underscored the contrast between the harmonious congressional deliberations and the nearly contemporaneous debates in the Constitutional Convention.[2] From July 9 to July 12, 1787, sectional anger erupted at Philadelphia as the convention argued about the three-fifths rule for apportioning representatives in the House of Representatives. A few northerners objected that allowing representation for slaves would encourage further slave importation from Africa. Delegates from South Carolina and Georgia demanded constitutional protection for slavery as the price for union. Subsequent conflicts in the convention and in the First Congress under the new Constitution showed how explosive the South would become in the face of any perceived threat to its most valuable form of property. Yet on July 13, the day after the Constitutional Convention provisionally accepted the three-fifths compromise, the Continental Congress, chaired by a southerner, adopted the Northwest Ordinance with its newly added Article VI, which had not appeared in the draft of July 11. A northerner cast the single dissenting vote. When the First Congress reenacted the Ordinance in 1789, the southerners who would soon become so outraged by cautiously worded antislavery petitions seem not to have sensed an abolitionist Trojan Horse or entering wedge.

Parallels between the slavery exclusions of 1735 and 1787 extend beyond slaveholder concurrence. Both the British and American governments hoped to attract enterprising white migrants who would rapidly settle a territory that reached toward a Spanish frontier. Some of the planners, at least, sought white settlers from a social class that could not afford to buy slaves—settlers who, as experience had shown, had been deterred from emigrating to the more prosperous plantation regions. Oglethorpe and his philanthropic supporters were thinking of British debtors and German peasants who could contribute to imperial self-sufficiency by producing such commodities as silk and wine. The later American developers were thinking of a less debased class of yeoman farmers who would clear the land of Indians and trees, cultivate grains, build roads, towns, churches, and schools, and eventually be capable of self-government. Despite this difference, both blueprints envisioned a fusion of individual opportunity and national interest that depended on maintaining the dignity of physical labor. One of the motives for excluding slavery, at least in the initial period of settlement, was the fear that whites would be demoralized and corrupted by the presence of black slave competitors.

Far more important, in the case of Georgia, was the need for a secure buffer zone between South Carolina and Spanish Florida. The British were alarmed by the Spaniards' success in encouraging black resistance in Carolina and offering a refuge for fugitive slaves. This anxiety deepened when Oglethorpe failed to capture St. Augustine and when the slave unrest exploded in the Stono Rebellion. The Spanish borderlands had a different but no less significant bearing on the Northwest Ordinance. Robert V. Remini, in his inaugural address to a conference on the Northwest Ordinance in 1987, its bicentennial year, graphically described the dangers of the mid-1780s, when southwestern settlers were prepared to transfer their allegiance to Spain if Congress refused to recognize their vital need for water transport to the Gulf of Mexico. Most southern leaders put the highest priority on securing from Spain the right to free navigation of the Mississippi River. Whatever tradeoffs led to the acceptance of Article VI, it seems likely that southerners expected the bargain to quiet most northern opposition to rapid westward expansion, including the demand for access to the Mississippi and for the undelayed admission of slaveholding states south of the Ohio River.

But as the trustees of Georgia soon discovered, an act prohibiting slavery is not self-enforcing. In 1735 slavery was universally sanctioned by the law of nations, and black slaves were openly sold and traded in England as well as in every New World colony. Petitions from white settlers in Georgia, including illiterates who could not sign their names, predicted that the colony would sink into ruin unless quickly supplied with black slaves. A few anti-slavery petitioners spoke of the Africans' natural right to freedom. They also argued that slaves would deprive white laborers and craftsmen of work and endanger the colony with bloody insurrections. But meanwhile, no institutions were effective in preventing Carolina planters from crossing the Savannah River with their slaves or even slave ships from landing their cargoes in Savannah. In 1749 the trustees finally capitulated and asked Parliament to repeal the prohibition.

Paul Finkelman has recently analyzed the ambiguities of the Northwest Ordinance with respect to slavery and has emphasized the failure of Congress to enact any enforcement legislation. As early as July 1788, the Franco-American slaveholders residing in the territory petitioned Congress to secure their slave property from the effects of what they considered an "Ex post facto law" that seemed to violate the terms of the Treaty of Paris of 1763 and the Virginia land cession of 1784. Like some of the earlier Georgian petitioners, the French settlers contended that the obnoxious law would depopulate parts of the territory. And, in actuality, some of the more affluent French slaveholders sought security in the Spanish territory across the Mississippi. Although Congress never took action to clarify the status of slaves living in the Old Northwest before 1787, Finkelman points out that the report of a three-member congressional committee that included James Madison "suggests how truly *uncommitted* the Founders were to ending slavery."[3] Governor Arthur St. Clair and other officials conveyed the same reassuring message to the inhabitants of the territory; namely, that Article VI pertained to the future introduction of slaves and was not intended to deprive present inhabitants of property they possessed at the time the Ordinance was passed. As Finkelman and other historians have shown, settlers continued to petition Congress to repeal or modify Article VI, while the territorial governments of Indiana and Illinois tried to attract slaveholders by giving sanction to various forms of involuntary servitude. Until the well-known electoral struggle of 1823–1824, there was a genuine possibility that Illinois would become a slave state. As in colonial Georgia, the issue turned on local conditions and demography. Fortunately, the Northwest was not adjacent to South Carolina and the Atlantic. From Finkelman's forceful arguments it might well be concluded that the Northwest Ordinance was no more significant as an anti-slavery measure than the British law of 1735 "for rendering the Colony of Georgia more Defencible."

But such a verdict would ignore the extraordinary power of antislavery ideology, which must be distinguished from Garrisonian immediatism. The principle that slavery should be excluded from the virgin West became the core of an antislavery and Republican party ideology that obscured the economic benefits of coerced labor and transformed the moral meaning of national interest. To develop this point I must first review recent reevaluations of slavery as part of a global capitalist economy. I will then turn to the misapprehensions that arise when immediatist standards and expectations are imposed on such measures as the Northwest Ordinance.

Historians have only begun to free themselves from the antislavery assumptions that permeated political economy from the time of Benjamin Franklin and Adam Smith. They still find it difficult to believe that an immoral and flagrantly unjust system of labor could be congruent with long-term economic and material progress. They intuitively reject the claims of Robert W. Fogel and other economists that slave labor was efficient, productive, adaptable, and immensely profitable. Whatever the short-term rewards, in the moral economy of history, the sin of slaveholding surely led to soil exhaustion, indebtedness, degenerate livestock, obsolete technology, dilapidated farms, and a society bereft of schools, towns, and enterprise. But this conventional imagery merges many independent variables and confuses the symptoms of an imbalanced economy with economic decline. It also obscures the crucial contributions of black slaves to the growth of a larger, interdependent Atlantic economy. The recent research of David Eltis, Seymour Drescher, Stanley Engerman, Rebecca J. Scott, and other scholars has moved beyond the now conventional view that black slave labor provided the foundation for the wealthiest and most dynamic New World economies before 1800; there is now impressive evidence that the economic importance of slavery *increased* in the nineteenth century along with the soaring global demand for such consumer goods as sugar, coffee, and cotton textiles. This demand could only be met by plantation production and coerced labor, including the hundreds of thousands of indentured Asian workers who eventually replaced many of the emancipated West Indian blacks.[4]

Contrary to traditional dogma, under most circumstances free labor was not cheaper or more productive than slave labor. In most of the New World, in any event, a sufficient supply of free labor was never available. And as the British learned to their dismay after emancipating nearly 800,000 colonial slaves, free laborers were unwilling to accept the plantation discipline and working conditions that made sugar production a highly profitable investment. The British West Indian colonies did not decline in their value to the British economy until the 1820s, when the effects of slave-trade abolition finally began to counteract rising worker productivity. Britain's suicidal, or as Drescher would have it, "econocidal" destruction of the world's leading producers of sugar and coffee provided an extra stimulus to the plantations of Cuba and Brazil and to the illegal slave trade that supplied them with labor.[5] And in Brazil the increasing concentration of slaves on coffee fazendas did not prevent the profitable use of slave labor in such varied enterprises as cattle ranching, food processing, construction, grain and root crop farming, textile manufacturing, jerked beef production, whaling, and even serving as deck hands on South Atlantic slave ships. In mid-nineteenth-century Brazil black slavery proved to be compatible with urban life and virtually every urban trade and skill. In mid-nineteenth-century Cuba black slaves were profitably employed in the most capital-intensive and highly mechanized sugar production. In both Cuba and Brazil, as Herbert Klein notes, slaves were "most heavily concentrated in the most dynamic regions of their respective societies on the eve of emancipation."[6]

David Eltis, in his monumental *Economic Growth and the Ending of the Transatlantic Slave Trade*, finds a symbiotic relationship between New World slavery and industrial capitalism. Slave labor produced most of the first luxury goods that reached a mass consumer market, particularly in England, and that therefore contributed to the labor incentives needed for English industrial work discipline. The dramatic drop in price for British manufactured goods reduced the cost of buying slaves on the African coast. While the price of slaves remained low and relatively stable in Africa during much of the nineteenth century, the price of slaves continued to rise in the New World, with minor fluctuations, as landowners sought to meet the mounting world demand for sugar, coffee, cocoa, tobacco, rice, and cotton. As Eltis convincingly argues, "for the Americas as well as for Britain at the outset of industrialization, there was a profound incompatibility between economic self-interest and antislavery policy."[7]

Despite Britain's vigorous and expensive efforts to suppress the Atlantic slave trade, approximately two-and-one-quarter million African slaves were imported into the Americas between 1811 and 1860. As Eltis has shown, it was not until the 1840s, a decade of massive European migration to the Americas, that the flow of free immigrants exceeded the flow of African slaves, even though the importation of slaves was by then almost entirely confined to Cuba and Brazil.[8] The symbiosis between slavery and industrial capitalism is perhaps most vividly indicated by the fact that the illicit Atlantic slave trade depended on British capital, credit, insurance, and the manufactured goods, including firearms, that were exchanged in Africa for slaves.[9]

One concludes from Eltis's iconoclastic study that British capitalism, as a source of human exploitation and suffering in the early industrial era, could have been even worse than it proved to be. Economic growth would probably have increased at a faster rate if Britain had not outlawed the slave trade and curbed the development of the rich plantation lands in Trinidad and Guyana. Consumers and cotton manufacturers would probably have benefited if British cruisers had protected slave ships bound for Texas instead of intercepting slavers in Brazilian waters. There is a subtle irony in the way that Eltis's neoclassical economic analysis exposes the pathological consequences of a world view that subordinates all human relationships to free-market choices and the supreme goal of achieving the largest national product.

But when the vitality and flexibility of nineteenth-century slavery are considered, the exclusion of the institution from any territory seems all the more remarkable. Before 1787 the single attempt to exclude slavery from a New World colony proved to be a hopeless failure. In 1790, when Britain sought to encourage white immigration to Canada as well as to the Bahamas and

Bermuda, the Imperial Act allowed the introduction of black slaves as a matter of course.[10] Britain failed to respect the French Convention's emancipation decree of 1794, which applied to territories that fell under British control. In 1802 Napoleon restored slavery in Guadeloupe and in the following year legalized both slavery and the slave trade. It is true that when the North American colonies had earlier begun to resist British taxation and to assert their own right to self-determination, they suspended or permanently prohibited the further importation of slaves; but unlike the other plantation societies of the New World, the southern colonies could rely on the rapid natural increase of their slave populations. Although the American Revolution encouraged genuine moral misgivings over the justice of human slavery, the state laws suspending or prohibiting the slave trade arose from a variety of motives. These included the desire of some southerners to maintain high slave prices and to dominate labor markets in the West; the fear of many northerners that slave competition would undermine the livelihood of white workers; and the more widely shared conviction that the Republic's security and welfare required greater racial homogeneity.

When historians ponder the mystery of Article VI, they customarily quote Whatever the legacy of the Revolution, in 1787 slavery was supported by the laws of every state except Vermont, New Hampshire, and Massachusetts. Why would representatives from slaveholding states agree without argument to ban the institution from the vast territory north of the Ohio River? It was improbable that the Northwest could ever benefit from the economies of scale associated with gang labor on sugar and cotton plantations, but in 1787 no one could foresee the cotton gin or the rich Black Belt extending across Alabama and Mississippi. As the later history of the Northwest suggests, slaves would have lowered labor costs in various occupations ranging from tobacco and hemp production to mining and construction work. It is well to remember that the Virginia border then extended north to central Ohio, that the lower third of Illinois still extends below northern Kentucky, and that Cairo, Illinois, lies farther south than Richmond, Virginia.

When historians ponder the mystery of Article VI, they customarily quote a revealing passage from William Grayson's letter of August 8, 1787, to James Monroe. Grayson, the Virginian who had presided over Congress when the Ordinance was approved, explained, "The clause respecting slavery was agreed to by the Southern members for the purpose of preventing Tobacco and Indigo from being made on the N.W. side of the Ohio as well as for sev'l other political reasons." While we have no reason to doubt the accuracy of this report, aside from a mistake in copying "indigo" instead of "hemp," it is not immediately clear why southerners feared competition more from the Northwest than from the Southwest.[11] In 1787 tobacco exports were rising. If western expansion threatened to lower the price of certain slave-grown staples, it would also raise the price of slaves and offer new opportunities to slaveholders who were willing to migrate. It is true that Grayson and other Virginians had a personal interest in developing the lands of Kentucky and Tennessee and that by 1787 many observers assumed the Northwest would be settled by New Englanders. But the exclusion of slavery would still appear to be a costly surrender of principle, especially for the Deep South.

Representatives from the Deep South, who fought so bitterly to protect their constitutional right to import slaves from Africa, might well have seen Article VI as a restriction that would limit the future demand for slave labor and thus reinforce arguments for a constitutional or congressional prohibition of the slave trade. On July 13 the Constitutional Convention had not yet faced the extremely divisive question of the Atlantic slave trade, and of course no one could predict the outcome of the Constitutional Convention or assume that a new constitution would be adopted.[12] However one interprets the evidence, excluding slavery from such an immense territory appears to be a dangerous precedent and a drastic means either for limiting competition or for the contradictory goal of ensuring that slavery could expand into the southwest. In any event, the latter objective would be virtually guaranteed by the terms of the land cessions of the southern seaboard states.

It is possible, of course, that the southern congressmen never expected the prohibition to be effective or permanent. Or Staughton Lynd may well be right when he offers the hypothesis of a secret compromise in which southerners accepted Article VI as a low price for the three-fifths clause and the fugitive slave clause in the federal Constitution.[13] But regardless of the varying views on this question, the intentions of the framers are of minor significance when compared with the ideological consequences of creating free soil.

An instructive analogy can be drawn between Article VI and Lord Mansfield's famed Somerset decision of 1772. Like the Continental congressmen, Lord Mansfield had no intention of endangering the institution of slavery. The question he faced was whether the law of England allowed Charles Stuart, a resident Virginian, to seize his runaway slave, James Somerset, and lock him in chains aboard a ship scheduled to sail to Jamaica. After granting a writ of *habeas corpus*, ordering the ship's captain to bring Somerset to court, Mansfield first sought an out-of-court settlement. Fearing the effects of a judicial opinion on the status of ten thousand or more black slaves held in

England, he advised resident planters to appeal to Parliament for appropriate legislation. In an earlier trial Mansfield had announced, "I would have all masters think them free, and all Negroes think they were not, because then they would both behave better." After hearing the opposing arguments of counsel, which would either have legitimated or abolished slavery on English soil, the chief justice searched for the narrowest possible ground on which to base his decision. He affirmed that slavery must be based on positive law and could not be "introduced by courts of justice upon mere reasoning or inferences from any principles, natural or political." In discharging Somerset, Mansfield went no farther than to say English law did not permit a master to seize his servant and forcibly transport him out of the country.[14]

The Somerset decision did not immediately emancipate the slaves living in England or prevent colonists from bringing slaves into the country. Mansfield continued to rule that slaves were not entitled to sue for back wages. Yet the popular press gave wide publicity to the arguments of Somerset's counsel and increasingly interpreted Mansfield's decision to mean that the air of England was too pure for slavery, or in William Blackstone's earlier formulation, that the moment a slave lands in England, "[he] falls under the protection of the laws, and with regard to all natural rights becomes *eo instanti* a freeman." Slavery lingered in England for some two decades and was not officially abolished until 1834, but masters had no legal remedies when slaves in increasing numbers simply walked away into freedom. Advertisements for runaways virtually disappeared by the late 1780s, when abolitionism acquired a mass appeal.[15]

Like the Northwest Ordinance, the Somerset decision deterred slaveholders from migrating across a boundary loaded with risk. The analogy should not be pressed, since a densely populated industrializing nation over three thousand miles from the nearest plantation economy can hardly be compared with an American frontier. Yet both the edicts became mythologized as antislavery landmarks. Salmon Chase might well have been referring to Somerset when he proclaimed that by a "single act" the Founding Fathers had made slavery illegal and had "impressed upon the soil itself an incapacity to bear up other than freemen." And even the Somerset case was not devoid of racist implications. When Somerset's chief counsel, Sergeant Davy, exclaimed that the air of England was too pure for a slave to breathe in, he was not inviting more slaves to come and breathe the freedom-giving air. He made it clear that the air of England was too pure for a black to breathe in. He wished to prevent an influx of blacks, "for now and then we have some Accidents of Children born of an Odd Colour." Unless a law were passed to prevent such immigration, Sergeant Davy said, "I don't know what our Progeny may be, I mean of what Colour."[16] Racial prejudice was of course far more virulent and widespread in the United States, especially in the Northwest. The determination to avoid the degradation and dishonor of slave labor also involved the exclusion of the race that slavery had degraded.

Although antislavery ideology was closely related to the need to valorize and legitimate free labor, it cannot be reduced to economic self-interest. The popular hostility to slavery that emerged almost simultaneously in England and in parts of the United States drew on traditions of natural law and a revivified sense of the image of God in man.[17] From the time of Granville Sharp and Anthony Benezet, Anglo-American abolitionists were moved by a profound conviction that man-stealing and slaveholding were morally wrong. No material rewards could justify the kidnapping and sale of innocent Africans or the reduction of human beings to the status of domesticated animals. When Sharp wrote in 1788 to the Pennsylvania Abolition Society on behalf of the London abolitionists, he stressed that "in addressing the Representatives of a commercial nation on an affair in which its interests and its justice are inseparable, we cannot for a moment abandon the fundamental principle of our association, that no gains, however great, are to be put in competition with the essential rights of man, and that as a nation is exalted by righteousness, so it is equally debased and debilitated by the revenues of injustice."[18]

This very letter also illustrates another aspect of pre-immediatist antislavery thought. Along with his emphasis on uncompromising moral principle, Sharp explained why the London Abolition Society had limited its purpose to eradicating the slave trade. Individual members might look forward to slave emancipation, he said, but this objective could be obtained only by "such gradual and temperate means as the colonial assemblies may adopt." This extreme caution, it appears in retrospect, sprang from the very values that led to the condemnation of slavery. Slavery could not be tolerated as a necessary and permanent evil because it deprived human beings of the responsibilities of free choice and of the recompense for labor, including private property, on which freedom depended. This meant that the ultimate goal of freedom could not be achieved by coercive means that destroyed the very fabric of law, consent, and property.

Even the Quakers, who established the first model of collective emancipation, proceeded gradually and with great caution as they dealt with the symptoms of "slavery withdrawal." Beginning in the late 1750s they investigated the problem of members who were actively engaged in the slave trade; in Philadelphia they adopted disciplinary measures that fell short of disownment. It took some twenty years for the Society of Friends to disengage itself from slaveholding even in the northern states; legal complications prolonged the process in North Carolina.

Four years after the passage of the ambiguous Northwest Ordinance, the French *Amis des noirs* issued a seemingly clear and uncompromising dictum on the status of slaves. Since no man could alienate his natural freedom, the French abolitionists said, "the slave is always free," regardless "of contrary laws, customs, and practices. . . . Accordingly, the restoration of a slave's freedom is not a gift or an act of charity. It is rather a compelling duty, an act of justice, which simply affirms an existing truth—not an ideal which ought to be." But despite this eloquent rhetoric the reformers concluded "that the immediate emancipation of Negro slaves would be a measure not only fatal for our colonies, but a measure which, since our greed has reduced the blacks to a degraded and impotent state, would be equivalent to abandoning and refusing aid to infants in their cradles or to helpless cripples."[19] Such examples add perspective to the emancipation acts of Pennsylvania, Connecticut, and Rhode Island, which preceded the Northwest Ordinance and which applied only to the future-born children of slaves, not to the slaves then living.

Paul Finkelman seems surprised and somewhat outraged by his discovery that "whatever it was supposed to accomplish, Article VI had little immediate impact on the legal status of slaves in the area that would become the states of Indiana and Illinois, where the bulk of the slaves in the territory lived." He suggests that "had there been a full-fledged debate over Article VI a clearer sense of its meaning might have emerged."[20] Apart from the fact that a full-fledged debate would have destroyed, in all probability, any chance of agreement on an antislavery provision, what I find surprising is the absence of any formal exemption of the Franco-American slaveholders from the effects of Article VI. In 1798, when Congress debated a motion to extend the exclusion clause of the Northwest Ordinance to Mississippi Territory, the advocates of slave exclusion acknowledged that the present settlers who had arrived under the laws of England, Spain, or Georgia could not with justice be deprived of their property.[21] The same presumption prevailed in 1804 when Congress considered various proposals for restricting slavery and the slave trade in Louisiana. Yet despite the contradictions between Article VI and a section of the Northwest Ordinance promising that Franco-Americans could retain the laws and customs then in force among them "relative to the descent and conveyance of property," the new federal Congress did nothing to clarify the issue and refused to comply with petitions requesting sanction for even the kind of age-limited servitude found in the gradual emancipation acts of the northern states. Although Congress also failed to veto territorial laws allowing indentured servitude and barring the residence of free blacks, the principle of prohibiting slavery remained intact.

Finkelman is surely right when he points to the discrepancy between the later abolitionist image of the Northwest Ordinance and the continuing vitality of slavery in the region. But one need not be as cynical or disillusioned about the Ordinance as he seems to be. For one thing, the unsuccessful struggle to legalize slavery in Illinois must be balanced against the unsuccessful struggle to abolish slavery in Kentucky. Initially led by such evangelical ministers as David Rice, David Barrow, and Carter Tarrant, the latter effort was revived in 1833 by James G. Birney's Kentucky Society for the Gradual Relief of the State from Slavery. Significantly, a large number of antislavery spokesmen from the Upper South eventually found a refuge from mob violence or peer-group hostility in the Northwest. It was not by accident that Edward Coles, the young Virginia antislavery slaveholder who pressed Thomas Jefferson to match his words with actions, later became the governor of Illinois who led the antislavery faction to victory. In 1856 Coles sketched the history of the "marvellous" Ordinance which had preserved freedom in all the states north of the Ohio River. According to Coles, the Ordinance had won more popular sanction than the Constitution as its principles were extended to the territory obtained by the Louisiana Purchase north of the 36°30' latitude and even to the Oregon Territory before being repealed by the Kansas-Nebraska Act. Needless to say, Coles regarded this repeal as a repudiation of the Founding Fathers' wisest legacy and as a possible prelude to "the awful realities of civil war."[22]

Finkelman voices skepticism about the claims of the aging Coles, who was born seven months before the Northwest Ordinance was enacted. Finkelman presents a brilliant but bleak account of the persistence of slavery in parts of the Old Northwest during sixty-one years of Coles's life. But these statistics must also be put in perspective. In 1820 there were still over 10,000 slaves in New York and more than 7,500 in New Jersey; in Illinois there were only

917; in Indiana 190. Although the Pennsylvania abolition law had been enacted seven years before the Northwest Ordinance, there were more slaves in Pennsylvania in 1820 than in Indiana. Finkelman seems especially disturbed by the fact that slavery lingered in Illinois until the constitution of 1848 finally abolished it. He does not mention that the census of 1840 records only 331 slaves or that in 1840 there were still a few slaves left in Pennsylvania, Connecticut, and Rhode Island. In other words, a lag of sixty years was not unusual in cases of gradual emancipation. In New Jersey, where an emancipation statute won assent only in 1804, slavery survived until 1846, and a few blacks remained in virtual bondage until the Civil War.[23]

Finkelman might logically reply that the language of Article VI did not imply gradual emancipation. But as he carefully demonstrates, the Northwest Ordinance said nothing about enforcement and failed to clarify the options open to new states. This very ambiguity was probably essential for the initial congressional consensus; it also converted the Ordinance into a charter document, as Andrew R. L. Cayton and Peter S. Onuf have argued, which was subject to conflicting interpretations.[24] The resulting uncertainty had one striking and incontrovertible consequence: it deterred slaveholders from moving across the Ohio River. The Northwest Ordinance, reinforced by flagrantly racist legislation and public opinion, maintained a preserve for whites until there was no possibility that states created from the Northwest Territory would legalize black slavery.

In 1820, for example, there were almost twice as many blacks in Missouri as in Ohio, Indiana, and Illinois combined. Blacks constituted less than 1 percent of the population in each of the three northwestern states, but 30 percent of the population of neighboring Kentucky. Had there been no Article VI, this incredibly lopsided distribution would surely not have prevailed. Parts of Indiana and Illinois, in particular, would have been inundated by the northern edge of the stream of slaves that rolled across Kentucky and Tennessee toward Missouri and Arkansas.

The timing of the Northwest Ordinance contributed to a pattern of boundary making that contained ominous implications for the future of slavery. From England to New England, Pennsylvania, and the Northwest, geographic lines marked off zones where free labor was to be the exclusive norm. If southerners wrongly assumed that even nonslaveholding westerners would prove to be allies, they rightly assumed that New York and New Jersey would soon join the ranks of emancipating states. When they accepted the premise that Congress could define and demarcate free-labor territory, they failed to anticipate the corollary that slavery would increasingly be seen as an exceptional or artificial institution requiring the sanction of positive law. Eventually, of course, after northern politicians moved to exclude slavery from Arkansas Territory, Missouri, and all territories won in the Mexican War, many southern leaders repudiated the principle of free-soil boundaries and demanded what amounted to the nationalization of slavery. The slaveholders won many victories in judicial decisions involving the vexing and complex questions of slave transit, sojourn, and comity, culminating in the Dred Scott decision, but their ideological losses should not be overlooked. The creation and expansion of a free-soil world, however accommodating in certain respects, invited increasingly invidious comparisons between antithetical and seemingly irreconcilable social systems.

Alexis de Tocqueville was only one of the numerous travelers who descended the Ohio River boundary and exclaimed over the contrasting landscapes on the northern and southern shores. After presenting images of industry and sloth, of growth and decay, Tocqueville condensed the message of free-labor ideology in a single memorable sentence:

> On the left bank of the Ohio work is connected with the idea of slavery, but on the right with well-being and progress; on the one side it is degrading, but on the other honorable; on the left bank no white laborers are to be found, for they would be afraid of being like the slaves; for work people must rely on the Negroes; but one will never see a man of leisure on the right bank: the white man's intelligent activity is used for work of every sort.[25]

This dramatic polarity, however deceptive in terms of wealth and economic growth, was a legacy of the Northwest Ordinance. It provided the core of the Republican party's ideology, an ideology that seemed convincing to millions of northerners who had no sympathy for the abolitionist cause. At the end of the Civil War, Charles Sumner contended that the Confederate states had neither seceded nor become conquered provinces. Having forfeited their rights by an act of rebellion, he claimed, they had in effect reverted to the status of territories temporarily subject to congressional control. Since the Constitution provided no guidelines for Reconstruction, Sumner turned instinctively to the precedent of new beginnings, the precedent that had supposedly made the Old Northwest a model republican society.

Notes

1. For the citation of primary sources and a brief discussion of excluding slaves from Georgia, see David Brion Davis, *The Problem of Slavery in Western Culture* (Ithaca, N.Y., 1966), 144–50.

2. Paul Finkelman, "Slavery and the Northwest Ordinance: A Study in Ambiguity," *Journal of the Early Republic*, VI (Winter, 1986), 343–70; Staughton Lynd, "The Compromise of 1787," *Political Science Quarterly*, LXXXI (June, 1966), 225–50. See also J. David Griffin, "Historians and the Sixth Article of The Ordinance of 1787," *Ohio History*, LXXVIII (Autumn, 1969), 252–60; Peter S. Onuf, *Statehood and Union: A History of the Northwest Ordinance* (Bloomington, 1987), 85, 109–32; Donald L. Robinson, *Slavery in the Structure of American Politics, 1765–1820* (New York, 1971), 378–83, 403; David Brion Davis, *The Problem of Slavery in the Age of Revolution, 1770–1823* (Ithaca, N.Y., 1975), 152–59; Edward Coles, *History of the Ordinance of 1787* (Philadelphia, 1856).

3. Finkelman, "Slavery and the Northwest Ordinance," 364.

4. See, especially, David Eltis, *Economic Growth and the Ending of the Transatlantic Slave Trade* (New York, 1987); Rebecca J. Scott, *Slave Emancipation in Cuba: The Transition to Free Labor, 1860–1899* (Princeton, N.J., 1985); Herbert S. Klein, *African Slavery in Latin America and the Caribbean* (New York, 1986); Seymour Drescher, *Capitalism and Antislavery: British Mobilization in Comparative Perspective* (New York, 1987); and Robert W. Fogel's *Without Consent or Contract: The Rise and Fall of American Slavery* (New York, 1989). I am indebted to Professor Fogel for sending me preliminary drafts of the latter work.

5. Seymour Drescher, *Econocide: British Slavery in the Era of Abolition* (Pittsburgh, 1977); Eltis, *Economic Growth*.

6. Klein, *African Slavery*, 130, *passim*; Scott, *Slave Emancipation*, chapter 1.

7. Eltis, *Economic Growth*, 15.

8. Ibid., 24.

9. David Eltis, "The British Contribution to the Nineteenth-Century Transatlantic Slave Trade," *Economic History Review*, 2nd ser., XXXII (May 1979), 211–27.

10. It should be noted that in 1793, under the prodding of Lieutenant-Governor John Graves Simcoe, Upper Canada's legislature passed an act "to prevent the further introduction of slaves," which also provided for gradual emancipation. Robin W. Winks, *The Blacks in Canada: A History* (New Haven, 1971), 96–98.

11. William Grayson to James Monroe, August 8, 1787, James Monroe Papers (Manuscripts Division, Library of Congress, Washington, D.C.). I am indebted to Robert F. Berkhofer, Jr., for the information that Grayson originally wrote "tobacco and hemp" and also that he had extensive landholdings south of the Ohio River.

12. For an excellent and provocative analysis of the influence of the issue of slavery on the

Constitutional Convention, see Paul Finkelman, "Slavery and the Constitutional Convention: Making a Covenant with Death," in *Beyond Confederation: Origins of the Constitution and American National Identity*, ed. Richard Beeman, Stephen Botein, and Edward C. Carter II (Chapel Hill, N.C., 1987), 188–225.

13. Lynd, "Compromise of 1787."

14. Quotations are from "Pleadings, and a solemn judgement, on the question, Whether a slave continues to be a slave after coming into Britain?" *The Scot's Magazine*, XXXIV (June 1772), 298–99, and Drescher, *Capitalism and Antislavery*, 37. For discussions of the Somerset case see William M. Wiecek, *The Sources of Antislavery Constitutionalism in America, 1760–1848* (Ithaca, N.Y., 1977), chapter 1; Drescher, *Capitalism and Antislavery*, chapter 2; Davis, *Problem of Slavery in the Age of Revolution*, chapter 10.

15. William Blackstone, *Commentaries on the Law of England* (4 vols., Oxford, 1765–1769), I, 123.

16. The Case of James Somerset, a Negro, 20 *How. St. Tr.* 1 at 75; transcript of proceedings in the Court of King's Bench, 1772, pp. 57–60, 65, Granville Sharp Papers (New-York Historical Society, New York City).

17. This ideology is one of the main themes of Davis, *Problem of Slavery in Western Culture*.

18. Granville Sharp to the Pennsylvania Abolition Society, July 30, 1788, Correspondence Incoming, Pennsylvania Abolition Society Papers (Historical Society of Pennsylvania, Philadelphia).

19. Translated from *Adresse de la Société des Amis des Noirs, à l'assemblée nationale . . .* (2nd ed., Paris, 1791), 107–8.

20. Finkelman, "Slavery and the Northwest Ordinance," 360, 359.

21. *Annals of Congress*, 5 Cong., 2 sess., 1797–1798, pp. 1306–10.

22. Coles, *History of the Ordinance of 1787*, 21–33.

23. Arthur Zilversmit, *The First Emancipation: The Abolition of Slavery in the North* (Chicago, 1967), 218–22. My figures on slave and black populations, which must be taken as crude estimates, are based on *Historical Statistics of the United States: Colonial Times to 1970* (Washington, 1975); U.S. Department of Commerce, Bureau of the Census, *Negro Population, 1790–1915* (1918; reprint, New York, 1968); and the table in Eugene H. Berwanger, *The Frontier Against Slavery: Western Anti-Negro Prejudice and the Slavery Extension Controversy* (Urbana, Ill., 1971), 31.

24. Andrew R. L. Cayton and Peter S. Onuf, "The Northwest Ordinance: New Directions in Historical Writing," 4–5 (unpublished paper prepared for a symposium on the Northwest Ordinance, Indiana University, Bloomington, September 6–7, 1987).

25. Alexis de Tocqueville, *Democracy in America*, ed. J. P. Mayer, trans. George Lawrence (Garden City, N.Y., 1969), 345–46.

16

The Benefit of Slavery

Economic Growth and the Ending of the Transatlantic Slave Trade
David Eltis (1987)

*Capitalism and Antislavery: British Mobilization
in Comparative Perspective*
Seymour Drescher (1987)

Last year a casual tourist flying by Air Jamaica to Montego Bay could learn
in one sentence why the British freed their West Indian slaves. "When the
sugar industry began to decline," the airline's journal *Skywritings* reported in
"Jamaica A to Z," "slavery was finally abolished." Not a word about William
Wilberforce and the other abolitionist heroes buried in Westminster Abbey.
Even well-read Americans might not suspect that *Skywritings'* matter-of-fact
statement is the product of a momentous historiographical debate which
involves the third world's understanding of capitalism and the capacity of
parliamentary governments for meaningful social reform.

The debate itself has mostly been confined to scholarly journals and international professional meetings. But the sesquicentennial of British slave
emancipation, in 1984, showed how deeply the theories of Eric Williams,
the late prime minister of Trinidad and Tobago, have become entrenched in
official and popular ideology in the West Indies and in much of the former
colonial world. At public commemorations from England to Guiana, Williams's followers reiterated the arguments of Williams's *Capitalism and Slav-*

ery, originally published in 1944, and scorned any suggestion that Britain's slaves had been freed for humanitarian rather than from economic motives.

Williams's influence can be partly explained by his powerful prose and the seeming simplicity of his arguments. *Capitalism and Slavery* was also perfectly timed to nourish and reinforce the anti-imperialist ideology of young intellectuals, especially in the emerging third world, who sought a historical foundation for theories of economic dependency. As an Oxford-trained historian who eventually became the ruler of a former British colony, Williams spoke with even greater authority when he repeated and expanded his thesis in *From Columbus to Castro: The History of the Caribbean, 1492 to 1969*. The crucial point, however, is that Williams addressed two questions that have a profound bearing on relations between the West and the third world: Did the expansion of Western capitalism and the affluence of the first industrialized nations depend initially on the coerced labor of Africans, Asians, and Amerindians? Assuming that such ruthless violence prepared the way for the Industrial Revolution, did Britain's leadership in the nineteenth-century crusade to suppress the Atlantic slave trade and abolish chattel slavery demonstrate that "the spread of moral convictions," as John Stuart Mill put it, could sometimes take precedence over material interests?[1]

Although Williams's thesis is subject to varied interpretations, its principal arguments support two broad conclusions. First, Williams maintained that European merchant capitalism created the immensely lucrative plantation system, fueled by the Atlantic slave trade, and that profits from this overseas system provided much of the capital in England that financed the Industrial Revolution.

Williams's second conclusion derived from the assumption that the American War of Independence initiated a period of irreversible economic decline in the British Caribbean and also coincided with Britain's decisive shift from mercantilism toward laissez-faire capitalism. By the early nineteenth century, according to Williams, the slave colonies had become an impediment to Britain's economic progress. Blighted by inefficient labor, depleted soil, and indebtedness, these former cornucopias of wealth were sustained only by mercantilist subsidies that led to chronic overproduction for the protected British market. While Williams acknowledged that a "brilliant band" of abolitionists won fame by conducting one of the "greatest propaganda movements of all time," he insisted that sentimental history should not be allowed to obscure the essential truth: "Overproduction in 1807 demanded abolition [of the slave trade]; overproduction in 1833 demanded emancipation."

With respect to the first conclusion, no one can doubt that slave labor was indispensable for European settlement and development of the New World. It is no less certain that the expansion of the slave plantation system from fifteenth-century Sicily to nineteenth-century Cuba, Brazil, and North America contributed significantly to Europe's economic growth. But economic historians have cast considerable doubt on the narrower proposition that the slave trade or even the plantation system as a whole created a major share of the capital that financed the Industrial Revolution.

It is Williams's second conclusion, however, that David Eltis and Seymour Drescher challenge in the books under review. In 1977, in an aggressive treatise loaded with statistical tables and organized like a lawyer's brief, Drescher sought to destroy the accepted belief that the British slave system had declined in value before Parliament outlawed the slave trade in 1807. Using statistics on British overseas trade, a criterion on which Williams had heavily relied, Drescher's *Econocide* showed that the value of British West Indian exports to England and of imports from England increased sharply from the early 1780s to the end of the eighteenth century. He also demonstrated that the British West Indian share of total British overseas trade rose to high peaks in the early nineteenth century and did not begin a long-range decline until well after Parliament deprived the colonies of fresh supplies of African labor.

After assessing the profitability of the slave trade and the increasing value of the British West Indian colonies, Drescher contended that the British slave system was expanding, not declining at the beginning of the nineteenth century. The abolition act of 1807 came at a time when Britain not only led the world in plantation production but had the opportunity, thanks to naval power and wartime conquests, of nearly monopolizing the slave trade and gaining a preponderant share of the growing world market for sugar and coffee. Neither Drescher nor the scholars who endorse his arguments have explained why so many contemporary observers and later historians accepted the view that the West Indies were in decline as a result of obsolete and wasteful farming techniques, soil exhaustion, rising production costs, indebtedness, bankruptcies, and declining white populations. Further study might show that the experience of the older and smaller colonies, such as

Barbados and the Leeward Islands, was more influential than the rich frontier regions in shaping popular imagery. It is also easy to confuse the symptoms of an imbalanced economy with economic decline. Drescher might have avoided some criticism if he had more clearly distinguished profitability from the structural defects and social impoverishment of the British slave colonies. Nevertheless, after a decade of debate it is clear that *Econocide* undercut a vital part of the Williams thesis.

David Eltis's book boldly expands Drescher's arguments against the putative economic decline of slavery, but as we shall later see, he can also be read as reformulating some of Williams's central points. A work of prodigious and meticulous scholarship, Eltis's book will be studied and debated well into the twenty-first century. No other scholar has so far rivaled Eltis in tracing the connections between industrialization in Europe and coerced labor in the Americas; in reconstructing the costs, profits, and techniques of the nineteenth-century Atlantic slave trade; in deciphering the covert activities of large multinational slaving firms; in mastering the details of slave ship tonnage, mortality, and voyage time; or in moving on a global scale from the plantations of Cuba and Brazil back to the sophisticated African slave-trading networks extending from Upper Guinea to Mozambique. Although clear and readable, *Economic Growth and the Ending of the Transatlantic Slave Trade* is a technical work that suffers, especially in the important first two chapters, from too much condensation. But Eltis's provocative arguments will require historians to reconsider the entire Anglo-American antislavery movement as well as the place of coerced labor in an emerging industrial and free market Atlantic world.

Historians have only begun to free themselves from the antislavery assumptions that permeated conceptions of political economy from the time of Benjamin Franklin and Adam Smith. We still find it difficult to believe that a flagrantly unjust system of labor could be compatible with long-term economic and material progress. But despite the many valid criticisms directed against Robert William Fogel and Stanley L. Engerman's *Time on the Cross* (1974), more recent research has confirmed their contention that slave labor could be efficient, productive, and adaptable to a variety of trades and occupations ranging from mining and factory work to the technologically modernized Cuban sugar mills. Indeed, in Cuba and Brazil as well as in the southern United States slavery continued to flourish until governments moved after 1860 to abolish it. In rejecting theories that slavery was doomed by its inherent limitations and by economic decline, Eltis rejects the tacit assumption that blacks were incapable of mastering advanced technology; yet at times he also echoes the precise reasoning slaveholders used against their abolitionist foes.

Eltis's argument about the use of coerced labor in the Atlantic economy can be summarized as follows. Slave labor on the plantations of the New World and Indian Ocean colonies attained its maximum economic importance *after* Britain and the United States outlawed the overseas slave trade and during the half-century, between 1816 and 1865, when Britain spent some £12 million (a staggering sum at that time) in an attempt to suppress the international slave traffic by patroling the African coasts, raiding African trading posts, bribing and coercing other nations to sign anti-slave trade treaties, seizing suspected slave ships, creating courts of mixed commission, and even sending cruisers to attack ships in Brazilian waters.

Slavery became more valuable to the Atlantic economy, according to Eltis, because economic growth created a soaring demand for such consumer goods as sugar, coffee, tobacco, and cotton textiles, all of which could be produced cheaply by slaves. In Britain alone, from 1785 to 1805 "sugar consumption rose 80 percent and cotton imports quadrupled despite prices that increased in real terms." By 1850, after Britain had finally equalized sugar duties and begun importing cheap slave-grown Cuban and Brazilian products, sucrose constituted a larger part of the diet of the working class than of the upper class, and national sugar consumption soon rose to a billion pounds a year.[2] Meanwhile, Britain's preeminent textile industry could not have survived without an expanding supply of cotton, almost all of which was produced by slaves until the end of the American Civil War.

At the beginning of the nineteenth century Britain possessed rich, uncultivated lands in Jamaica and especially in the newly acquired colonies of Trinidad and Demerara, in Guiana. Jamaica alone was exporting five times as much coffee as Cuba and Rio de Janeiro combined, and the British colonies were producing over half the sugar consumed by the North Atlantic nations. Even with a wholly inadequate supply of slaves, Demerara was emerging as a promising source of cotton for the British market.

But in marked contrast to the United States, where the slave population achieved a high rate of natural growth and where in fifty years some nine hundred thousand bondsmen were transferred from the eastern seaboard to the old Southwest, Brazil and most of the Caribbean colonies depended on slave populations that were shrinking. This attrition could be overcome only by the import of fresh laborers from Africa. In the twenty-seven years between Britain's abolition of the slave trade in 1807 and the emancipation of slaves in the colonies in 1834, the slave population declined by 25.3 percent in the new sugar colonies and by 10.8 percent in Jamaica.[3] The British government succeeded not only in stopping the flow of labor from Africa to the British colonies but also in restricting the sale or movement of slaves from the older, more densely populated islands to the highly productive frontier zones. This antislavery policy raised production costs and prevented British planters from exploiting the expanding world market. It also gave an enormous stimulus to entrepreneurs in Cuba and Brazil, who continued to import African labor. Even so, the British colonies were able to export more sugar than Cuba and Brazil together until Parliament abolished slavery itself in 1834. The economic consequences of emancipation became fully apparent only after 1838, when Britain abolished an experimental system of slavelike apprenticeship.

As Eltis convincingly argues, "for the Americas as well as for Britain at the outset of industrialization, there was a profound incompatibility between economic self-interest and antislavery policy." With considerable dismay the British learned that free laborers were unwilling to accept the harsh plantation discipline and working conditions that made sugar cultivation a highly profitable investment. European immigrants shunned the plantation regions of the New World and, in any event, it was not until the 1840s that the transatlantic flow of free immigrants exceeded the flow of African slaves, even though the importation of slaves was by then almost entirely confined to Cuba and Brazil. To save the plantations of Jamaica, Trinidad, and Guiana from complete ruin, Britain resorted to indentured African and Asian immigrants. But the hundreds of thousands of East Indian "coolies" who eventually arrived in Trinidad and Guiana could not reverse the effects of slave emancipation or restore the British colonies to their earlier competitive advantage.

Ironically, Britain's industrial growth greatly reduced the cost of the manufactured goods that were used to purchase slaves on the African coast. At the very time when British officials were engaged in bribery, spying, and violations of international law to suppress the foreign slave trade, it was British capital, credit, insurance, and manufactured goods that made this illicit trade so profitable. Despite the policing actions of the British navy, between 1811 and 1860 approximately 2.25 million African slaves were imported into the Americas, for the most part illegally. Eltis estimates, after an analysis of demand and supply, that without British naval, diplomatic, and ideological pressure, approximately 290,000 more Africans would have been shipped across the Atlantic. He also estimates that an open British slave trade between 1811 and 1830 would have resulted in the transport to the Americas of at least 250,000 additional Africans. However one calculates the impact of British efforts at suppression, the short-term results fell far short of the goals of the abolitionists. Unfortunately, Eltis seems more impressed by the costs and illegal tactics of British policy than by its long-term effects of clearing slave ships from the seas, encouraging foreign antislavery movements, and weakening slavery throughout the world.[4]

But as Eltis makes clear, the economic costs of abolitionism were high; they went well beyond the expense of enforcing anti-slave trade treaties and paying £20 million compensation to British slaveholders. During the first six decades of the nineteenth century there was an ample supply of slaves on the African coasts and the price remained relatively low and stable. Yet throughout the American plantation societies, slave prices continued to rise in response to labor shortages. If free market conditions had prevailed, labor costs would have been reduced on New World plantations, consumers would probably have paid considerably less for sugar, coffee, and cotton goods, and British merchants could have sold more manufactured goods in markets extending from Brazil and the West Indies to Africa. As Eltis remarks: "In national income terms a much more effective way of using the African squadron would have been to station it off the Texas coast to generate and protect an illicit slave trade from Cuba to the U.S. South—and later to recognize and protect the Confederacy in 1862."

One concludes from Eltis's iconoclastic study that capitalist self-interest, as a source of human exploitation and suffering in the early industrial era, could have been even worse than it proved to be. If Britain had not outlawed the slave trade, emancipated nearly eight hundred thousand slaves, and promoted abolitionism throughout the world, economic growth might have increased at a faster rate. There is a subtle irony in the way that Eltis's neoclassical economic analysis exposes the pathological consequences of a world view that subordinates all human relationships to free-market choices and the supreme goal of achieving the largest national product.

Why, then, did the British government adopt and pursue antislavery policies for such a prolonged period? Most abolitionists probably agreed with Granville Sharp "that no gains, however great, are to be put in competition

with the essential rights of man, and that as a nation is exalted by righteousness, so it is equally debased and debilitated by the revenues of injustice."[5] But this was hardly a principle that could guide the leaders of the
world's most powerful and economically expansive nation.

Seymour Drescher's *Capitalism and Antislavery* provides a fresh approach to
the politics of abolitionism for anyone who seeks an answer to the conun-
drum Eltis exposes. Rejecting interpretations based either on economic interest or the moral vision of abolitionist "Saints," Drescher emphasizes the
distinctive political culture that led a significant proportion of the British
population to oppose slavery. In December 1787, Drescher claims, "two-
thirds of Manchester's eligible men subscribed to the first petition for the
abolition of the slave trade."[6] In the 1780s, 1790s, 1810s, and 1830s antislavery petitions outnumbered those on any other single issue, including parliamentary and religious reform. In 1833 almost 1.5 million people signed
petitions demanding slave emancipation; one of these 5,252 petitions was a
monstrous roll, nearly a half-mile long, bearing the signatures of 187,000
women.

Drescher has gone far beyond previous historians in examining provincial
newspapers and reconstructing the broad-based, populist characteristics of
British abolitionism. By making informed comparisons with other countries,
especially France, he has also dramatized the remarkable distinctiveness of
the active British opposition to slavery, which cut across lines of class, party,
and religion. This support from the unenfranchised mass cannot be explained
by economic interest, at least in any conventional sense of the term. As
Drescher argues, it depended on widespread literacy and a tradition of political consciousness and activism. And the antislavery movement was itself a
vehicle for political experiment and training—for preparing men and even
women to form societies, gather petitions, and demand pledges from political
candidates.

To account for the strength of this popular feeling, Drescher maintains
that the conditions of everyday life in British capitalist towns led to a growing
consciousness of the cultural and moral disparities between life in England
and life in the colonies. Although Englishmen had long prided themselves
on living in "an island of liberty in a world filled with slaves," they had
willingly accepted such a geographic division along with the wealth that
poured in from benighted regions "beyond the line." By the late eighteenth
century, however, the British public not only refused to tolerate the intrusion

into England of colonial institutions but began to insist that British standards of freedom be extended to the high seas and colonial plantations.

While a similar argument has been advanced by other historians, including this reviewer, Drescher's account raises numerous questions that can be only briefly noted here. He ignores the deep intellectual and cultural transformation that provided the imagery, sensibility, and ideas for the antislavery movement. Drescher often refers to the large effects of capitalism but fails to explain the local political and economic conditions that united most of Manchester's entrepreneurs and artisans, for example, in a common cause. From Drescher's book we never learn why antislavery, among dozens of competing reforms, won such overwhelming support that abolitionists were virtually unopposed in most regions. By 1833 the ratio of signatures for immediate emancipation to those against was more than 250 to one.

Although Drescher refers vaguely to "molders of public opinion," he is so hostile to any idea of influence "from above" that he tells us little about the local activists who organized meetings, disseminated tracts, and solicited petition signatures. At times, indeed, Drescher writes as if "mobilization" of opinion were a self-sufficient force; when discussing the initial mobilization in Manchester, for example, it is "Manchester" itself that launches the petition campaign, aims for a mass enrollment of its male inhabitants, and begins "its long search for a myth which 'would elevate its citizens above the prosaic level of their daily working life.'" Similarly, Drescher tells us nothing specific about the way public opinion influenced legislation. The careless reader, overlooking Drescher's point that Parliament spurned mass petitioning against Catholic emancipation, might conclude that Britain was governed in the early nineteenth century by plebiscite.

These shortcomings are greatly outweighed by Drescher's insights and by the comparative perspective that enables him to demonstrate, for example, that "French antislavery was clearly distinguished by an inability to combine a stable élite leadership with a mass appeal." But why was it England, a nation deeply affected by the world's first industrialization and increasingly divided by class and religious struggles, that found a way of uniting a stable elite leadership with mass appeal—and in a cause that threatened specific property rights and social order, to say nothing of the economic benefits that David Eltis has so forcefully underscored? Eltis himself provides the clue that may help future historians round out Drescher's account of popular mobilization and explain why important antislavery measures were proposed by otherwise conservative statesmen and approved with little organized dissent by the House of Lords.

Whereas Drescher tends to idealize British traditions of liberty, Eltis is fully aware of the continuing attempts in the seventeenth and much of the eighteenth century to ensure the industriousness of British workers by low wages and Draconian vagrancy laws. Such notables as Bishop Berkeley, Francis Hutcheson, and Andrew Fletcher even advocated enslavement as the best means to discipline the beggars and idle rogues who roamed the country. Eltis connects this acceptance of coerced labor with a preindustrial preoccupation with competitive exports and low labor costs.

By the late eighteenth century, however, a growing home market was beginning to alert capitalists to the importance of "want creation" and to incentives such as higher wages as a means of increasing both worker productivity and the number of consumers. "For owners of capital," Eltis points out, "a population responsive to market forces was a basic prerequisite [for optimum level of consumption], and if that population had no other means of supporting consumption than through wages, so much the better." Significantly, it was products grown by slaves, such as sugar, coffee, tobacco, and cotton, that had stimulated so many new wants at every level of British society and that were "forerunners of the great mass of products in modern high-income societies that are purchased in the expectation that they will satisfy nonsubsistence or psychological needs." The contradiction between the coerced labor used to produce plantation products and the consumer demand that was changing British attitudes to wage labor sheds a wholly new light on Drescher's dichotomy between the metropolis in the British Isles and the colonial frontier in the Caribbean. It also brings us back to Eric Williams.

In a statement that he unfortunately fails to develop, Eltis observes that

the important aspects of the relationship between capitalism and abolition that Eric Williams was searching for were, first, that British employers had less need for coercion by the second half of the eighteenth century and that, second, both draconian vagrancy laws at home and predial [i.e. plantation] slavery in the colonies were examples of coercion. In the light of a system that relied on voluntary labor to satisfy individual wants going beyond subsistence needs, forced labor appeared not only inappropriate but counterproductive.

This reformulation of the question asserts the importance of ideology—specifically, an ideology of free labor that would be understood in increasingly conflicting ways by workers and employers but that could nevertheless unite many of them in condemning chattel slavery in distant colonies.

I doubt that Williams's orthodox leftist followers would be satisfied by even a well-developed theory relating British antislavery to a free-labor ideology. Yet such a theory, based on empirical evidence, would confirm some of Williams's most important insights: that the slave system contributed to structural transformations in British life that made abolitionism acceptable; that British leaders became committed to colonial labor reform only when they were convinced that free labor would be less dangerous than slavery and more beneficial for the imperial economy as a whole. In contrast to Williams's cynicism, however, such a theory would not diminish the moral vision and accomplishments of the abolitionists. It would show that, given a fortunate convergence of economic, political, and ideological circumstances, the world's first industrial nation could transcend narrow self-interest and achieve genuine reform.

Notes

1. Anyone interested in the continuing debate over the Williams thesis should consult Barbara Solow and Stanley L. Engerman, eds., *British Capitalism and Caribbean Slavery: The Legacy of Eric Williams* (Cambridge University Press, 1987); Stanley L. Engerman, "The Slave Trade and British Capital Formation in the Eighteenth Century: A Comment on the Williams Thesis," *Business History Review*, 46 (Winter 1972), pp. 430–443; Seymour Drescher, *Econocide: British Slavery in the Era of Abolition* (University of Pittsburgh Press, 1977); Roger Anstey, *The Atlantic Slave Trade and British Abolition, 1760–1810* (Macmillan, 1975); Seymour Drescher, "Eric Williams: British Capitalism and British Slavery," *History and Theory*, 26/2 (1987), pp. 180–196; Selwyn H. H. Carrington and Seymour Drescher, "Debate: Econocide and West Indian Decline, 1783–1806," *Boletin de Estudios Latinoamericanos y del Caribe*, No. 36 (June 1984), pp. 13–67; Walter E.

Minchinton, "Williams and Drescher: Abolition and Emancipation," *Slavery and Abolition*, 4 (September 1983), pp. 81–105; Barbara L. Solow, "Caribbean Slavery and British Growth: The Eric Williams Hypothesis," *Journal of Development Economics*, 17 (1985), pp. 99–115; Seymour Drescher, "The Decline Since *Econocide*," Slavery and Abolition, 7 (May 1986), pp. 3–24; David Brion Davis, "Reflections on Abolitionism and Ideological Hegemony," *American Historical Review*, 92 (October 1987), pp. 797–812.

2. Sidney W. Mintz, *Sweetness and Power: The Place of Sugar in Modern History* (Viking, 1985), p. 143.

3. B. W. Higman, *Slave Populations of the British Caribbean, 1807–1834* (Johns Hopkins University Press, 1984), p. 72. Higman provides a detailed and informative analysis of the extremely complex problem of slave population growth and decline.

4. In considering the significance and consequences of slave-trade suppression, Eltis mentions the frequent famines of west-central Africa and the improved nutrition and taller stature that Africans gained in the New World; the shortage of prime-age males that increased work pressures for slave women in field gangs; the accelerated development of "a wholly Creole Afro-American society"; and the impetus given to direct European political and economic intervention in Africa when Africans failed to meet the British abolitionists' "culture-bound expectations" (pp. 238–240).

5. Letter to the Pennsylvania Abolition Society, July 30, 1788, Pennsylvania Abolition Society Papers, Correspondence Incoming, Historical Society of Pennsylvania.

6. The most detailed and illuminating account of antislavery petitioning in Manchester can be found in a pioneering but unpublished M.A. thesis by E. M. Hunt. Hunt shows that the petition signatures were not obtained in 1787, as Drescher says, but in January 1788, when the petition prepared by a committee of manufacturers, clergymen, and civic leaders of both parties was submitted to a large public meeting and when copies were later left for signature at eleven public houses, stationers' offices, and other such sites (E. M. Hunt, "The North of England Agitation for the Abolition of the Slave Trade, 1780–1800," M.A. thesis, University of Manchester, 1959, pp. 77–83). The ability of Manchester's elite to obtain petition signatures for even an illiberal cause can be seen from the popular support given to Pitt's Sedition Bills of 1795, which far exceeded that of the nation at large (see Drescher, *Capitalism and Antislavery*, pp. 82–83).

17

Capitalism, Abolitionism, and Hegemony

Attention is turning once again to the almost simultaneous appearance of industrial capitalism and antislavery sentiment in Great Britain. Since the publication of Eric Williams's *Capitalism and Slavery*, more than a generation ago, the relation between these two broad forces has provoked considerable debate. As Howard Temperley demonstrates, the issues have acquired high ideological voltage in the Third World as well as in Britain and the United States.[1]

Williams and his many followers have sought to portray Britain's antislavery measures as economically determined acts of national self-interest, cynically disguised as humanitarian triumphs. Roger Anstey, who led the way in undermining Williams's case for economic motivation, viewed Christianity's role in abolitionism as nothing less than "a saving event within the context of Salvation History."[2] While few of Williams's opponents have shared this explicit faith in slave emancipation as a step toward historical redemption, it has been difficult to find a middle ground that rejects Williams's cynical reductionism but that takes account of the realities of class power. A historian who scrutinizes the moral pretensions of the abolitionists or who observes, to borrow a phrase C. Vann Woodward has applied to the American Civil War, that West Indian emancipation enabled Britain to add an immense sum to the national "treasury of virtue" and to bank on it for "futures in moral credit," runs the risk of being classified as a follower of Eric Williams. Yet national pride is especially dangerous and deceptive, as

Reinhold Niebuhr reminded us, when it is based on the highest achievements of human history.[3]

In 1975, in *The Problem of Slavery in the Age of Revolution, 1770–1823*, I suggested that British abolitionism served conflicting ideological functions but that it helped, in this initial period, to reinforce the hegemony of capitalist values. This view has evoked fruitful criticism from Seymour Drescher, Thomas L. Haskell, and Betty Fladeland, among others.[4] Since I bear some responsibility for the misinterpretations that have been given to my "thesis," I would like to take this opportunity to restate and clarify my argument and to assess some of the criticisms.

I should first emphasize that my hegemonic argument fills only a few pages in a 570-page volume and that it applies only to British history in a limited period from the 1790s to 1823, with some brief speculations reaching ahead to the 1830s. In this volume I did not extend the concept of hegemony to America or France, where abolition movements emerged in wholly different contexts. Certainly I advanced no general theory of abolitionism per se as an instrument of hegemonic control. I have never meant to suggest that abolitionism can best be understood as a device for deflecting white working-class discontent or that it was not part of the wider egalitarian and liberalizing movement I described in *The Problem of Slavery in Western Culture* (1966).

It is important to distinguish the *origins* of antislavery sentiment, a subject I discussed at length in the first volume, from the *conditions* that favored the widespread acceptance of antislavery ideology among various governing elites. This is a distinction that Thomas Haskell continually blurs. In all my work I have taken pains to emphasize the importance of religious sources of antislavery thought and the religious transformations that made slave emancipation a symbolic test of the efficacy of Christian faith. In *The Age of Revolution* I do not say, and here Haskell misquotes me, that the "origin" of the new humanitarian sensibility lay in "the ideological needs of various groups and classes."[5] I do maintain that "the continuing evolution" of antislavery opinion "reflected the ideological needs of various groups and classes."[6] I had in mind the ideological needs generated by the French Revolution and the early Industrial Revolution, by war, nationalism, and religious revivalism. At issue are the uses made of antislavery doctrine and rhetoric as the movement pulled away from the Painite radicals of the early 1790s, won legitimacy from government ministries in 1806–7, was appropriated by the aristocratic African Institution, and was then reshaped by wealthy merchant philanthropists.

In *The Age of Revolution* I had to deal with Britain in the period from 1793 to 1823, decades of reactionary politics and domestic repression that should not be confused with the era of social ferment and reform that accompanied West Indian slave emancipation and the abolition of apprenticeship. The crucial question, therefore, was not why groups of enlightened Britons, Frenchmen, and Americans attacked slavery from the 1760s to the 1780s, but why this single reform cause, which attracted significant radical support in the early 1790s and which some conservatives denounced as a Jacobin-front movement, won growing acceptance in the early nineteenth century from British political and social elites otherwise obsessed with the fear that social reform would open the gates to revolution.

During the long period from the late 1790s to 1823, the British public showed little interest in the slavery issue except at the end of the Napoleonic wars. In 1814 an eruption of petitions expressed outrage at the prospect that the government would allow France to resume the Atlantic slave trade, which Britain had earlier renounced on moral grounds. This brief popular outburst drew on nationalistic pride and was orchestrated by abolitionist leaders who were eager to demonstrate to the courts of Europe that "with a single voice" the English people demanded international suppression of the slave trade. The cause served the purpose of Wellington and Castlereagh, who actively cooperated with the abolitionists. Castlereagh even requested a digest of anti-slave-trade evidence that could be translated into French in preparation for the Congress of Vienna. It was a notably reactionary and repressive British government that tried to influence French public opinion and bribe Spain and Portugal into ending or restricting the Atlantic slave trade.

Historians have often exaggerated the continuity of popular antislavery agitation from the late 1780s to the 1830s. The crucial antislavery measures from 1800 to 1823 were not the result of public pressure. Government leaders and a few influential abolitionists were responsible for the decisions to curtail and then stop the flow of African slaves to Guiana and other foreign colonies conquered by Britain, and then to prohibit the British slave trade to all foreign nations and colonies. The successful abolition bill of 1807 originated in the House of Lords; the prevailing public apathy and ignorance of the question prompted Wilberforce to publish and widely circulate *A Letter on the Abolition of the Slave Trade; Addressed to the Freeholders and Other Inhabitants of Yorkshire*. The later campaign to establish a central registry of all colonial slaves aroused little public interest, though it was seen as an essential preparatory step toward emancipation. Even in 1823 and 1824, when an organized emancipation movement got under way, the abolitionists who solicited petitions and organized auxiliary societies were surprised by the general public ignorance concerning West Indian slavery. Yet the governing elites had become increasingly committed to colonial labor reform. Why should colonial slavery have seemed so repugnant to such groups?

In pursuing this question I should have made it clearer that by "ideology" I did not mean a fixed set of ideas and doctrines used to promote concrete class interests. When referring to an ideology as a "mode of consciousness," I was thinking of a perceptual lens, a way of viewing social reality that helps to define as well as to legitimate class, gender, or other collective interests. Keeping this elasticity in mind, it is important to draw a distinction between the motives of individual reformers and the ideological context that gave hegemonic meaning to their rhetoric and influence.

When in 1786 Thomas Clarkson published his prize-winning Cambridge University essay on the horrors of the African slave trade, he clearly had no intention of condoning British child labor in factories and mines. But Clarkson's proslavery opponents like Gilbert Francklyn and Jesse Foot immediately contrasted the alleged comfort and security of West Indian slaves with the oppression of English workers and the plight of English children exposed to the "pestilential vapour" of factories. Francklyn pointedly asked why the universities did not offer prizes "for the best dissertation on the evil effects which the manufactures of Birmingham, Manchester, and other great Manufacturing towns, produce on the health and the lives of the poor people employed therein?" He proceeded to show how Clarkson's rhetorical techniques could be applied to the specific consequences of the early Industrial Revolution.[7]

Such antiabolitionist counteroffensives had appeared even earlier and they would become a dominant theme of British and later American proslavery writing. Similar points were made by radical labor spokesmen who were in principle opposed to all forms of economic and political bondage. Given the venom of the debate, no abolitionist could plead ignorance of the charge that moral outrage was being directed against oppression overseas while similar or worse oppression was complacently tolerated at home. In 1818, for example, Sir Francis Burdett asked why William Wilberforce could be shocked by the enslavement of Africans and yet support in Parliament a seditious meetings bill and the suspension of habeas corpus, measures that allowed Englishmen to be seized and treated like African slaves.

Theoretically, abolitionists faced by such challenges could condemn all forms of social oppression and simply give priority to the slave trade or chattel slavery as the most flagrant and remediable crimes against humanity. This course would entail a disavowal of the proslavery writers' claims and at least a private expression of regret over the unintended consequences of extolling free wage labor. As a second alternative, exemplified by some of the later Garrisonians and labor reformers, the abolitionists could claim that both distant and nearby evils arose from a common cause. As a third choice, they could deny any comparability between black slaves who were subjected to constant physical coercion and English workers who faced merely the threat of starvation, which was termed a "liberal motive" and a "rational predicament" by the reformer who drafted the 1833 slave emancipation act.[8]

In response to proslavery indictments of the wage-labor system, most abolitionists accentuated the moral contrast between what they conceived of as the free and slave worlds. Their greatest hope, after all, was to end the involuntary shipment of Africans to the New World and to transform black slaves into cheerful, obedient, and grateful laborers whose wants could be satisfied only by working voluntarily for wages. This hope rested on the assumption that the British system of labor had achieved a reasonable balance between freedom and order and could serve as a norm against which harsher regimes should be measured. I am not suggesting that early abolitionists were mostly conservatives who accepted the status quo and opposed domestic reforms, though some of them fit this description. But the sharp contrast they drew between British and colonial society had ideological meaning, especially at a time when there was a growing need to valorize wage labor as a universal norm, when the Industrial Revolution was introducing new forms of exploitation and suffering, and when it was by no means clear that the British working class was less victimized than West Indian slaves.

For example, early in 1807 at a depressing stage in Britain's war against Napoleon, James Stephen the elder, who was the abolitionists' master strategist, singled out British depravity in Africa and the West Indies as the cause for God's vengeance. Stephen specifically excluded domestic sins and proceeded to marvel over the "social happiness [that] has been showered upon us with singular profusion." "In no other part of the globe, are the poor and helpless so well protected by the laws, or so humanely used by their superiors. . . . If it be as the protector of the poor and destitute, that God has entered into judgment with us, we must, I repeat, look to Africa, and to the West Indies, for the causes of his wrath."[9]

Stephen was a deeply religious man who was genuinely concerned with collective guilt and retribution. We can be almost certain, from what we know of him, that he did not consciously intend to use his abhorrence of slavery and the slave trade, which he had observed first-hand in the West Indies, as a means of diverting attention from domestic suffering. Though as a boy he and his mother had lived in debtors' prison, he honestly believed, at least after marrying into the Wilberforce family and allying himself with paternalistic Tories, that Britain's treatment of the poor could not be a cause for divine displeasure. Later in 1807 Stephen played an important role in securing the abolition of the British slave trade, a law hailed by political leaders as the most altruistic act since Christ's crucifixion and as proof that Britain waged war for human brotherhood.

From the time of the Mosaic Exodus, slavery and redemption have been extremely powerful paradigms involving the ultimate questions for both individual and collective life: the passage from present misery and degradation to a land of Canaan. Apart from their religious meanings, these paradigms are capable of being extended to a wide range of social experiences with oppression and liberation, or of being confined to the historical sufferings of a particular people. According to Rousseau, "man is born free—and everywhere he is in chains." But since Rousseau, at least, there has always been a tension between such generalizing proclamations and attempts to dramatize the horrors of a special instance of human bondage.

For James Stephen, Wilberforce, and the government leaders who deplored the African slave trade and who moved toward gradualist antislavery policies, it was essential to maintain a sharp distinction between the evils of the colonial slave world and the ostensibly free institutions that had been imperiled both by French tyranny and English Jacobins. The constant comparisons in abolitionist literature between the agony of black slaves and the smiling, contented life of English "husbandmen" was not fortuitous. Abolitionists repeatedly reminded Britons that the Somerset decision of 1772 had outlawed slavery in England. At a time when many of the peoples of Europe were said to be "enslaved" by French despotism, it was crucial to define England as a "free" nation—both in the sense of having no slaves and of having successfully resisted foreign domination. With the growth of nationalism in the Napoleonic era, *freedom* increasingly signified membership in a nation that had resisted or thrown off foreign tyranny. When national leaders were perceived as the protectors of liberty in this collective sense, it was more difficult to accuse them of fostering various forms of domestic oppression.

If the slave colonies helped England to define itself as free soil—much as Communist countries enable the United States to define itself as the leader of the free world—they also helped to specify the nature of freedom. The

African slave trade defined, by negative polarity, the conditions necessary for consensual and acceptable labor transport. It was unacceptable for an employer to claim ownership of the person of an employee, to sell husbands apart from their wives, or children apart from their parents. It was acceptable, on the other hand, to buy the labor of adults or children even under conditions that led to the separation of families and that made a mockery of the worker's supposed consent.

British selectivity, as I suggested in *The Age of Revolution*, must be understood in terms of historical context. The government's first interventions in the colonial labor system coincided with an urgent domestic problem of labor discipline and labor management—not yet the problem of an industrial proletariat but of an immense rural labor force that had been released from traditional restraints and controls but not yet deprived of the independence of preindustrial village culture. Many Britons, including abolitionists, felt ambivalent toward the changes accompanying early industrialization. Tensions mounted between the advocates of hard-headed utilitarianism and the defenders of traditional paternalism or evangelical benevolence. The issue of slavery provided a meeting ground for these diverse groups and for members of different propertied classes who longed to ensure stability while benefiting from the economic changes under way.

> Because the slave system was both distinctive and remote, [I wrote,] it could become a subject for experimental fantasies that assimilated traditional values to new economic needs. An attack on the African slave trade could absorb some of the traditionalist's anxieties over the physical uprooting and dislocation of labor. . . . By picturing the slave plantation as totally dependent upon physical torture, abolitionist writers gave sanction to less barbarous modes of social discipline. For reformers, the plantation offered the prospect of combining the virtues of the old agrarian order with the new ideals of uplift and engineered incentive. Abolitionists could contemplate a revolutionary change in status precisely because they were not considering the upward mobility of workers, but rather the rise of distant Negroes to the level of humanity. . . . British antislavery provided a bridge between preindustrial and industrial values; by combining the ideal of emancipation with an insistence on duty and subordination, it helped to smooth the way to the future.[10]

I have quoted at length from this passage because I have sometimes been interpreted as arguing that British abolitionism was a "screening device" designed to distract attention from metropolitan exploitation.[11] In actuality, I was trying to suggest a far more complex model in which the colonial plantation system served as a projective screen or experimental theater for testing ideas of liberation, paternalism, and controlled social change that were prompted in part by domestic anxieties. As one might expect in a society as deeply divided as early industrial Britain, different audiences drew contradictory conclusions from the experiments in overseas reform. But it is difficult to deny that the abolition cause offered both national and local ruling elites an increasingly attractive opportunity to demonstrate their commitment to decency and justice.

In the passage quoted above I was also concerned with the implications of sharply separating slavery from other kinds of coerced labor and social domination. It is noteworthy that even Thomas Clarkson, who retained much of the liberal spirit of the late 1780s and early 1790s, found nothing inequitable about coerced labor. Any state, he said, might legitimately use convicts to work in mines or clear rivers. What outraged Clarkson and other early abolitionists was the claim of personal proprietorship that justified arbitrary and unlimited authority. The slave owner's claims contrasted sharply with those of the idealized British squire, whose authority was constrained by law and custom; and with the rights of the rising capitalist, who was content to purchase labor in the market like any other commodity.

Above all, the slave system came to epitomize an inherent and inescapable conflict of interest, a kind of warfare sublimated or suspended from the time the original captive was subdued. For a time the more moderate abolitionists searched for means to ameliorate this conflict, hoping that an end to further slave imports, for example, would persuade masters to promote their slaves' welfare as part of their own long-term self-interest. Yet the continuing negative growth rate of the West Indian slave population seemed to show that the system itself was unreformable and would lead to eventual genocide. This impression was reinforced by the slaveholders' truculent resistance to missionaries, moral uplift, the abolition of Sunday markets, restrictions on the flogging of women, and other benevolent measures. The whole thrust of the British antislavery movement, by the early 1820s, was aimed at creating a natural harmony of interests between planters and black workers, a relation similar to the assumed mutuality between British landlords and tenants.

In arguing that antislavery mirrored the needs and tensions of a society increasingly absorbed with problems of labor discipline, I was not saying that such needs and tensions are sufficient to explain the emergence and ultimate direction of antislavery thought. While emphasizing the importance of class and social context, I specifically warned against "the simplistic impression that 'industrialists' promoted abolitionist doctrine as a means of distracting attention from their own forms of exploitation."[12] My main theme was that antislavery cannot be divorced from the vast economic changes that were intensifying social conflicts and heightening class consciousness; that in Britain it was part of a larger ideology that helped to ensure stability while accommodating society to political and social change.

Even in Britain, where the cause won significant support from the governing elites, there were both conservative and radical aspects to abolitionist thought. Some readers have focused exclusively on the first part of my argument, in which I claimed that the abolitionists' acts of selectivity "helped to strengthen the invisible chains being forged at home." But I also emphasized that abolitionism "bred a new sensitivity to social oppression," "that it provided a model for the systematic indictment of social crime," and that it "ultimately taught many Englishmen to recognize forms of systematic oppression that were closer to home."[13] To illustrate the radical potentialities of antislavery thought I quoted from Friedrich Engels precisely because he showed how abolitionist perceptions and locutions had become universalized by the 1840s; even a resident alien, with no roots in the abolitionist movement, appropriated the language and perspective of Anglo-American abolitionists when he exposed the "slavery" of Manchester's working class. As early as 1817, when Wilberforce and his friends in the Liverpool cabinet feared that England was on the verge of revolution, another radical alien pointed to the connections between the oppression of West Indian slaves and the oppression of England's poor. Iain McCalman has discovered that Robert Wedderburn, a Jamaican mulatto whose slave mother was born in Africa, edited a London periodical, *Axe Laid to the Root*, which called for a simultaneous revolution of West Indian chattel slaves and English wage slaves. Associated with Thomas Spence, Thomas Evans, and other London radicals, Wedderburn popularized a plebeian antislavery rhetoric in the taverns and hayloft chapels of London's underworld.[14]

Social movements often serve opposing or contradictory functions, especially if they endure for any length of time. As I have already indicated, slavery and emancipation have long been extraordinarily complex paradigms, since they are capable of almost infinite extension to both material and spiritual states. Even in the 1820s antislavery agitation led American radicals like Langton Byllesby and Thomas Skidmore to the conclusion that black slavery was not only the quintessential American crime but that it revealed deep structural flaws that enabled a fortunate few to live off the labor of the so-called free majority. On the other hand, when radical American reformers later contended that the wage system was slavery, that conventional marriage was slavery, and that submission to any government using coercion was slavery, their rhetoric surely diluted the charge that Negro slavery in the South was a system of exceptional and intolerable oppression. As Christopher Lasch has observed with respect to our own time, the language of radical protest was impoverished when it was appropriated by fat people, short people, old people, and other such groups who claimed that they were as much oppressed as racial minorities: "Since interest-group politics invites competitive claims to the privileged status of victimization, the rhetoric of moral outrage becomes routine, loses its critical edge, and contributes to the general debasement of political speech."[15]

While acknowledging that abolitionism was always double-edged and set precedents for attacking practices and institutions that most abolitionists condoned, we should remember that even in America it was the wealthy Tappan brothers and their associates, not Thomas Skidmore, who shaped the basic character of the antislavery movement, at least in the 1830s. For their part, spokesmen for the radical labor movement in New York City had concluded by 1850 that it was essential "to abolish Wages Slavery before we meddle with Chattel Slavery." Faced with the workers' hatred for middle-class moralizers and with their persistent racial prejudice against free black competitors, labor leaders wished to postpone emancipating slaves "who are better off than to be let loose under the present Competitive System of labor. . . ."[16] The abolition movement was neither monolithic nor unchanging; in the United States, in contrast to Britain, it presented a fundamental challenge to economic, political, and religious establishments. Yet it also served various hegemonic functions, particularly by promoting a free-labor ideology as the antithesis of the Slave Power it attacked.

The concept of hegemony is easily discredited by misconstruction or misunderstanding—by attacking the argument, for example, that a discrete capitalist class imposed a form of false consciousness upon a passive populace, duping people with antislavery propaganda designed to divert attention from the women and children in the mills and mines. It is now clear that by the early 1830s, in both England and the United States, the movement attracted significant support from artisans and other skilled workers; that in England the swelling "pressure from without" ran ahead of the elite antislavery leadership, embarrassing Thomas Fowell Buxton in his negotiations with government ministers; and that a few reformers moved from an apprenticeship in the abolitionist campaign to more radical activism as Chartists or labor reformers.[17] But these facts in no way invalidate the hegemonic argument when properly understood.

Hegemony, as Eugene D. Genovese has written, implies no more than the ability of a particular class to contain class antagonisms "on a terrain in which its legitimacy is not dangerously questioned."[18] Ideological hegemony is a process that is never complete or total; it can be understood in different ways by opposing groups or classes as long as it limits the terms of debate, heads off more fundamental challenges, and serves to reinforce the legitimacy of the ruling groups and existing order. Obviously antislavery agitation had very different meanings in 1814, 1833, and 1838, and a detailed analysis would be required to show the degree to which abolitionism stabilized or destabilized Britain's social and political order at a particular moment in time. But a few preliminary points can be made in response to the common view of an expansive, one-directional surge of democratic consciousness.

No doubt many British workers empathized with colonial slaves and understood abolitionist principles in ways that would have deeply troubled Wilberforce, Buxton, and Zachary Macaulay. But rank-and-file abolitionists could not escape the fact that the governing classes had appropriated the cause and defined the terms of the debate. Britain's landlords, merchants, and manufacturers had made it clear that there were varieties of exploitation that would no longer be tolerated in England or on the high seas; that there were forms of labor, even in the distant colonies, that would have to be brought more in line with metropolitan standards. This affirmation of moral standards helped to legitimate both the existing system of class power and the emerging concept of free labor as an impersonal marketable commodity. The 1833 Emancipation Act gave assurance to Britons of various classes that there were limits to the rapid socioeconomic changes taking place: workers could not literally be reduced to chattel slavery; owners of even the most questionable form of private property could not be deprived of their capital without generous compensation.

While the politics of slave emancipation were extremely complex, the act of 1833 fostered the illusion that the newly reformed Parliament had become an almost democratic assembly that would respond to the voice of a moral majority. The succession of antislavery victories and official commitments, beginning with the order-in-council of 1805 restricting the slave trade to conquered colonies, vindicated trust in the government's basic sense of justice. It is no wonder that when various British groups wanted to dramatize their own oppression or lack of freedom, they complained that their condition was at least as bad as that of West Indian slaves. Defenders of colonial slavery had opened this door, and the argument implied two propositions: first, that to receive attention one had to meet the "slavery test" by enumerating horrors equivalent to those in abolitionist literature; second, that since Parliament and the middle-class public were attuned to this language, the same techniques that had brought Parliament to bestow liberty on West Indian slaves would also bring freedom and justice at home.

In effect, the antislavery radicals were addressing the governing classes as follows: wage labor under present conditions leads to even worse misery than chattel slavery; since you responded to moral arguments in abolishing the slave trade and in freeing the colonial slaves, you should now relieve the distress of England's poor. But this reinforcement of ruling-class standards is precisely what is meant by ideological hegemony. Denunciations of "wage slavery" were a way of expressing outrage and resentment over working conditions in industrial Britain and America. But as Christopher Lowe points out, there could be no lower standard than to ask that free laborers be treated better than slaves.[19] Everyone knew that white workers were not really slaves. The analogy, whatever its emotive power, invited a rhetorical response celebrating the benefits of the market and the inestimable privilege of being free to change employments. The dichotomous terms of this debate forced radicals to prove that in some fundamental respects wage earners were no freer or better off than slaves.

There can be no doubt that abolitionism contributed to more radical kinds of social criticism. Especially in the United States, where slavery was abolished in a cataclysm of violence, radical labor leaders and socialists found that parallels between black and white slavery retained resonance well into the twentieth century.[20] But analogies with chattel slavery may also have retarded the development of a vocabulary that could depict more subtle forms of coercion, oppression, and class rule. To be a free worker was to be as unlike a Negro slave as possible. Most opponents of slavery equated unjust domination with a legalistic conception of property rights in human beings. This absolutist approach often made it difficult to distinguish the forms of domination concealed by voluntary contracts and the "bundle of powers" that could be exercised over nominally free workers.

I have already responded implicitly to many of the criticisms of my hegemonic thesis, but Seymour Drescher's forceful arguments deserve some further comment.[21] There is a seeming disjunction between Drescher's attacks on the hegemonic thesis (especially in "Cart Whip and Billy Roller") and his substantive findings on popular political mobilization. In his essay "Paradigms Tossed," he accuses me and other "historians of ideology" of "accepting Williams's premise that humanitarian ideals cannot alone explain the emergence and triumph of antislavery. . . ." But this premise has been accepted by Reginald Coupland, Roger Anstey, and virtually every historian of the antislavery movement, including Drescher himself. Even the abolitionists never presumed that humanitarian ideals could alone account for their triumphs.

In a number of statements Drescher also seems to question those historians who accept his main critique of the Williams thesis but who continue to seek "alternative explanations somehow grounded in fundamental economic development." He cites Peter C. Emmer's conclusion that even if Drescher's *Econocide* overturned most of the factual grounding of the Williams thesis, there still "remains something unassailable in this thesis concerning the connection between economics and abolition." Since Drescher never reveals his own stand on this issue and moves on to expose the deficiencies of the "ideological historians" who have sought to find indirect links between abolitionism and economic change, many readers may assume he rejects any connection between humanitarian ideals and economic or ideological interests. Yet Drescher affirms that British abolitionism became "engrafted onto other everyday practices of commercial capitalism." He refers to the slave-sugar b⸻ weapon of consumer capitalism." It was only in Britain, ⸻ very ideology "became rooted as a national social move-⸻ ge of the Industrial Revolution." Drescher seems pos-⸻ he finds that the petition campaign of 1787 originated ⸻ ancashire and was launched by "a portion of Man-⸻ manufacturing interests that had led the petition ca⸻ ed customs union with Ireland. What are we to mak⸻ een capitalism and antislavery? One need not doubt Thor⸻ s sincerity as a radical abolitionist to suspect that antislavery and capitalist enterprise formed part of a coherent world view.

Drescher's research on petitioning and popular mobilization has greatly enriched our understanding of British abolitionism. Historians were long aware that the abolitionist leaders were eager to advertise their cause as emanating from the voice of the united people. Although some of the more conservative London abolitionists feared that popular agitation would get out of hand, no pains were spared to circulate petitions at public meetings and in taverns and workshops as well as churches. We can never know the motives of most petition signers, but Drescher has demonstrated with graphic new detail the extraordinary popularity of the cause. One should add that in 1833 slave emancipation was no less popular in the House of Commons, where the final bill passed by an overwhelming majority. But why should so many Britons of different rank and background be concerned about Negro slavery, an institution thousands of miles away across the Atlantic?

Drescher never quite confronts this question. He does note that "the abolitionist crowd" "was not seeking a local rectification of a deviation from a traditional moral order, but demanding increasing overseas conformity to an emerging metropolitan moral order." This is precisely the argument that I and other "ideological historians" have made. But why should so many Britons *care* about overseas conformity? Why should Manchester's capitalists and artisans want to extend their "everyday political and economic activity" to a campaign that would bring them no tangible political or economic rewards? When there were so many competing human rights and humanitarian causes, why should colonial slavery take center stage? Free-labor ideology—which Drescher wrongly sees as somehow inconsistent with his own approach— provides a plausible answer. The anti-slave-trade petitions, Wedgwood's medallions, the slave-ship prints, the innovations in public communication— all symbolized the "progressive" spirit of Lancashire's labor system and cotton boom.

Drescher pictures British abolitionism as part of a larger liberating, modernizing process. I accept this view with one crucial reservation: the process was also oppressive, exploitive, and controlling. Drescher frames the debate in binary terms of either this or that. It is inconceivable that a social movement could both inspire working-class reforms and provide the moral capital to legitimate a new alliance of elites. Yet the evidence suggests that abolitionism served different social functions and had different meanings for various groups and classes. As Drescher has shown, the antislavery petitions of 1823 and 1824 stimulated petitions for political reform and other domestic causes. But Thomas Clarkson, who canvassed the country for many months soliciting antislavery petitions and organizing nearly 200 antislavery societies, emphasized that only the daily flow of petitions from all parts of the country would support the *government* as it withstood the "threats and clamor of interested persons." Clarkson also reassured Lord Liverpool that the petitions were "respectable beyond all precedent" and showed a complete unity of

Whigs and Tories, of Churchmen and Dissenters, of supporters and opponents of Liverpool's administration.[22] No one could make this claim for the petitions calling for domestic reform.

The theory of ideological hegemony presupposes continuing conflict over the meaning of shared beliefs and commitments. The key question is not whether abolitionism "hegemonized" the working class, as Drescher puts it, but the degree to which the movement encouraged other forms of protest or reinforced the moral authority of local and national elites. When Clarkson traveled through England, Wales, and Scotland, he sought out chief magistrates, vicars, curates, bankers, solicitors, industrialists, and dissenting clergymen. Some of these "leading men" opposed organizing a local antislavery society and argued that the matter should be left entirely to the government. Other seized the opportunity to lead a local meeting. Some groups favored immediate emancipation and a boycott of all slave produce. In Carlisle, however, an antislavery committee expressed the fear that a consumer boycott would be most injurious to the slaves, who would either starve or "retire into the woods and lead there a *savage* life."[23] It would require a detailed study of numerous towns and districts to sort out the local meanings of antislavery and to determine the degree to which the movement destabilized local structures of power.

Drescher's most valuable contribution is his elucidation of the distinctive political culture that enabled the people to exert pressure on the British government. His discussion of Continental countries suggests that a "highly articulate political life" was a necessary precondition for a successful antislavery movement. One should note, however, that the United States had not only met that test but had moved far beyond Britain in devising institutions for the expression of popular sovereignty. American abolitionists tried to follow Britain's example of popular political mobilization, but with extremely disappointing results. Drescher does not seem to appreciate how weak and isolated the American abolitionists were, at least until the rise of the Republican party. Even by the late 1850s there was no groundswell of opinion demanding slave emancipation.

Surely the British people were not morally superior to the Americans; there must have been as many humanitarians per capita in the United States as in Britain, and evangelical Christianity reached a larger proportion of the American population. But in the United States, unlike Britain, slave emancipation threatened vital metropolitan interests. In Britain, where Drescher notes that abolitionism "lacked the ingredient of potential metropolitan upheaval," the governing elites could tolerate and even encourage reforms that redeemed the national character and enhanced their own authority. In contrast, Drescher finds that French antislavery was "distinguished by an inability to combine a stable élite leadership with a mass appeal."[24] That is what I meant by hegemony.

Notes

1. Howard Temperley, "Eric Williams and Abolition: The Birth of a New Orthodoxy," in *British Capitalism and Caribbean Slavery: The Legacy of Eric Williams,* ed. Barbara L. Solow and Stanley L. Engerman (Cambridge, England, 1987), pp. 229–257.
2. Roger Anstey, "Reflexions on the Lordship of Christ in History," *Christian,* 3/1 (Michaelmas, 1975), 69–80. See also David Brion Davis, "An Appreciation of Roger Anstey," in *Anti-Slavery, Religion, and Reform: Essays in Memory of Roger Anstey,* ed. by Christine Bolt and Seymour Drescher (Folkstone, England, 1980), pp. 11–15.
3. C. Vann Woodward, *Thinking Back: The Perils of Writing History* (Baton Rouge, 1986), p. 112; Richard Wightman Fox, *Reinhold Niebuhr: A Biography* (New York, 1985), p. 181.
4. See especially Seymour Drescher, "Cart Whip and Billy Roller: Antislavery and Reform Symbolism in Industrializing Britain," *Journal of Social History,* 15/1 (Sept., 1981), 3–24; Drescher, *Capitalism and Antislavery: British Mobilization in Comparative Perspective* (New York, 1987); and Drescher, "Paradigms Tossed: Capitalism and the Political Sources of Abolition," in *British Capitalism and Caribbean Slavery,* pp. 191–208; Thomas L. Haskell, "Capitalism and the Origins of the Humanitarian Sensibility," Part 1, *The American Historical Review,* 90/2 (April, 1985), 339–361; and Part 2, *The American Historical Review,* 90/3 (June 1985), 457–566; Betty Fladeland, *Abolitionists and Working-Class Problems in the Age of Industrialization* (Baton Rouge, 1984). David Eltis's *Economic Growth and the Ending of the Transatlantic Slave Trade* (New York, 1987) and Robert William Fogel's *Without Consent or Contract* (New York, 1989) extend my own arguments and show that they are not incompatible with the main empirical findings of Drescher and Fladeland. I am grateful to Professors Eltis and Fogel for allowing me to read early versions of their own extremely important manuscripts. I am also much indebted to Christopher Lowe, a Yale graduate student, whose seminar paper on "Ideology, Hegemony and Class Rule in *The Problem of Slavery in the Age of Revolution*" helped to clarify my own thinking.
5. Haskell, "Capitalism," Part 1, p. 344.

6. Davis, *The Problem of Slavery in the Age of Revolution, 1770–1823* (Ithaca, N.Y., 1975), p. 42.

7. Cited in Davis, *Problem of Slavery in the Age of Revolution*, pp. 462–463. Since I am responding to misreadings of this book, I will draw most of my examples from it.

8. Davis, *Slavery and Human Progress* (New York, 1984), p. 218.

9. Quoted in Davis, *Problem of Slavery in the Age of Revolution*, pp. 366–367. Wilberforce also warned in 1807 that Britain's afflictions might be a prelude to much worse divine punishment if the nation persisted in the criminal slave trade (*Letter on the Abolition of the Slave Trade* [London, 1807], pp. 4–6).

10. Davis, *Problem of Slavery in the Age of Revolution*, pp. 466–467.

11. See especially Drescher, "Cart Whip and Billy Roller," p. 4.

12. Davis, *Problem of Slavery in the Age of Revolution*, p. 455.

13. *Ibid.*, pp. 455, 467–468. Seymour Drescher has greatly amplified these themes, which do not contradict my position, as he seems to think. No doubt I should have cited more varied examples of the linkage between denunciations of colonial slavery and wage slavery, and I was unaware of the language in petitions that Drescher has discovered. It was my intention to explore this subject in a succeeding volume on the "Age of Emancipation." Drescher does not seem to deny that Wilberforce, Stephen, Macaulay, Clarkson, Cropper, Buxton, and the other national leaders of the early period were unsympathetic to the wage-slavery argument, which they associated with their enemies.

14. Iain McCalman, "Anti-Slavery and Ultra-Radicalism in Early Nineteenth-Century England: The Case of Robert Wedderburn," *Slavery and Abolition*, 7 (September 1986), 99–117.

15. Christopher Lasch, "The Great American Variety Show," *New York Review of Books*, Feb. 2, 1984, p. 36.

16. Sean Wilentz, *Chants Democratic: New York City and the Rise of the American Working Class, 1788–1850* (New York, 1984), pp. 162–168, 183–190, 382.

17. For a discussion of the pressure exerted on Buxton and the Parliamentary abolitionists, see Davis, *Slavery and Human Progress*, pp. 195–202. Seymour Drescher's *Capitalism and Antislavery* emphasizes the broad-based, popular character of the antislavery movement. For abolitionist Chartists, see Betty Fladeland, "'Our Cause being One and the Same': Abolitionists and Chartism," in *Slavery and British Society, 1776–1846*, James Walvin, ed. (Baton Rouge, 1982), pp. 69–99.

18. *Roll, Jordan, Roll: The World the Slaves Made* (New York, 1974), p. 26.

19. Lowe, "Ideology, Hegemony and Class Rule," p. 7.

20. Barry Herbert Goldberg, "Beyond Free Labor: Labor, Socialism and the Idea of Wage Slavery, 1890–1920," Ph.D. dissertation, Columbia University, 1979.

21. I address some of Thomas Haskell's arguments in "Reflections on Abolitionism and Ideological Hegemony," *The American Historical Review*, 92/4 (Oct. 1987), part of which replicates this essay. The entire debate with Haskell is contained in Thomas Bender, ed., *The Antislavery Debate* (Berkeley, California, 1992).

22. Thomas Clarkson to John Gibson (?), March 7, 1824, Howard University Library; Clarkson to Lord Liverpool, May 3, 1823, British Library Add. MS 38,416, fols. 391–392.

23. Thomas Clarkson, MS Diary, 1823–1824, National Library of Wales.

24. Drescher, *Capitalism and Antislavery*, p. 53.

Part IV

The Violence of Slavery as Experienced

18

The White World of Frederick Douglass

Frederick Douglass
William S. McFeely (1991)

If Abraham Lincoln ultimately transcended the racism that infected most of his white countrymen, he could never forget the virulence, omnipresence, and political usefulness of the disease. When Lincoln, a Republican moderate, spoke out in 1856 against the geographic extension of slavery, Illinois Democrats accused him of "the most ultra abolitionism" and the *Illinois State Register* claimed that "his niggerism has as dark a hue as that of [William Lloyd] Garrison or Fred Douglass."[1] Two years later, during his great debates with Senator Stephen A. Douglas, Lincoln found himself more closely tied to Frederick Douglass, the most celebrated black leader in America—and to the bugaboo of "racial amalgamation."

Stephen Douglas, in his attacks on Lincoln and the "Black Republicans," repeatedly referred to his near namesake as one of Lincoln's "advisers," as an architect of the conspiracy to destroy the old Whig party, abolitionize the North, and propagate the doctrine of racial equality. In view of Lincoln's "conscientious belief that the negro was made his equal, and hence is his brother," Douglas proclaimed, amid bursts of laughter, "he is worthy of a medal from father [Joshua] Giddings and Fred Douglass for his Abolitionism." On two occasions, at Freeport and Jonesboro, the Little Giant reinforced his appeals to racial hatred with the image of a black man—in this case Frederick Douglass himself—fraternizing as an equal with a young (in one version, "beautiful") white lady. Referring to an incident in 1854, when Frederick Douglass had reportedly come to Illinois in order "to speak on behalf of Lincoln, [Lyman] Trumbull and abolitionism against that illustrious Senator [Lewis Cass]," Stephen Douglas recalled, "Why, they brought Fred Douglass to Freeport when I was addressing a meeting there in a carriage driven by the white owner, the negro sitting inside with the white lady and her daughter." "Shame," cried the Jonesboro crowd. As Douglas made clear when he debated Lincoln at Freeport, where the response of the audience was mixed, the kind of man who thought that his wife should ride in a carriage with a Negro, "whilst you drive the team," "of course will vote for Mr. Lincoln."[2]

After trying repeatedly to overcome the stigma of "niggerism," Lincoln could not have been pleased when in the fourth debate Stephen Douglas presented a copy of a recent speech made by Frederick Douglass "to a large convention" in Poughkeepsie, New York. Although Stephen Douglas said he had no time to read from the speech, he affirmed that Lincoln's "ally" "conjures all the friends of negro equality and negro citizenship to rally as one man around Abraham Lincoln, the perfect embodiment of their principles, and by all means to defeat Stephen A. Douglas." ("It can't be done," yelled the crowd.)[3]

Douglas's summary was quite accurate. Frederick Douglass, as William S. McFeely tells us, was by then the most famous runaway slave in America. In a long and eloquent address commemorating West Indian emancipation, he eventually turned to the current political contest in Illinois, since he considered Stephen Douglas "one of the most restless, ambitious, boldest and most unscrupulous enemies with whom the cause of the colored man has to contend." "It seems to me," Frederick Douglass quipped,

> that the white Douglas should occasionally meet his deserts at the hands of a black one. Once I thought he was about to make the name respectable, but now I despair of him, and must do the best I can for it myself. (Laughter.) I now leave him in the hands of Mr. Lincoln, and in the hands of the Republican Party of Illinois, thanking both the latter.

Having exposed Stephen Douglas's hopeless dilemma of trying to reconcile the doctrine of popular sovereignty with the Dred Scott decision, Frederick

Douglass quoted with admiration the central passages from Lincoln's recent "House Divided" speech.[4]

But Douglass was far from being a consistent supporter of Lincoln, even after his first cordial meeting with the president in 1863. He was outraged after the election of 1860 by Lincoln's "slave-hunting, slave-catching and slave-killing pledges," by which he meant Lincoln's commitment to enforce the Fugitive Slave Law of 1850, and he exploded with anger in 1862 when Lincoln became involved in colonization schemes based on his long-held view that "a universal feeling," such as the refusal of "the great mass of white people" to extend equality to blacks, "whether well or ill-founded, can not be safely disregarded."[5] As James M. McPherson has pointed out, Negro-phobia was rampant in the dismal summer of 1862, and racial fears "constituted the [Republican] party's Achilles' heel." Looking for indirect means to prepare public opinion for slave emancipation and convinced that "support for colonization was the best way to defuse much of the anti-emancipation sentiment that might otherwise sink the Republicans in the 1862 elections," Lincoln summoned a committee of free blacks from the District of Columbia for a meeting at the White House.[6]

No extenuating circumstances can excuse Lincoln's supercilious tone as he told the members of the delegation that the black presence was to blame for the Civil War and lectured them on their duty to persuade people of color to emigrate to the coal mines of Central America. This was perhaps Lincoln's worst moment. Yet various black leaders, such as Martin Delany and Henry Highland Garnet, had been better prepared than Douglass to reflect on the basic "fact" or reality that Lincoln tried to describe: the perpetuity of racial conflict and the seemingly hopeless future that black people faced in the United States. Acknowledging that "your race are suffering, in my judgment, the greatest wrong inflicted on any people," Lincoln grimly observed that "you are cut off from many of the advantages which the other race enjoy. The aspiration of men is to enjoy equality with the best when free, but on this broad continent, not a single man of your race is made the equal of a single man of ours, Go where you are treated the best, and the ban is still upon you."[7]

With good cause blacks denounced Lincoln's address in protest meetings in a number of Northern cities, although a few dissenters agreed that white supremacy and prejudice could never be overcome. Douglass shrewdly noted that

The tone of frankness and benevolence which [Lincoln] assumes in his speech to the colored committee is too thin a mask not to be seen through. The genuine spark of humanity is missing in it, no sincere wish to improve the condition of the oppressed has dictated it. It expresses merely the desire to get rid of them, and reminds one of the politeness with which a man might try to bow out of his house some troublesome creditor or the witness of some old guilt.

Douglass called Lincoln "a genuine representative of American prejudice and Negro hatred" who revealed "all his inconsistencies, his pride of race and blood, his contempt for Negroes and his canting hypocrisy."[8]

In one year the exigencies of war had produced revolutionary changes and prospects that wholly transformed Douglass's view of Lincoln. The Emancipation Proclamation, coupled with the enlistment of black troops in the Union army, showed that a Union victory would depend on black military manpower as well as on the destruction of slavery. In Douglass's eyes, "Once let the black man get upon his person the brass letters, U.S.; let him get an eagle on his button, and a musket on his shoulder and bullets in his pocket, and there is no power on earth which can deny that he has earned the right to citizenship."[9] Douglass soon became the most famous government agent recruiting black troops throughout the North; his son Lewis, a sergeant major in Colonel Robert Gould Shaw's celebrated Fifty-Fourth Massachusetts, was one of the lucky survivors of the assault on Fort Wagner.

Despite his conviction that military service could help win the "double battle" against Southern slavery and Northern racial prejudice, Douglass became increasingly angered by the government's refusal to appoint blacks as commissioned officers; by the disparity in pay between black and white Union soldiers; and especially by Lincoln's lack of response to the Confederate government's announced policy of executing or enslaving black prisoners of war. Fortunately, Lincoln issued an order to retaliate against the latter atrocity before Douglass traveled to the White House on August 10, 1863, to present the grievances of his people.

In a letter written shortly after the interview, Douglass emphasized that he "[w]as received cordially and saw at glance the justice of the popular estimate of his qualities expressed in the prefix *Honest* to the name Abraham Lincoln." Nearly four months later, in a speech to an antislavery convention, Douglass elaborated on this point: "I never met with a man, who, on the first blush, impressed me more entirely with his sincerity, with his devotion to his country, and with his determination to save it at all hazards."

Lincoln had good-naturedly referred to a speech Douglass had made attacking "the tardy, hesitating and vacillating policy of the President of the United States." The president had then defended himself by stressing the tactical importance of timing and preparation in view of the fact that "the colored man throughout this country was a despised man, a hated man."[10] McFeely concludes that Douglass "felt at ease in [Lincoln's] presence, with no sense of inferiority," and "came away convinced that once Lincoln had taken a position favorable to the black cause, he could be counted on to hold to it." For his part, Lincoln, who later summoned Douglass to the White House to discuss a desperate plan to encourage slaves to seek freedom behind Union lines, was reported to have said that Douglass was "one of the most meritorious men in America."[11]

In one of the characteristic insights that give unity to his fine biography, McFeely writes that Douglass's first visit with the president in "the Executive Mansion itself, was a crowning achievement for the [slave] boy who had once sneaked into Wye House," the Eastern Shore of Maryland mansion of Colonel Edward Lloyd, who employed as his plantation manager Aaron Anthony, Frederick Douglass's original owner. The progression from Wye House to the White House brings us to an extremely complex question: Frederick Douglass's relationships with whites.

Although Douglass (originally named Frederick Bailey) experienced the appalling cruelties of slavery, the wrath of Negrophobic mobs, and the more subtle slights and cuts of unconscious racism, he also had a series of unique encounters with white people that seemed to refute Lincoln's basic assumption about the universality and intractability of racial prejudice. From his early childhood as a slave boy who could only fantasize about the identity of his white father, Douglass, who was extraordinarily attractive, encountered whites who played with him, nurtured him, protected him, educated him, guided him, praised him, saved his life, endowed him with financial support, cheered and applauded him, loved him, and honored him. It was not out of character for Douglass at age sixty-six to marry a white woman twenty years younger than he; or for him to return as a celebrity to the plantation manor, where, as McFeely puts it, "the once-slave sipped madeira with a great-grandson of the lord of Wye House, whose portrait, still on its walls, the slave child had once surreptitiously studied with wondering imagination."

McFeely is sensitive to the nuances of Douglass's relationships with whites and portrays these ties and close relations without ever suggesting a betrayal of race on Douglass's part or even a desire to be white. McFeely also does his best to animate Douglass's intimate relationships with blacks: with Betsy Bailey, his heroic grandmother who provided him with an example of resourcefulness when he spent his first six years in her small cabin; "good Father Lawson," a Baltimore lay preacher; John and Henry Harris, field hands and close friends with whom the seventeen-year-old Douglass risked life and limb in an abortive conspiracy to escape bondage; Anna Murray, the free black woman whom Douglas married after they successfully fled from Baltimore to the North; Thomas James and other free black abolitionists who gave protection, support, and encouragement to the fugitive couple as they finally found refuge in New Bedford, Massachusetts. If these ties with an African-American community remain shadowy, it is not a shortcoming of McFeely's research, which is more extensive than that of any previous Douglass biographer. The surviving record, including what McFeely calls Douglass's "three unidentical autobiographies," shows, along with an unswerving dedication to racial equality, a constant attraction to the white world.

As a small child Frederick developed a close friendship with Daniel Lloyd, the lonely son of the patriarch of Wye House. Though Daniel was five years older, the two boys played and sported about the estate; Frederick attentively studied the behavior of Daniel's private tutor, brought from Massachusetts to educate the aristocratic colonel's son. At age seven, McFeely writes, Frederick "simply knew that he belonged inside the great house . . . [and] was ready to move in. There was only the fundamentally silly problem that, by accident, he was a slave." Slave or not, he was made into "something of a pet" by Lucretia Anthony Auld, his owner's daughter and the wife of Thomas Auld, who acquired title to Frederick through inheritance (and who may well have been his father).

Drawing on a masterful study by Dickson J. Preston,[12] McFeely captures Douglass's complex and ambiguous relationship with the Auld family: Lucretia and Thomas, Thomas's brother, Hugh, his wife, Sophia, and the latter couple's young son Tommy. Douglass's later attacks on the Aulds, which were part of his indictment of the entire slave system, "do not fully hide the fact," McFeely points out, that the adults "were four perplexed and limited people struggling to respond to the needs of an unusual boy who was also a slave."

The Aulds made a number of extraordinary decisions that unintentionally prepared the way for Douglass's successful escape into freedom and for developing his brilliant talents as an orator, writer, and social critic. In 1826, when Frederick was eight, Lucretia and Thomas decided to send him to Baltimore to live with Hugh and Sophia, who owned no slaves. In the normal course of events, as the Aulds well knew, Frederick would have remained within the stunting environment of the Eastern Shore and would probably have grown up to be a field hand, in continual danger of being sold like many of his relatives into the Deep South. When Sophia Auld welcomed Douglass into her home as a genuine human child, he later recalled, he encountered for the first time "a white face beaming with the most kindly emotions," a woman who became "more akin to a mother, than a slaveholding mistress." Except for one brief but frightening interruption when he was forced to return to Eastern Shore and was in danger of being sold, Frederick lived in this "haven of cheerful affection" until he was fifteen, a household, as McFeely writes, "that gave him the security and a neighborhood that gave him the stimulation he needed to expand his wonderfully curious mind."

Treating Frederick like the older half-brother of her own son Tommy, Sophia read passages of the Bible to both boys and began to teach Frederick to read. Despite Hugh's disapproval and strong misgivings about subverting the foundations of white supremacy, he took no effective steps to prevent Frederick from studying Tommy's spelling book, reading the newspapers, hanging around the docks with a gang of boys oblivious to slavery, or buying and studying his own copy of a book entitled *The Colombian Orator,* a compilation of great speeches extolling liberty and conveying the message, in McFeely's phrase, that "oratory was power."

As the precocious slave boy weathered the storms of adolescence, he became increasingly aware that his fate lay in the hands of Thomas Auld, the master in whom he hoped to find, according to McFeely, "an uncle, an older brother, perhaps even a friend." Or, one might add, a father. When Thomas, now a shopkeeper in St. Michaels, Maryland, arranged for the return of the fifteen-year-old from Baltimore, Frederick futilely hoped that Thomas's religious conversion would "rescue him through either manumission or the creation of some special world within slavery." McFeely is convinced that "Frederick loved Thomas, and that love was returned," despite Douglass's brutal treatment by the farmer to whom Douglass was hired out and despite his later attempts to deny the complexity of his feelings toward Auld. The crucial fact is that Thomas Auld finally saved the rebellious teenager from an armed posse of would-be lynchers, resisted immense public pressure to sell Frederick out of the state, and sent him back to Baltimore to learn to be a skilled laborer, with the promise "that if he worked diligently at a trade (and stayed out of trouble) he would set him free when he became twenty-five." As McFeely astutely concludes, when Douglass finally achieved his great goal of freedom,

> he would be a debtor. Frederick Bailey owed his chance to seek freedom not to the camaraderie of the brave Henry Harris, but to the largesse of an ambiguous Thomas Auld. For his freedom—for his life—he would for the rest of that life be beholden to a white man whom he had loved and whom he now had to remember to loathe.

After his triumphal speech in 1841 to a wildly enthusiastic abolitionist audience in Nantucket, Douglass's relationships with individual whites were far too numerous and labyrinthine to be easily summarized or characterized. As he took up a career of ceaseless touring, public speaking, and agitating, often removed for extended periods from his illiterate wife and his growing children, white abolitionists traveled with him, roomed and dined with him, invited him to their houses, joined him in facing hostile crowds, and sat with him at night when he was denied a bed or berth because of his color. Douglass never expressed greater gratitude than he did to William A. White, a Harvard graduate and abolitionist agent whose head was gashed and teeth knocked out when he saved the already injured Douglass from a possibly lethal blow at the hands of a racist Indiana mob. "I shall never forget how like two very brothers we were ready to dare, do, and even die for each other," Douglass wrote to White, recalling that his friend had left a "life of ease and even luxury . . . against the wishes of your father and many of your friends" to do "something toward breaking the fetters of the slave and elevating the despised black man."

Like numerous white abolitionists, Douglass suffered a painful break with the overbearing and doctrinaire William Lloyd Garrison, whom he continued to respect as a courageous pioneer. One may detect covert racism in the efforts of some white abolitionists to keep Douglass in a subordinate role, in their criticism of his "ingratitude," and in their indignation over his intimacy with Julia Griffiths, an Englishwoman who became an adoring companion and a kind of business manager for his newspaper, the *North Star*. But in reading McFeely's biography, one is struck by the absence of racism or subservience in Douglass's long and rich friendships with abolitionists like Amy and Isaac Post, Abby Kelley, Parker Pillsbury, Gerrit Smith, and Ottilia Assing, a German admirer and probable lover about whom McFeely presents important new material.

The fact that Douglass was accepted by many whites as a respected equal—especially during his nearly two years in Ireland, Scotland, and England in 1845–1847, where he became a celebrity, and "people of the highest rank," as his publisher wrote, "contend[ed] for his company"—helps to explain his underlying optimism about the imminent conquest of racial prejudice. No black leader I know of was more acutely sensitive to white condescension or more aware of the ubiquity in the Northern United States of the refrain, "*We don't allow niggers in here!*"[13] But no other leader was so sanguine on the prospects for racial equality and racial integration, or so convinced that these goals were part of a more general struggle for women's rights, temperance, and social uplift. The very qualities that made Douglass such an effective and eloquent critic in the pre-emancipation era have rendered his legacy increasingly open to question.[14]

Horace Greeley summed up a central antislavery and Republican dogma regarding the effects of slavery on human progress: "Enslave a man and you destroy his ambition, his enterprise, his capacity. In the constitution of human nature, the desire of bettering one's condition is the mainspring of effort."[15] Clearly enslavement had no such effect on the "mainspring" of Frederick Douglass, and he presents a special problem for his modern biographers. Modern academia, devoted as it is to producing elites, has long professed a deep suspicion as well as distaste for upward mobility. McFeely almost conveys a shudder when he mentions Douglass's "best-known stock-in-trade lecture," on "Self-Made Men." Yet when every allowance is made for the blacks and whites who educated Douglass and who gave him indispensable support, his life still adds up to a stunning case of individual achievement—an achievement that defied the prevailing system, not one that showed that merit was rewarded "regardless of race."

Occasionally, McFeely's portrait is marred by remarks revealing the shadow of the Douglass he would like to find—a convivial populist who, having worked as a caulker and field hand, never lost a taste for merging and carousing with the proletariat. McFeely shows little sympathy for Douglass's remarkable self-discipline, temperance, ambition, and commitment to bourgeois moral values. Yet the very traits that made Douglass a great writer, powerful orator, and one of his century's most trenchant critics of slavery, racism, and sexual inequality were inseparable from his drive for self-improvement. It was this confidence that social democracy could actually be advanced when individuals are enabled to overcome seemingly insuperable obstacles that provided a bridge of respect between Douglass and Abraham Lincoln.

Notes

1. *The Collected Works of Abraham Lincoln*, Vols. 1–9, Roy P. Basler, editor (Rutgers University Press, 1953), Vol. 2, p. 344.
2. *The Collected Works of Abraham Lincoln*, Vol. 3, pp. 3, 5, 6, 10, 55–56, 105. Jonesboro, located toward the southern tip of Illinois, was far more hostile to abolitionists than was Freeport, in the extreme north of the state.
3. *The Collected Works of Abraham Lincoln*, Vol. 3, pp. 171–172.
4. *The Frederick Douglass Papers, Series One: Speeches, Debates, and Interviews*, John W. Blassingame, editor (Yale University Press, 1979), Vol. 3, pp. 233–237. As the editors of the Douglass papers note, Douglass raised the issue that Lincoln posed some weeks later in his famous "Freeport question," "although forms of the question had been extant for some time" (p. 234, note 36). For Douglass's visit to Illinois in 1854, including his views of Stephen Douglas and play on the common name, see *Frederick Douglass Papers*, Vol. 2, pp. 541–559.
5. *The Collected Works of Abraham Lincoln*, Vol. 2, p. 256.
6. James M. McPherson, *The Battle Cry of Freedom: The Civil War Era* (Oxford University Press, 1988), pp. 506–509; *The Collected Works of Abraham Lincoln*, Vol. 5, pp. 370–375; David W. Blight, *Frederick Douglass' Civil War: Keeping Faith in Jubilee* (Louisiana State University Press, 1989), pp. 122–147. McFeely writes that President Lincoln "had only two private conversations with Douglass—and none with other black leaders, except for the famous meeting with *creole de couleur* gentlemen from New Orleans just before the president's death . . ." (p. 235). Since the first interview with Douglass was not *entirely* "private" (Senator Samuel C. Pomeroy was present), this appears to be an error. But McFeely may not regard the brief responses of the black delegation headed by Edward M. Thomas to constitute a "conversation," even if these were the first free African Americans to have an official audience with an American president.
7. *The Collected Works of Abraham Lincoln*, Vol. 5, pp. 371–375.

8. Blight, *Frederick Douglass' Civil War*, p. 139.

9. McPherson, *Battle Cry of Freedom*, p. 564.

10. *Frederick Douglass Papers*, Vol. 3, p. 607.

11. Gabor S. Boritt, *Lincoln and the Economics of the American Dream* (Memphis State University Press, 1978), p. 174. In 1865, McPherson notes, "Lincoln went out of his way to welcome Frederick Douglass to the inaugural reception on March 4," and also admitted blacks for the first time to White House social functions (*Battle Cry of Freedom*, p. 840).

12. Dickson J. Preston, *Young Frederick Douglass: The Maryland Years* (Johns Hopkins University Press, 1980), reviewed in *The New York Review* by George M. Fredrickson, June 27, 1985.

13. See Douglass, *My Bondage and My Freedom* (Arno Press reprint, 1968), pp. 371–373.

14. For the ambiguities of Douglass's literary legacy, extending from Booker T. Washington to Malcolm X and Eldridge Cleaver, see David L. Dudley, *My Father's Shadow: Intergenerational Conflict in African American Men's Autobiography* (University of Pennsylvania Press, 1991).

15. Quoted in Eric Foner, *Free Soil, Free Labor, Free Men: The Ideology of the Republican Party before the Civil War* (Oxford University Press, 1970), p. 46. Douglass showed precisely how the wounds inflicted by slavery were used to stigmatize the victims: "Ignorance and depravity, and the inability to rise from degradation to civilization and respectability, are the most usual allegations against the oppressed. The evils most fostered by slavery and oppression are precisely those which slaveholders and oppressors would transfer from their system to the inherent character of their victims. Thus the very crimes of slavery become slavery's best defence. By making the enslaved a character fit only for slavery, they excuse themselves for refusing to make the slave a freeman" (*Frederick Douglass Papers*, Vol. 2, p. 507).

19

Life and Death in Slavery

Celia: A Slave
Melton A. McLaurin (1991)

Bloody Dawn: The Christiana Riot and Racial
Violence in the Antebellum North
Thomas P. Slaughter (1991)

On occasion, as with the two excellent books under review, a gifted historian may discover a remarkable story about ordinary people that illuminates the laws, themes, and disputes of history. This interplay between private lives and public events enables the reader, who knows in retrospect how the official scroll of time will unfold, to recapture the contingency of the past, to enter a world when, for example, no one could predict how long the Fugitive Slave Law would be in effect or know whether Kansas would become the next slave state.

Robert Newsom and Edward Gorsuch, the murdered slaveholders who are the subject of the books by Melton A. McLaurin and Thomas P. Slaughter, were not owners of great plantations but rather presided over prosperous family farms. Gorsuch ruled a homestead in Baltimore County, Maryland, that had belonged to his family for nearly two centuries. Between 1819 and 1822 Newsom and his family had migrated from Virginia to the new slave state of Missouri, where they had settled in the rich river bottom lands of Callaway County, due west of St. Louis and almost precisely in the center of the state. In 1850 Newsom was sixty years old, Gorsuch fifty-five. Both were fathers of grown children and were respected members of their border state communities. McLaurin's portrait of Newsom as "the self-sufficient yeoman farmer," "the fulfillment of the Jeffersonian dream" applies equally well to Edward Gorsuch.

Neither Newsom nor Gorsuch was rich, but for both of them a lifetime of hard work and shrewd management had brought satisfying rewards. Newsom's farming region was noted for its healthy herds of livestock and its impressive crops of wheat, rye, corn, and oats. In 1850 Newsom owned, in addition to his eight hundred acres of land, eighteen horses, six milch cows, twenty-seven beef cattle, seventy pigs, twenty-five sheep, and two oxen. Gorsuch owned twelve horses, fifty pigs, thirty sheep, some forty cows, and flocks of chickens and ducks. Both Newsom and Gorsuch had been able to provide opportunities and advantages to their children. Even in 1855, when Newsom was sixty-five and a widower, he shared his house with two daughters who were nineteen and thirty-six, to say nothing of the latter's four children, who ranged in age from twelve to four.

These family farmers, almost archetypal of the mid-nineteenth-century American, one a western "pioneer," the other a settled native of the East and a "class leader" in the local Methodist Episcopal church, seem far removed from the popular image of the cotton-growing slaveholder. Yet in 1850, 36 percent of the slave labor force had nothing to do with cotton cultivation; 43 percent lived on plantations or farms with fifteen or fewer slaves.[1] Edward Gorsuch owned twelve slaves including four young adult field hands. Robert Newsom owned five male slaves including a five-year-old boy. Then, in 1850, he purchased a girl named Celia, who was about fourteen, the same age as his own youngest child, Mary. There was nothing unusual about such ownership of human beings. The neighbors of Newsom and Gorsuch, including the business and professional men in towns like Fulton, Missouri, commonly bought their first slave, often a household servant, when they began to become prosperous. What distinguished Newsom and Gorsuch was the fact that both of these aging farmers were murdered by their own slaves.

Blacks who lived on farms or small plantations had little opportunity to form slave communities that might provide some protection from white surveillance, interference, instruction, domination, and exploitation. The historical controversy over the black family has seldom recognized that families headed by the mother were 50 percent more frequent on plantations with fifteen or fewer slaves than on larger units, or that black women were more sexually vulnerable to white men when they lived apart from genuine slave communities.[2] Nothing could dramatize this point more forcefully than McLaurin's eloquent account of how Robert Newsom purchased the teenage Celia for his own sexual pleasure. As McLaurin puts it: "Newsom seems to have deliberately chosen to purchase a young slave girl to fulfill this role [as a sexual partner], a choice made the more convenient by the ability to present the girl as a domestic servant purchased for the benefit of his daughters." Presumably because it had been about a year since his wife had died, the sixty-year-old farmer could not even wait until he had driven Celia home from neighboring Audrain County. He raped the girl on the way.

McLaurin is both scrupulous and imaginative in his interpretation of the evidence, which sometimes presents glimpses of slavery that are almost never revealed in other accounts but which then becomes mute at the most frustrating points. There can be no doubts about Celia's own suffering, anguish, and humiliation during the five years that Newsom kept her as his sexual slave. Newsom may well have granted her favors and expressed affection— he built her a comfortable brick cabin with a large fireplace, and assumed that she would always welcome his nocturnal visits. He never acknowledged, however, the two children she bore, who were almost certainly his own progeny. Celia's later actions gave expression to a kind of accumulated hatred few males could ever feel.[3]

The most intriguing questions concern the thoughts of Newsom's family and even neighbors, such as William Powell, who led the search when Newsom disappeared and who interrogated Celia and finally got her to confess. Though McLaurin considers the possibility "that Newsom managed to conceal his relationship with Celia from the family. Or, [that] family members might have chosen to ignore the relationship, to convince themselves that it did not exist," it seems inconceivable that Celia's sexual relations with Newsom could have been kept a secret. Virginia Waynescot, Newsom's eldest daughter, who was either a widow or separated from her husband, had managed her father's household since her mother's death. The mother of four children, the youngest apparently conceived after her husband died, Virginia would certainly have noticed her father's movements to Celia's cabin, only fifty yards from the family home, as well as the birth of Celia's presumably light-skinned children. The same can be said of Virginia's sister Mary and her brothers Harry and David, all of whom lived in the Newsom house after Celia had replaced their mother. Citing the example of Senator James Henry

Hammond, who passed on a slave mistress to his son, McLaurin even speculates that David, at age seventeen, may have hoped to share Celia's sexual favors.

In dealing with the sexual exploitation of black women McLaurin might have said more about the conflict between Victorian images of respectability and the world of male boasting, outhouse talk, and whispered exclamations over black female sensuality. Certainly Celia's public trial for murder, which revealed the facts of her sexual relationships, must have been the main subject of gossip in central Missouri. Evidence that many of the citizens in the region were sympathetic to Celia suggests a significant division of opinion regarding the sexual exploitation of a teen-age slave, even on the part of slaveholders. McLaurin could well have said more on this point.

He does consider, however, the possible feelings of Newsom's daughters. The comments of Southern women in other cases suggest that the daughters might have sympathized with Celia and deplored their father's behavior; more likely, McLaurin writes, they regarded Celia as "the dark, sensual temptress who seduced their father." In any event, Mary and Virginia were financially dependent on Newsom, who also supported Virginia's four children. In view of the patriarchal structure of Southern society, the sisters were unlikely to take up Celia's cause, even when she privately appealed to them in 1855 to put a stop to their father's sexual advances, citing pregnancy and a long illness as her reasons.

Celia had an even more pressing reason. She had fallen in love with George, one of Newsom's young slave workers, who had begun spending time at her cabin and who demanded that she cease sexual relations with their master. Much has been made in historical literature about the powerlessness of male slaves to "protect" their wives and lovers. George proved to be a feckless protector, since he implicated Celia when Newsom suddenly disappeared. He helped the Newsom family search for his master's remains, and he then deserted Celia and fled the farm as soon as she got into trouble. But initially George stiffened Celia's own formidable courage and made her resolve that she would confront Newsom. To retain George's affection, Celia decided on a Saturday night in June 1855 that she would resist Robert Newsom—at first with words and then, if necessary, with a club she had prepared for such a purpose.

This decision obviously involved grave risks. Even when she had later been convicted of murder and was about to be hanged, Celia stuck to her story that neither George nor anyone else had been an accomplice. Yet in June she was pregnant and ill and could hardly expect that a stick would deter a healthy farmer who had raped her and who could easily have her flogged for insubordination or sold her apart from her small children in the more lucrative slave markets of the Deep South. By Celia's account, Newsom ignored her pleas and warnings; he kept advancing until she struck him on the head; as he sank down and then threw up his arms as if to catch her, she grabbed the club with both hands and hit his skull with all her might (in her final confession, she said that as soon as she first struck Newsom, without intending to kill him, "the Devil got into me, and I struck him with the stick until he was dead").

Panicked at first by Newsom's death, Celia finally decided to burn the body in her large fireplace. Without commenting on the symbolism, McLaurin vividly describes Celia's success in picking out and crushing Newsom's bones and in later persuading Virginia Waynescot's son Coffee to remove his grandfather's ashes. Nothing is known about the response of Celia's own children, who must have been awakened by the heat of the fire and the stench of their father's burning corpse.

McLaurin juxtaposes the story of Celia's inquest and trial, extending from June to October 1855, with the rising national furor over attempts to legalize slavery in Kansas Territory. As a result of the Kansas-Nebraska Act passed in the preceding year, which repealed the Missouri Compromise and delegated the decision on slavery to "popular sovereignty," members of the proslavery and free-soil factions rushed to the contested ground of Kansas, due west of Celia's Missouri. The vigilante tactics used in Kansas by Missouri's "border ruffians" presented a sharp contrast with the procedural correctness of Celia's trial. At a time of such national turmoil over slavery, Judge William Hall, a Democrat with strong Unionist feelings, was determined to show that a slave like Celia could receive what he considered a fair trial. But the Kansas issue inflamed Missouri politics in ways that may have worked as much against Celia as in her favor.

McLaurin's main point, however, is that Celia's trial revealed deep and disturbing truths about the institution which Democratic politicians and officials were determined to impose on Kansas even against the will of a majority of settlers. A century earlier John Woolman, the great Quaker reformer, had insisted that no human beings were saintly enough to avoid being corrupted by the kind of power slaveholding entailed. Woolman had spoken in general terms and had not addressed the special corruption of limitless power over women—as evidenced, for example, by the absence of any laws against the rape of slave women. Although nineteenth-century abolitionists called attention to the sexual abuse of female slaves, Southern reformers failed to enact any legislation to protect women, although they enacted other laws that showed concern for the safety and well-being of human property. They dared not infringe on the owner's control over the reproductive capacities of his female slaves. In effect, the law not only condoned Newsom's kind of behavior but stripped slaves of most distinctions of gender.[4]

Since Celia confessed that she had killed her master, Judge Hall might easily have arranged a perfunctory defense leading to a quick trial and execution. He probably got more than he bargained for when he chose John Jameson, a seasoned trial lawyer and former congressman, to represent Celia, as well as two young attorneys who had been well-trained in legal research. All three were slaveholders or came from slaveholding families, but Jameson clearly believed that Celia was morally innocent. He and his young assistants were determined to prove that she was not guilty of murder, even if this meant challenging some of the basic premises of American slavery.

Jameson knew that everything hinged on Judge Hall's instructions to the jury. Jameson's success in bringing prominent and respected witnesses to the stand would mean nothing unless the issue of Celia's motives could be made central to the jury's deliberations. In principle Judge Hall could have instructed the jury that Celia was innocent of first-degree murder if she had acted in self-defense, fearing for her life; or if she had not intended to kill Newsom; or if she had struck him "without deliberation and premeditation, and in the heat of passion." Jameson managed to present evidence on these points, but when it came to the argument over the jury's final instructions, Judge Hall sustained objections from the prosecution, and made no reference in his charge to such mitigating circumstances.

Apparently the defense lawyers anticipated this outcome and adopted another strategy which was, as McLaurin writes, "as bold as it was brilliant." They shifted the argument from self-defense, which some Southern courts had extended to slaves accused of capital crimes, to sexual honor. Missouri statutes, according to the defense, entitled "any woman" to use deadly force to protect her honor when a man attempted to compel her against her will to have sexual intercourse. Moreover, in Jameson's view the law held that the woman's previous sexual conduct conferred no absolute right, even on the part of a slave master, to compel the slave woman to have sexual intercourse with him. The defense built its elaborate argument on the premise that the words "any woman" in an 1845 Missouri statute applied to slaves as well as to free white women. McLaurin rightly points out that this "radical" request to "extend the protection of the general statutes to Missouri's slave population" would in effect have nullified "the underlying concept of slave codes" and threatened "the very foundations of the institution of slavery."

Although McLaurin underscores the moral implications of the personal choice Judge Hall now had to make, he interprets the judge's denial of the defense's instructions as "practically a foregone conclusion." Jameson, however, by no means accepted the inevitability of Celia's conviction and execution for first-degree murder. Accusing Hall of delivering "illegal" instructions to the jury before Celia's conviction, the defense moved for a new trial. Two days before Celia was scheduled to be sentenced, she and a black male convict were somehow allowed to "escape" from the Callaway County jail (the male convict was promptly returned, however). Celia's lawyers took no steps to free her but sought to prevent her execution before a ruling could come from the Missouri Supreme Court. In a personal appeal addressed to a newly elected member of the court, the defense claimed that a majority of Callaway's citizens opposed Judge Hall's refusal to issue a stay order to prevent Celia's execution: "The greater portion of the community here are much interested in her behalf."

McLaurin skillfully builds suspense by combining an account of a proslavery army gathering around the well-armed antislavery town of Lawrence, Kansas, with a discussion of the political views of the three justices of the Missouri Supreme Court who on December 14 finally examined Celia's case and found no grounds for an appeal or for a stay of the execution. Celia, who had been returned to custody, went to the gallows on December 21. McLaurin could find no record of what happened to her two children (her third pregnancy ended in miscarriage), though he notes the possibility that a nine-year-old girl owned in 1860 by one of Newsom's sons was in fact "Celia's daughter, and his half sister." Without ever moralizing McLaurin conveys the raw horror and "psychic costs" of a legal and thoroughly American institution that condoned the rape, sexual abuse, and hanging of a girl known only as Celia.

Edward Gorsuch, the Maryland farmer who in status and success so closely resembled Robert Newsom, must have had misgivings about the ethics of perpetual servitude. He adopted the policy of setting his slaves free at the age of twenty-eight. In *Bloody Dawn*, the historian Thomas Slaughter cautions us not to marvel at such seeming generosity. While taking account of Gorsuch's Quaker ancestry, the moral influence of his church, and his reputation for honor, fairness, and liberality, Slaughter makes the point that farmers in northern Maryland had less need for a permanent year-round labor force as they shifted from tobacco production to livestock and cultivating wheat. The continuing demand for slaves in grain-producing regions like Callaway County, Missouri, casts some doubt on the adequacy of this explanation. But certainly in northern Maryland the number of slaves had declined dramatically by 1850, and no other slave state came close to Maryland in either the absolute or relative size of its free black population.[5] As Slaughter notes, Gorsuch could easily have sold any slaves for whom he had little use in the markets of the Deep South. Instead, he offered them freedom and even seasonal jobs and a place to live if they wanted to continue working for him.

Slaughter describes Gorsuch as "a good man" who, presumably like most masters, repeatedly misjudged the character of his slaves. Events would show, he writes, that Gorsuch was also "a stubborn, foolhardy, and hot-tempered man." He could not comprehend why, in 1849, after he had learned that some of his slaves had been stealing and selling his wheat, four of the young men should have fled his farm and headed north to the free state of Pennsylvania. All four had been promised their freedom when they turned twenty-eight, and Gorsuch saw himself as an exemplary Christian master who could be counted on for fair and just treatment. He blamed Abe Johnson, the free black who had tried to market the stolen wheat, for deluding his "boys" and luring them away from the warmth and security of the farm. Because the issue involved his sense of honor and his own self-image as a master who was respected and even loved by his servants, Gorsuch could not simply write off the escape as a tolerable financial loss or a premature manumission. He became obsessed with finding some way to communicate with the fugitives, confident that he could persuade his "boys" to return.

Gorsuch's slaves were among the 279 fugitives who escaped from Maryland in the year preceding July 1850. This mostly northward trickle of slaves from Maryland and other states hardly threatened to undermine the South's system of labor, but it infuriated Southerners, who increasingly feared a loss of national acceptance of an institution that Northerners clearly wished to exclude from the western territories and that had already been abolished in the British, French, and Danish colonies, to say nothing of the Hispanic-American republics. As part of the momentous Compromise of 1850 the South demanded and won a rigorous new fugitive slave law which allowed a master like Gorsuch to seek the aid of a federal commissioner, who could issue warrants, gather posses, and force bystanders or other Northern citizens to help catch any black who was alleged to be a runaway slave.

The law denied African Americans a jury trial and the right to testify in their own defense, accepted an affidavit by the claimant as sufficient proof of ownership, and awarded commissioners ten dollars for returning a fugitive to the claimant and only five dollars for freeing a captive wrongfully held. The federal government therefore in effect sanctioned not only Southern slavery but the kidnapping of free blacks in the North. Despite white acquiescence in many parts of the North, this act provoked a decade of civil disobedience, legal challenge, and active resistance.[6]

Indignant over his own slaves' lack of gratitude, Edward Gorsuch soon became one of the first white victims of that resistance. For two years he responded to every lead and rumor that might enable him to locate and communicate with his errant "boys." Then in late August 1851 he received a letter from an informant in Lancaster County, Pennsylvania. It reported that Gorsuch's slaves had found a refuge within the rural African American community in southeastern Pennsylvania and provided detailed instructions on how to reclaim them. Against the advice of his son Dickinson, Gorsuch boarded an express train for Philadelphia on September 8, expecting to be joined by a small party of relatives and neighbors. The fugitive-slave commissioner appointed Henry H. Kline, known among blacks as "a professional kidnapper of the basest stamp," as the marshal to lead the Gorsuch posse. Gorsuch never suspected that he was blundering toward the headquarters of a black mutual-protection organization—a group of fugitives and their supporters who, as Slaughter puts it, "had practiced the arts of guerrilla warfare and had gained confidence in their ability to fight."

After several mishaps, the armed posse of six marched before dawn on the morning of September 11 toward the stone house of William Parker, a tall mulatto fugitive known as "the preacher," who had emerged as the brave leader of black resistance against kidnappers and the racist assaults of the nearby "Gap Gang." The seven blacks in Parker's house, including two of Gorsuch's fugitives, had received news of the expedition and were armed to resist. They were not impressed by Marshal Kline's warrants, though Parker's brother-in-law feared that the blacks' cause was hopeless. After an exchange of shots, the blacks requested time to consider Gorsuch's appeal to surrender, perhaps because they were "just stalling for time," as Slaughter suggests, "until friends could respond to the summons of the horn" that Parker's wife Eliza had blown from the attic.

Slaughter barely mentions one of the most remarkable incidents of this initial standoff, as later recalled by Parker: a debate between the black "preacher" and the Methodist "class leader" on the biblical justifications for slavery.[7] At a moment when the fortified blacks might have killed or wounded members of the posse, the leaders exchanged citations from Scripture that echoed the arguments that were then raging in theological schools, colleges, and learned journals. The blacks at Parker's house then broke into a popular spiritual about Judgment Day and dying on the field of battle with glory in the soul.

The arrival of neighbors soon complicated matters. Castner Hanway, a white miller and Parker's nearest neighbor, rode up on a work horse, soon followed by Elijah Lewis, the local postmaster and shopkeeper. In response to Eliza Parker's horn blasts, scores of blacks, many of them armed with guns, began to converge on the house. The intentions of Hanway and Lewis are unclear, but they refused to assist Marshal Kline and sensibly advised him and the posse to leave in order to avoid bloodshed. This infuriated Kline, who saw the need to flee but who warned Hanway that he would be subject to the stiff penalties provided by the Fugitive Slave Act for refusing to aid a marshal. If Gorsuch could not at that moment recover his slaves, Kline argued, he could at least be assured that the courts would find the miller financially liable for the value of his property. Like others in his party, Gorsuch was convinced that only a white like Hanway could be the leader of such organized resistance. Yet as Kline and other members of the posse began to withdraw, only Gorsuch refused to be intimidated by the immense crowd of African Americans who kept brandishing their weapons in mock battle.

The climax came when Gorsuch went back to Parker's house and finally confronted one of his slaves, who in freedom had taken the name Samuel Thompson. "Old man, you had better go home to Maryland," Thompson said. "You had better give up," Gorsuch answered, "and come home with me." Like Celia, Thompson then struck his master on the head, but with a pistol instead of a club. He hit Gorsuch again when the white man tried to rise from his knees, and then shot the patriarch who claimed to own and even care for him. Others fired bullets into Gorsuch's body or gouged his head with corn cutters. According to one legend, widely believed in the South according to Slaughter, the African American women mutilated Gorsuch's body and cut off his penis. Other whites were wounded in the accompanying melee but managed somehow to escape. Gorsuch became a Southern martyr.

There is something elemental in the confrontations between Gorsuch and Thompson and between Newsom and Celia. The master, backed by legal authority, asserts a claim that flows from his sense of omnipotence and need of recognition, as Hegel put it, by a "slavish consciousness" "which embodies the truth of his certainty of himself."[8] Yet both Thompson and Celia no longer see themselves as slaves. As the master persists, they issue warnings and then strike out in protest, not with a lethal blow but with one that brings the master to his knees. Once the barrier of authority has been broken, the slaves lose all restraint. Once unleashed, rage leads to the mutilation or consumption of the master's body—to the total negation of honor, respect, and lordship.

The "Christiana Tragedy" resulted in what Slaughter calls "the largest mass indictment for treason in the history of our nation." Partly because the law of treason was so confused, thirty-eight men were charged on 117 separate counts of "levying war" against the government. Yet William Parker and many other black suspects, including Gorsuch's four fugitives, escaped to Canada. National attention therefore shifted to the trial of Castner Hanway, an alleged abolitionist and leader of the blacks and the defendant against whom the government believed it had the strongest case. Opponents of the Fugitive Slave Law, including the powerful abolitionist establishment, flocked to Hanway's defense and helped to secure his acquittal. To the outrage of Maryland and other Southern states, charges were then dropped against other white and black defendants.

Slaughter's admirably researched book describes Hanway's trial and devotes much attention to the general history of race relations and violence in southeastern Pennsylvania. Unfortunately, the story of Gorsuch trails off into an account of other unrelated riots, crimes, and trials. This material is often fascinating, but the reader never learns what happened to Parker and the other black fugitives in Canada, or how the acquittal of Hanway influenced abolitionist resistance and impinged on other fugitive-slave cases. Slaughter's conception of social history is both informative and limited. His prose conveys his loathing of all varieties of "social control"; he even links the use of animals in medical research with "our violent past," including the violent past of slaveholders. Yet like so many social historians of his generation, he is warmly sympathetic to the "working-class culture of drunken recreational violence." Whatever one thinks of such bias, Slaughter, along with McLaurin, has reconstructed a sequence of events that goes to the heart of American slavery.

Notes

1. Robert William Fogel, *Without Consent or Contract: The Rise and Fall of American Slavery* (Norton, 1989), pp. 44, 179.
2. Fogel, *Without Consent or Contract*, p. 179.
3. There is a growing literature, especially by feminist legal scholars, on the "battered woman syndrome" and on abused women who kill men in self-defense.
4. Ironically, the abolitionists remained ignorant of Celia's treatment and her motives for killing Newsom, which would have provided ideal material for sensational moralizing. William Lloyd Garrison's *Liberator* ran a brief account of Newsom's death in a feature called "Catalogue of Southern Crimes and Horrors."
5. In 1850 slaves constituted 97.1 percent of the black population of Missouri, but only 54.7 percent of the black population of Maryland. Only 17 percent of Baltimore County's population was black, and only 3.2 percent were slaves (Barbara Jeanne Fields, *Slavery and Freedom on the Middle Ground: Maryland During the Nineteenth Century*, Yale University Press, 1985, pp. 2, 11–13).
6. After the Wisconsin Supreme Court declared the Fugitive Slave Act unconstitutional, the U.S. Supreme Court, in *Ableman* v. *Booth* (1859), upheld the law's constitutionality and asserted the supremacy of federal law and federal courts over the states.
7. Jonathan Katz gives a fuller account in *Resistance at Christiana: The Fugitive Slave Rebellion, Christiana, Pennsylvania, September 11, 1851, A Documentary Account* (Thomas Y. Crowell, 1974), pp. 88–90. Slaughter seems uninterested in the religious side of the fugitive slave question, which was absolutely central for many abolitionists and other Americans, and he fails to discuss any sermons on the Christiana trial.
8. My use of Hegel draws on my own book, *The Problem of Slavery in the Age of Revolution, 1770–1823* (Cornell University Press, 1975), pp. 559–562.

20

The Ends of Slavery

Narrative of a Five Years Expedition
against the Revolted Negroes of Surinam
John Gabriel Stedman, transcribed for the first time from the
original 1790 manuscript, edited by Richard Price and Sally Price (1988)

The Overthrow of Colonial Slavery, 1776–1848
Robin Blackburn (1988)

The Arrogance of Race: Historical Perspectives
on Slavery, Racism, and Social Inequality
George M. Fredrickson (1988)

Robin Blackburn's monumental book *The Overthrow of Colonial Slavery* re-
produces on the front of its dust jacket the extreme right-side portion of
John Trumbull's patriotic painting *The Death of General Warren at the Battle
of Bunker's Hill*. A young American lieutenant, "wounded in the sword hand,
and in the breast," as Trumbull described the scene, turns in hesitation as he
flees the American redoubt on Breed's Hill, wondering if he should sacrifice
his life in a vain attempt to save General Joseph Warren. Close by his side
stands "a faithful negro," actually a black combatant named Peter Salem,
who holds in readiness a cocked flintlock musket. So at the outbreak of the
American Revolution, a black rifleman stands shoulder to shoulder with a
white American patriot holding a sword in his left hand and wearing a
plumed hat.[1]

General Thomas Gage's Redcoats were not the only European troops shipped out to quell a colonial revolt. During the week in June 1775 when the Americans inflicted over one thousand casualties on the British at Bunker Hill, Captain John Gabriel Stedman reported that a detachment of Dutch colonial troops in Suriname had, while wading through a deep marsh, been ambushed by the rebels they were pursuing. As we learn from the account Stedman later wrote, now published for the first time in an accurate edition, the news jolted Stedman's professional marines, who had been sent over from Holland more than two years earlier, into a state of high alert.[2]

In Suriname, in contrast to the North American colonies, the rebels in this "First Boni War" (1765–1777) were all escaped black slaves or the descendants of fugitive slaves. Such people were called maroons throughout the Caribbean islands and *marronnage* had been a chronic problem for Europeans from the time of their first settlements in the New World; communities of maroons appeared and often flourished in the wilderness from Río de la Plata to Virginia.[3] Nowhere, however, were maroons more successful in defending their independence than in the Dutch colonies of Guiana, particularly in the colony of Suriname. Today the six tribes descended from these maroons, living primarily in the interior rain forests, make up over 10 percent of Suriname's population.

In 1760 and 1762, after a century of struggle, the two major groups of Surinamese maroons—the Djuka and Saramaka—had won treaties from the Dutch colonists acknowledging their independence and even promising a regular supply of arms and supplies. But in the colony of Berbice, to the west of Suriname, the black slave population rose in a mass revolt in 1763, seizing control of much of the sugar colony until troops sent from Holland, Suriname, and other neighboring colonies finally crushed the rebels' dreams of founding an independent black kingdom.

Although the Djuka and Saramaka of Suriname had pledged themselves to return fugitive slaves (as had Jamaican maroons in 1739), their inland communities were an inducement to slaves to desert. In the late 1760s and early 1770s new maroon groups in Suriname began to coalesce in the forests, close to the plantations on the banks of the Cottica and Commewijne rivers. As these rebels set plantations ablaze and massacred their white inhabitants, more black slaves took to the woods. White settlers fled in panic to Paramaribo, the capital of Suriname, and it soon appeared that the entire colonial economy was on the brink of collapse. As Stedman's *Narrative* makes clear, "the revolted Negroe Slaves . . . may with truth be called the Terror of this Settlement if not the total loss of it—." A New World Haiti might well have emerged in some form without benefit of French Revolutionary ideology.[4] It was to prevent such an outcome that the Dutch States-General dispatched a corps of professional soldiers, later followed by reinforcements, to assist the jaded colonial troops.

The son of a Scots army officer and his Dutch wife, Stedman had grown up partly in Scotland and partly in Holland, joining at age sixteen the Scots Brigade that served the Dutch government. Proud of his physical strength and exploits at brawling, drinking, and wenching, Stedman was also an acute and intelligent observer who had a talent for drawing and an ardent interest in flora, fauna, and ethnography. His hot temper and the toughening exposure to frequent violence and death failed to blunt his unusual sensitivity to human or animal suffering. Fluent in English, Dutch, and French, he learned to speak Sranan, the creole language of Suriname's slaves and many whites. Stedman was ideally prepared to write what Richard and Sally Price, its editors, accurately term "one of the richest, most vivid accounts ever written of a flourishing slave society."

After retiring from military service in his early forties, Stedman settled in England and began drafting an account of his experiences abroad based on his notebooks and the log he had kept of daily events. The Prices, during their years of research in Holland, England, Suriname, and the United States, discovered that Stanbury Thompson, an English antiquarian who had acquired Stedman's diaries around 1940 from a London junk dealer and had sold them before his death in the late 1960s, had flagrantly distorted the text in his 1962 edition of Stedman's *Journal.* In addition to locating the original manuscript diaries and arranging their sale to the James Ford Bell Library at the University of Minnesota, the Prices found fifteen of Stedman's drawings and watercolor paintings, which as anthropologists they assure us are "ethnographically careful and accurate—considerably more so than many of the engravings modeled after [them]."

Stedman finished his long *Narrative* in 1790 and was later pleased when Joseph Johnson not only agreed to publish the book but engaged four engravers, including Francesco Bartolozzi and William Blake, to cut plates. Stedman established close ties with Blake, whose sixteen engravings included scenes of slave life that helped form the core of international abolitionist iconography for generations to come. What Stedman didn't know was that in 1794 Johnson hired William Thompson, a professional editor and man of letters, to rewrite the entire manuscript. In 1795, when Stedman saw the "mard" and bowdlerized printed book, "full of lies and nonsense," he exploded in anger and claimed to have burned two thousand copies. Although Johnson finally agreed to reinstate portions of Stedman's text, the Prices conclude that the edition finally published in 1796 was an "unhappy compromise."

It was the 1796 *Narrative*, however, that became a classic, was republished in twenty editions and translated into six languages. In 1978, thanks to the alert eye of Professor Stuart B. Schwartz, a distinguished Latin American historian now at Yale University, Richard Price found Stedman's original 1790 manuscript at the James Ford Bell Library. So after the passage of two centuries, we now have a superbly edited critical edition of the book Stedman actually wrote.

The 1790 *Narrative* is mostly written in direct, earthy prose that evokes the emotional response of a young European captain to the naked breasts of "beautiful Negroe Maids," to the clouds of ravenous "muskitos," to the tremors of tropical fever, and to the delight of stripping off all his sweat-soaked clothing and diving daily into the cool depth of a Surinamese river, a therapeutic secret confided to Stedman by Cramaca, a wise old slave. Cramaca also convinced Stedman that the motion from vigorous swimming would protect him from alligators and piranhas, or "p—k biters," as Stedman called them in his diary.[5]

Stedman's first editor deleted such references to nudity as well as frequent passages expressing anger and contempt for Colonel Fourgeoud, Stedman's commanding officer. He also diluted Stedman's portrayal of Suriname as a cornucopia of sexual pleasure for European males, who could choose between casual one-night stands or acquiring a slave mistress who, in addition to providing sex, "preserves their linnens clean and decent, dresses their Victuals with Skill, carefully attends them/they being most excellent nurses/during the frequent illnesses to which Europeans are exposed in this Country."[6] Thompson could not eliminate references to Joanna, Stedman's own beautiful mulatto mistress, but the 1796 edition gives no sense of Stedman's loving admiration of Joanna's dignity and superior talents, or of his belief in racial equality, repeatedly underscored by such affirmations as "in every respect I look on [the African Negro] as my brother," or "I love the African Negroes, which I have showed on numberless occasions."

Thompson's most significant revisions, the Prices believe, pertain to Stedman's views on race, slavery, and moral justice. The 1796 edition was published when British troops had suffered appalling casualties in order to preserve plantation slavery in the Windward Islands and were struggling to restore the institution in Saint Domingue, where black rebels and the French government had tried to abolish it. Stedman, as a retired army officer and conservative royalist, surely had sympathy for the British Caribbean troops and may well have approved the attempt to transform his *Narrative* into a proslavery tract. By the mid-1790s even the most conservative abolitionists were being denounced as covert Jacobins.[7]

In 1792 Stedman refused to sign one of the immensely popular petitions against the slave trade. Even in the 1790 manuscript he urges the reader to consider the "Proof" presented in an obdurate proslavery work by James Tobin, a wealthy planter who had written a blistering response to the Reverend James Ramsay, perhaps the most cautious and conservative of British abolitionists. Indeed, throughout the 1790 edition Stedman repeats the standard proslavery arguments that were voiced in Parliament and marshaled in pamphlets commissioned by the Committee of West India Planters and Merchants. Britain's tropical colonies, he wrote, could not be cultivated without the labor of African slaves; the colonies would inevitably be lost if Parliament interfered by adopting "rash" measures, a lesson supposedly proved by the recent American War of Independence; many of the West Indian slaves were treated with indulgence and enjoyed such diversions as fishing, swimming, dancing, making baskets and musical instruments, and socializing with their friends and families; they were infinitely happier and more secure than European soldiers, sailors, paupers, and prostitutes, or for that matter the millions in Europe who "annually expire under the name of Liberty, loaded with the pangs of want & disease, and crushed under the galling chains of oppression."[8]

But these proslavery passages seem perfunctory and lifeless, as if dutifully inserted to prove Stedman's "Manly" impartiality to potential subscribers and the readers of travel literature. Far from counterbalancing Stedman's descriptions of appalling torture, brutality, and slaveholder debauchery, unforgettably illustrated by Blake's engravings, the proslavery arguments could lend strength to the belief that Stedman was an objective eyewitness, untainted by effeminate abolitionist sentimentality. As Stedman first glimpsed Surinamese society, after stepping ashore, he saw a most miserable Young Woman in Chains simply covered with a Rag round her Loins, which was like her Skin cut and carved by the lash of the Whip in a most Shocking Manner. Her Crime was in not having fulfilled her Task to which she was by appearance unable. Her punishment to receive 200 Lashes and for months to drag a Chain of several Yards in length the one end of which was Lock'd to her ancle and to the other End of which was a weight of 3 Score pounds or upwards. She was a beautiful Negroe Maid.

The first image, which Stedman sketched for pictorial evidence, paled by comparison as he went on to witness blacks being mutilated, dismembered, and slowly burned to death. Confirming Voltaire's famous description of Surinamese slavery in *Candide*, Stedman echoed the judgment of Candide's dismembered black informant by estimating that in the slave colonies "in 20 Years two millions of People are murdered to Provide us with Coffee & Sugar." Stedman expressed particular outrage over the white "overgrown Widows, Stale Beauties, and overaged Maids" who out of jealousy disfigured, tortured, or killed young slave women. When Stedman tried to stop the merciless flogging of a beautiful slave girl who had refused to submit "to the loathsome Embraces" of an overseer, he learned that such interference always called for the redoubling of the punishment, and walked away imploring "the curse of Heaven to be poured down upon the whole relentless fraternity [of overseers]." Two years later he succeeded in rescuing "a Negro boy and a Girl Suspended from a high beam . . . in the most Agonising Tortures, and with theyr Shoulders half out of Joint," and swore "to Demolish the Overseer for inflicting this New mode of torture Without he Promis'd to forgive them which Miraculously did—."

The 1790 *Narrative* rivals the most radical abolitionist literature in its scathing portrayal of a slave society. As Stedman saw, the root of the problem lay in the corrupting temptations of unlimited power. There was no law or impartial authority that could prevent whites from killing slaves with impunity, from cutting off their ears or slitting their noses "from private Peek," or smashing out their "*Teeth* for Tasting the Sugar Cane Cultivated by themselves." It was no wonder, Stedman wrote, that slaves seized every chance to assemble armies of rebels in the forest "to Seek Revenge & Liberty." Stedman not only expressed frequent admiration for blacks, including a magnificent swimmer named Philander, "the Finest Man without Exception that Ever I saw in all my Life," but took pride in looking like a mulatto after cutting his hair short, having his skin darkened by the tropical sun, and his bare feet toughened by years of marching through the forests. During his seven agonizing campaigns against the rebels, Stedman also tried to learn from their "Masterly Manoeuvers" and built "a High Palace on 12 Stakes in imitation of *Bonys* [Boni] the Prince of the Rebels."

In many ways Stedman exemplified the preracist and pre-abolitionist mentality of a sensitive, outgoing man of the world who knew that life was filled with pain and death and who took slavery as much for granted as the disease and suffering he and his fellow soldiers experienced in the rain forests of Suriname. Though outraged by the extraordinary excesses of the plantation system, he was content in the end to propose modest political and legal reforms and to intersperse descriptions of exotic "Quadrupedes–Birds–Fishes–Reptiles, trees, Shrubs–Fruits & Roots" with recollections of sadistic brutality.

Stedman's perceptions of slavery were influenced by one crucial phenomenon that has been disconcerting for modern historians, especially those of the left. From Stedman's account it is clear that Suriname could never have survived without the aid of black soldiers who were carefully selected from the slave population and offered their freedom. Stedman called them "rangers," likening them to the rangers who fought the Cherokee in North America. Where the white troops were continually baffled and cut off from their supplies by the rebels, the black rangers knew the techniques of bush fighting and guerrilla warfare; in 1772 they had even discovered the secret underwater paths of communication to the main rebel base, thereby enabling the whites to capture it. "It will ever be my Opinion," Stedman wrote, "that *one* of these free negroes, was Preferable to half a Dozen White men in the *Woods* of Guiana, which Seemed their natural Element."

Stedman was astonished by the bravery of these black troops, by "theyr fidelity to the Europeans," and by their "implacable bitterness against the rebels," whom they mutilated or killed on the spot. The bitterness was mutual, since the rebels viewed the rangers as "Traytors—and betrayers of theyr Countrymen." In one instance, at least, the rebels were beaten back by plantation slaves who had been armed at the last minute by their master. While it should be emphasized that planters could never count on such performance and that Stedman often speaks of plots and insurrections, the fact remains that in the 1790s the British relied increasingly on "slaves in Red Coats" in their attempts to conquer Saint Domingue and defend their own slave colonies. Without the aid of such black power, including informers who revealed impending uprisings, it seems probable that the West Indian slaveholder regimes would have been overthrown during the last third of the eighteenth century.[9]

If Robin Blackburn fails to give this question the attention it deserves, it is one of the few weaknesses of his vast, complex, and powerful narrative that describes and accounts for the abolition of colonial slavery from the American Revolution to the revolutions of 1848. Blackburn, who edits the *New Left Review* in London, is the first historian since Eric Williams to present a comprehensive interpretation that connects the destruction of slave systems to the American and French revolutions, to the colonial revolts against imperial authority, and to the triumph of industrial capitalism in Britain. But Blackburn, profiting from and admirably synthesizing the vast scholarship produced since the publication of Williams's influential book *Capitalism and Slavery* (1944), is far less rigid and doctrinaire than Williams, much more attuned to the workings of politics. Unlike Williams, he includes slavery throughout the Western hemisphere (though he curiously fails to mention Canada).

In many respects Blackburn succeeds in his aim to move beyond the works of Williams, Eugene D. Genovese, and the present reviewer "to construct a Marxist narrative of the actual liberation struggles in the different areas of the Americas and to establish to what extent antislavery, either in intention or result, transcended the bourgeois democratic or capitalist dynamic." We can leave it to self-professed Marxians to debate just what is Marxist in his narrative. Blackburn emphatically rejects economic determinism and in fact shows relatively little interest in the economics of slavery or the development of new consumer markets. He repeatedly stresses the contingency of events, the unpredictable confluence of military, political, and ideological developments, and the irreducible importance of individual choice.[10] "The overthrow of slavery," he writes when discussing the impact of the French Revolution in Saint Domingue, "required conscious and dedicated protagonists as well as favourable conditions." He may well give too much attention to "elite" leaders to satisfy those who favor history "from the bottom up," though in Saint Domingue the black elite were less dedicated than the black masses.

All this said, no one can mistake Blackburn's sympathies or his casting of good guys and bad guys. In Saint Domingue, patriot "bands" clash with royalist "gangs." For him, the French Jacobins, who generally opposed interference with the Atlantic slave trade, are far more admirable than the American revolutionaries who outlawed slave imports and in 1777 adopted the first constitution in history (Vermont's) that prohibited slavery outright. Plebeian abolitionists are somehow more authentic than bourgeois abolitionists, especially those bourgeois motivated by Christian benevolence. Like C. L. R. James, the Marxist author of *Black Jacobins*, a major study of the Haitian revolution, Blackburn would like to convey "a marvellous sense of the eruption of the masses in history," and at one point he concludes that

> part of the grandeur of the great French Revolution is that it came to sponsor slave emancipation in the Americas; and part of the grandeur of the great Revolution in St. Domingue/Haiti is that it successfully defended the gains of the French Revolution against France itself. . . . Haiti was not the first independent American state but it was the first to guarantee civic liberty to all inhabitants.

As these samples indicate, Blackburn's rhetoric is sometimes haunted by a Marxist scenario of what should have happened. Remarkably, this ghost from the past seldom impedes Blackburn's quest to understand what did happen. Indeed, his flexibility, open-mindedness, and balanced judgments are characteristic of the best recent "Marxist" writing on slavery. It may not be coincidental, at a moment when Marxism is being subjected to intense self-scrutiny around the world, that Blackburn views the British antislavery movement as an instrument for progressive adaptation that eventually rendered the capitalist "ship of state more seaworthy in a storm."

Blackburn's highly readable narrative presents the political and social setting of the gradual emancipation acts in the northern United States, the violent overthrow of slavery in Haiti, the less decisive undermining of the institution during the Latin American wars of independence, the outlawing of the slave trade in 1808 by Britain and the United States, Britain's legislative emancipation in 1834 of some 800,000 colonial slaves, and the final eradication of slavery in the French and Danish colonies during the revolutions of 1848. It is welcome news that Blackburn, having published *The Making of New World Slavery* in 1997,[11] is preparing a final volume, *Nemesis of the Slave Power*, concentrating on the final struggle for emancipation in the three societies in which black slavery gained strength during the first half of the nineteenth century: the southern United States, Cuba, and Brazil (in Suriname and the other Dutch New World colonies, slavery persisted until 1863 but was of marginal economic importance).

The present volume, while containing informative chapters on the French and Haitian revolutions, Latin America, and the French restoration of slavery in the early nineteenth century, quite rightly centers on Britain. For it was Hanoverian Britain, the world's leading slave-trading nation, that executed a dramatic volte-face that led to costly efforts to eradicate the entire Atlantic slave trade and encourage abolitionist movements throughout the world. Most students of the question agree that Britain's conversion to antislavery ideology was related in some way to the Industrial Revolution, the need to legitimize and honor wage labor, and the bitter struggles over various demands for domestic reform. But as Seymour Drescher and David Eltis have argued, Britain's antislavery policies actually ran counter to the nation's economic self-interest.[12]

Blackburn agrees, in his central conclusion, "that slavery was not overthrown for economic reasons but where it became politically untenable." His rejection of economic causation extends to the historically naive theory that the spread of capitalism and market values cultivated new habits of thought, such as "thinking causally," which gave efficacy to the Golden Rule and made possible new and enlarged conceptions of moral responsibility, exemplified in abolitionism and other humanitarian movements.[13] Blackburn's narrative, so rich in significant detail, demonstrates the fallacy of divorcing an abstract "humanitarian sensibility" either from the political and class struggles within the British metropolis or from the militant actions of the colonial planters, the free blacks, and the slaves themselves.

Moreover, as Blackburn observes, abolitionists found it extremely difficult to win over merchants and manufacturers involved in trades that employed slaves precisely because "markets set up a structure which appeared to erase individual responsibility for the pattern of resultant action. Very often bankers and trustees would have been negligent of their clients' interests if they had not seized profitable openings available to them in the slave-related sector."

Although Blackburn tends to underestimate the religious sources of both white and black activism, he recognizes that the radical Agency Committee of the British abolitionists instructed its lecturers "to make clear that the central objection to slavery was humanitarian and religious," and that the movement "derived strength from its association with the critique of the operation of pure market forces, rather than their celebration."

Blackburn captures the dynamic tension between antislavery as a means of demonstrating the liberality of a privileged class or political regime and antislavery as a vehicle for challenging all hierarchical establishments. In the late eighteenth-century world of political upheaval and intrusive commercialization, antislavery and patriotism served "as secular correlates to [the evangelical religious] search for new meanings and a more stable and satisfying order, alike in the public and private spheres. The challenge to empire was accompanied and preceded by a generalised malaise, what might be called the 'legitimation crisis.'" By 1806, as the British government strained to maintain support for a seemingly interminable war and to stave off moves for major domestic reforms, various leaders began to see abolition of the slave trade as "the only reform measure which was simultaneously widely popular, agreed between leading members of the government and within the realm of the 'art of the possible.'" The final passage of abolition, according to Blackburn,

> dignified and elevated Britain's resistance to Napoleon and bid for global hegemony. The self-confidence of the ruling class was boosted and at least some of the ground-swell of democratic patriotism evident in 1804–6 harnessed to the war effort. . . . The passage of abolition offered symbolic satisfaction to middle-class reform while preserving unchanged the substance of oligarchic power. . . . Just as abolitionist legislation helped the oligarchy to assert its right to rule and deflect middle-class agitation for reform, so in the industrial districts middle-class abolitionism helped manufacturers to outface menacing combinations, cement ties with other respectable persons and assert their social conscience. The Luddites sought to halt or deflect capitalist industrialisation by threats of violence; the abolitionists proclaimed the need to pacify market relations and base them on a minimum respect for personal inviolability and autonomy.

But these conservative, legitimizing functions of the antislavery movement by no means stifled domestic protest or movements for radical reform, which in fact drew upon the techniques abolitionists used to call mass meetings, obtain hundreds of thousands of petition signatures, interrogate political candidates, and arouse and inform armies of disfranchised artisans, farmers, and women. Blackburn quite rightly stresses the ambiguous and changing character of the British antislavery cause. As "the least controversial reform" in an age of sharp class conflict, it attracted the crucial support of Lords Grenville, Grey, Derby, and other enlightened members of the oligarchy along with middle-class evangelicals and plebeian radicals like Robert Wedderburn, the son of a Jamaican slave woman, who preached to crowds in a large Soho hayloft chapel, calling for a republican revolution in England and a mass insurrection of West Indian slaves.

Except for some inconsistent rhetoric, Blackburn recognizes the contributions slaves and free blacks made to their own emancipation without succumbing to the romantic view that the black masses finally intimidated British policy makers, forcing them to choose emancipation as the only alternative to revolution. As Stedman's *Narrative* makes clear, the victories of black rebels in Suriname and Berbice failed to shake the resolve of the slaveholding Dutch.[14] Even the traumatic lesson of the Haitian revolution did not deter the French from restoring slavery in Guadeloupe and shipping at least 125,000 new slaves to their Caribbean colonies after the conclusion of the Napoleonic wars. Despite major slave revolts in Barbados in 1816, in Demerara in 1823, and in Jamaica in 1831, Blackburn concludes that for British rulers this slave resistance was not by itself "a decisive consideration."

Thanks to the restraint of the slaves, who hoped to strengthen the hand of their antislavery friends in Britain, these nineteenth-century revolts resulted in few white casualties. In Stedman's time the Guianese rebels had killed and terrorized whites throughout the interior. But in Demerara, one of the Dutch Guianese colonies later annexed by the British, thousands of rebels apparently inflicted only one casualty upon the governor's outnumbered forces, and were content to demand "Our right" and to plead for their own lands and three days a week to work for themselves. For this insubordination some 250 slaves were killed and many more flogged or imprisoned.

In the great Jamaican revolt of 1831 slaves burned cane fields and destroyed hundreds of buildings but killed few whites. Some 540 slaves were either executed or killed in the fighting by black and white colonial troops. As Blackburn points out, "the very revulsion prompted by the idea of slavery can lead to an oversimplified view of how easy it was to end it. . . . The odds were stacked against slave resistance. . . . Unifying the oppressed was extraordinarily difficult." If Britain had been willing to pay the political and economic costs, the West Indian garrisons could easily have been reinforced and slave resistance could have been contained, as it had been during the previous two centuries.

This conclusion should not distract attention from the decisive impact on

British public opinion of slave resistance and free black demands for equal rights. While much is still to be learned about the convergence of events that led to British emancipation, Blackburn goes beyond previous historians in illuminating the cumulative effect of diverse forces and the way antislavery became intermingled with other social and political contests. In the last analysis, the connection between capitalism and antislavery was indirect, in the sense that antislavery sentiment was promoted, however erratically, by the class conflicts and governmental structures that industrial capitalism produced.

Blackburn explicitly rejects the view that abolitionism was an instrument of capitalist "social control." He acknowledges that "abolitionism as an ideology was capable of directly articulating a fairly comprehensive projection of bourgeois ideals and capitalist disciplines." Yet in various countries the movement tended to alienate industrialists and business leaders and attract bourgeois reformers who had, he writes, "a generous and even utopian side to them." Major abolitionist leaders, such as Joseph Sturge in England, Victor Schoelcher in France, and (though not mentioned by Blackburn) Wendell Phillips in the United States, "remained eminently bourgeois without ever being in the mainstream or even specifically pro-capitalist." The one point missing in this otherwise accurate analysis is the central importance of religious commitment, at least among the British and American foes of slavery, blacks as well as whites.

Blackburn, whose treatment of United States history is rather superficial, gives little attention to race. And he is no doubt right when he concludes that "the blockages and delays encountered by British and French abolition stemmed more from the solidarity of the propertied classes than from racial solidarity." In the United States, however, historians have often begun with the central issue of "race relations" and have then approached slavery and antislavery as subsidiary parts of this larger field. This description applies to the work of the eminent Stanford historian George M. Fredrickson, who moved from a brilliant chapter on "The Meaning of Emancipation," in *The Inner Civil War: Northern Intellectuals and the Crisis of the Union* (1964), to write *The Black Image in the White Mind: The Debate on Afro-American Character and Destiny, 1817–1914* (1971) and *White Supremacy: A Comparative Study in American and South African History* (1981).

In *The Arrogance of Race* Fredrickson has assembled seventeen essays that diverge sharply from Blackburn's work in tone, method, and assumptions, to say nothing of style. This is not to imply that Fredrickson is in any way parochial, since he has been a pioneer in comparative history and devotes one essay in this volume to an analysis of white responses to slave emancipation in the American South, Jamaica, and the Cape of Good Hope. In his introduction and in the two essays published here for the first time, Fredrickson acknowledges his great intellectual debt to Max Weber, who has long provided him with a "pluralistic, multicausal approach as a point of departure for historical analysis," in contrast to "a Marxist class determinism or an idealist cultural determinism." Since Blackburn has also adopted a pluralistic, multicausal approach, one must still ask how the concept of race fits in with Fredrickson's laudable goals.

Having been attacked by neo-Marxians for elevating race above class, Fredrickson shows that he has always opposed the attempts by some historians "to find the origins of American racism in a cluster of deeply rooted or primordial [antiblack] sentiments brought from Europe by the early colonists and to play down the impact of the social and economic circumstances associated with the rise of plantation slavery." He has insisted, however, that "racism, although the child of slavery, not only outlived its parent but grew stronger and more independent after slavery's demise."

Fredrickson has an admirable ability to move from abstract theory to specific historical events, allowing each level of analysis to illuminate the other. His essays in *The Arrogance of Race* always show a sophisticated grasp of social theory as he moves from the limitations of planter-class paternalism to Lincoln's views of racial equality; from the historiographical legacy of C. Vann Woodward to the connections between colonialism and racism within "the full spectrum of multiracial societies resulting from the expansion of Europe and the development of a world capitalist economy." Written with clarity and elegance, this collection reconfirms Fredrickson's reputation as our leading authority on racism, antiracism, and the racial attitudes of whites.

Despite the strengths of Fredrickson's approach, the meaning of race itself remains curiously elusive. To what extent is race an ideological construction? How do we account for a man like Stedman, who for years fought black rebels and defended slavery and yet condemned racism as a moral insult to humanity? How could a black Jamaican-born tailor like Robert Wedderburn attract such an enthusiastic following among London's most oppressed and poverty-stricken whites, when in contemporary American cities a similar class of whites rejoiced in burning and looting black homes, schools, and churches? Why did definitions of blacks, mulattoes, quadroons—the very concept of "race"—differ so dramatically from one slaveholding region to another? Or for that matter, why did the riot in Nanjing become the occasion for such soul-searching by Chinese and Westerners over racism in China, a country far removed from any heritage of black plantation slavery? Are the concepts of race and class to be given equal ontological weight, as Fredrickson implies when he calls for an "interactionist approach" that refrains from giving theoretical priority to either category?

These are not questions one would expect to see resolved in a collection of essays concerned with biographical case studies, the historiography of southern race relations, and the promise of the comparative method. Whatever ambiguities still adhere to the historical construct "race," Fredrickson has led the way in lucidly tracing and analyzing the history of racism in America. And about the reality, iniquity, and persistence of American racism there can be no doubt.

Notes

1. Trumbull, who had watched the Battle of Bunker Hill from a distance, painted this scene in London in 1786. It now hangs in the Yale University Art Gallery. As Hugh Honour points out in his magnificent work, *The Image of the Black in Western Art*, Vol. IV: *From the American Revolution to World War I, Part I: Slaves and Liberators* (Harvard University Press, 1989), Trumbull's painting bore strong thematic and stylistic resemblances to John Singleton Copley's *The Death of Major Peirson*, in which a beplumed black soldier, fighting with the British who are resisting a French invasion of the Channel Island of Jersey, aims in Copley's words "his musquet at the French officer by whom his master was slain" (pp. 41–44). The two paintings, intended for American and British audiences respectively, reflect the fact that blacks fought on both sides in the American Revolution, many escaping by this means from slavery (for further illustrations and historical information, see Sidney Kaplan, *The Black Presence in the Era of the American Revolution, 1770–1800*, Smithsonian Institution Press, 1973).
2. Stedman later mentions the "Havock" of the Battle of Bunker Hill (p. 558) and encounters Tory refugees in Suriname, as well as American seamen who denounced Lord North and swore they would be willing to die in defense of American liberties.
3. The English word "maroon" and the French *marron* derived from the Spanish *cimarrón*, which first referred to domestic cattle that roamed off into the hills of Hispaniola.

See Richard Price, ed., *Maroon Societies: Rebel Slave Communities in the Americas* (Johns Hopkins University Press, 1979), and Gad Heuman, ed., "Out of the House of Bondage: Runaways, Resistance and Marronage in Africa and the New World," *Slavery and Abolition: A Journal of Comparative Studies*, Vol. 6, No. 3 (December 1985). For fascinating accounts and illustrations of the persistence of maroon culture in modern Suriname, see Richard Price, *First-Time: The Historical Vision of an Afro-American People* (Johns Hopkins University Press, 1983), and Richard Price and Sally Price, *Afro-American Arts of the Suriname Rain Forest* (University of California Press, 1980).

4. In effect, Palmares, the *mocambo* or "African state" in Brazil, fits this description. This large community of fugitive slaves resisted conquest through most of the seventeenth century. Unlike Haiti, of course, it did not have a formal constitution based on principles of the Euro-American Enlightenment.

5. In the 1790 *Narrative* Stedman avoids this term but refers to piranhas snapping off "the fingers and breasts of women and private Parts of Men." This passage was deleted from the 1796 edition and Thompson deleted the more graphic phrase from his edition of the *Journal*.

6. The Prices point out that Stedman himself censored the impersonal, commercial sexual exchanges recorded in his diary. He did make it clear, however, that European men were drained to exhaustion by their frequent relations with remarkably athletic black and mulatto women.

7. In an endnote the Prices carefully consider and then reject the possibility that Stedman's views on slavery may have hardened after 1790 and that he himself may have been responsible for some of the changes in the 1796 edition that they attribute to William Thompson, who had accepted commissions to write proslavery tracts at the time he was revising Stedman's manuscript. Their reasoning is partly convincing, but to this reviewer they fail to give sufficient weight to the proslavery passages in the 1790 manuscript and to the probable effects on a professional soldier and patriot of the "Black Jacobins" of Saint Domingue, Guadeloupe, and Grenada, who were killing thousands of Stedman's comrades.

8. For an informative description and analysis of proslavery ideology in Britain and the northern United States, which drew on the counterrevolutionary reaction of the late eighteenth and early nineteenth centuries, see Larry E. Tise, *Proslavery: A History of the Defense of Slavery in America, 1701–1840* (University of Georgia Press, 1988).

9. See especially Roger Norman Buckley, *Slaves in Red Coats: The British West India Regiments, 1795–1815* (Yale University Press, 1979), and David Geggus, *Slavery, War and Revolution: The British Occupation of Saint Domingue, 1793–1798* (Oxford University Press, 1981). This conclusion applies mainly to colonies populated by overwhelming black majorities. At the end of the eighteenth century Cuba and Puerto Rico had only begun to develop plantation economies.

10. Blackburn appears to find determinism in my own *Slavery and Human Progress*, which implies that "the unfolding of events is already pre-programmed" and which risks "trapping us in a closed history where the imperative of progress cannot be escaped"; that

was certainly not the message I intended to convey, though such idealistic determinism can be seen in many of the nineteenth-century writers I discussed.

11. See my review "A Big Business" in this volume.

12. See my essay "The Benefit of Slavery" in this volume.

13. This dubious thesis, which is reduced to ruins by Blackburn's narrative and explicit attack, can be found in Thomas L. Haskell, "Capitalism and the Origins of the Humanitarian Sensibility, Part 1," *American Historical Review*, Vol. 90, No. 2 (April 1985), pp. 339–361; "Capitalism and the Origins of the Humanitarian Sensibility, Part 2," *American Historical Review*, Vol. 90, No. 3 (June 1985), pp. 547–566. Critiques by John Ashworth and the present reviewer appear, along with a lengthy reply by Haskell, in the same journal, Vol. 92, No. 4 (October 1987), pp. 797–878. For the complete controversy see Thomas Bender, ed., *The Antislavery Debate* (University of California Press, 1992).

14. Blackburn discusses Stedman's 1796 *Narrative* in an endnote and quotes from Stedman the remarkable statement of a defiant rebel who in 1757 described to a representative of the government the slaves who had been abused and finally driven to the woods, "who by their sweat earn your subsistence, without whose hands your colony must drop to nothing, and to whom at last, in this disgraceful manner, you are glad to come and sue for friendship." Blackburn also refers to the black rangers recruited by the British and to black maroon leaders in Saint Domingue who practiced voodoo and cooperated with the British. He makes no effort to explain this betrayal of black solidarity.

21

White Wives and Slave Mothers

Life in Black and White: Family and Community in the Slave South
Brenda E. Stevenson (1996)

✳

Life in Black and White is an impressive example of the kind of local and regional history that for the last generation has transformed our understanding of the past. Brenda Stevenson has immersed herself so deeply in the private letters, diaries, school records, newspapers, and census schedules of Loudoun County, Virginia—and occasionally the records of some other Virginia counties—that she is able to bring to life a fascinating variety of Southern whites, black slaves, and free blacks while also providing a broad view of economic, demographic, and social change from the mid-eighteenth century to the Civil War. Stevenson also avoids the sentimentality and demonization that have characterized some of the best-known work on American slavery. As part of her major theme of racial differences between whites and blacks, she challenges prevailing beliefs regarding family life under slavery and thus contributes to the larger debate, which has taken many sharp turns during the past half-century, concerning the alleged weakness and pathology of the African-American family.

Loudoun County, stretching across rolling piedmont country east of the Blue Ridge Mountains and south of the Potomac, combined some of the characteristics of Virginia's tidewater plantation country with the ethnic and social diversity of border states like Maryland. Settled in the early eighteenth century by Quakers, Germans, Welsh, and Scotch-Irish, as well as by black slaves, the region also attracted such eminent planter families as the Carters, Byrds, Harrisons, Lees, Masons, Peytons, Janneys, and Powells. Both James Monroe and Robert E. Lee owned Loudoun estates, though neighboring Fairfax County was much richer.

As in tidewater Virginia, tobacco soon became the staple crop and for the few large planters the means to great wealth. Many of the richest eighteenth-century planters were "absentee" landlords like John Mercer, who owned plantations in three Virginia counties as well as in Antigua, in the Caribbean. It was not uncommon for a Loudoun planter to own land not only in other Virginia counties but in Maryland, Alabama, Mississippi, or Louisiana. This diversification had a cruelly divisive effect on slave families and communities, since large planters commonly separated family members as they transferred workers from one farm to another in accordance with economic need. Multiple holdings also allowed owners to shift their resources away from northern Virginia when the profits from tobacco began to decline. Because eighteenth-century farmers showed little interest in fertilizers or crop rotation, a steady decline in soil fertility, reinforced by a drop in tobacco prices, led to fallow fields and to a long-term shift from tobacco to wheat, barley, corn, oats, and rye.

The total population of Loudoun County was remarkably stable from the late eighteenth century to the Civil War. During those six decades when the U.S. population soared from 5,308,000 to 31,443,000, Loudoun County's continued to hover between 20,431 and 22,796. But its slave population reached a peak of 6,078 in 1800 and declined by more than a thousand in the next decade. The increasing sale of slaves, especially young men, to the west and south removed what would otherwise have been an uneconomical "surplus" resulting from the rapid natural reproduction of the slaves. The 1810s and 1840s marked brief intervals of agricultural prosperity that stimulated a modest growth of both white and slave populations.

The most striking statistics, however, show that the population of free blacks nearly quadrupled in number from 1800 to 1840, but declined in the 1850s. As Stevenson documents in her most powerful chapter, the decline was caused by one of the most shameful episodes of mass persecution in American history, when it became "illegal for free African Americans to own many kinds of businesses, to perform as medical practitioners, preachers, teachers, or entertainers. It even was difficult for them to do skilled and manual labor as boatmen, barbers, peddlers, or vendors." Virginia's laws even denied free people of color the right to learn how to read and write.

In view of the stereotypes of Southern planter society, the most surprising characteristic of Loudoun County's upper- and middle-class whites was their dedication to a kind of Puritan ethic. Many parents were eager to provide a broad, liberal education for their sons and even daughters, and some hoped that their sons would become doctors, lawyers, or engineers instead of planters. By the mid-1830s, with a declining white population of some fifteen thousand, the county could pride itself on twenty-one private academies or more advanced schools, including five that were for girls and seven that were coeducational. Leesburg, the county seat, had a library, hotel, churches, bank, general stores, artisan shops, and professional offices. According to Stevenson, fathers exhorted their sons to suppress their natural impulses, to "curb their appetite for frivolous spending," and to learn how to keep to a budget.

Stevenson quotes some typical parental advice: "Order, method and punctuality whether applied to one's finances, studies, recreation or physical needs is necessary for any type of accomplishments or success." This is not the mentality usually associated with a slave society, and one wishes that Stevenson had done more to show how Loudoun County and northern Virginia in general can be seen as typical of the South. It should also be added that Loudoun's white world was both hierarchical and patriarchal, and made virtually no effective provisions for the education or well-being of the poor.

Stevenson maintains that blacks and whites in antebellum Virginia led entirely different lives, especially with respect to their family structure, to the roles of men and women, and to the social relationships that helped to pass on distinctive African-American and European-American cultures. Accordingly, Stevenson devotes the first half of her book to the world of whites and the second half to the world of slaves and free blacks. If this organization tends to minimize the interaction between whites and blacks and occasionally gives the impression of two separate studies or even books, Stevenson, who is herself an African-American, succeeds not only in creating convincing white and black worlds but in viewing blacks through the eyes of whites and then whites through the eyes of blacks. She also points out, with respect to Loudoun County's toleration of aggressive miscegenation, that "over half of

Loudoun free 'blacks' were light-skinned enough to be considered 'mulatto' by 1860 census enumerators, as was more than a quarter of the local slave population."

Stevenson describes the lives of well-to-do whites with much empathy, showing how, at a time when marriage meant the total dependency of a wife on a husband, a father would be anxious that his daughter choose a man who could earn a good living and would not beat or exploit her. We can appreciate the frustrations of Elizabeth Conrad, the wife of a wealthy state legislator, who has so many children, guests, slaves, and household tasks to manage that she has no time to answer her husband's letters demanding she entertain his political supporters while he is away. Knowing what Elizabeth Conrad faces, we may find ourselves agreeing with Stevenson that "to his credit, Robert [her husband] did secure several house slaves to help Betty."[1] But when we later enter the minds of slave women, we see white women as "hell cats" or "devils" bent on "frequent scoldings and beatings, or [the] mishandling of slave children." Black men tended to view white women far more charitably, but they would remember a young master who "used to say, 'a man must be whipped, else he wouldn't know he was a *nigger*.'" No less memorable were the masters who used sale or the threat of sale as a means of control:

> "Boys git to cuttin' up on Sundays an' [dis]turbin' ole Marsa," one ex-slave explained. "[He] come . . . down to the quarters. Pick out de fam'ly dat got de most chillun an' say, 'Fo' God, nigger, I'm goin' to sell all dem chillun o' your'n lessen you keep 'em quiet.' Dat threat was worsen prospects of a lickin'. Ev'ybody sho' keep quiet arter dat."

Stevenson quotes the historian Jacqueline Jones as summarizing the conventional wisdom of the past generation of scholars who have studied the slave family in America: "The two-parent, nuclear family was the typical form of slave cohabitation regardless of the location, size, or economy of a plantation, the nature of its ownership, or the age of its slave community."[2] Stevenson challenges this consensus on the ubiquity of two-parent slave families; it is a view, she suggests, that emerged in the 1970s as part of a sweeping reinterpretation that portrayed slaves as having succeeded despite formidable obstacles in creating their own cultural world. Stevenson strongly argues that the slaves created their own cultural world, but she provides striking evidence that most slave children in Loudoun County did not grow up in two-parent homes. She asserts, on the contrary, that in colonial and antebellum Virginia the slaves' "most discernible ideal . . . was a malleable extended family that, when possible, provided its members with nurture, education, socialization, material support, and recreation in the face of the potential social chaos that the slaveholder imposed."

✳

To understand the significance of Stevenson's evidence and arguments regarding the slave family we need, at least briefly, to review the kinds of historical revisionism and counterrevisionism which have figured in the debates over public policy toward blacks, from the defenses of racial segregation in the 1930s and 1940s to justifications for affirmative action some forty years later.

For nearly fifty years after World War I, Ulrich Bonnell Phillips, a Southerner who taught at the University of Michigan and then at Yale, dominated the thinking of professional historians on American slavery. Despite his undisguised belief in Negro inferiority, Phillips's magisterial *American Negro Slavery* was still regarded as the authoritative work in its field when I was a graduate student at Harvard in the early 1950s. As late as 1967, when Eugene D. Genovese was a militant Marxist and an emerging authority on American slavery, he could boldly praise Phillips's achievements while deploring the racism that "corroded his enormous talent, and kept him short of the greatness he approached."[3]

No chapter or section in Phillips's long book is devoted to the subject of slave families. The relevant information, always given from the perspective of how slaves were treated, appears within discussions of large plantations, plantation management and labor, and slave law. In Phillips's presentation a kindly paternalism, combined with a concern for order, discipline, good health, and productivity, governed the planters' rules for the treatment of slave children, pregnant and nursing slave mothers, and slave marital unions. Thus the reader is told about small slave children playing in plantation "nurseries" under the supervision of older children and kindly-looking, elderly Negro women. Nursing mothers come in from the fields three times a day, always resting for a "cooling off" period before feeding their infants (for twelve months they are expected to do only three fifths of the work of a full-time hand). At the fifth month pregnant women are put in a sucklers' gang and prohibited from plowing or lifting. After giving birth they lie-in for a month, with a midwife giving constant care for the first week.

Slaves were said to increase "like rabbits," and Phillips tells of a woman "in her forty-second year [who] has had forty-one children and at this time is pregnant."[4] But slave fathers and even families are absent from his discussion. Phillips does mention planters who humorously encourage and reward slave courtship, who celebrate weddings with dinners and dancing, who punish slave adultery, and who even plead with neighbors to purchase a spouse and thus unite a divided couple. But since slave marriages had no legal standing, Phillips makes it clear that everything depended on the character or whim of the owner.

In 1956 Kenneth M. Stampp, in his revolutionary book *The Peculiar Institution*, demolished Phillips's portrait of benevolent paternalism and described the full horrors of human beings being owned in a laissez-faire society. In 1939 E. Franklin Frazier's *The Negro Family in the United States* had already argued that the Atlantic slave trade had severed American blacks from their African cultural heritage and that slavery, by depriving husbands and fathers of both authority and responsibility, had led to families headed by mothers, weak marital and parental ties, and a lack of restraint on individual impulses—marks of social disorganization which racism and poverty had perpetuated far into the twentieth century. Stampp confirmed this picture, at least with respect to slavery, and emphasized that because Southern laws never recognized slave marriages and endowed masters with total power, slaves were doomed to live "in a kind of cultural chaos."[5]

Like Brenda Stevenson, Stampp stressed that "the slave woman was first a full-time worker for her owner, and only incidentally a wife, mother, and home-maker." But this observation had quite different implications in the 1950s than it does today. Unlike Stevenson, Stampp could see no positive results from what has come to be termed a "matrifocal household," with fathers and husbands either absent or living "abroad" on other plantations. For Stampp "the general instability of slave families," accentuated by the frequent division and separate sale of family members, had certain logical but disastrous consequences: a "casual attitude" of many slaves toward marriage; "the indifference with which most fathers and even some mothers regarded their children"; and "widespread sexual promiscuity among both men and women," typified by a Kentucky slave woman "who had each of her seven children by a different father." Although Stampp was scrupulous in attributing such evils to slavery itself and not to African-American character or culture, and though he added that "the majority of slave women were devoted to their children, regardless of whether they had been sired by one or by several fathers," he made it plain that slavery inflicted considerable social damage upon the slaves.[6]

Since the 1960s this issue of social impairment, which seemed so central for such writers as Frazier and Stanley Elkins, has virtually disappeared from discussions of slavery. For decades historians have shied away from Stampp's evidence of "sexual promiscuity" and status-seeking among slaves. It is difficult to imagine the following words of Kenneth Stampp being written in the 1990s:

> In a society of unequals—of privileged and inferior castes, of wealth and poverty—the need to find some group to feel superior to is given a desperate urgency. In some parts of Virginia even the field-hands who felt the contempt of the domestics could lavish their own contempt upon the "coal pit niggers" who were hired to work in the mines. . . . A thousand-dollar slave felt superior to an eight-hundred-dollar slave.[7]

The turning point came in 1965 with the beginning of an explosive and still unresolved controversy over Daniel Patrick Moynihan's *The Negro Family in America: The Case for National Action*, a report aimed at changing public policy which drew on the work of Frazier and a recent, influential book by Stanley M. Elkins.[8] Since Moynihan was criticized by liberals and leftists and by African-American leaders, it is easy to forget that he was trying to dramatize the centuries of racial tyranny and abuse American blacks had suffered in order to justify an extensive national program of remedial action. If Herbert Gutman and Brenda Stevenson are correct when they suggest in different ways that the slaves' sexual values and family structures were actually healthier than those of contemporary Southern whites, it becomes more difficult to find a historical basis for affirmative action and other remedial programs. But Moynihan's emphasis on "deep-seated structural distortions in the life of the Negro American," leading to a "tangle of pathology" emanating from successive generations of the "fatherless matrifocal (mother-centered) family," infuriated a new generation that was skeptical of bourgeois sexual norms and eager to celebrate and romanticize a rebellious "Afro-American" past.

Herbert G. Gutman acknowledged that his major work, *The Black Family in Slavery and Freedom, 1750–1925*, published in 1976, had been conceived and written as a rebuttal to Moynihan. Gutman also criticized Frazier, Stampp, Elkins, and Genovese, among others, for not appreciating the extraordinary "adaptive capacities" of American slaves. For Gutman slavery was simply "an oppressive circumstance," analogous to the burdens and exploitations faced by lower-class immigrants and day laborers. While his book was by no means the first to shift historians' attention from the injustice of slave treatment to the strength of slave culture and resistance, Gutman's impressive research established the foundation for the consensus on the two-parent slave household described by Jacqueline Jones in the quotation cited earlier.

Gutman claimed that in all parts of the South, on plantations large and small, most slaves lived in households headed by two parents, although this did not mean that they had a system of "nuclear" families. The slaves' practices in naming children, Gutman argued, provided evidence that they were strongly conscious of grandparents and linkages among generations. Though slaves, in Gutman's view, showed a healthy tolerance of premarital sex and childbirth, they then settled into long-lasting marriages despite the constant threat of separation by sale. In Gutman's often informative pages there are no emasculated males, no Sambos, no white preachers marrying slaves or exhorting them on the responsibilities of family life.[9] Indeed there are few whites at all. And according to this cheerful account, the black family remained strong and vigorous through much of the Jim Crow era and even after the first large migrations to the cities of the North.

In his desire to refute the traditional image of slaves as passive victims, Gutman overreacted to the point of denying the realities of power—not only physical power of a sort that immigrants seldom felt, but the subtle cultural and psychological influences that emanate from superior power when it is exercised with conviction for any length of time. Gutman's extremely influential book reflected the rigid, idealistic, and romantic dichotomies of the 1960s, when, for a moment, power hardly seemed to matter. A central question is the degree to which slave family life, far from being a wholly autonomous force as Gutman maintained, became subject to rules which whites pragmatically chose to ensure the stability and profitability of the slave system.

I still think that the most convincing attempt to engage this question is Eugene D. Genovese's *Roll, Jordan, Roll: The World the Slaves Made*, published two years before Gutman's *The Black Family*. In many ways the two books point to similar conclusions. Genovese addressed "the ill-fated Moynihan Report" and "the conventional wisdom according to which slavery had emasculated black men, created a matriarchy, and prevented the emergence of a strong sense of family." Genovese's slaves courageously create a "world of their own" built on the "life-affirming" and earthy perspective of African religions, a world which rejects the white sin-obsessed standards of premarital chastity but which takes "a stern view of postmarital philandering."

But if Genovese indulges at times in 1960s romanticism, his strong slave families emerge from constant testing and negotiation within a complex situation of white paternalism. The masters, according to Genovese, "understood the strength of the marital and family ties among their slaves well enough to see in them a powerful means of social control." And Genovese also acknowledges that "the pressures on the family" documented by Frazier, Stampp, Elkins, and others "were extraordinary and took a terrible toll." The legends of matriarchy, of emasculated but brutal males and fatherless children, Genovese writes, "rest on unquestionable evidence, which, being partial, has misled its interpreters." He eloquently concludes that "the wonder is not that many slaves slipped into the insensitive and even brutal patterns of life they were being pushed toward by a demoralizing social system, but that so many others, possibly a commanding majority, fought for human ground on which to live even as slaves."[10]

Brenda Stevenson's intensive study of Loudoun County, reinforced by research on other parts of the state, appears to refute both Genovese and Gutman on the matter of two-parent slave families. In addition to analyzing numerous slave lists and registers as well as the results of the federal census, Stevenson draws on recorded interviews with elderly former slaves from Virginia. At first glance, she seems to make a case for the matriarchal, "father-absent" household and "disorganized" family structure described by Frazier, Elkins, and Moynihan. Yet according to Stevenson, Virginia's slaves ended up in matrifocal or father-absent households not only because of the consistent practice of selling young males to the cotton-producing regions of the Deep South, or because large absentee planters like George Washington shifted individual slaves from one farm to another without much regard for family unity, but also because the slaves themselves wanted it that way. One must quickly add that Stevenson's evidence for the predominance of matrifocal households and extended families is much stronger than her evidence for the preferences and ideals of slaves. But if the pendulum of historical studies is swinging back toward an emphasis on matriarchy, we now discover in Stevenson's book that matriarchy can be a good thing. After reading in the first half of the book about the debasement of white women and the strains and pressures of white marriage and child-rearing, one sees certain attractions in the slaves' extended and surrogate families, which, Stevenson suggests, may have owed something to African tribal traditions.

On the other hand, Stevenson presents a far too sanguine picture of black child-rearing and cooperation. While she argues that the increasing sale and export of young women in the 1850s tended to undermine even the matrifocal slave families, she for the most part ignores whether slavery impaired the social relations and psychological capacities of many slaves. The same criticisms Bertram Wyatt-Brown made with respect to Gutman's book can be applied to Stevenson's own account. She largely fails, as Wyatt-Brown wrote of Gutman,

> to deal directly with the social ills that so often play a role in family disorganization: venereal disease, desertions, violence inside and outside the home, child abuse and neglect, criminal examples in neighborhood and street, sexual rivalries and infidelities, abusive racial language (demeaning another as well as oneself), card gambling and numbers, drinking and other forms of self-destructive activity.[11]

Moreover, we have very little evidence regarding the marital preferences and ideals of slaves. Stevenson shows quite conclusively that free blacks in Virginia preferred monogamous marriage and two-parent households, a fact that casts considerable doubt on her thesis about slave preference. Once slaves were manumitted, their choices must have reflected, for the most part, the desires they could not fulfill as slaves. Even the experience of typical slave households is open to quite different interpretations. For example, Genovese and Gutman tend to include "abroad marriages"—i.e., marriages with slaves on other plantations—in the category of two-parent families, whereas Stevenson does not. Genovese says that slaves often preferred to marry off the plantation since this would allow them a much greater variety of choice of mates, and visiting their wives would enable them to get away regularly from a prison-like environment. By living apart, moreover, they would "not have to witness the beatings and humiliations their loved ones took."[12] Gutman adds that slaves strongly desired marriages outside their own local groups as a result of African traditions regarding incest. Although there is much overlap between Stevenson's and her predecessors' pictures of abroad marriages, of the devastation of slave sales, and of the crucial importance of slave grandparents and other kin or surrogate parents, Stevenson has drawn a much sharper line between the worlds of blacks and whites than either Genovese or Gutman did.

I wish she had gone much further in showing how this sharp racial divide affected the behavior and social norms of both blacks and whites. For example, Stevenson presents some fascinating examples of white adultery and divorce, and in one passage suggests how the presence of blacks in the South altered the perception of a white wife's infidelity:

> To put it crudely but aptly, whites married, blacks copulated. Whites did not just marry, they stayed married. Blacks moved promiscuously from one partner to the next, or so the racialized mythology of the day went. In the American South, therefore, where notions of racial difference shaped social hierarchy and expectations so profoundly, marriage and divorce in European American communities took on incredible significance, privately and publicly.

Does this mean that the great racial divide helps to explain the point Alexis de Tocqueville made when he wrote that Americans considered nothing *"de plus précieux que l'honneur de la femme"*? Perhaps one can argue that as market forces and democratic ideals eroded one traditional boundary after another, the preservation of female sexual purity, particularly that of wives, became a crucial aspect of whiteness, of maintaining a safe distance from what whites perceived as the world of African sexual power and menace. In retrospect, may it be more than a coincidence that the "sexual revolution" of the 1960s arrived at the same time as the movement for black civil rights?

Notes

1. For a fascinating collection of letters written by white women in the Old South, including members of the Conrad family, see Joan E. Cashin, editor, *Our Common Affairs: Texts from Women in the Old South* (Johns Hopkins University Press, 1996). No less revealing is Carol Bleser, editor, *Tokens of Affection: The Letters of a Planter's Daughter in the Old South* (University of Georgia Press, 1996).
2. Quoted from Jones, *Labor of Love, Labor of Sorrow: Black Women, Work and Family from Slavery to the Present* (Basic Books, 1985), p. 32. It should be stressed that Jones, like Stevenson, recognizes the importance of "abroad marriages," in which couples lived on separate plantations and were dependent on their owners' permission to visit

each other. Jones also has much to say about the slaves' extended families and kin networks.

3. Genovese, *In Red and Black: Marxian Explorations in Southern and Afro-American History* (University of Tennessee Press, 1984), pp. 259–298. It is a mark of Brenda Stevenson's openness of mind that her endnotes cite Phillips various times, an indication that his work is still an indispensable source for students of American slavery.

4. Phillips, *American Negro Slavery: A Survey of the Supply, Employment and Control of Negro Labor as Determined by the Plantation Régime* (D. Appleton, 1918; reprinted, Louisiana State University Press, 1966), p. 299.

5. Stampp, *The Peculiar Institution: Slavery in the Ante-Bellum South* (Knopf, 1956), p. 340.

6. *The Peculiar Institution*, pp. 340–349.

7. *The Peculiar Institution*, pp. 338–339. With regard to sexual promiscuity, the historian John Blassingame saw little difference between what Herbert Gutman referred to as wholesome "pre-nuptial intercourse" and "bridal pregnancy" and what Frazier had earlier described as "slave licentiousness." As Blassingame added, "nineteenth-century clerics had the best of both worlds when they described such practices as 'ante-nuptial fornication.'" Blassingame, review of Herbert G. Gutman, *The Black Family in Slavery and Freedom, 1750–1925*, in *The New Republic*, December 4, 1976, p. 27.

8. Elkins, *Slavery: A Problem in American Institutional and Intellectual Life* (University of Chicago Press, 1959). Elkins brilliantly pressed the theme of social and psychological damage to an extreme point. He argued that in a free-for-all capitalist environment, where no institutional restraints could mitigate the slaveholder's power, slave marriages and families were essentially meaningless. Each slave faced the unrestricted authority of his owner, and this absolutism resulted in the psychological infantilization of many slaves. Hence there was some basis in reality, Elkins argued, for the numerous descriptions of the typical American slave as the "docile but irresponsible, loyal but lazy, humble but chronically given to lying and stealing . . . childlike [Sambo]" (p. 82).

9. As John Blassingame pointed out, "Contrary to Gutman's assertions, thousands of plantation diaries testify to the influence exercised by whites on slave marriage and family life. Antebellum white ministers regularly preached to black congregations about family obligations, and thousands of slaves were married in white churches. While giving due recognition to the resilience of the slaves, one should not forget that they lived in close contact with whites. The African became an Afro-American, partially because he borrowed from whites." (See Blassingame's review of Gutman.) This same criticism applies to Brenda Stevenson's book, which in its earlier dissertation form was co-directed by Professor Blassingame. If there are great merits to Stevenson's decision to devote five chapters to white families and then five chapters to black families, the inherent bias of this organization would have benefited if it had been balanced by a stronger black presence in the first half of the book and a stronger white presence in the second.

10. Genovese, *Roll, Jordan, Roll* (Pantheon, 1974), pp. 452, 467, 469, 491.

11. Wyatt-Brown, review of Gutman, *The Black Family in Slavery and Freedom, 1750–1925*, in *Commentary*, January 1977, p. 77. Stevenson does very briefly discuss alcohol abuse among slaves.

12. Genovese, *Roll, Jordan, Roll*, pp. 474–475.

22

Terror in Mississippi

*Tumult and Silence at Second Creek: An Inquiry
into a Civil War Conspiracy*
Winthrop D. Jordan (1993)

*Witness for Freedom: African American Voices
on Race, Slavery, and Emancipation*
Edited by C. Peter Ripley, Roy E. Finkenbine,
Michael F. Hembree, and Donald Yacovone (1993)

*Free at Last: A Documentary History of
Slavery, Freedom, and the Civil War*
Edited by Ira Berlin, Barbara J. Fields, Steven F. Miller,
Joseph P. Reidy, and Leslie S. Rowland (1992)

✳

"The Negro," Frederick Douglass proclaimed at the beginning of the Civil
War, "is the key of the situation—the pivot upon which the whole rebellion
turns." Investing his hope in the "desperate insurrectionary movements of
slaves," Douglass saw that his belief in the centrality of racial justice was
hotly contested in the North, and knew that justice depended far more on
the mysterious workings of providence than on the intentions of white Americans. Late in 1860, at a meeting in Boston honoring the martyrdom of John
Brown, Douglass had been heckled and then attacked by hired thugs before

he and his followers were thrown out of the hall by the police. African Americans who sought to aid the Union cause frequently encountered a response similar to the insults hurled by some Cincinnati policemen: "We want you d——d niggers to keep out of this; this is a white man's war."[1]

Since Abraham Lincoln disavowed any intention of interfering with slavery in the existing states and since Confederate officials insisted that virtually all slaves were content and grateful servants, loyal to their masters' cause, how could the Negro be a "key" or "pivot" in the nation's decisive crisis? The claim Douglass made would have seemed absurd even to several generations of historians in the twentieth century. In the 1930s, for example, a popular biography of General Grant affirmed that

> the American negroes are the only people in the history of the world . . . that ever became free without any effort of their own. . . . [The Civil War] was not their business. . . . They twanged banjos around the railroad stations, sang melodious spirituals, and believed that some Yankee would soon come along and give each of them forty acres of land and a mule.[2]

This dominant view was challenged by a few black historians, best typified perhaps by Benjamin Quarles; and by the pioneering Marxist historian Herbert Aptheker, who wrote about blacks in the Union army and navy as well as about slave plots and insurrections. But only in the civil rights era, beginning in the mid-1960s, did historians such as James McPherson, Willie Lee Rose, George P. Rawick, and Leon Litwack bring the struggle for racial equality into the mainstream of historical writing and suggest exactly how the Negro became "the pivot upon which the whole rebellion turn[ed]."

By 1976 the ideological climate encouraged the funding of two long-term projects of extraordinary value that reinforce and give meaning to Douglass's thesis. The editors of the *Black Abolitionist Papers* project, led by C. Peter Ripley of Florida State University, examined thousands of manuscript collections and newspapers in Great Britain and Canada as well as in the United States. They then produced on seventeen reels of microfilm, now available in many research libraries, a huge collection of letters, essays, speeches, pamphlets, and editorials documenting the African American movement to abolish slavery and combat racial discrimination.

Between 1985 and 1992 Ripley and his associates published five volumes of selected documents, superbly edited and annotated, which represent less than 10 percent of the primary sources on microfilm. Two of these volumes dramatize the international aspects of America's racial conflicts, presenting documents about the thousands of blacks who emigrated to Canada and the scores of black abolitionists, including many fugitive slaves, who toured Great Britain where enthusiastic audiences attended their lectures, read their publications, and donated funds to their cause. *Witness for Freedom* is a one-volume distillation of the black abolitionist material intended for the general reader and for classroom use. Since so much of the subject matter is unfamiliar even to nonspecialist historians, the introduction, chronology, and glossary are extremely valuable.[3]

The Freedmen and Southern Society Project, conducted by a group of scholars led by Ira Berlin, has now published four volumes of primary sources (selected from the National Archives) under the general title *Freedom: A Documentary History of Emancipation, 1861–1867*. These immensely valuable works document the enlistment and military service of almost 200,000 black soldiers and sailors, most of them former slaves; the gradual disintegration of the slave system; and the emergence during the Civil War of free labor in the upper and the lower South. The volumes include the testimony of blacks and whites, soldiers and civilians, slaveholders and slaves. Like Peter Ripley's *Black Abolitionist* volumes, Berlin's *Freedom* series enriches and transforms our understanding of America's greatest dilemma in the most crucial years of decision. Historians will mine these collections for generations to come. Fortunately, *Free at Last*, the one-volume abridged version of *Freedom*, gives the general reader a powerful sense of "how a people with little power and few weapons secured its freedom against the will of those with great power and many weapons."

Historical documents can be a liberating antidote to silence. Winthrop D. Jordan implies as much in the title of his new book, *Tumult and Silence at Second Creek*, and in the twenty key documents that conclude this fascinating narrative. Like the works edited by Ripley and Berlin, Jordan's account of a conspiracy by plantation slaves to organize a large-scale revolt in the Second Creek neighborhood of Adams County, Mississippi, at the beginning of the Civil War is a venture in historical therapy; it is an attempt to overcome generations of denial and repression concerning the relations between blacks and whites in America and the ultimate meaning of the Civil War.

This effort to lift the curtain of silence that fell over the discovery of the Mississippi plot, and the execution of some forty slaves who were accused of taking part in it, should not be confused with a "multicultural" policy of alloting a certain quota of historical space to every ethnic group.[4] That kind of history is wholly consistent with the traditional cinematic and historiographical depictions of the Civil War in which each battle, each regiment, each contestant gets its due. Instead, Jordan, Ripley, and Berlin try to lead us out of a Plato's cave of Civil War legend. As we hear the aspirations, the pain, the rage of African Americans—as opposed to "the happy-go-lucky, lovable ol' darkies of magnolia-blossom historic legend"—we come to realize that tyranny is a central theme of American history, that racial exploitation and racial conflict have been central to American culture.

As Jordan makes clear, however, the "lovable ol' darkies" were not merely a legend (the shadows in Plato's cave were only partly illusory). He quotes from a remarkable letter sent by the daughter of a Mississippi planter-politician to her husband, a Confederate officer at the front in Virginia:

> [The servants] have *all* behaved extremely well, indeed I cannot utter the least complaint of them, they are deeply interested and very sympathizing with us all. They often speak to me about the war and there was great rejoicing in the kitchen at the news of our recent glorious victory in Virginia. What would those miserable abolitionists say to such manifestations of devotion and affection on the part of the poor maltreated slave, whose heart, according to them, is only the abode of hatred and revenge against their master—They know nothing of the bond that unites the master and servant[,] of its tenderness and care on the one side, and its pride fidelity and attachment on the other.

These words of Louisa Quitman Lovell were written in late July 1861, three months after rebellion had begun to simmer among slaves in the vicinity of Natchez, where she lived, and two and a half months after some hitherto trusted carriage drivers had been hanged for suspected plotting. As Jordan notes, "Mrs. Lovell was not writing for any public but herself and her husband. She believed what she wrote." One might add that she was also engaged in a private debate with the abolitionists and was eager to shape her experience in ways that would refute them. The "legend" of paternalism, in other words, could guide and order southern behavior. Lemuel Parker Conner, the wealthy planter who left a transcript of the rebellious slaves' words when they were later interrogated near Natchez, had always remembered to add, in letters to his wife when he was away from home, "Howdy to the servants."

As early as the 1820s many Southerners were eager to become "popular" with their slaves. African Americans were by no means invulnerable to such expressions of care. In 1937, when the WPA Federal Writers' Project sponsored the interviewing of large numbers of elderly former slaves throughout the South, a local historian in Natchez recorded the reminiscences of Charlie Davenport, a Negro who had once been owned by Gabriel B. Shields on a large plantation across Second Creek, just south and east of Natchez, and whose enslaved father William had somehow escaped, joined the Union army, and fought in the Vicksburg campaign.

Charlie Davenport was the only veteran of slavery whose recorded interview referred to the planned uprising along Second Creek, and Jordan warns that the document must be treated with great caution. Mrs. Edith Wyatt Moore, who interviewed Davenport, was white and thus represented the voice of authority in a rigidly segregated caste society based ultimately on terror. Jordan even sees certain parallels and continuities between this complacent WPA interview and Lemuel Conner's transcript of the Second Creek examinations of slaves, who spoke after being whipped and tortured. Certainly the elderly Davenport was aware that he was telling a white audience, in the midst of a long economic depression, about his memories of slavery. Still, Jordan's exhaustive research shows that many of Davenport's factual statements are confirmed by other sources.[5]

Insisting that "us didn't 'blong to no white trash," Davenport expressed great pride in his master, "one ob de richest en highest quality gentlemen in de whole country," and took special delight in the character of the Surgets, the wealthy family of his mistress: "Dey wuz de out fightenist, out cussinest, fastest ridin, hardest drinkin, out spendinest folks I ebber seed. But Lawd, Lawd, dey wuz gentlemen eben in dey cups." Davenport clearly hated the overseer, "a big, hard fisted Dutchman" named Charles Sauter, who beat Charlie when he was a child until "I thought I'd die," proclaiming that "from now on you works in de field." But Davenport claimed that "our houses wuz clean en snug. We wuz bettah fed den I is now en warmer too, kaize us had blankets en quilts filled wid home raised wool. I jist loved layin in de big fat feather bed a hearin de rain patter on de roof."

Like many of the former slaves interviewed in the 1930s, Davenport contrasted his own relatively benevolent plantation with others that were far less generous. After recalling the slaves' garden patches, the hunting and fishing, and his own support for Jefferson Davis, Davenport mused that "Marse Randolph Shields"—the descendant of his owner—"is a doctor way off in China.

I 'bleeves day would look aftah me now if day knowed I wuz on charity."
Davenport then concluded with thoughts that confirmed the white racial
mood in 1937 and that presumably brought a glow to the heart of Mrs.
Moore:

> How I gwine to know 'bout de rights or wrongs ob slavery? Fur ez I
> is concerned I wuz bettah treated ez a slave den I is now. Folks says
> hit wuz wicked but fur all I kin see de colored folks aint made much
> use ob day freedom. Day is all in debt en chained down to somethin
> same ez us slaves wuz. . . . Day aint no sich thing ez freedom. Us is all
> tied down to somethin.

Today it is highly unfashionable to discuss the effects of paternalism in either
the antebellum or post-Reconstruction periods. Jordan, who is primarily interested in Davenport's brief account of the planned slave uprising, does not
really consider how the prevailing Southern white ideology, to which Charlie
Davenport had been subjected during his long life as a "free Negro," might
have shaped his recollections and his assessment of slavery. One way of dealing with the question of submission and its effects can be found in the
speeches and writings of black abolitionists. A militant fugitive slave named
J. Sella Martin assured audiences in Britain that American slaves were anything but "content." But let us suppose, Martin said in a speech at the Bristol
Athenaeum,

> it were the fact that the black man was contented in bondage, suppose
> he was contented to see his wife sold on the auction-block or his daugh-
> ter violated or his children separated from him, or having his own
> manhood crushed out of him, I say that is the heaviest condemnation
> of the institution, that slavery should blot out a man's manhood so as
> to make him contented to accept this degradation, and such an insti-
> tution ought to be swept from the face of the earth.

Of course a slave's seeming contentment could be a way of making the
best of a grisly situation in which ill humor or any sign of "surliness" became
an excuse for whipping. Jordan has discovered that at Aventine Plantation,
where Charlie Davenport was born and reared, the overseer called the roll
of hands three times every Sunday, and male and female slaves who had in
some way offended the master were put in the "stock" by the head or by the
legs and then given lashes. In fact, in 1859 a slave named Davenport, prob-

ably Charlie's father, was put in the stock and given thirty-nine lashes for "being saucy and clinching his hands against the overseer." Many of the rebels who took part in the Adams County conspiracy lived on plantations noted for lax or erratic discipline. Jordan has good reason for suggesting "that the slaves on Aventine rejected joining [the rebels'] Plan *because* they were kept under unusually rigid and efficient discipline."

Davenport recalled that one night when he was "a little boy" "a strange nigger come en he harangued de ole folks but dey wouldn't budge." This "powerful big black feller named Jupiter" reported that "De slaves had hit all worked out how dey wuz goin to march on Natchez aftah slayin all dare own white folks." In one of the two versions of Charlie's report, the rebels were determined to take the land after killing "dey white folks." But Davenport said nothing (that we know of) about rape or sexual relations with white women, a subject that figures prominently in Conner's transcript of the slave interrogations. He did not condemn the rebels' plan or express any judgment concerning the capture and hanging of Jupiter, except to say "Dey didn't need no trial kaise he was kotch rilin [caught riling up] de folks to murder." He had a simple explanation for the passivity at Aventine: "Us folks wouldn't jine 'em kaise what we want to kill Ole Marse fur?" Whatever its other shortcomings, this testimony from an allegedly loyal slave, combined with other evidence that Jordan has turned up in one of the most remarkable feats of detective work achieved by a modern historian, makes it virtually certain that scores of slaves in Adams County, Mississippi, were prepared for a major uprising in the first months of the Civil War.

✱

Historians celebrating slave resistance have pointed with undisguised delight to the great conspiracy led by a slave named Gabriel, which traumatized Virginia's leaders in 1800;[6] to a more enigmatic revolt in Louisiana in 1811, when some two hundred slaves marched toward New Orleans before being met by a military force and defeated; to Denmark Vesey's success in 1822 in enlisting some of the most trusted servants in Charleston in a plot to seize the city and kill its white inhabitants; and to Nat Turner's seventy-odd rebels, who in 1831 killed some sixty white men, women, and children as they stormed through Southampton County, Virginia. The rarity of such plots and uprisings by no means proves that slaves were happy or content: during the millennia for which we have records of human bondage revolts have been extremely uncommon. Nevertheless, the alleged passivity of Southern slaves during the Civil War, when Union troops invaded the Confederacy from many directions and when hundreds of thousands of Southern white males departed for the front, has been used to bolster traditional racist ideology and to challenge the thesis advanced by Douglass about the ultimate meaning of the war.

In 1940 a leading historian of the South, Clement Eaton, could write without qualification that "the slaves were remarkably peaceful and tractable during the Civil War despite the provocation to rebel."[7] Yet Eaton had examined the central document of Jordan's book: Lemuel Conner's transcript, then in the possession of a Conner descendant in Natchez. Jordan discovered the record of the plot in 1971 when an archivist at Louisiana State University Library, who now happens to be Jordan's editor and publisher, brought it to his attention. "This discovery," according to the dust jacket of his book, "led him on a twenty-year search for additional information about the aborted rebellion." Eaton had even read two other key documents used by Jordan, both of them letters written by slave owners in mid-May 1861 to the governor of Mississippi, reporting that many slaves, having "been induced to believe Lincoln's troops would be here for the purpose of freeing them all," had plotted to kill their masters and either rape or take "as *Wives*" "such of the females as suited their fancy." Both letters said that white men had been involved in the conspiracy and that slaves had been hanged.

Eaton adapted this material to the racial assumptions of his time and to the purpose of his book, which was to show how slavery and the sectional conflict led to an erosion of Jeffersonian ideals and to the suppression of free thought and speech in the Old South. Though not an apologist for slavery, Eaton viewed the institution as relatively benign and its victims as totally incapable of a large-scale and vengeful insurrection. The details of the Adams County plot, somewhat garbled, appear within a long chapter on the Southern fear of "servile revolt"—"a pathological fear of their slaves, not at all justified by actual danger." As Eaton moves from one alarm to another, he speaks of "the black terror," "dark rumors and imagined plots," "contagious fear," "hallucinations," "phobia," "melodramatic reports," and "imagined insurrectionists."

No doubt there is much justification for Eaton's emphasis on Southern excitability and virtual hysteria over the specter of infiltration by abolitionist agents. Before assessing Jordan's claims, it is also salutary to consider Eaton's description of how evidence was "extorted from the negroes by unmerciful whippings." In 1856, according to a Memphis newspaper, no fewer than forty victims of such torture were hanged for plotting insurrection. If Southern whites wanted to believe that abolitionists were inciting the slaves to revolt, they could presumably force some slaves to confirm their fears.

Eaton tends, however, to associate these procedures with the frenzied mob; intelligent Southerners, he assures us, discounted rumors of plots and rebellion. Here he was quite wrong. One must turn to Jordan to find that the Adams County "Examination Committee" or "Vigilance Committee," which was organized to deal with the plot, was made up of the region's leading citizens and planters. Moreover, any decision by this extra-legal body to privately execute slaves meant a substantial loss of property. If the slaves had been condemned after a legal trial at the Adams County Circuit Court, which would have brought unwanted publicity, the owners would have been entitled to compensation equal to half the value of each slave. In view of these circumstances and the careful attentiveness suggested by Lemuel Conner's transcript, there are grounds for believing that the committee was intent on obtaining the truth regardless of the methods used. It is significant that two former slaves later testified that the committee had tried them while other slaves were being hanged at the racetrack just east of Natchez, and had then released them after friendly witnesses affirmed their innocence. One of these slaves had been gang-whipped until he repeatedly fainted and, before his reprieve, had even been taken to the gallows to be hanged.

Jordan skillfully reconstructs details of the slaves' conspiracy as well as the social world of the great cotton plantations surrounding the boisterous town of Natchez, which was said to contain more millionaires than any city in America. Many plantation owners lived in the town itself, while slaves far outnumbered whites in the countryside. Slaves in the Natchez region began plotting in May 1861, soon after news flashed over various grapevines that war had begun and that Northern troops, sometimes associated with "abolitionists," could be expected to capture New Orleans and march toward Natchez. That expectation is one of the few things that seem clear about the plot: for the most part, the precise details of how the slaves planned to fight and take power remain vague. It would be interesting to know whether any slaves suspected that some abolitionists were black. At that very moment black abolitionists in the North were invoking the memories of Nat Turner, Denmark Vesey, and John Brown, while calling, in effect, for a black revolution. There seems no doubt that the war made it possible for the plotters to believe they would have the support of the Union army when it arrived in Mississippi.

Ironically, while slaves in Mississippi and other states knew that a man named Lincoln was the "enemy" of their owners and expressed their confidence that Lincoln intended to free all slaves, black abolitionists reacted with anger and dismay when black volunteer units were barred from serving in the Union armed forces. They were equally bitter when Lincoln countermanded General Frémont's proclamation freeing the slaves of all Confederate activists in Missouri, and when both Lincoln and Congress excluded slavery from their definition of the war's objectives. Many white abolitionists appreciated Lincoln's desperate need to maintain support in the slaveholding border states and build as much unity as possible within the racist North. By withholding criticism of Lincoln and supporting what William Lloyd Garrison called the "death-grapple with the Southern slave oligarchy," white reformers believed that black bondage would eventually be destroyed.[8] But in May 1861, when self-styled white Minute Men just north of Natchez were hanging slave carriage drivers who were suspected of organizing opposition and investigating white foreigners suspected of collaborating with blacks, the leading newspaper of the black abolitionists advised black military units in the North to drill and stand ready "as Minute Men, *to respond when the slave calls.*"

The black "Minute Men" who were eventually accepted into the Union army in large numbers could not have heard the calls from Mississippi even if they had been able to invade the state. Perhaps the most significant thing about the "tumult" at Second Creek is the silence that enveloped it. In contrast to widespread discussion of the Gabriel, Vesey, and Turner affairs, the newspapers were entirely mute; there were no speeches, pamphlets, or official messages about the conspiracy. Even Jordan, who has drawn on census data, diaries, plantation records, "road duty books," and inscriptions on gravestones, has no idea why Lemuel Conner wrote down some of the answers he heard nineteen or twenty slaves give to the markedly unrecorded questions of their examiners. Since knowledge of a major slave conspiracy was nearly erased in Mississippi, it seems likely that memories of other tumults were also effaced and that we have a very imperfect picture of slave resistance in general.

In both the Caribbean and North America black informers frequently divulged to white authorities news of an impending slave revolt. That did not happen at Second Creek. Instead, several ringleaders made the fatal mistake of talking in front of "Mas Benny," the eight- or nine-year-old son of the overseer of a large plantation. Jordan can only speculate on how young Benny Austen might have caught the horrified ears of adults when he reported that "the whipping business would stop." The committee interrogated slaves in September and October 1861. According to the testimony, the slaves of nine Second Creek planters were directly involved in what Jordan calls "the Plan," and three other planters and a gunsmith were also specified as victims.

With one exception, the slaves seem to have had no strong religious faith, in marked contrast to Nat Turner and various other African American rebels. The group included no skilled artisans. All were illiterate except for three men owned by the permissive Dunbar widows, who like other planters were, according to Conner's record, slated for death. One of the Dunbar slaves had a gun, but most of the insurgents intended to use hoes and axes to kill white people in the countryside before marching on Natchez and then, so they hoped, joining forces with Union troops.

In 1864, after Union soldiers had occupied Natchez, a captain from Wisconsin visited a local widow and teacher after attending church. As talk turned to the 1861 plot, Mrs. Henry gave Captain Bennett an account of the way the slaves had been tortured in the interrogations. Bennett wrote in his diary that "the outrages . . . surpass any thing I ever heard or read of. . . . The cruelty of the chivalrous gentry of Natchez would put to blush the warmest advocates of the Spanish Inquisition as practiced in the dark ages of Popery." This information, coupled with other evidence Jordan presents, raises difficult questions about the meaning of the Conner transcript and other reports of what the slaves supposedly said. Jordan is acutely aware of these difficulties, but in the end he is too willing to accept the recorded testimony at face value, particularly regarding the slaves' intent to rape.

There were clearly limits on what white questioners could force the slaves to say. Billy and Obey refused to talk at all. Surely no interrogator pressured Dennis to report that two other slaves, Simon and George Dunbar, had predicted "Northerners make the South shit behind their asses." Simon was also quoted as saying "he hoped to see the day when he would blow down a white man who called him a damn rascal"—the latter term, as Jordan explains, implying at that time "inferiority of *class*." Jordan makes an excellent case for the authenticity of many such statements. Many of the blacks were filled with rage and resentment, and the examinations gave them a chance for self-assertion, for shocking some of the whites they had planned to murder. Knowing that they would soon be hauled to the gallows, they had little to lose.

This is the perspective from which Jordan interprets the frequent report that specific slaves intended to "take," "ravish," and "ride" specific white women, often the wives or daughters of their owners. For them, apparently, nothing could exemplify the meaning of freedom better than inverting the slave/master relationship: kill the master, possess and ravish the white mistress or daughter, and seize the land. Since Jordan completed his manuscript, the reports of systematic raping of a great many Bosnian women have added new meaning to the view of rape as a means of revenge, a weapon of war and dishonor. Some of the Second Creek slaves even spoke of taking the white women as "wives," implying that white women would actually desire their embraces once they had become victors and free men. This thought moves Jordan to make the following analysis:

> While today we recognize the powerful and indeed central element of violence in the act of rape, we greatly oversimplify a complicated mixture if we call it only an act of vicious violence and nothing more, for surely it includes hatred and attraction, aggressive humiliation and sexual assertiveness, brutality, vengeance, lust, eros and thanatos, perverse devotion and devotion to perversity. We know that the "act of love," even in a loving context, can involve a great deal of aggressiveness and that such feelings and behavior are embedded in our mammalian natures.

Yet it is worth recalling that in fact none of the Mississippi blacks is known to have attacked a white woman; and Jordan himself, in his monumental book *White Over Black*,[9] has led all other historians in exposing the long traditions of white fantasy concerning black sexuality. In a footnote citing that book and defending its thesis, he refers to his argument "for treating assertions about the sexual aggressiveness of black men as a function of white insecurities and domination." In *Tumult and Silence* he even summarizes the long tradition in America, going back to the seventeenth century, of imagining that black slaves were planning to kill their white masters and rape the best-looking white women.

For their part, as Jordan notes, white women never seemed to share this sexual phobia, at least in the pre–Civil War period, and they seldom if ever made allusion to black rapists in their letters and diaries. Even more to the point, there is not a shred of evidence that black insurrectionists in America ever had sexual contact with a single white woman, though Nat Turner's band of killers had total power over numerous white women and girls. I can add that in my own reading I have seen no evidence of rape in the great slave uprisings in Barbados in 1816, in Demerara (Guiana) in 1823, or in Jamaica in 1831. The silence of sources does not prove that occasional rapes never occurred, but if Jordan's interpretation is correct, the Second Creek rebels were unique in their lust for specific white women.

At one point Jordan toys with imagining "the snide hostility of the question" asked by the interrogators: *"Which one of the ladies was you going to take, boy?"*[10] But he fails to pursue the question whether the conspirators were forced to testify falsely to such a question. If they were, this could undercut his new thesis regarding black sexual power and even imperil his other readings of the Conner transcript. In view of traditional white male preconceptions, why should we not expect the examiners to have asked, "What did you intend to do with the ladies?" "Who was Simon [or Albert or Peter] going to ravish?" "After you killed Master and Mrs. Mosby, did you plan to ride Miss Anna?" And if the slaves were being savagely whipped or tortured in other ways, why wouldn't they have told the inquisitors what the inquisitors wanted to hear? Testimony taken under such circumstances is of course legally worthless and is especially suspect regarding a volcanic issue like rape, which evoked in the minds of the inquisitors a dark mythology seething with "brutality, vengeance, lust, eros and thanatos."

While we will never know the true intentions of the Second Creek conspirators, Jordan presents a convincing case that they did conspire to mount a revolt and that the issue of freedom dominated the minds of Mississippi whites and blacks from the moment they knew there was a Civil War. This basic point, which made the Negro "the pivot" of the war, is eloquently confirmed by the documents collected by the two great projects I have described above.

By July 31, 1863, a black woman named Hannah Johnson gave advice to President Lincoln on two critical matters. The daughter of a slave who had escaped north from Louisiana, Hannah had a son who had fought at "Fort Wagoner" with the famous Massachusetts Fifty-fourth regiment, and "was not taken prisoner, as many were." Unaware that Lincoln had just promised to retaliate against Confederate prisoners if captured black soldiers were killed or enslaved, Ms. Johnson urged Lincoln to take this step without delay: "They have lived in idleness all their lives on stolen labor and made savages of the colored people, but they now are so furious because they are proving themselves to be men. . . . You must put the rebels to work in State prisons to making shoes and things, if they sell our colored soldiers, till they let them all go."

Hannah Johnson was also shocked by reports that Lincoln would "take back" the Emancipation Proclamation:

[D]on't do it. When you are dead and in Heaven, in a thousand years that action of yours will make the Angels sing your praises I know it. Ought one man to own another, law for or not, who made the law, surely the poor slave did not. so it is wicked, and a horrible Outrage, there is no sense in it, because a man has lived by robbing all his life and his father before him, should he complain because the stolen things found on him are taken. Robbing the colored people of their labor is but a small part of the robbery their souls are almost taken, they are made bruits of often. You know all about this. . . . We poor oppressed ones, appeal to you, and ask fair play. Yours for Christs sake.

Notes

1. Quoted in James M. McPherson, *The Negro's Civil War: How American Negroes Felt and Acted during the War for the Union* (Pantheon, 1965), p. 22.
2. Quoted in McPherson, *The Negro's Civil War*, p. viii. W. E. Woodward's *Meet General Grant* was published in 1928, but I remember my parents and their friends reading it with admiration some ten years later.
3. Seven of the eighty-nine selections are taken from works not included in the *Black Abolitionist Papers* volumes, which for various reasons exclude Frederick Douglass and such earlier figures as David Walker.
4. Jordan stresses that we can never know the exact number of slaves that were executed. At one point he cautiously states that "at least twenty-seven slaves and very probably more were hanged." But in July 1862 the Confederate provost marshal of Natchez in-

formed the state's governor that "within the last twelve months we have had to hang some forty for plotting and insurrection and there have been about that number put in irons."

5. There are two versions of the Davenport interview, which Jordan prints as Documents Y and Z at the end of his book. The differences need not concern us here.

6. Douglas R. Egerton has published a comprehensive study, *Gabriel's Rebellion: The Virginia Slave Conspiracies of 1800 and 1802* (University of North Carolina Press, 1993), which reinforces my point about erroneous white expectations of black rebels raping white women.

7. *Freedom of Thought in the Old South* (Duke University Press, 1940; Peter Smith reprint, 1951), p. 105. Eaton received his Ph.D. from Harvard in 1929 and indicates in his preface of 1939 that the book was a revised version of a doctoral dissertation directed by Arthur M. Schlesinger, Sr.

8. James M. McPherson, *Battle Cry of Freedom: The Civil War Era* (Oxford University Press, 1988), p. 312. Most white abolitionists later changed their minds and became harshly critical of the Lincoln administration until the President finally gave notice of an impending emancipation proclamation.

9. *White Over Black: American Attitudes Toward the Negro, 1550–1812* (University of North Carolina Press, 1968).

10. While at times Jordan seems to hesitate on this issue, he also states unequivocally, without any reasoned defense of the position, "If we take the rebels seriously, then, we have to accept what they said when they talked of 'taking' and 'ravishing' certain white women. They had their own reasons that seemed to them entirely sufficient.

Part V

From the Construction of Race to the American Dilemma and the Feminist Revolution

23

Constructing Race: A Reflection

Although political rhetoric often conceals this truth, as we enter a new millennium, no issue in America is as sensitive, potentially explosive, and resistant to resolution as the issue of race. To understand the meanings of race in the future, we must first uncover the historical and cultural contexts of the past in which separate human races were conceived. Since responsible scientists have long discredited any biological or genetic definition of racial groups, historians have increasingly recognized that the so-called races of mankind are the fortuitous and arbitrary inventions of European and American history, the by-products, primarily, of Europe's religious, economic, and imperial expansion across the seas of the earth.

The arbitrary and cultural character of race has often been illustrated by contrasting the North American "Negro," defined to include anyone with even a slight trace of African ancestry, with the complex gradations of racial intermixture found in Latin America. Why is someone who has seven white European great-grandparents classified as "black"? We no longer speak of an Alpine race, a Mediterranean race, or a Hebrew race. But by what logic can the natives of Karachi, Madras, Yokohama, Manila, and Canton be conflated as "Asian"? And by what means did the Irish, Jews, and Arabs, at one time regarded as barbarous and even subhuman, become "white"? If race differentiates and divides groups of people, how important has it been as a means of unification? Of course, racial categories are no less *real* even when deprived of biological substance. Like serfdom, social castes, and royal or noble "blood," concepts of race influence perception, including self-perception, and can above all represent a shared historical experience, such as that of Amerindians and African Americans in the United States.

If there is wide agreement that races, including the "white race," have been socially constructed or invented through history, there remain some momentous questions that historians and other scholars have not resolved. Are human beings universally inclined to dehumanize people who differ from them in physiognomy, phenotype, language, religion, social status, and even gender? When we categorize people by such criteria, temporarily repressing what we share and accentuating our differences, does the resulting Otherness inevitably debase and demean even if it sometimes emits a surreptitious appeal? Is racism simply a variant on intergroup prejudice, hostility, and genocide, such as that between Tutsis and Hutus in East Africa or Serbs and Muslims in the Balkans? And if antiblack racism can erupt in modern Japan, China, and Russia, countries far removed from the historical effects of black slavery, should we conclude that this kind of racism is universal, immutable, perhaps inevitable?

When an earlier generation debated the origins of antiblack racism, attention tended to fall on underlying economic forces and on whether African-American slavery preceded or followed the emergence of collective and deeply rooted prejudice. This question may have been not so much resolved as superseded as a new generation of scholars has opened new perspectives on the subject. The articles published in the special issue of *William and Mary Quarterly* (January 1997) generally move toward subtle and often extremely complex transformations in culture and perception. In "*Othello* and Africa: Postcolonialism Reconsidered," Emily C. Bartels stresses the "experimental," "random," and "disjointed" nature of England's early overseas ventures as she reconstructs the historical context of Shakespeare's great play. After showing that the truly great cultural divide in *Othello* separated Venetians from the Turks, not the Moor, Bartels challenges the widespread postcolonialist insistence on "a linear or inevitable progression from expansionism to racism, exploration to domination." While she acknowledges that English culture by Shakespeare's time was already "filled with stereotypes of Africans as embodiments of evil, blackened by sin, driven by lust, and hungry for murder and revenge," Bartels points out that the English applied similar negative imagery to "sodomites," Jews, and other groups. Until the mid-seventeenth century, she insists, there was a significant "disjunction between a world that would acknowledge and embrace a Moor of Venice" and "one that would rather put him in chains, like a circumcised dog."

Alden T. Vaughan and Virginia Mason Vaughan agree with Bartels that the English interest in Africa was only marginal, but they present a far grimmer picture of incipient racism in their essay "Before *Othello:* Elizabethan Representations of Sub-Saharan Africans." According to the Vaughans, the earliest English accounts of sub-Saharan Africa focused on the people's collective difference, setting them apart as "a special category of humankind." As sixteenth-century travel reports moved away from classical myths and fantasies, they expressed a growing contempt, rather than admiration, for a people already associated with slavery, sin, and bestiality. "By and large," the Vaughans conclude, "the evidence suggests denigrative images of sub-Saharan Africans transcended class, gender, age, and levels of literacy."

Robin Blackburn's "The Old World Background to European Colonial Slavery" moves from literary and travel literature to the complex and varied conditions that prepared the way for the Atlantic slave system. On the one hand, Blackburn discusses the disappearance of slavery and serfdom from most parts of western Europe as the economies changed from feudal business and agriculture to free commerce and capitalism. Ironically, this revolutionary emergence of regions of freedom and affluence created the consumers' market for sugar, tobacco, coffee, cotton, and other commodities that would be produced by New World slaves. On the other hand, Blackburn emphasizes that neither economic change nor the Renaissance and Reformation led to a significant repudiation of the *principle* of slavery, although Christian states seem to have followed the Muslim example of forbidding the forcible enslavement of their co-religionists. Hence, the Portuguese, Spaniards, Dutch, French, and English had few qualms about purchasing pagan or even Muslim slaves along the West African coast. After reviewing the steps that led to the African slave trade, Blackburn concludes that the racial slavery practiced on New World plantations was "quite unlike what had existed in any part of the Old World."

Students of American slavery are aware that in the eighteenth and nineteenth centuries the biblical curse of Canaan, the son of Ham, was probably the central justification for racial slavery. In "The Sons of Noah and the Construction of Ethnic and Geographical Identities in the Medieval and Early Modern Periods," Benjamin Braude demolishes much of the conventional wisdom concerning the Christian and Jewish interpretations of this crucial theological foundation of antiblack racism. If medieval and early modern Europeans had not believed that all human beings were the descendants of Noah's sons, Braude argues, their treatment of Jews, Muslims, Africans, and Native Americans would have been even worse than it turned out to be. But as Braude examines the numerous contradictory texts of such works as *The Travels of Sir John Mandeville*, he documents centuries of ambiguity and disagreement concerning the geographical assignments of Noah's sons, Ham, Shem, and Japhet. Even in the fifteenth century, as the Portuguese began shipping African slaves to Lisbon and the Atlantic islands, other Christians associated sub-Saharan Africa with Prester John and the Ethiopian Christians who lived in Jerusalem or made their way to Rome. After illuminating the highly diverse ways in which Christians and Jews interpreted Genesis 9 and 10, Braude suggests that it was only in the period from 1589 to 1625 that the institution of African slavery began to influence English views of Noah's curse as an explanation for both blackness of skin and perpetual servitude.

Historians of early America must always remind themselves that the English were latecomers and that the Atlantic slave system was an Iberian (and Italian and African) creation. James H. Sweet, in "The Iberian Roots of American Racist Thought," questions the conventional equation of racism with capitalism as he traces antiblack imagery and rhetoric back through feudal Castile and Andalusia to medieval Muslim distinctions between black and light-skinned slaves. Stressing long-term continuity, in contrast to Bartels and Braude, Sweet concludes that, by the fifteenth century, "race, and especially skin color, defined the contours of power relationships. . . . Biological assumptions that were familiar to a nineteenth-century Cuban slaveowner would have been recognizable to his fifteenth-century Spanish counterpart." In assessing this claim we must remember Braude's warning against projecting modern assumptions into the past. Yet Sweet's quotations indicate that Africans were likened to animals for many centuries before Columbus, a point that connects his essay with Jennifer L. Morgan's " 'Some Could Suckle Over Their Shoulder': Male Travelers, Female Bodies, and the Gendering of Racial Ideology, 1500–1770."

To the question of race Morgan fuses the crucial element of gender, showing that a single male traveler like Richard Ligon could exclaim in the Cape Verde Islands over a "Negro of the greatest beauty and majesty," a woman comparable to an English queen, and then express complete disgust over African slaves in Barbados whose breasts "hang down below their Navels, so that when . . . weeding, they hang almost to the ground, that at a distance you would think they had six legs." As Morgan demonstrates, this English animalization of Africans centered on the transformation of women from beautiful mothers and lovers to lecherous and totally promiscuous beasts who bit off penises, slept with a new man each night, copulated with apes, experienced no pain at childbirth, and allowed their children to run about stark naked, "their private members all open." According to Morgan, the icon of distended breasts signified an inferiority that wholly justified the domestication in America of such dehumanized humans as African slaves.

It would be difficult to imagine a greater contrast when we turn next to representations of American Indians in Karen Ordahl Kupperman's "Presentment of Civility: English Reading of American Self-Presentation in the Early Years of Colonization." Drawing on the biblical belief in humanity's common origin, early English travelers and settlers expressed delight over points of likeness that they and the Indians shared. Their writings implied that both they and the Indians were attempting to "read" each others' bodies and behavior with similar questions in mind. To Englishmen, Indians were far from being a separate race; they were "borne white" and were later somewhat darkened by the sun and, like the ancient English, by the use of dyes. Kupperman convincingly connects the growing popularity of English manuals on deportment, posture, and civil "carriage," as signs of the inner self, with the great emphasis of English observers on Indians' aristocratic bearing, restraint, and modesty. The North American natives not only were tall and well proportioned but stood straight as arrows. According to Kupperman, the English were particularly struck by the modesty of Indian women, the majesty of Indian kings "who acted like kings," and the success with which Indian elites maintained order and distinction. At a time when the English were beginning to express fear that their own society was breaking down, the Indian example was reassuring. Yet the same writers who admired the Indians' "natural" boundaries of gender, class, and status voiced much optimism over the prospects of Christianizing and civilizing these innocent and dignified people.

The final essay, Joyce E. Chaplin's "Natural Philosophy and an Early Racial Idiom in North America: Comparing English and Indian Bodies," moves on from the idealized stage described by Kupperman to show how English colonists racialized Indian bodies without resorting to a "paradigm shift," such as rejection of the belief in a common human nature and origin. Chaplin begins by describing the ancient European discourse of "natural philosophy," an amalgam of Aristotle and the Hippocratic and Galenic traditions that explained human bodily variations in nonracial, environmental terms. As the colonists tried to explain the ghastly Indian mortality from disease in terms of natural philosophy, they increasingly gravitated toward conceptions of inferiority and superiority, suggesting that the Indians were not naturally suited for the American environment. Although Anglo-Americans often praised Indian pharmacology, they interpreted the Indians' susceptibility to disease as a kind of racial failing. According to Chaplin, the ancient discourse of natural philosophy enabled the white colonists to construct a *physical* identity for themselves as the truly "native" Americans.

Beginning in 1950, when Oscar and Mary Flug Handlin published an immensely influential article in the *William and Mary Quarterly*, the theory that antiblack racism was an indeterminate product of contingent conditions focused narrowly on the records of a few decades in seventeenth-century Virginia. Such evidence, as later analyzed, expanded, and interpreted by Edmund S. Morgan, T. H. Breen, and Stephen Innes, seemed to confirm the generalization Eric Williams made in 1944 in his seminal *Capitalism and Slavery*: "slavery was not born of racism: rather, racism was the consequence of slavery."[1]

In 1968, Winthrop D. Jordan's authoritative *White over Black* severely qualified this maxim and rightly moved the locus of the "origins debate" backward in time and eastward across the Atlantic—in Jordan's first chapter—to Elizabethan England. After examining "the unthinking decision" that led to the adoption of slave labor in British North America, Jordan brilliantly analyzed the cultural evolution of American racial attitudes in the eighteenth century, concluding with an understood commitment "toward a white man's country." Jordan's book was the pioneering precondition for the papers of the Omohundro Institute's April 1996 seminar "Constructing Race: Differentiating Peoples in the Early Modern World, 1400–1700." Yet with respect to one introductory point in *White over Black*, Braude, David Goldenberg, Paul Freedman, Ephraim Isaac, and other scholars have now shown that Jordan seriously distorted the Talmudic and rabbinic interpretations of the biblical Curse of Canaan, implying a Jewish origin of antiblack racism (an innocent error that has proved to be especially unfortunate in view of Louis Farrakhan's anti-Semitic campaign to blame Jews for inventing racism and Jordan's own negative but legitimating review in the *Atlantic Monthly* of the Nation of Islam's vicious propaganda tract, *The Secret Relationship between Blacks and Jews*.[2] Like numerous other scholars, Jordan also projected modern perceptions of blacks into premodern Europe, thereby constructing a linear and continuous progression of racist thought in Europe that now appears to evaporate in the light of Braude's meticulous research on the construction of

racial identity in medieval and early modern Europe. This position is reinforced by the articles of Bartels, Blackburn, Morgan, and Chaplin.

It takes much mental discipline to picture educated Europeans who may
never have seen a map, a Bible, a calendar, or a clock. Muslim geographers
benefited from the detailed ethnographic reports of Muslim merchants and
travelers whose inexhaustible curiosity about *Dar al-Harb*, the lands of infidelity, arose from the certitude of men who have found the ultimate religious
truth, but Europeans had no clear, fixed sense of political or continental
boundaries. In his longer seminar paper, Braude contrasts the immensely
erudite eleventh-century *History of India* by the great Muslim scholar al-
Biruni with *The Travels of Sir John Mandeville*, "a monument to the ignorance
of medieval Christendom" but nonetheless the most widely read work of
travel between 1350 and 1600, a true best-seller survey of the world's Others,
a copy of which Columbus probably took with him to America.

At a time when Muslims studied and admired the achievements of Hindu,
Chinese, and classical civilizations, even learned Europeans marveled at Mandeville's (the true authorship is unknown) accounts of anthropophagi, of
anthills of gold dust, and of men whose heads grew beneath their shoulders.
Yet like virtually all Christian writers, Mandeville took for granted the unity
and common origin of humankind. This consensus gave added significance
to the biblical curses of Cain and Canaan (or Ham), which were linked to
Africa and slavery, as Braude demonstrates, much later than historians have
previously supposed. Except in Iberia, where Christians struggled against the
Moorish infidel, the most immediate and sometimes threatening Others in
the eyes of literate western Europeans were, first, the small minority of
"Christ-killing Jews" and, second, the great mass of serfs, villeins, and rustic
peasants.

While historians and other scholars frequently speak of dehumanization,
they have seldom grasped the significance of the ultimate weapon for excluding humans from empathy, equal fellowship, and the Golden Rule: bestialization, which, significantly, was closely associated with human enslavement from the time of the earliest civilizations.[3] This theme, which Morgan
develops with particular insight, runs through many of the essays. There is
a profound meaning behind Aristotle's remark that the ox was the poor man's
slave. Anyone familiar with the history of Christians representing Jews as
horned beasts, swine, and vermin or the ways in which blacks have been
animalized in the United States—and Jordan was a pioneer in exploring that
theme—will be stunned by the discoveries of Freedman, a medievalist on

whom Braude draws, regarding Europe's bestialization of the "lower orders" over a period of many centuries.[4]

Of course, animals can be loved, admired, and even worshipped, and comparisons of people to animals can be a means of endearment or praise, as some Englishmen learned to their surprise from American Indians. But that was not the message when the literate likened peasants to wolves, asses, dogs, pigs, and baboons with muzzles, snouts, and paws or when humorists constantly played on the theme of the rustics' filth and affinity for huge farts and excrement. Rustics were frequently said to be "worse than Jews" or as "inept and wicked" as Jews. Yet unlike the supposedly scheming and avaricious Jews, rustics' resemblance to animals signified a level of ignorance, stupidity, and gullibility that might occasion pity and laughter as well as contempt. Animality could also suggest the peril of murderous violence and the need for surveillance and discipline. As Freedman notes, bestialization usually involves an oscillation between the discovery of both animal and human traits. If a villein or peasant was "like" an ox or pig, it was precisely because he or she was also something more than an ox or pig, something that made the comparison meaningful. Like the later African slaves in the New World colonies, the peasants were productive, useful, even necessary. Unlike the black slaves, they were not from an alien land, though they were often described as being "black" as a result of their constant exposure to the sun, soil, and manure.

Is it possible that the stereotype of the black, beastly European rustic, personifying the human Id, became a template for the later representations of the Negro slave? Freedman devotes an entire chapter of his prizewinning book to the ways in which the biblical curses of Cain and Ham (really Canaan) were applied to European serfs and peasants. While the malformed Cain "represented the ur-peasant," the tiller of the ground who killed his shepherd brother after God rejected his offering, Ham came to be regarded as the progenitor of the unfree, including northern serfs. Apart from controversies over the biblical sources of human servitude and inequality, Freedman points out that "the entire discourse about the filthy, wicked or bestial peasantry is an extended commentary on the notion of natural slavery, that some are fit [as Aristotle had observed] by their nature for labor." Medieval writers used every imaginable figure and device to prove that the subservience of farm laborers was rooted in nature and therefore just. By mocking the animal-like peasants, satirists in particular could define the standards of chivalric, civilized men. To be sure, rustics were at least nominally Christians and therefore theoretically equal in the eyes of God. In time, the peasantry could be emancipated, romanticized, and nationalized. They could even become, as in Russia, the "soul" of the nation.

This precolonial snapshot of European dehumanization provides a wider context for viewing and comparing the first English perceptions of Native Americans with the first English representations of sub-Saharan Africans. As readers digest the information conveyed especially by Morgan, Kupperman, Chaplin, and the Vaughans, even well-informed historians may be astonished by the remarkable contrast between these first English depictions of Indians and Africans.

As the essays indicate, the English in North America not only admired and paid tribute to the natives but eagerly looked for evidence of a common humanity. From Virginia to New England, Englishmen marveled over the *aristocratic* bearing and posture of Native Americans, a feature that presumably exempted them from being identified in any way with the English lower classes. English writers seemed no less surprised and pleased by the "modesty" of Indian women, whose status as wives or virgins could be detected by subtle cultural insignia. Because Native Americans were associated with Nature, their sensitivity to status appeared to legitimate England's hierarchical social structure. The precise opposite could be said of Africans, who, as Morgan suggests, seemed to dissolve even the boundaries between the sexes. According to Kupperman, English writers actually looked to the Indians' customs and culture for solutions to what they perceived as the growing social problems of their own homeland.

When we first read the late sixteenth- and early seventeenth-century accounts, we know in the back of our minds that when the Indians begin to resist the white settlers' desires and expectations, they will quickly become unredeemable "savages." They will be killed, enslaved, sold to the West Indies, and hunted like animals. As Kupperman puts it, the Indians will be increasingly thought of as "as permanently other—and permanently lower." Nevertheless, the Englishmen's initial conviction of commonality, reinforced by a continuing dependence on Indians for trade and military alliance, worked against the kind of racist separation and degradation associated with Africans. For example, in a 1996 paper on Anglo-Iroquois diplomacy from 1744 to 1776, Timothy J. Shannon underscores the lengths to which both English and Indians went at their feasts and dances to overcome their immense cultural differences and to ritualize their shared humanity.[5] When English negotiators considered it an honor to accept Iroquois names and other gifts, we see the very antithesis of rituals of dehumanization.

As we turn to Africa, it is worth noting that several of the essays cite John Thornton's 1992 study of the early Portuguese commercial interaction with West Africans.[6] There is a certain resemblance between the English negotiations with the Iroquois and the scenes Thornton describes of mimetic cultural influence and mutual exchange, especially in Kongo and Angola. Indeed, the Africans, whose steel and textiles rivaled those of Europe, were far more powerful than any Native Americans. But, unfortunately, the Africans were selling and even buying slaves from the Portuguese, and the relatively egalitarian relationship of the fifteenth and sixteenth centuries created the Atlantic slave system. And the articles by the Vaughans, Sweet, and Morgan describe extremely negative characterizations of a race or people who were increasingly associated with human bondage.

The Vaughans' article presents such a striking contrast to the roughly contemporary English depictions of Indians described by Kupperman and Chaplin. The Vaughans find that, from the mid-sixteenth century onward, English writers accentuated the *differences* between themselves and sub-Saharan Africans, a point also underscored by Morgan. In the words of Robert Gainsh, after a voyage in 1554 to equatorial Africa, the blacks were "a people of beastly lyvyng, without a God, lawe, religion, or common wealth." The imagery of "blacke beasts" and "brutish blacke people" recurs throughout the descriptions the Vaughans and Morgan cite, though there is not yet any argument that Africans are a separately created species. Nakedness, reports of cannibalism, and the proximity of "wild and monstrous beasts and serpents" all reinforce the impression of tropical animality. Kupperman explains why the constantly clad English viewed even well-dressed Indians as "naked," a term that in America expressed more curiosity than contempt. In Africa, however, "nakedness" tied in with Gainsh's report that, like animals, "women are common: they contracte no matrimonie, neyther have respecte to chastitie."[7] In other words, all the boundaries and constraints that distinguish humanity have disappeared.

One must remember, as Bartels and the Vaughans stress, that English interest in Africa was always limited and secondary to interest in America and that about a century elapsed between the first Portuguese commercial ventures along the West African coast and the first English eyewitness accounts of West Africa.[8] Yet the Vaughans conclusively show that in the late Elizabethan period a plethora of travel narratives, plays, poems, and visual material conveyed an overwhelmingly negative view of Africans. Indeed, this prejudicial climate even led Queen Elizabeth, in the waning years of her reign, to call "repeatedly, though unsuccessfully, for the expulsion from the realm of 'the great numbers of negars and Blackamoores' who had become a 'great annoyance of hir owne leige people.'" This was a full two generations before England became seriously involved in the African slave trade.

How do we account for this extraordinary contrast between Africans and Native Americans? As Morgan notes, Indians could also be portrayed as cannibalistic savages or as conforming to Aristotle's definition of "natural" slaves. Yet no one can doubt the general proposition that Englishmen regarded Indians with a kind of respect and admiration very seldom extended to sub-Saharan Africans. Although much of the difference probably arose from the circumstances of trade, disease environments, and conquest—until the late nineteenth century, tropical diseases prevented colonization of the region south of the Sahara and north of South Africa—another possibility may be worth investigation. At a time when the English were congratulating themselves on being the world's first truly "free" people, could it be that Africans provided a scapegoat for removing some of the negative imagery long projected on villeins and peasants? This hypothesis would harmonize with Kupperman's suggestion that North American Indians represented a mirror of gentility in which the English could find sanction for their own class system.

On quite different paths, some historians have pointed to a generally negative tradition regarding Africa that extends back through Leo Africanus, various editions of *Mandeville's Travels*, Benjamin of Tudela, and Isidore of Seville, to such classical writers as Pliny the Elder and Herodotus. The naked Americans, on the other hand, living in apparent freedom and innocence, awakened memories of terrestrial paradise and the Golden Age described by the ancients. Of course, Iberians also created a literature on Indian cannibalism and human sacrifice. But even Columbus fell under the spell of the gentle natives on the Gulf of Paria who wore golden ornaments and lived in a land of lush vegetation and delicious fruits. He concluded in August 1498 that he had arrived on the "nipple" of the earth, which reached closer to Heaven than the rest of the globe, and that the original Garden of Eden was nearby.

In addition, as Braude observes, the long-standing conviction that American Indians were the Lost Tribes of Israel linked the New World with the vision of an imminent millennium.

Sweet points out that the centuries of warfare between Christians and Muslims in southwestern Europe, culminating in the Christian Reconquest of Portugal and Spain, nourished the image of white Christians overcoming dark-skinned Moors. Since the Berber dynasties (Almoravids and Almohades) had deployed armies that included thousands of black slaves, *all* of Africa became equated in many Christian minds with the Islamic enemy. Historians have also speculated on the possibility of Zoroastrian, Gnostic, or Manichaean influence on the changing religious meanings of blackness, as exemplified by the black devils and torturers in European medieval art. Yet there is a danger of exaggerating the contrast between Africa and the New World. The Spanish and Portuguese slaughter and enslavement of the Berber-like Canary Islanders has quite rightly been seen as a prelude to the slaughter and enslavement of Caribbean, Mexican, Central American, and Brazilian Indians.

The myth of a racially tolerant Latin America has tended to divert attention from the scholarly literature on slavery and race in the Iberian peninsula, especially in the fifteenth century, and in earlier Muslim states from North Africa to Persia and even India. Sweet makes a valuable contribution by synthesizing a vast amount of evidence to support his conclusion that "Iberian racism was a necessary precondition for the system of human bondage that would develop in the Americas during the sixteenth century and beyond." He also challenges the conventional Marxist equation of racism with capitalism by emphasizing the religious foundations of much racist thought, including the Spanish anti-Semitic obsession with "purity of blood"—a subject also discussed by Blackburn—and by observing that certain aspects of racism to be found in Iberian societies "preceded the emergence of capitalism by centuries."

It should be emphasized that these points do not detract from the thesis of Eric Williams that views slavery as the ultimate source of racism. Sweet cites estimates ranging from 80,000 to 150,000 for the number of slaves shipped to Portugal from sub-Saharan Africa in the fifty years before Columbus's voyage of 1492. Some of these bondspeople were exported to Castile and other European and Mediterranean markets; others were purchased from caravan traders in North Africa and sent to Sicily. Much earlier, after the Islamic conquests of Egypt and Tripoli, the Nilotic and central Sudanese states regularly delivered slaves to the north as part of a commercial pact or as a form of tribute, and by the fifteenth century literally millions of African slaves had been imported into Islamic lands from Spain to India. Therefore, when the fourteenth-century Arab historian Ibn Khaldūn asserted that blacks "have little [that is essentially] human and possess attributes that are quite similar to those of dumb animals," he and numerous other Islamic writers were constructing or passing on stereotypes of *slaves*—stereotypes that had been applied since earliest antiquity to slaves of numerous ethnicities and of non-African origin.[9]

It is true, as Sweet makes clear, that Arabs and Berbers increasingly consigned blacks to the lowliest and most degrading forms of labor, denying them the privileges often given to *mamluks* or white slaves. This was partly because European slaves could often be ransomed and, as monarchs like Ivan the Great took steps to protect their subjects, because white slaves were in increasingly short supply. Though many Arabs came to equate slavery with sub-Saharan phenotypes, the prevalence of racist stereotypes did not lead to a racist system of laws or to a widespread system of plantation production. Still, from the tenth century onward, a growing body of Arabic literature tried to defend blacks from prejudice, and poets of African or mixed African parentage cried out: "If my color were pink, women would love me / But the Lord has marred me with blackness"; or "Though my hair is woolly and my skin coal-black, / My hand is open and my honor bright"; or "My color is pitch-black, my hair woolly, my appearance repulsive." "I am a black man," a famous singer and musician wrote on seeking lodging in Damascus: "Some of you may find me offensive. I shall therefore sit and eat apart."[10]

There is a seeming conflict between, on the one hand, the continuity implied by such examples together with the dehumanizing images of black slaves documented by Sweet and the Vaughans and, on the other, the more optimistic sense of contingency and openness conveyed by Braude, who argues that there were no medieval Christian or Jewish traditions regarding the suitability of Africans for slavery.

Braude's painstaking research highlights the danger of projecting a relatively modern consensus, such as identifying the biblical Ham with Africa, onto medieval texts. Clearly, Noah's portentous curse could be used to justify the subordination of European serfs or to explain the immense and reckless power of Asian invaders. The lack of any single or consistent cultural tradition concerning Africa meant that popes could look forward to Ethiopian Christian missions to Rome from Jerusalem or Ethiopia itself, that in scenes of the Nativity a non-kneeling Magus could be depicted with Negroid features, and that similar features could appear in northern European paintings and statues of St. Maurice, the Theban martyr who by the mid-thirteenth century had become a Germanic saint heading the conquest and Christianization of pagan Slavs and Magyars![11]

But does this contingency and flexibility rule out the possible transfer and acculturation of antiblack stereotypes, along with a familiarity with black slavery, from Muslims to Iberian Christians and Jews and from Iberians to the budding maritime powers of northern Europe? We should note that from the Treaty of Windsor, in 1386, Portugal and England were strongly allied. English ships, like African slaves, were a common sight in Portuguese Madeira, where Columbus once lived.

There is a related and parallel issue regarding the continuity and evolution of slave systems from the medieval Mediterranean to the New World. Blackburn maps out with great skill and coherence the events and changing institutions in the Old World that finally led to the Atlantic slave system. Yet he insists that the New World plantation colonies developed a unique form of racial slavery that differed from the slavery in any part of the Old World.[12] This paradox of continuity and uniqueness emerges in Darwinian evolution, in human families, and in all historical change. Is it not possible, then, to recognize the highly distinctive characteristics of New World racial slavery while also stressing the crucial importance of the Black Sea slave trade, the Italian colonies in the Mediterranean, the westward movement of sugar cultivation, and the shift to African slave labor on the plantations of the Atlantic islands?

With respect to a related and perhaps more controversial matter, Stephen P. Bensch has called attention to the tendency of historians "to regard medieval slavery as a static, moribund institution doomed to extinction in the transition from slavery to feudalism." Bensch feels it necessary to insist "that slavery did not remain a static category in the West over a period of a thousand years."[13] With such imaginative work as Ruth Mazo Karras's *Slavery and Society in Medieval Scandinavia*, a new generation of medieval historians seems to be moving beyond rigid Marxist "stages" and what Pierre Bonnassie has termed the "furious polemics" within the Marxist camp.[14] New clarity on how and why slavery disappeared from western Europe can only further our understanding of "the enslavement" of the Western Hemisphere.

Finally, these essays as a whole point to the amazing convergence of seemingly unrelated events in the revolutionary period from the mid-1400s to the mid-1500s: the Christian alarm over "the Terrible Turk" as the Ottoman empire pushed westward, capturing Constantinople and thereby cutting off the Italian slave markets on the Black Sea coasts, diminishing Europe's supply of sugar, and diverting Italian investment, enterprise, and colonizing experience to Seville and Lisbon; the final Christian Reconquest of Granada and the Portuguese and Spanish colonization of the Atlantic islands, coupled with the beginnings of the maritime slave trade from West Africa to Iberia and the colonies; the westward extension of sugar cultivation, especially to São Tomé and Brazil, and the rise of Antwerp as a sugar refining and distributing center for northern Europe; the development in western Europe of a more urbanized market for foreign luxuries; the opening of direct oceanic commerce with Asia, and the discovery and colonization of America; the Protestant Reformation; the invention of printing and the diffusion of capitalist print culture, which revolutionized popular knowledge of the Bible and other sources of information; the growing conviction in western Europe that sub-Saharan Africans were the descendants of Ham or Cain and thus destined to be perpetual slaves. The list could be lengthened, but we can already see many of the tools, instruments, and conditions for "constructing race."

Notes

1. Williams, *Capitalism and Slavery* (Chapel Hill, 1944), 7.
2. *Atlantic Monthly*, September 1995, 109–14. See the January 1996 issue for letters and Jordan's lame reply (pp. 14–15). For references to the works by Goldenberg and Isaac see Braude's article, note 57. Let me stress that I am not implying in any way that Jordan is guilty of anti-Semitism, but he has helped the cause of anti-Semites.
3. David Brion Davis, *From Homicide to Slavery: Studies in American Culture* (New York, 1986), 213, and *Slavery and Human Progress* (New York, 1984), 4; "At the Heart of Slavery," in this volume; Karl Jacoby, "Slaves by Nature? Domestic Animals and Human Slaves," *Slavery and Abolition*, 15 (April 1994), 89–97. This will be a major theme of my book *The Problem of Slavery in the Age of Emancipation: Dilemmas of Race and Nation*.
4. I wish to thank Paul Freedman for permitting me to draw on his book *Sanctity and Savagery: The Images of the Medieval Peasant* (Stanford, Calif., 1999) well before it was published.

5. "Dress, Deportment, and Social Ritual in Anglo-Iroquois Diplomacy, 1744–1776," paper delivered at the Milan Group in Early U.S. History, 8th Biennial Symposium, June 20, 1996.

6. Thornton, *Africa and Africans in the Making of the Atlantic World, 1400–1680* (Cambridge, 1992).

7. Morgan attributes this quotation to John Lok, "borrowing verbatim from Richard Eden's 1555 translation of Peter Martyr" (p. 179, n. 34). The Vaughans, citing Eden and Willes and Hakluyt, write that "authorship of the otherwise anonymous report of the second voyage to Guinea is attributed to Gainsh in the running heads of Hakluyt" (p. 25 n. 17).

8. Although the English first sailed along the Guinea coast in 1530, it was only the voyages of the 1550s that led to printed descriptions of sub-Saharan Africans.

9. In addition to the essay by Sweet, see Davis, "Slaves in Islam," in this volume, and *Slavery and Human Progress*, 32–54; Bernard Lewis, *Race and Color in Islam* (New York, 1971), and *Race and Slavery in the Middle East: An Historical Enquiry* (New York, 1990); and Gernot Rotter, *Die Stellung des Negers in der islamisch-arabischen Gesellschaft bis zum XVI Jahrhundert* (Bonn, 1967).

10. Lewis, *Race and Slavery in the Middle East*, 28–30.

11. See especially Jean Devisse, ed., *The Image of the Black in Western Art*, 2 vols. (New York, 1979).

12. Blackburn apparently forgets the Portuguese colony of São Tomé, in the Gulf of Guinea, where in the early 1500s thousands of black slaves toiled on sugar plantations that would be difficult to distinguish from those later created in Brazil.

13. Bensch, "From Prizes of War to Domestic Merchandise: The Changing Face of Slavery in Catalonia and Aragon, 1000–1300," *Viator*, 25 (1994), 4–5.

14. Karras, *Slavery and Society in Medieval Scandinavia* (New Haven, 1988); Bonnassie, *From Slavery to Feudalism in South-Western Europe*, trans. Jean Birrell (Cambridge, 1990), 8; Debra G. Blumenthal, "'Implements of Labor, Instruments of Honor': Muslim, Eastern, and Black African Slaves in Fifteenth-Century Valencia," Ph.D. diss., University of Toronto, 2000.

24

The Culmination of Racial Polarities and Prejudice

The classic, authoritative eleventh edition (1910–1911) of the *Encyclopaedia Britannica* can well be seen as a great compendium of the knowledge and wisdom of the nineteenth century, updated in final form for the twentieth century.[1] The authors of the essays, often long and beautifully written, include many of the most famous writers and scientists of the time. The subject "Indians, North American," commands thirty double-column pages of fine print, covering nearly two hundred tribes, fifty-five "stocks," much technical information on Indian languages, and a sober assessment of the Indians' then present "condition" and "progress."

The subject "Negro" warrants less than five double-column pages, but in the second part, "Negroes in the United States," Walter Francis Willcox, a Cornell professor of social science and statistics and the chief statistician of the U.S. Census Bureau, presents a cautiously optimistic and highly statistical view of the post-Reconstruction condition of African-Americans, and cites three works each by Booker T. Washington and W. E. B. Du Bois.[2] The first and more generalized essay, by Thomas A. Joyce, an anthropologist at the British Museum's Department of Ethnography, draws on a far more international scholarly literature and conveys the impression of cautious objectivity. For example, Joyce states at one point that "the negro is largely the creature of his environment, and it is not fair to judge of his mental capacity by tests taken directly from the environment of the white man, as for instance tests in mental arithmetic."

Yet Joyce shows no hesitation on the key issue:

Mentally the negro is inferior to the white. The remark of F. Manetta [in *La Razza Negra nel suo stato selvaggio* (Turin, 1864), p. 20], made after a long study of the negro in America, may be taken as generally true of the whole race: "the negro children were sharp, intelligent and full of vivacity, but on approaching the adult period a gradual change set in. The intellect seemed to become clouded, animation giving place to a sort of lethargy, briskness yielding to indolence . . ." the arrest or even deterioration in mental development is no doubt very largely due to the fact that after puberty sexual matters take the first place in the negro's life and thoughts.

This basic white consensus, embodied in such influential and "progressive" works as Ulrich Bonnell Phillips's *American Negro Slavery* (1918) and W. E. Woodward's popular *A New American History* (1936), was in many ways the product of the historical changes described in eight essays, to which this article is a conclusion, in a special issue, "Racial Consciousness and Nation Building in the Early Republic," in the Winter 1999 *Journal of the Early Republic*. As the essays vividly suggest, the ways in which slaves were freed in the North, together with the "removal" of the Indians from the south-eastern states and the expansion and defense of racial slavery in the South, exerted a profound influence on the meaning of emancipation in the Civil War and the ultimate abandonment of Reconstruction. The resulting white consensus on Negro inferiority, greatly reinforced by Euro-American pseudo-science and popular media such as film, became a massive blight or ideological pathogen against which generations of black and white scholars and activists have struggled.

In the antebellum period a few white radicals, such as Gerrit Smith and John Brown, emerged from the racist Platonic cave of misperception and succeeded in viewing the world through African-American eyes.[3] Yet as Smith and Brown discovered, the truth of equality was too overwhelming to bear. If Africans and people of African descent were truly equal and capable of all the mental achievements of whites, then the whites' recognition of guilt should resemble Michelangelo's faces of the Damned in the Sistine Chapel's *Last Judgment*.[4] This vision of guilt would include not only the four centuries of the ghastly Atlantic slave trade and New World slavery, the many decades of Jim Crow and the thousands of lynchings, but also the long-term effects of what the black abolitionist Theodore S. Wright termed in 1836 "the spirit of prejudice," which, like the atmosphere everywhere felt by [the colored man] . . . withering all our hopes, and oft times causes the colored parent as he looks upon his child, to wish he had never been born. . . . This *influence* cuts us off from everything; it follows us up from childhood to manhood; it excludes us from all stations of profit, usefulness, and honor; takes away from us all motive for pressing forward in enterprises, useful and important to the world and to ourselves.[5]

As Wright and other black writers emphasized, this humiliating and dehumanizing prejudice could be self-reinforcing in the sense that white contempt and denial of hope could lead to despair and patterns of behavior that provoked more prejudice. Given the genuine progress made since World War II, it is extremely difficult for today's historians to imagine the psychological *effects* of enslavement and rabid racism on black aspirations and behavior in the nineteenth and early twentieth centuries.[6] Even in the 1930s and 1940s, at the time of Stepinfetchit and *Native Son*, the number of African-American college graduates, doctors, lawyers, generals, and business executives in the year 2000 would have seemed incredible.[7] Of course we still have a long way to go in freeing ourselves from the heritage of the white racist consensus symbolized by the 1911 *Encyclopaedia Britannica* article. But meanwhile, the moral shock of facing the realities of our past can easily oversimplify history by moralistically dividing its actors into "the children of light and the children of darkness."

For many years there has been a strong tendency to write history in the constant shadow of "what should have happened," from the perspective of the late twentieth century. Precisely because both masters and slaves were complex human beings, their relationships often defy easy formulas and expectations. The fashionable and continuing emphasis on slave resistance, while correcting the *Gone with the Wind* mythology, makes it virtually impossible to explain why slavery could be so economically productive and successful over long periods of time, why slave prices in the South continued to rise through the 1850s and well into the Civil War, and how two or three adult white males could control one hundred or two hundred slaves on an isolated Caribbean or southern plantation. It is also easy to forget that negrophobia has sometimes been closely related to negrophilia, much as antiSemitism and philosemitism have "bled over into each other," as the historian Harold Brackman puts it.[8] But above all, if we are to understand the workings of historical evil, we must strive to *understand* (which must always be distinguished from exoneration) the minds not only of slaves and free blacks but of masters, blackface minstrels, colonizationists, anti-abolitionists, and leaders of lynch mobs (how can one understand World War II without seeing the world through the eyes of Hitler, SS troops, and their commanders?).

The eight excellent essays in the *Journal of the Early Republic* collection point to the 1830s as a time of critical change for African and Native Americans, a transformation that led, I would conclude, to a "culmination of racial polarities" during the century that followed. Of course no matter when a historian begins a particular inquiry or narrative, there is always a "before." Without questioning the centrality of the 1830s (and some of the essays do move back into the eighteenth century), I think it is important to take note of a number of recent discoveries regarding the much earlier Euro-American "construction of race," particularly a 1996 seminar that met in Colonial Williamsburg and then produced a special issue of the *William and Mary Quarterly.*[9] Thus before discussing a few of the questions raised in the Winter 1999 *Journal of the Early Republic*, I would like to summarize some of the antecedents and preconditions that help to put early or mid-nineteenth-century racial developments in broader perspective.

As the medievalist Paul Freedman has shown, "whiteness studies" should turn first to the symbolism of social class in medieval Europe. For many centuries the aristocracy, clergy, and commercial classes looked upon serfs and peasants with contempt, derision, and sometimes fear. Unlike Jews, Muslims, heretics, and lepers, who were also degraded and dehumanized, the servile peasants constituted a large majority of the population and furnished the physical labor on which the elites depended. Therefore, as Freedman emphasizes, the images of the medieval peasant could combine a mockery of filth, stupidity, and bestiality with occasional tributes to the peasants' simplicity, piety, and closeness to God. Yet the need to justify vast inequality and subjugation led to the conclusion that the lower classes were the progeny of Cain or Ham (as Freedman points out, it was in the Islamic world, with its heavy traffic in African slaves, that Noah's curse of Ham's son Canaan was first widely used to link blackness with slavery).[10] Medieval Europeans also elaborated Aristotle's argument that many humans are simply born and constructed to do heavy toil. And especially in France, serfs and peasants were "often depicted as dark-skinned or 'black,' either by reason of their labor in the sun and their proximity to the earth, or as a sign of their overall hideousness."[11]

The discovery that medieval European peasants were often perceived as "black" by whites who stayed out of the sun and never handled dirt and manure fits in with Peter Kolchin's report that some nineteenth-century Russian nobles "actually claimed that whereas they had white bones peasants had black bones." And according to Kolchin, "Russian noblemen saw the peasants as inherently different from themselves, possessing the same lazy, childlike character that American slaveholders ascribed to blacks."[12]

Despite some ambiguity over the meaning of dark skin color—exemplified in medieval Europe by the statues and paintings of the noble African knight, Saint Maurice, and the black king or Magus in depictions of the Nativity scene—European Christian culture was already receptive to negative views of "black."[13] As the distinguished medievalist William Chester Jordan has put it: "Allegorically the words 'Jew' and 'Blackness' conjured the Devil; morally they denoted evil; and mystically they evoked the Day of Judgment."[14] Since medieval Europeans hardly ever viewed sub-Saharan Africans in person, their first impressions of dark-skinned humans would probably have come from religious paintings of the devil, his torturers, or a black or swarthy crucifier of Christ.[15]

Despite these predispositions, there can be no doubt that slavery produced racism, in the sense that the negative stereotypes that had been applied to slaves and serfs since antiquity, regardless of ethnicity, were ultimately transferred to black slaves and then to most people of African descent after bondage became almost exclusively confined to blacks. On the other hand, there is a sense in which people of dark skin were "made to order" for Europeans who had struggled for centuries to find markers that would help to justify class polarities and also identify, even at some distance outdoors, people who could be classified as "natural slaves." This is not to say that European maritime nations consciously planned to found New World colonies based on African slave labor. Black slavery was almost always a delayed and unexpected choice. Yet when Columbus sailed from Spain in 1492, African slaves were already producing much of Europe's sugar on the Portuguese plantation colonies of Madeira and São Tomé. And there is much evidence to support James H. Sweet's conclusion that "The Muslims created a plethora of racist ideas, but it was the Iberians who, in conjunction with a rising demand for slave labor, turned these ideas into a coherent ideology. . . . Iberian racism was a necessary precondition for the system of human bondage that would develop in the Americas during the sixteenth century and beyond."[16]

The Muslim societies from Spain and north Africa to the Mideast never developed racism in a judicial or institutional way, but as they increasingly drew on sub-Saharan supplies of slave labor, Arabic and Persian literature conveyed most of the antiblack stereotypes adopted by Euro-Americans in the eighteenth and nineteenth centuries. Ibn Khaldūn (1332–1406), one of the greatest historians and social thinkers of the Middle Ages, drew a significant line between white slaves and black slaves, and concluded that "the Negro nations are, as a rule submissive to slavery, because [Negroes] have little [that is essentially] human and have attributes that are quite similar to those of dumb animals." Khaldūn added that "most of the Negroes of the first zone [the tropics] dwell in caves and thickets, eat herbs, live in savage isolation and do not congregate, and eat each other."[17] In other medieval Arab and Iranian works the black "appears as a kind of monster or bogeyman," "ugly and misshapen," "naked and licentious." According to a thirteenth-century Persian writer, the east African "Zanj differ from animals only in that 'their two hands are lifted above the ground.' . . . Many have observed that the ape is more teachable and more intelligent than the Zanji."[18]

The frequent likening of blacks to animals is especially significant in view of the theory that slavery was originally modeled on the domestication of animals (Aristotle remarked that the ox was "the poor man's slave"), as well as the common use of bestialization as a way of dehumanizing humans and depriving them of all respect, honor, and dignity.[19] In a sense, enslavement has been the most extreme expression of this all-too-human desire for individual or group supremacy, achieved by subjugating "the Other."

The widespread existence of Islamic antiblack racism from the tenth century onward is confirmed by the response of black and colored writers, who cried out, for example, "If my color were pink, women would love me / But the Lord has marred me with blackness"; "though my hair is woolly and my skin coal-black / My hand is open and my honor bright." "I am a black man," a famous singer and musician wrote on seeking lodging in Damascus: "Some of you may find me offensive. I shall therefore sit and eat apart."[20]

There has been little study of the transmission of racist ideas from Muslims to Christians (or Jews) in the Iberian Peninsula. Gomes Eanes de Zurara, the Portuguese royal chronicler who in the mid-fifteenth century described the capture and sale of the first African slaves shipped to Portugal, referred ambiguously to the blacks who had already been enslaved by the Moorish prisoners "in accordance with ancient custom, which I believe to have been because of the curse which, after the Deluge, Noah laid upon his son Cain ["Caim," a Latin word in the orginal text], cursing him in this way:—that his race should be subject to all the other races in the world."[21] In 1625 the English Reverend Samuel Purchas also drew upon an account of Muslim slavery to make a more explicit linkage between Noah's curse, blackness of skin, and slavery.[22] Nevertheless, as Benjamin Braude makes clear, Europeans long associated Ham with Asia, and the Noachic curse was more of an ex post facto justification than an original motive for enslaving black Africans.

But the centuries of warfare between Christians and Muslims, culminating in the Christian Reconquest of Portugal and Spain, certainly did nourish the image of white Christians overcoming dark-skinned Moors—an impression reinforced by the fact that Berber armies included thousands of black slaves. James Sweet affirms that "the Portuguese were undoubtedly influenced by the attitudes of their Muslim trading partners along the Saharan littoral," and by the fact that many black slaves toiled in salt mines and fields on the Saharan frontier.[23] Whatever the sources of influence, the African slaves shipped to Lisbon in the fifteenth and sixteenth centuries were stripped naked and marketed and priced exactly like livestock. A. C. de C. M. Saunders and other scholars have documented the grim plight of slaves and free blacks in Portugal from the 1440s to the 1550s. Since protective laws were not enforced, the main curb on racism was the fraternization and occasional marriage with members of the lowest classes of whites—a situation that in some ways anticipated social relations in parts of Latin America and in what Ira Berlin has termed "the charter generation" period of slavery in North America.[24] For many centuries the interaction between blacks and whites of the lowest servile orders prevented racial polarization in the most rigid and modern sense.

One can only speculate on possible Portuguese lines of influence in England. From the Treaty of Windsor, in 1386, England was strongly allied with the nation that initiated and long dominated the African slave trade (English ships, like African slaves, were a common sight in Portuguese Madeira). While the English long showed little interest in Africa and became heavily involved in the slave trade only in the late seventeenth century, they seemed especially prone to racist views of Africans as early as the 1550s. According to the early voyager Robert Gainsh, the Negroes were "a people of beastly lyvyng, without a God, lawe, religion, or common wealth." African women, Gainsh continued, "are common: for they contracte no matrimonie, neyther have respecte to chastitie." Images of "blacke beasts" and "brutish blacke people" recur throughout the Elizabethan traveler descriptions that Emily C. Bartels and Alden T. Vaughan and Virginia Mason Vaughan have examined.[25] In effect, this new research confirms the judgment Winthrop D. Jordan made in 1969:

> They [English commentators] knew perfectly well that Negroes were men, yet they frequently described the Africans as "brutish" or "bestial" or "beastly." The hideous tortures, the cannibalism, the rapacious warfare, the revolting diet . . . seemed somehow to place the Negro among the beasts. . . . Slave traders in Africa handled Negroes the same way men in England handled beasts, herding and examining and buying.[26]

In view of the much later American colonization movement, it is important to note that Queen Elizabeth, in the waning years of her reign, "called repeatedly, though unsuccessfully, for the expulsion from the realm of 'the great numbers of negars and Blackamoores' who had become a 'great annoyance of hir owne leige people.'"[27] Two centuries later, when London received numerous blacks who had been freed by the British during the American War of Independence, Granville Sharp and other philanthropists founded Sierra Leone as a refuge for a people who were generally prevented from finding jobs or becoming integrated into English society.[28]

The essays in the "Constructing Race" collection point to an extraordinary contrast between the first English representations of Africans and those of Native Americans, who were often perceived as the descendants of the ten Lost Tribes of Israel, whose conversion would thus bring on the millennium. If the beastly, "black" European peasant personified the human Id and became a template for the later depictions of the Negro slave, English observers marveled over the *aristocratic* bearing and posture of Native Americans, who were said to be "borne white" and who seemed to share no characteristics with the English lower classes. Indeed, because Indians were associated with Nature, the "modesty" of their women and their sensitivity to status appeared to legitimate England's vast hierarchical social structure. According to Karen Ordahl Kupperman, English writers actually looked to the Indians' customs and culture for solutions to what they perceived as the growing social problems of their own homeland.[29]

Of course English settlers, like other Europeans, would soon look upon some Indians as unredeemable "savages" who could be slaughtered or enslaved and sold to the West Indies. Still, the Englishmen's initial conviction of commonality, reinforced by a continuing dependence on Indians for trade and military alliance, worked against the kind of racist separation and degradation associated with Africans. A further theme of pragmatism can be seen

in the fact that white settlers in frontier South Carolina used Indian scouts
to hunt down fugitive black slaves but also relied on armed slaves to ward
off repeated attacks by Native Americans.[30]

As we have seen, then, one can trace a continuity of negative and dehumanizing images of black Africans from medieval Muslims to fifteenth- and
sixteenth-century Iberians and on to sixteenth- and seventeenth-century
northern Europeans and Euro-Americans. Yet racism was clearly nourished
by the haphazard and somewhat fortuitous spread of black slavery from Portugal, the Mediterranean, and Atlantic Islands to the Spanish New World
colonies, Brazil, Barbados, Virginia, and then most of the Western Hemisphere (it is difficult to imagine an eighteenth-century European monarch,
after the New World slave system was solidly in place, following the example
of Portugal's Manuel I, who in 1491 helped to persuade the ruler of the
Kongo to be baptized as João I, and who even accepted an embassy in 1513
from the Empress of Ethiopia).[31] Though the continuities of negative imagery
are important as preconditions, I think it is a mistake to imagine a teleological
picture of racism developing in a linear or inevitable progression.

The complexity and fortuity of racial attitudes can be illustrated by a
number of random examples: the decision of a seventeenth-century Massachusetts court to return kidnapped captives to Africa;[32] the highly dignified
and individualized portraits of blacks by a galaxy of great Renaissance and
early modern painters; the alliances of various kinds between American indentured servants, sailors, and black slaves; the popularity among London's
poor in the early nineteenth century of the ultra-radical Spencean preacher,
Robert Wedderburn, a mulatto son of a Jamaican slave who was inspired by
the Haitian Revolution and edited the periodical *Axe Laid to the Root;*[33] and
finally, the international fame of Olaudah Equiano and Phillis Wheatley, to
say nothing of Toussaint Louverture and Frederick Douglass.

Above all, until the late eighteenth century, antiblack racism seldom permeated entire white populations or became a tool for political manipulation.
It was not until the mass emancipation of slaves became *thinkable*—starting
with the judicial decisions and cautious legislation of the Northern states in
the early 1780s and culminating with the Haitian Revolution and the French
emancipation decree of 1794—that race took on new and highly explosive
popular meanings.

As Lois Horton and Joanne Melish make clear, the consequences of gradual emancipation in the North coincided with the ending of white indentures
and with a white democratization that increasingly separated the white work-

ing class from a competitive population of former slaves who, in the words of one early mulatto preacher, "have been taught to view themselves as a rank of beings far below others," a people whom whites thought of as "despised, ignorant, and licentious."[34] As Northerners repressed and effaced their own historical experience with slavery in an effort to claim the distinction of "free soil," they converted the free blacks, as Melish perceptively shows, into a "marooned" population of "unaccountable strangers." Even black abolitionists could not agree on a confusing question: were white prejudice and black degradation the result of their own ancestors' bondage? Or of the continuing existence and expansion of black slavery in the South? The former answer, concerning slavery in the North, might well alienate white abolitionists, since they wanted to think of the North as historically "free," and even more important, Northern abolition would then underscore the long-term complexity and difficulties of emancipating slaves. In striking contrast to the British abolitionists like Thomas Clarkson, who never had to live with the consequences of emancipation and who narrated a succession of triumphs that gave the illusion of continuity from outlawing the slave trade in 1808 to the ending of slavery and apprenticeship in 1834 and 1838, American abolitionists failed to honor or celebrate their preceding generations' truly difficult struggles to abolish slavery in the North. From the time English Quakers posed embarrassing questions to Pennsylvania Quakers about the consequences of emancipation in the 1780s, American abolitionists were deeply perplexed by the issue of the free African-Americans' "condition."[35]

Even the most radical French abolitionists could first assert that no society could legitimate the crime of slavery and that "the restoration of a slave's freedom is not a gift or an act of charity . . . [but rather] a compelling duty, an act of justice, which simply affirms an existing truth," and then quickly add that "since our greed has reduced the blacks to a degraded and impotent state, [an immediate emancipation] would be equivalent to abandoning and refusing aid to infants in their cradles or to helpless cripples."[36] Though some modern historians are inclined to view such statements as examples of blatant hypocrisy, even former slaves often agreed that the institution was psychologically "degrading" and debilitating, and entailed serious problems of self-confidence, self-perception, and aspiration. The notion that slaves needed "preparation" for freedom became discredited—despite the biblical model of the Israelites' forty years of preparation in the wilderness—by measures like Britain's "apprenticeship," which merely prolonged the exploitation of black labor. Yet given the deprivations of bondage, it was hardly unreasonable to think of some kind of rehabilitation, as opposed to abandoning freedpeople in the midst of an increasingly racist and competitive society. In view of the efforts of missionaries to "civilize" the Cherokees, for example, it is remarkable how little thought abolitionists and liberal legislators gave to the issue of providing freed slaves with the skills, education, and self-confidence needed to become truly "free" in the dominant white and capitalist culture.

Nevertheless, as James Brewer Stewart makes clear, from the beginning of Northern emancipation African-American leaders hammered away at the crucial need for uplift, self-improvement, and the achievement of "respectability." White abolitionists then repeated similar appeals, which echoed much of the rhetoric concerning the "civilizing" of Southeastern Indians (and as Daniel K. Richter shows, the misguided efforts of Quakers to "civilize" the Miamis and other Northwestern tribes). To put matters in perspective, we should remember that the 1820s was a decade of unprecedented urbanization, when *white* workers were still consuming extraordinary quantities of alcohol and were only beginning to adjust to the clock-determined regimen of factory discipline. Indeed, the powerful temperance movement was in part directed by the goal of making workers more responsible and productive.

The 1820s also witnessed the birth of the Second Great Awakening, which led converts like Theodore Dwight Weld to campaign for schools that combined intellectual study with manual labor, before Weld became a radical abolitionist who reached out to and worked with the black community in Cincinnati. The movement for black uplift, upward mobility, and respectability was thus part of a much broader effort to democratize the onset of modernity and to create a more unified and socially responsible citizenry.

Such words jar or even anger some modern historians brought up in an antibourgeois, anti-elitist tradition. Though they take pride in their own status and usually try to train their own children to be courteous, neat, considerate, well-mannered, highly skilled, and well-informed, such historians and other writers tend to romanticize the supposedly communal, anti-individualistic behavior of a vaguely premodern, pre-"market revolution" era.[37] With respect to American race relations, this means the mixing of blacks, both slave and free, with mostly lower-class whites in grog houses, cellar bistros, oyster houses, lottery stalls, and houses of prostitution. If a dominant theme of American history has been upward mobility into an increasingly diverse middle class, one of the tragic costs of this dramatic improvement in education and standard of living has been a widespread disdain and contempt for those left behind, at least temporarily—for those who still lived as our ancestors did, i.e., the ancestral indentured servants, criminals, and steerage-traveling immigrants from whom most white Americans are descended. Yet even the harshest critics must admit that no nation in history has attracted so many millions of immigrants (and would-be immigrants) from all parts of the world. Nor has any other nation given such newcomers, at least over a number of generations, such a range of opportunities.[38]

But the most serious consequence of downgrading the importance of the black quest for uplift and self-respect is the way it minimizes and detracts attention from the truly central point: the racist white backlash against every form of black elevation, upward mobility, and "self-improvement." As Stewart, Melish, David R. Roediger, and Lois Horton all show, the freeing of slaves in the North led to a concerted movement—which in effect lasted at least until the 1940s—to keep the Negro "in his place." White mobs repeatedly attacked black schools, churches, fraternal societies, abolitionist printing presses, and other symbols of African-American elevation and integration into white American society. Despite such pressures, some antebellum blacks did become prosperous or achieve higher education, sometimes abroad, but their lives were filled with insult and peril.

This vehement and continuing hostility to black uplift and self-improvement, to the specter of blacks becoming more like middle-class whites, is difficult to explain. I can think of a number of possible causes. One can point to the enduring stigma of slavery, which has been a handicap in various cultures including parts of Africa. The cultural gap that separated African-Americans from Anglo-Americans was probably even wider than that experienced by Irish, German, Polish, Italian, and eastern European Jewish immigrants. And as Jon Gjerde and David Roediger make clear, many immigrants found that antiblack racism was the easiest route to assimilation and winning acceptance as "white," respectable Americans. As Gjerde puts it: "By becoming white, they were able to etch out a niche amid the uncertainties of the early national era. In an effort to make certain that the larger society differentiated them from the nonwhite, the unfree, and disempowered, these immigrants became among the most vociferous advocates of a herrenvolk republic."[39] In a now classic work Edmund S. Morgan argued years ago that lower-class white Southern farmers made a similar discovery by the early eighteenth century.[40] If free blacks no longer served as what Senator J. H. Hammond termed "the mud-sills of society" and began climbing to the highest floors, the entire edifice of American democratic society might collapse as if struck by an earthquake of 9.8 on the Richter scale.

Building on the work of William G. McLoughlin, Theda Perdue, and other historians, James P. Ronda shows that even the Southeastern Indians who were in effect deported to the West took with them many black slaves and the racist standards and values of the white slaveholding society. Thus the Cherokee Constitution of 1839 barred anyone "of negro or mulatto parentage" from holding "any office of profit, honor, or trust under this government."[41] Like most of the Southern states, the Cherokee nation se-verely restricted slave manumissions and made it a crime to teach any slave or free Negro (not of Cherokee blood) to read or write. Efforts to exclude and expel free blacks take on added meaning when we read of the prohibi-tions of intermarriage with "any slave or person of color" "under pain of corporal punishment."[42] If Cherokees and Choctaws could not become white, they could at least take pride in being "red" and try to prevent their tribes from becoming black.[43]

There is a mountain of evidence suggesting that at the very core of op-position to black upward mobility lay a frantic, obsessive fear of what ante-bellum Americans termed "amalgamation" ("miscegenation" was a product of the Civil War years). In other words, white (and even many Native) Amer-icans assumed that the growth of genuine social equality would inevitably lead to racial intermixture, including intermarriage. In retrospect, this deep apprehension seems wholly irrational, since blacks were supposedly ugly and physically repulsive, and as matters developed there has been so little black-white intermarriage between emancipation in 1865 and 1999 that the inci-dence today is still well below one percent of all marriages[44] (this is especially remarkable when compared with the intermarriage rate between Jews and Gentiles [about 52 percent of marriages involving Jews]). Yet the antebellum white obsession seems to have been based on four factors: (1) the actual high incidence of sexual intermixture in the South, where white men continued to exploit slave women; (2) the visible blending of races in the Luso-Hispanic world, a point driven home by news reports and debates over annexation during the Mexican War; (3) a long popular tradition regarding the blacks' superior sexuality; (4) and probably most important, the whispered awe re-garding the grossly misunderstood meaning of certain dominant and recessive genes. Thus while we now know that African ethnic groups embody far more genetic diversity than that found between, let us say, a given African group and Chinese or Europeans, whites were dumbfounded for many centuries by the observation that even grandchildren of a single black grandparent shared many of the somatic features of a "Negro."

When Fray Prudencio de Sandoval wanted to make the same point in 1604 about the Christian descendants of Jews (*Conversos* or *Marranos*), he took it for granted that everyone knew that if Negro men "should unite themselves a thousand times with white women, the children are born with the dark color of the father. Similarly, it is not enough for the Jew to be three parts aristocrat of Old Christian for one family line [i.e., one Jewish ancestor] alone defiles and corrupts him."[45] This Spanish obsession with "purity of blood" (*limpieza da sangre*) was clearly one of the sources of modern racism and rested to a large extent on the generational dominance of dark skin and kinky hair, which had little if anything to do with other, more "internal" genetic traits.[46] But for many white Americans, at least vaguely aware of the rapid natural increase of the slave population in the South, it appeared that if slavery were abolished and racial intermixture spread to the North, the U.S. would soon become "a nation of Negroes."

Nevertheless, despite the general white hostility to black upward mobility, despite the number of leaders from Jefferson, Madison, and Monroe to Clay and Lincoln who favored the "colonization" of free blacks outside the U.S., despite the notorious Fugitive Slave Law and Dred Scott decision, there were more moments of toleration and openness than one might expect. In 1843, for example, abolitionists succeeded in repealing the Massachusetts law forbidding racial intermarriage—a revolutionary step that the nation as a whole would not take until *1967*, with the landmark Supreme Court decision of *Loving* v. *Virginia*.[47]

Even the white crowd that responded to the Lincoln-Douglas debate in Freeport, Illinois, was more open to racial social equality than David Roediger's essay suggests. He points to a revealing moment when Stephen Douglas's backers "chanted over and over" "'White men, white men.'"[48] Actually, they voiced these words only once (but did repeat "white, white"), and the sexual context is crucial for an understanding of the wholly opposing viewpoints. In an effort to besmirch Lincoln and "the Black Republicans," Senator Douglas accused Lincoln of relying on Frederick Douglass, the famous former slave, as one of his three advisers (Frederick Douglass later made sport of this in a speech in Poughkeepsie, New York).[49] Stephen Douglas then asserted that he had earlier seen the black leader in Freeport, riding in a magnificent carriage: "a beautiful young lady was sitting on the box seat, whilst Fred

Douglass and her mother reclined inside, and the owner of the carriage acted as driver." This image of a former slave cavorting as an equal with two seemingly prosperous white women evoked an amazing response: "Laughter, cheers, cries of 'right, what have you to say against it,' &c." When Douglas angrily replied, "I saw this in your own town," someone shouted, "'What of it[?]' There were further cries of "'Good, good,'" and cheers, mingled with hooting and cries of 'white, white.'" It was only after Douglas added that "another rich black negro" was campaigning in the state "for his friend Lincoln as the champion of black men," that someone yelled, "'White men, white men.'" Yet other voices chimed in: "'[W]hat have you got to say against it,'" "'that's right,' &c."[50]

We need to learn more about such diverse points of view within the general public, especially since historians are far too inclined to generalize on the basis of region, class, religion, and ethnicity. James Stewart is surely right when he points to a profound shift in the abolitionists' perception when they realized that "moral suasion" had failed and that the growing nationalism of the Jacksonian period demanded an acceptance of the racial status quo—an agreement never to question the South's controversial and now "peculiar" institution which undergirded the system of racial control in the North. As abolitionists saw the necessity of somehow regenerating the entire society, perhaps by endorsing slave violence, they became more alienated from the general public. Yet as Lacy K. Ford, Jr., brilliantly demonstrates, Southerners themselves continued to harbor more reservations about racial slavery than most of us have recognized. Even in the Deep South, where the economic necessity of slave labor could hardly be doubted, legislators feared black majorities and attempted without success to prohibit the commercial influx of slaves for sale or hire; indeed, Louisiana and Mississippi, fearing an insurrection if the states became a dumping ground for rebellious blacks, even developed "character tests" for imported slaves.

Daniel K. Richter's insightful essay on the way well-meaning Quakers misinterpreted "Indianness" provides a theme that unites the eight articles in the *Journal of the Early Republic* series. During the once-celebrated era of "Jacksonian democracy," white Americans became increasingly entangled in a web of misjudgments and contradictions as they generally abandoned efforts to uplift, include, and assimilate Indians and blacks. Jackson himself dissociated the westward removal of Indians from any ideal of a civilizing process and eventual integration. The parallel hope of removing African-Americans from a hopelessly prejudiced society failed, largely because leaders in the Deep

South saw the project as an abolitionist Trojan horse (despite the vehement attacks on colonization from free blacks and the Garrisonians). Yet in the end many blacks and Indians were doomed for a prolonged period to a kind of colonization—the first group in urban ghettos, the second in often arid and ambition-stifling reservations.

Notes

1. The first edition, published in three volumes, appeared in 1768–1771; the eleventh has twenty-nine volumes.
2. Professor Willcox is the only scholar I've met and talked with when he was well over the age of 100. In the mid-1950s, when I was still in my twenties, he honored me with a request to write his biography, a project I felt incapable of doing.
3. John Stauffer, "The Black Hearts of Men: Race, Religion, and Radical Reform in Nineteenth-Century America," Ph.D. dissertation, Yale University, 1999.
4. It's interesting to note that Michelangelo included the face of a black man among the Elect, in the Last Judgment (*The Complete Work of Michelangelo* [New York: n.d.], 250).
5. Theodore S. Wright, in *Friend of Man* (Utica, N.Y.), October 27, 1836, reprinted in *The Black Abolitionist Papers*, ed. C. Peter Ripley (5 vols., Chapel Hill, 1991), III, 184.
6. One of the most successful recent attempts to deal with this issue is Bertram Wyatt-Brown, "The Mask of Obedience: Slave Psychology in the Old South," found on the internet, http://www.clas.ufl.edu/users/bwyattb/sambo2.htm.
7. Even more mind-boggling, for someone living in 1940, would have been the black "Dionysian" males recently discussed by Orlando Patterson—i.e., Michael Jordan, O. J. Simpson, Michael Jackson, Dennis Rodman (*Rituals of Blood: Consequences of Slavery in Two American Centuries* [Washington, D.C., 1998], 235–82), to say nothing of General Colin Powell, who might well have been elected president of the United States.
8. Harold Brackman, personal e-mail to the author, August 16, 1999.
9. "Constructing Race," Third Series, LIV, No. 1 (January 1997). Though I did not attend the seminar, I wrote the introduction to the published papers; see "Constructing Race: A Reflection" in this volume.
10. Freedman, *Images of the Medieval Peasant* (Stanford, Calif., 1999), 89. However, as Bernard Lewis points out, the Hamitic story "was by no means generally accepted by Muslim authors," though "for the sellers and buyers of black slaves, the curse of Ham provided both an explanation and a justification" (*Race and Slavery in the Middle East:*

An Historical Enquiry [New York, 1990], 125). Freedman notes that the Hamitic justification for serfdom was especially prevalent in Germany but not in Italy. Benjamin Braude, in his invaluable essay, "The Sons of Noah and the Construction of Ethnic and Geographical Identities in the Medieval and Early Modern Periods" (*William and Mary Quarterly*, LIV [January 1997], 103–42), presents a detailed picture of the mistakes, contradictions, and inconsistencies in the European (and historians') interpretations of Noah's biblical curse.

11. Freedman, *Images of the Medieval Peasant*, 139.

12. Kolchin, *Unfree Labor: American Slavery and Russian Serfdom* (Cambridge, Mass., 1987), 170, 186.

13. *The Image of the Black in Western Art, II: From the Early Christian Era to "The Age of Discovery,"* ed. Jean Devisse and Michel Mollat (2 vols., New York, 1979).

14. William Chester Jordan, "The Medieval Background," in *Struggles in the Promised Land: Toward a History of Black-Jewish Relations in the United States*, ed. Jack Salzman and Cornel West (New York, 1997), 53.

15. Ibid., 58.

16. Sweet, "The Iberian Roots of American Racist Thought," *William and Mary Quarterly*, LIV (January 1997), 162, 166.

17. Ibid., 147–48; Lewis, *Race and Slavery in the Middle East*, 53, 122. Lewis provides French as well as English translations of Ibn Khaldun's remarks on blacks being an inferior kind of humanity, much closer to the "animaux stupides." In parts of the Arab world the word for slave, *'abd*, became limited to black slaves and was even extended to free blacks.

18. Lewis, *Race and Slavery in the Middle East*, 46–48, 96; Lewis, *Race and Color in Islam* (New York, 1971). The term "Zanj" referred generally to the kind of East African blacks who for many centuries had been shipped as slaves to the Persian Gulf, where, in the Tigris-Euphrates delta they rose in revolt from 869 to 883 C.E. For many other racist passages, see Gernot Rotter, *Die Stellung des Negers in der islamisch-arabischen Geselschaft bis zum XVI Jahrhundert* (Bonn, 1967).

19. David Brion Davis, "At the Heart of Slavery" in this volume, and "Introduction: The Problem of Slavery," *A Historical Guide to World Slavery*, ed. Seymour Drescher and Stanley L. Engerman (New York, 1998), ix–xviii.

20. Lewis, *Race and Slavery in the Middle East*, 28–30.

21. Gomes Eannes de Azurara [Eanes de Zurara], *The Chronicle of the Discovery and Conquest of Guinea . . . Now First Done into English by Charles Raymond Beazley, M.A., F.R.G.S., and Edgar Prestage, B. A. Oxon* (2 vols., London, 1886–87), I, 54; Braude, "Sons of Noah," 127–28. The captives included light-skinned Muslims, who appealed for ransom in the form of five or six Black Moors who would be traded, once they were returned to Africa, for each of the three men who had apparently been free when captured. Since the above translation may be open to doubt, the original text reads as follows: "E aquy avees de notar que estes negros postoque sejam Mouros como os outros, som porem servos daquelles, per antiigo costume, o qual creo que seja por causa da

maldicom, que despois do deluvyo lancou Noe sobre seu fillho Caym, pella qual o mal-disse, que a sua geeracom fosse sogeita a todallas outras geeracooes do mundo, da qual estes descendem" (Gomes Eannes de Azurara, *Chronica do Descobrimento e Conquista de Guiné* [Paris, 1841], 93). Azurara later speaks contemptuously of the blacks, who lived "like beasts," and "in a bestial sloth," and may well have been referring to a Muslim interpretation of Noah's curse, though as Braude points out, he inaccurately referred to Josephus's *Antiquity of the Jews*. Cain was often confused with Canaan, and there were also difficulties in translating the Hebrew and Latin words for Canaan and Cain.

22. Braude, "Sons of Noah," 137–38. Drawing on George Sandys's description of a Mus-lim slave caravan, Purchas's book six of *Hakluytus Posthumus, or Purchas His Pilgrimes* (1625–26) is all the more revealing since in the earlier editions he had celebrated the unity of all humankind, "without any more distinction of colour, Nation, language, sexe, condition, all may bee *One* in him that is ONE." As Braude observes, the growth of New World slavery was beginning by 1625 to bring a change in English attitudes toward the Curse of Ham (p. 138).

23. Sweet, "The Iberian Roots of American Racist Thought," 162.

24. Saunders, *A Social History of Black Slaves and Freedmen in Portugal, 1441–1555* (Cam-bridge, England, 1982); Berlin, *Many Thousand Gone: The First Two Centuries of Slav-ery in North America* (Cambridge, Mass., 1998).

25. Alden T. Vaughan and Virginia Mason Vaughan, "Before *Othello*: Elizabethan Repre-sentation of Sub-Saharan Africans"; Emily C. Bartels, "*Othello* and Africa: Postcolonial-ism Reconsidered," *William and Mary Quarterly*, LIV (January 1997), 19–64. The Vaughans conclude that the few exceptions only prove the rule: "Elizabethan images of Africa featured an unbalanced, sometimes ambiguous, but overwhelmingly derogatory picture of a segment of the world's population that the English had theretofore scarcely known at all" (p. 44).

26. Jordan, *White over Black: American Attitudes Toward the Negro, 1550–1812* (Chapel Hill, 1969), 28.

27. Vaughan and Vaughan, "Before *Othello*," 42.

28. For one of the several studies of blacks in Britain, see James Walvin, *Black and White: The Negro and English Society, 1555–1945* (London, 1973).

29. Kupperman, "Presentment of Civility: English Reading of American Self-Presentation in the Early Years of Colonization," *William and Mary Quarterly*, LIV (January 1997), 226. For French Canadian and other efforts to idealize Native Americans, in contrast to blacks, see David Brion Davis, *The Problem of Slavery in Western Culture* (New York, 1988), 165–181.

30. Berlin, *Many Thousands Gone*, 66, 69; James H. Merrell, "The Racial Education of the Catawba Indians," *Journal of Southern History*, L (1984), 363–384; Philip D. Morgan, *Slave Counterpoint: Black Culture in the Eighteenth-Century Chesapeake and Lowcountry* (Chapel Hill, 1998), 477–483.

31. Robin Blackburn, *The Making of New World Slavery: From the Baroque to the Modern, 1492–1800* (London, 1997), 117–118. "Ethiopian envoys reached Venice in 1402.

Ethiopian pilgrims made their way perhaps as far as Rome in 1408. An Italian, Pietro Rombulo, was in Ethiopian service for most of the first half of the fifteenth century. The Ethiopian community in Jerusalem sent regular missions to Rome" (Braude, "Sons of Noah," 126).

32. Elizabeth Donnan, ed., *Documents Illustrative of the History of the Slave Trade to America* (Washington, D.C., 1930–1935), 3, 4–9; John Winthrop, *Winthrop's Journal "History of New England," 1630–1649*, ed. James K. Hosmer (2 vols., New York, 1908), II, 251–253.

33. Iain McCalman, ed., *The Horrors of Slavery and Other Writings by Robert Wedderburn* (New York, 1991).

34. Melish, "The 'Condition' Debate and Racial Discourse in the Antebellum North," *Journal of the Early Republic* (Winter 1999), 651–673.

35. The letters between London and Philadelphia Quaker Meetings in the 1780s show that "The Philadelphia Quakers were extremely reluctant to send London detailed information on the condition of emancipated blacks, arguing that the cause of emancipation must be defended on its higher grounds, not on a possibly misleading study of the consequences. When London Meeting for Sufferings finally received the information they sought, early in 1788, they rejoiced over the progress made by certain free blacks, and indicated that the heart-warming stories sent from Philadelphia had resolved various doubts." Quoted from David Brion Davis, *The Problem of Slavery in the Age of Revolution, 1770–1823*, with a new preface (New York, 1999), 232–233, footnote 28.

36. *Adresse de la Société des Amis des Noirs, à l'assemblée nationale, à toutes les villes de commerce, à toutes les manufactures, aux colonies, à toutes les sociétés des amis de la constitution* (1st ed., Paris, 1791), 76; (2nd ed., Paris, 1791), 107–108.

37. For a brilliant questioning of the "market revolution" concept, see Richard Lyman Bushman, "Markets and Composite Farms in Early America," *William and Mary Quarterly*, 3rd Series, LV (July 1998), 351–374.

38. I once suggested that this "continuing desire of millions of people to immigrate to the United States from all quarters of the world [could be seen] as a kind of uncelebrated revolution in slow motion" (*Revolutions: Reflections on American Equality and Foreign Liberations* [Cambridge, Mass., 1990], 3).

39. Jon Gjerde, "'Here in America There Is Neither King Nor Tyrant': European Encounters with Race, 'Freedom,' and Their European Pasts," *Journal of the Early Republic* (Winter 1999), 575.

40. Morgan, *American Slavery, American Freedom: The Ordeal of Colonial Virginia* (New York, 1975), especially 316–387.

41. James P. Ronda, "'We Have a Country': Race, Geography, and the Invention of Indian Territory," *Journal of the Early Republic* (Winter 1999), 753.

42. Ibid., p. 754.

43. While the Indians tried to exclude whites, other than missionaries and government officials, it is highly significant that whites could *become* Cherokees by renouncing their

whiteness—an option not open to blacks (except for those who already had some Cherokee ancestry).

44. In 1960 marriages between blacks and whites constituted about 0.125% of all marriages in the U.S.; in 1997, 0.568% (*The New York Times World Almanac and Book of Facts, 1999* [Mahwah, N.J., 1999], 877). My statement is also based on a private discussion with the Harvard sociologist Orlando Patterson.

45. Fray Prudencio de Sandoval, *Historia de la vida y hechos del emperador Carlos V*, vol. 82 of *Biblioteca de autores espanoles* (Madrid, 1956), 319.

46. Despite this Spanish desire for "purity of blood," which seems to have arisen from the mass conversion of Jews and subsequent intermarriages, I have already mentioned the wider acceptance of black-white intermixture in the Spanish colonies. This was partly the result of a drastic shortage of white Spanish women, coupled with the unifying influence of the Catholic Church. The Luso-Hispanic cultures also placed a great premium on marrying a lighter-skinned spouse and producing as light-skinned children as possible.

47. James Oliver Horton and Lois E. Horton, *Black Bostonians: Family Life and Community Struggle in the Antebellum North* (New York, 1979), 70; *Loving v. Virginia*, 338 U.S. 1 (1967). As the Hortons point out, free blacks did not actively participate in the repeal of the law against interracial marriage; they were far more interested in the successful integration of Boston's schools. In 1843 white abolitionists and other advocates of repeal tried to assure the public that legalizing black-white marriages would result in *less*, not more racial intermixture.

48. David Roediger, "The Pursuit of Whiteness: Property, Terror, and Expansion, 1790–1860," *Journal of the Early Republic* (Winter 1999), 580–600.

49. John W. Blassingame, ed., *The Frederick Douglass Papers: Series One: Speeches, Debates, and Interviews*, III, 1855–63 (6 vols., New Haven, 1985), 233–237. At one point Douglass said, "It seems to me that the white Douglas should occasionally meet his deserts at the hands of the black one. Once I thought he was about to make the name respectable, but now I despair of him, and must do the best I can for it myself. (Laughter.) I now leave him in the hands of Mr. Lincoln" (237).

50. Paul M. Angle, ed., *Created Equal? The Complete Lincoln-Douglas Debates of 1858* (Chicago, 1958), 156.

25

The American Dilemma

Two Nations: Black and White,
Separate, Hostile, Unequal
Andrew Hacker (1992)

The Dispossessed: America's Underclasses
from the Civil War to the Present
Jacqueline Jones (1992)

✳

In 1854 a perceptive Scottish bookseller, publisher, and promoter of public knowledge named William Chambers posed the following question: Did the United States "contain within itself the germs of dissolution?" Chambers was not thinking of a civil war between slaveholding and nonslaveholding states. Recording his impressions after a tour of the country in a book entitled *Things As They Are in America*, Chambers pointed to the "rigorous separation of the white and black races" in the North as well as the South, and noted that every white person with whom he conversed on this subject "tended to the opinion that the negro was in many respects an inferior being, and his existence in America an anomaly."

Chambers concluded that "we see, in effect, two nations—one white and another black—growing up together within the same political circle, but never mingling on a principle of equality." After surveying the depth and extent of racial discrimination and white hypocrisy, and observing that blacks were "condemned to infamy from birth," Chambers would hardly have been surprised to learn that in 1992 a distinguished political scientist would conclude, in a book entitled *Two Nations*, that "[e]ven today, America imposes a stigma on every black child at birth." For Chambers, who knew that the fate of America would profoundly affect "the whole civilized world," the long-range question was whether the blacks, once the great majority were liberated from slavery, would "grow up a powerful alien people within the commonwealth, dangerous in their numbers, but doubly dangerous in their consciousness of wrongs, and in the passions which may incite them to acts of vengeance."

Both a consciousness of wrongs and acts of vengeance were painfully evident in Los Angeles and other cities following the announcement on April 29, 1992, of the jury's verdict in suburban Simi Valley. The columns of smoke, the unrestrained looting, perhaps above all the view from a helicopter of blacks savagely beating and apparently trying to kill Reginald Denny, the hapless white truck driver, seemed to confirm Chambers's grim prophecy, which echoed earlier prophecies of racial warfare made by Jefferson, Tocqueville, and countless white leaders in the pre–Civil War era, particularly those, like Jefferson, Madison, John Marshall, Henry Clay, and Lincoln, who favored plans for gradually "colonizing" the black population in Africa, the Caribbean, or Central America.

Although Andrew Hacker never mentions Chambers and provides little historical background for his discussion of contemporary racial inequality, he quotes Tocqueville's prediction that sooner or later black Americans would "revolt at being deprived of almost all their civil rights," as well as Tocqueville's observation that "[t]he danger of a conflict between the white and the black inhabitants perpetually haunts the imagination of the Americans, like a painful dream." Hacker suggests that the fundamental issues have changed little since Tocqueville's time. Nor is Hacker more optimistic in 1992 than Tocqueville was in 1835. According to Hacker, "there are few signs that the coming century will see [the racial chasm] closed." Even aside from the unwillingness of most white Americans to invest in redistributive programs, racial tensions, Hacker affirms, "serve too many important purposes to be easily ameliorated, let alone eliminated or replaced."

By coincidence, *Two Nations* was published six weeks before the great Los Angeles riot. Advertised as "the first book since Gunnar Myrdal's 1944 classic

An American Dilemma to offer an up-to-date and profound analysis of the conditions that keep blacks and whites dangerously far apart in their ability to participate fully in the American Dream," this short book has become a kind of guide or almanac for understanding the crisis of the inner city.[1] Hacker is highly skilled in presenting statistics in an interesting and readable way. His clear discussion of measurable differences, supplemented by statistical tables, has provided reporters and commentators with a wealth of information on the structure of black families and the disadvantages suffered by blacks in employment, housing, and schooling, and the high incidence of black crime, among other subjects. He has also been harshly attacked, particularly by the sociologists Orlando Patterson and Chris Winship, for confusing race with class, for ignoring some of the impressive gains that blacks have made, and for misusing statistical averages in ways that identify all African Americans with a stereotyped underclass.[2]

Significantly, Hacker borrowed his title not from Chambers but from Disraeli's *Sybil, or The Two Nations*, which was concerned with the appalling division between social classes in early Victorian Britain.[3] Hacker even quotes Disraeli on his opening page, equating the difference between Britain's rich and poor with the gulf that still divides America's whites and blacks: "Two nations, between whom there is no intercourse and no sympathy; who are as ignorant of each other's habits, thought, and feelings, as if they were dwellers in different zones, or inhabitants of different planets." Although Hacker says very little about social class, he does at one point acknowledge the existence of a "white underclass" and recalls that sociology textbooks used to dilate "at length about families like the Jukes and the Kallikaks, who remained mired in squalor from generation to generation." Emphasis on race, Hacker suggests, has something to do with the diversion of public attention from poverty-stricken whites. By concentrating attention on a black underclass, he writes, we make white poverty seem "atypical or accidental. . . . At times, it almost appears as if white poverty must be covered up, lest it blemish the reputation of the dominant race."

Unfortunately Hacker does not say much more about this crucial point. The use of racial animosity as an antidote to, and substitute for, class divisions has a long history which provides an important background to his subject. During the colonial period, when black slaves worked alongside white indentured servants in Virginia's tobacco fields, lawmakers countered the threat of biracial rebellion by fostering a sense of white solidarity. White servants were increasingly accorded privileges and protections denied to slaves, including, upon the termination of their services, the promise of land, money, a musket, and a respectable suit of clothes. As Edmund S. Morgan has pointed out, aristocratic planters succeeded in persuading Virginia's small farmers that "both were equal in not being slaves."[4]

The presence of millions of black slaves in the pre–Civil War decades helped sustain the illusion of equality for American whites and immigrants—the "equality of condition" that so captivated Tocqueville and other European visitors. The actual inequalities between social classes were also blurred by the visibility in most cities of a separate caste of "free" blacks, who were deprived of civil rights, excluded from white schools, and confined to menial employments. Beginning in the so-called Age of Jackson, white Americans of diverse backgrounds have anxiously tried to cast off any characteristics identifying them as members of a "lower" class, that is a class lower than the one with which they identify, precisely because they have believed in America as a land of opportunity—a land in which no fixed barriers prevent one from acquiring the skills, tastes, and demeanor, as shown in one's behavior as a consumer, that denote success. Andrew Hacker bases much of his moral argument on the unacknowledged privileges and benefits that most Americans derive from having white skin. This point would have been reinforced if he had related it to the dialectical and historical connections between American slavery and American freedom, between the belief in an inferior, servile race and the vision of classless opportunity.

The use of race as a substitute for class has further implications that have seldom been explored. The very notion of America's exceptionalism—the "American Dream" of a land of promise where, as Hacker affirms, there is "a greater obligation" than in other nations "to achieve amity and equity in relations between the races"—was originally made possible by the availability of cheap, coerced labor to clear and cultivate the most fertile lands and to produce export crops for which there was seemingly an unlimited demand. From the early West India trade of the northeastern colonies to the cotton exports that helped pay for northern railroads and industrialization, America's economy depended largely on slave labor.

Yet by the time of the American Revolution, this material circumstance appeared to contradict everything the emerging nation stood for. For most of the Founding Fathers, as for numerous clergymen and journalists, slavery became the fatal defect in an otherwise boundless and perfectable social order. In 1786 petitioners to the Virginia legislature repeated the familiar argument,

That the Glorious and ever memorable Revolution can be Justified on no other Principles but what doth plead with greater Force for the emancipation of our Slaves in proportion as the oppression exercised over them exceeds the oppression formerly exercised by Great Britain over these States.

As Jefferson confessed to an audience of French rationalists, "Indeed I tremble for my country when I reflect that God is just; that his justice cannot sleep forever."

If slavery was seen by some as the primal curse, the only obstacle preventing Americans from fulfilling the nation's high destiny, the prevailing ideology affirmed that it was the African Amercians' incapacity for freedom and responsible citizenship, not their indispensable role in the economy as productive field hands, that stood as the major roadblock to slave emancipation. In a remarkable example of displacement of moral responsibility, the sin, corruption, and brutality of slavery spilled over to infect the victims themselves, who were mired, according to a popular phrase, in "irremediable degradation." Even ardent critics of slavery became attached to the image of stunted minds and withered souls, of human beings rendered incapable of moral choice or benevolent feeling. Of course the doctrine of black inferiority had many sources, including the widespread belief that Africans were the descendants of Cain or Ham, who had been condemned to perpetual servitude, according to twisted biblical interpretation, by Noah's curse of Canaan. But paradoxically, the view of slavery as America's original sin also contributed to the image of helpless Negroes as the embodiment of sin, in the sense that they were ruled by animal passions and deprived of the capacity for moral and intellectual improvement in a civilized society.

Hacker briefly summarizes James Baldwin's theory that white people "need the nigger" because "the nigger" signifies the precise traits—"lust and laziness, stupidity and squalor"—that whites cannot tolerate within themselves: "By creating such a creature, whites are able to say that because only members of the black race can carry that taint, it follows that none of its attributes will be found in white people."

One should add that most abolitionists, who were acutely attuned to the sins of white people, struggled to end their own complicity with evil by demanding the emancipation and uplift of all blacks. Still, the abolitionists faced a dilemma that has continued to perplex other reformers: the more they highlighted the injurious effects of oppression, the more dehumanized and incapable the victims appeared to be.

For a time evangelical abolitionists could rely on visions of an imminent millennium or a moment of transfiguring change. Reformers also resorted to the device of romantic racialism, idealizing the "childlike, affectionate, docile, and patient" traits that allegedly characterized the African race and that were needed to humanize an overly competitive and rationalistic white society.[5] But by 1864 Samuel Gridley Howe, a radical abolitionist, supporter of John Brown, and president of the American Freedmen's Inquiry Commission, took comfort in the thought that most of the black population, the "blameless" victims of slavery, "was doomed to disappear because of inherited weaknesses that would put them at a disadvantage in the inevitable competition."[6]

Howe's prediction that African Americans would gradually become extinct in the racial struggle for survival fulfilled the wish that had always been embodied in the Great White Dream of black colonization, a dream that President Lincoln continued to endorse well into the Civil War. The United States, a chosen nation, *E pluribus unum*, signaling a new order to the ages, could carry out its godlike mission and potentialities—if only . . . Had the curse of slavery and a black population been foisted upon innocent colonists by perfidious Albion, as Jefferson and numerous other Founders maintained? Or had the nation begun with a Faustian bargain, obligating all future generations to pay the debt? However conceived, "the Negro problem" meant that blacks were associated metaphysically with everything that compromised or stood in the way of the American Dream—with finitude, failure, poverty, fate, the sins of our fathers, nemesis. In short, with dark reality.

While this analysis points to a complex pathology regarding race at the core of American culture, I would argue that race in the genetic sense of color is not an ultimate reality; nor can I agree with Hacker that the "idea of race is primeval." Class and race are both products of contingent social and historical forces. There was nothing inevitable or "natural," for example, about attaching the label "Negro" to a man or woman whose ancestors were half or even seven-eighths European and whose other forebears were divided among highly diverse nations and tribes in the vast continent of Africa. For many generations light-skinned and straight-haired "Negroes" took on the identity of whites, and some southern courts even validated such "crossing" for people of visible color who had acquired reputations of "respectable" character. Class, in other words, could take precedence over race.

If Hacker's claims were correct concerning the overwhelming value of whiteness and the insurmountable liabilities of blackness in contemporary America, our college classes would not contain so many young people who could easily pass for white but who make it clear that they are proud to be African Americans. Still, no one can doubt that the pathology of race has become a pervasive and deeply threatening American reality. After stressing that one million black males are now confined in prisons and jails, or could be returned to prison from parole or probation, Hacker writes that "blacks do not consider it paranoid to wonder whether they might someday find themselves behind barbed-wire enclosures, as happened to Americans of Japanese descent during the Second World War."

Hacker is exceptionally good at unmasking white pretenses and excuses, at exposing the anxieties, hypocrisies, and contradictions of white liberals in particular. For example, in discussing the reactions of a typical white liberal to black criticism in a racially mixed group, Hacker writes that the white liberal is apt "to stammer plaintively, either retracting what he said or protesting that he had been misunderstood. Here, as elsewhere, liberals stand in dread of black disfavor, which must be mollified by admitting to oversight or error."

But Hacker sometimes tends to emphasize the physical fact of race, and not the perceptions of it, and to exaggerate the actual polarization between blacks and whites—as opposed to the ways a racist culture has traditionally attempted to polarize the two groups. In other words, Hacker is still partially trapped by the tendency I have been discussing to make racial differences displace all other explanations of behavior, a tendency reinforced, as we shall see, by a comparison of statistical averages without sufficient reference to the progress made in the past fifty or one hundred years. It is not "race," as Hacker writes, that "has made America its prisoner since the first chattels were landed on these shores," but rather the ideological purposes that the idea of race has served.

Given Hacker's account, one could hardly imagine the scene, which I observed just days ago, of black and white house painters working and joking together and singing along with the same pop music on the radio; or black students with high SAT scores winning top academic awards at an Ivy League university and a mostly white public high school; or equal numbers of blacks and whites working together to build an elegant Jehovah's Witness church in a white Connecticut suburb; or interracial couples whose marriages are as successful as those of other people; or hard-working, aspiring black families who live in the inner city and who are determined to see their children move into the middle class. The reader of *Two Nations* might have assumed that the violence in Los Angeles was essentially a conflict between blacks and whites and not "the nation's first multi-ethnic urban riot," to use Tim Rutten's phrase, a complex battle between classes and ethnic groups in which some of the shops and businesses of blacks were destroyed along with those of Koreans, Chicanos, and Iranian Jews.[7]

When we overlook the ways in which race and class overlap and interact, explanations tend to shift toward characteristics that are supposedly distinctive to each race. This can be hazardous because such characteristics tend to derive from personal impressions that may well be contradicted by people who have quite different experiences. Thus Hacker writes that teachers of black children "should be tolerant of more casual approaches to syntax, time, and measurement," and that "it has been found that black pupils are more apt to work to full potential if their teachers identify with them in a caring and solicitous way." He cannot mean that white pupils do better when their teachers are aloof and uncaring, but there is an unfortunate looseness about such views. Hacker writes that "black children are also more attuned to their bodies and physical needs," which makes it harder for them to sit still in class, and he appears sympathetic to claims that they have different "learning styles" from those of whites. Each of these statements calls to mind contradictory cases; they remind one of the romantic racialism of the past.

While Hacker explicitly rejects all theories of hereditary inferiority, believers in such doctrines may derive ammunition from this approach—especially from his argument that colleges should drop the requirement of a Ph.D. degree for blacks who are able to "communicate" in other ways and that medical schools should make special accommodation for blacks "who have an intuitive flair for diagnosing maladies" or "personalities that put patients at ease." These recommendations seem to be based on Hacker's disturbing conclusion that "racial bias remains latent not only in the multiple-choice method, but in the broader expectations set by the modern world," including "the European structure of technology and science" and "administrative systems based on linear modes of reasoning." Nothing will betray the cause of equal rights more decisively, I fear, than the idea that mathematics or linear thought is "white." Indeed, in some of his other writings Hacker has explicitly rejected such views, for example when he raised the question whether standards should be lowered for black cardiac surgeons or in his statement in *The New York Review of Books* that:

On more than a few college campuses, and within many school administrations, whites seem to feel they must gain black approval if they are both to live with themselves and keep the peace. They fail to see how condescending they are when they encourage blacks and other ethnic groups to promote fantasy as history or as science. Whether such self-indulgent attitudes will be outgrown is a large question for the decade ahead. . . .

We live in a demanding age that requires—and rewards—technical and organizational skills. It is simply irresponsible to tell children of an underclass that their salvation lies in flights of rhetoric.[8]

＊

An exclusive concentration on race not only diverts attention from the white and Latino underclasses but also obscures the economic and political causes of black poverty, which is then almost inevitably associated with racial traits. Jacqueline Jones, a historian at Brandeis University and the author of the prize-winning book *Labor of Love, Labor of Sorrow: Black Women, Work, and the Family from Slavery to the Present,* is one of the few scholars who have succeeded in clarifying, in specific historical discussions, the extremely complex relationships between race and class. Her new history of America's various underclasses therefore provides a valuable antidote to the current obsession with race. By the late 1980s, Jones explains,

> the grip of the black "underclass" on the American imagination served to obscure the historical and economic processes that by this time had created a multitude of "underclasses," people who were neither black nor the residents of Northern cities. By the late twentieth century a growing population of immigrants from Latin America, the Philippines, China, India, and Southeast Asia, combined with structural transformations in the American economy that affected the previously secure white working class, revealed the political—and moral—limitations of a continuing focus on race and urban residence as the defining characteristics of the poor.

To accept such an analysis is not to denigrate Hacker's book, which is filled with important insights as well as significant and often surprising information. But Jones's *Dispossessed* enables one to read Hacker with greater care and profit, and to recognize that in some ways his book has already become a "primary source," more valuable perhaps as evidence of the way that pessimistic white liberals who are appalled by endemic racism are now responding to racial inequality than as a guide for understanding what policies might be helpful. When Hacker acutely describes liberal white behavior, including the desire to be liked by blacks and to be cleared of all taint of racism, he will, I suspect, make many readers squirm and instantly confess, "that's me."

Although Jones stresses the oppressive economic forces that have subjected various groups to poverty regardless of race, she in no way neglects the unique vulnerability of African Americans to exploitation, from the time they were denied land and transformed into a dependent, sharecropping labor force following their emancipation from slavery. But she shows that the end of slavery narrowed the gap between southern blacks and landless whites. Both groups were subject to the will of planters determined to find a substitute for slave labor by restricting the mobility of workers and their options for employment. Restoring a staple-crop plantation system in the South, along with lumber camps, sawmills, coal mines, and phosphate pits, depended on preserving a vast supply of subservient, low-skilled labor that could be counted on for intensive work at certain times of the year. Jones describes how, between the late 1860s and the 1930s, southern blacks and whites often worked under similar conditions. As sharecroppers they sometimes signed the same kind of annual labor contracts; occasionally, as in the Populist movement of the 1890s and the Southern Tenant Farmers Union of the 1930s, blacks and whites joined forces in a common cause. But racism, like human sin, was always there to be reasserted. The lowliest white could easily be reminded that the most accomplished black was a disfranchised nigger, a frightening example of what human nature could become, a man who deserved contempt, caricature, dishonor, and violence.[9]

Jones has little to say about the psychological and cultural effects of such prolonged oppression of both whites and blacks. She is surely right when she argues that "the desire among men and women for a stable job and a settled home place has transcended class, cultural, and racial lines; the white middle class has had no monopoly on the virtues of hard work, love of family, and a commitment to schooling for their children." Still, the aspirations of blacks were inevitably withered in a society that confined African Americans to the heaviest, dirtiest, or most servile kinds of work and that demanded their obsequious respect for all whites. Locked in a system of unending debt, paying interest charges as high as 71 percent to plantation stores, black sharecroppers had little experience with money and found it difficult to save for

The American Dilemma 353

the future. A tenant farmer might seek opportunity during the slack season by "shifting" to a sawmill or phosphate mine, a kind of migration that inevitably weakened some families. But southern society denied blacks virtually any opportunity for developing managerial skills or even, in rural districts, for establishing their own businesses to serve a black clientele. Nor were states that had made it a crime to teach slaves to read enthusiastic about black education. As late as 1940, when the two decades of greatest migration to the North had just begun, five years was the median for years of school completed by blacks in the South; a bare 5 percent of the black population had graduated from high school.

An understanding of poverty in late-twentieth-century America requires some knowledge of the gradual collapse—or modernization—of the old southern plantation economy, the migration northward and westward, between 1910 and 1960, of some nine million white and black workers, and the subsequent decline of the kind of heavy industry that once furnished jobs for such unskilled or semiskilled labor. This is the main subject of Jones's book, which is especially successful in showing the continuity between the southern plantation regime and postindustrial poverty. She gives a vivid account of the most arduous, dangerous, and degrading kinds of work as she follows migratory men and women from job to job as they worked in turpentine stills, coal mines, coastal canneries, and seafood processing plants. It is startling to read that in this unprecedented emigration from the South, whites outnumbered blacks (even though the proportion of blacks in the South fell from 90 percent to 50 percent). Jones also points out that most of the poor in the U.S. today are white and live well outside the central cities.

In a particularly striking passage, Jones finds that one group of southern migrants encountered an especially hostile reception in midwestern towns and cities:

Municipal officials considered them lazy, promiscuous, rapidly proliferating welfare-seekers, a drain on the public treasury, a stain on the city's image. Educational officials tracked their children for failure in the public schools, and medical authorities decried their persistent superstitions in all manner of ailments, such as rinsing out a child's mouth with urine to cure a rash called thrush. Employers expressed mixed feelings; the migrants provided cheap labor, but they were unreliable, inept at any kind of machine work, slow on the job, and unambitious.

Landlords told them that they need not apply, citing their large families, allegedly deplorable housekeeping practices, and presumed violent proclivities (with the knife as the weapon of choice). Their neighbors native to the North soon developed a repertoire of jokes that focused on the migrants' ignorance of city ways, their primitive Southern origins, their slovenly appearance and demeanor. . . . Shiftless, evasive, and untrustworthy, they supposedly lived for the moment and squandered their weekly paychecks on trinkets and drink. Once in their new homes, they apparently remained willing and able to tolerate the most degrading living and working conditions, "immune to discomforts that sorely try other Americans."

This portrait of "native-born, Protestant, English-speaking whites . . . from the southern Appalachian Mountains" underscores the consequences of class prejudice and suggests that the "Negro traits" that whites found most repellent had more to do with class than with race—though as I have argued here, the rhetoric of race has long been used as an antidote to, or substitute for, class divisions. According to Jones, some northern employers and realtors expressed a preference for "a good clean colored person" over the heavy-drinking Appalachian white who was incapable of saving money and who would suddenly disappear from his job if he decided to visit relatives back home in the South. Like the stereotyped "Negro," the southern poor white, who emerged from the same backward region that had long been dominated by a slave economy, seemed to lack the essential inner faculty required for self-discipline and for intellectual and moral improvement.

Yet as Jones goes on to show, during World War II "countless Southern black migrants watched poorly educated whites from Kentucky or Tennessee take advantage of skin color and kin ties to secure jobs" in the defense industries of the Midwest. Although one-third of the Appalachian whites were illiterate, they were repeatedly hired in preference to better-qualified blacks and had a much easier time obtaining on-the-job training. It is true that blacks working in the steel, automobile, railroad, and meatpacking industries earned wages that would have been unthinkable in the South. Between 1940 and 1944 the percentage of black men employed in industry nearly doubled; the proportion who worked as farmers fell from over 41 percent to 28 percent. But unlike most blacks, the white Appalachians often owned cars that allowed them to move around urban regions in search of better jobs. Unlike blacks, they were not excluded from segregated working-class and middle-class suburbs. Although white and black migrants entered the northern urban labor market at the same time, the whites, according to Jones, tended to lose their accents within a generation and to scatter and blend into the middle-American landscape.

To be sure, not all of the Appalachian whites became suburbanites. In examining white slums and pockets of rural poverty, Jones demonstrates that whiteness is not always a benefit and points to social evils that have too often been associated with the inner city alone: malnourished and lead-poisoned children, alcohol and drug abuse, violence, teen-age pregnancy, a high proportion of households headed by women, and estranged youths who drop out of school as soon as possible. Jones questions the traditional belief "that poverty [in] the countryside was somehow cleaner, healthier, more wholesome, and less degrading than its inner-city counterpart." But she also traces the history of the modern black ghetto—including what Hacker terms its "self-destructive spiral" and "self-inflicted genocide." Jones emphasizes the continuing disruptive influence of federal government policies that encouraged the virtual eviction of farmers and agricultural workers from the South, created wartime job opportunities in the North, opened the way for the flight from the city of both the white and black middle classes, and then, in the Reagan years, cut back on a large number of human services and shifted responsibility to already overburdened state and city governments.

Since the federal government has had a large part in producing the malaise of today's inner cities—including the raising of expectations of racial justice which have then been repeatedly dashed by lack of public support—the government clearly seems to have a responsibility to rectify evils that continue to perpetuate, as William Chambers put it, the "rigorous separation of the white and black races." Even apart from justice, we may well be confronting what he called the nation's "germs of dissolution" at a time when no nation will be able to afford the luxury of underclasses—of dependent, hostile, unproductive, alienated populations. It should now be clear that market forces and moral exhortations are insufficient to improve the quality of urban life and of the potential urban labor force. Only a huge, coordinated program, guided by unprecedented imagination and sensitivity, can provide the jobs, the skills, and ultimately the incentives that are needed to overcome America's historical "curse," including its pathology of race, and make full use of the nation's human resources.

No doubt such words will sound naive and dated, as Hacker's own caution about solutions makes clear. Even apart from the widespread disenchantment with governmental power, racial attitudes are being reshaped by what might be termed a loopback effect, in which the self-destructive behavior of a relatively small number of black men accentuates the symbolic menace of race. Contrary to much popular writing, the gains made by most African Americans in the past fifty years are little short of miraculous when judged by standards of the preceding century. Between 1947 and the late 1960s, a period that witnessed the collapse of the entire structure of legal segregation in the South, black household income more than doubled and the percentage of households earning less than $10,000 (in 1987 dollars) dropped from 68 percent to 31 percent.[10] Although the slowing of economic growth soon brought a reversal of these trends except for the most prosperous blacks, the 1964 Civil Rights Act contributed to impressive gains for black workers in obtaining both better-paid work and jobs that had previously been denied to blacks.

Yet the erosion of racism, especially in the 1990s, soon gave a new emphasis to considerations of class at a time when school credentials and character references were becoming required conditions for success. Many blacks who were successful in school, who scored well on tests, who exhibited the "right" traits of character, became social workers, firemen, policemen, insurance adjusters, schoolteachers, military officers, government clerks and administrators, lawyers, mayors. Those who were left behind, particularly young men, included a high proportion of people who were estranged from the system and who often behaved in ways that clashed with the norms of a market and technology-driven society. This outcome was aggravated by the government's withdrawal from social service programs, by the decline of urban industrial employment, by the narrowing of choice to lowly service-related jobs, and by the cumulative effects of the sexual revolution, Black Power, the heavy use of drugs, especially crack, and the growing obsession with violence on the part of television networks and the press generally.

Just when the rise of a substantial black middle class was beginning to create more positive racial stereotypes for whites, the aimless rebellion of black ghetto gangs and the callous cutbacks in federal social and economic programs had the combined effect of restoring racial fears to the center of attention. As muggings became commonplace and black crime soared in the 1980s, young black physicians and professional athletes were more frequently stopped by police and searched. Black college students watched scared whites flee before them on the street. Many blacks who have made a relative success in life have expressed deep resentment over this confusion of identities, especially when they are mistaken for rapists or thugs. Keenly aware that most of the victims of black crime are black, they may also have relatives in the inner city and know that, by a slight shift of fate, they might have dropped out of school and joined a gang. While successful blacks often resent white exhortations to discipline "their own people," the plight of the black underclass may also strengthen their sense of racial solidarity and weaken their ties with white liberals, some of whom might welcome black neighbors of their own social class.

We seem, in other words, to have entered another period when race has preempted class. Perhaps Americans will never overcome their endemic pathology of race until they are finally able to confront both the underlying reality of class divisions in America and the destructive myth of a classless society.

Notes

1. It does not detract from the usefulness of Hacker's study to call attention to a more detailed, balanced, and scholarly volume published by the National Research Council of the National Academy of Sciences, *A Common Destiny: Blacks and American Society*, edited by Gerald David Jaynes and Robin M. Williams, Jr. (National Academy Press, 1989), which Hacker reviewed in *The New York Review*, along with seven other books, on October 12, 1989.

2. "White Poor, Black Poor," *The New York Times*, May 3, 1992, Section 4, p. 17.

3. Hacker's subtitle, "Separate, Hostile, Unequal," echoes the conclusion of the *Report of the National Advisory Commission on Civil Disorders* in 1968.

4. *American Slavery, American Freedom: The Ordeal of Colonial Virginia* (Norton, 1975), p. 381.

5. George M. Fredrickson, *The Black Image in the White Mind: The Debate on Afro-American Character and Destiny, 1817–1914* (Harper and Row, 1971), p. 102.

6. Fredrickson, *The Black Image in the White Mind*, p. 163. The quotation is Fredrickson's paraphrase of Howe's position.

7. Tim Rutten's account of the Los Angeles riot appeared in *The New York Review*, June

11, 1992. He noted that a majority of the people arrested by the Los Angeles police between midnight April 30 and the following Monday were Latinos, many of them recent immigrants, not blacks. For the burning and destruction of black-owned businesses, see *The New York Times*, May 18, 1992, p. 1. It is interesting that Priscilla Feldsher, a thirty-five-year-old black woman who with her mother had founded successful chiropractic and skin-care clinics that were burned out in the riot, praised the Koreans for qualities she hoped blacks would emulate: "The Koreans have a different type of community. . . . They help each other. They lend to each other. We aren't a good example because we had to do everything ourselves. No banks financed us. No relatives financed us" (p. B8). It should be pointed out that Hacker gives more attention to the black middle class in some of his essays in *The New York Review*, particularly in the issue of April 23, 1992.

8. See *The New York Review*, April 23, 1992, p. 30, and *The New York Review*, October 24, 1991, p. 18.

9. Partly because Jones is so concerned with victimization rather than with economic development and underdevelopment, it is useful to supplement her book with Jay R. Mandle's short survey of recent scholarly literature on the economic history of African Americans, *Not Slave, Not Free: The African American Experience since the Civil War* (Duke University Press, 1992).

10. Mandle, *Not Slave, Not Free*, p. 106.

26

The Other Revolution

*Joyous Greetings: The First International
Women's Movement, 1830–1860*
Bonnie S. Anderson (2000)

*Not for Ourselves Alone: The Story of Elizabeth Cady Stanton
and Susan B. Anthony*
Geoffrey C. Ward, based on the documentary
film by Ken Burns and Paul Barnes (2000)

*Not for Ourselves Alone: The Story of
Elizabeth Cady Stanton and Susan B. Anthony*
A documentary film by Ken Burns and Paul Barnes (2000)

✳

Writers have long attached the word *revolution* to technological innovations
such as the now current "e-commerce, biotech, and information revolutions."
But when we think of "real revolutions" we are still inclined to envision
guillotines, barricades, Bolsheviks, and the execution of Tsar Nicholas II and
his Romanov family. Yet when one looks carefully at the Taliban rule in
Afghanistan as an example, even if somewhat extreme, of the kinds of patriarchy that governed orthodox Christians, Muslims, Jews, and ancient Mes-
opotamians reaching back for millennia and that shaped even much later
secular and socialist forms of male domination, it becomes clear that the

revolution of all revolutions has been the relatively recent, peaceful, and still continuing equalization of men and women.

Whereas the Taliban prohibit women from being educated, there are now more women than men as students in America's four-year colleges and universities, and the proportion of women continues to rise in American law schools, medical schools, graduate schools, and the armed forces.[1] The Western world is still in the midst of a profound change in gender relationships, and as more women are employed or pursuing professional careers, there has also been a wholly new sensitivity to sexual harassment and the "gender-friendliness" of the workplace.

Of course it is partly to protect Afghan women from sexual harassment that the Taliban (like the Middle Assyrian Laws from the fifteenth to the eleventh centuries B.C.E.) require women to wear head-to-toe veils or burkas and forbid them from speaking to nonfamily males or walking outdoors except in the company of a close male relative.[2] Protection from rape and predatory males has often been one side of monopolizing the sexual life and reproductive capacity of particular women, the favored women who did not become prostitutes (who could not wear veils). As Gerda Lerner and other feminist historians have shown, similar restrictions pervaded patriarchal cultures until relatively recent times. Women were not only subordinated to males but were deprived of their own history and of any part in the creation of law, symbolic values, and the structures of meaning.[3]

Though a few isolated voices in medieval and early modern Europe challenged Aristotle's positive equation of women with slaves and domesticated animals,[4] it was not until the late seventeenth and early eighteenth centuries that writers like Mary Astell and Daniel Defoe called for a female university and condemned marriage without love as "conjugal lewdness." The eighteenth century was flexible enough to enable Laura Bassi to receive a doctoral degree in philosophy from the University of Bologna in 1732, and to allow a few exceptional women to enter the professions and "Republic of Letters." Thus Madame du Châtelet conducted experiments in physics and translated Newton's *Principia* into French. Yet even Rousseau, often considered the most radical of the *philosophes*, did all he could to reinforce the traditional image of women.[5] The true pioneers in challenging patriarchal restrictions were, first, French feminists,[6] including a few males like the Marquis de Condorcet, who were freed by the French Revolution to write radical books and tracts in the early 1790s; and second, the Anglo-American Quakers who had taken the lead in condemning all slave trading and slaveholding, and whose beliefs empowered "the inner light" of hundreds of traveling women ministers.

The French feminists could draw on the principles of the French and Scottish Enlightenment, especially the distinction between the corruptions and hierarchies of manmade history and the equality that had supposedly existed in a primitive state of nature (of course their opponents pointed to the way "nature" had distinguished men from women, endowing the latter with the responsibilities of bearing and raising children). But even by the mid-eighteenth century various writers in France, Scotland, and even Sweden attempted to explain how oppressive customs and conventions had led to the "cruel tyranny" of male domination. As Karen Offen has made clear, these appeals to nature and human perfectibility were reinforced by the growing literacy of privileged women in France and other western European countries, and by the assertion of female equality in novels, plays, poetry, and treatises on law and political economy. Even before the French Revolution, arguments for the equality and political importance of educated mothers had provoked a backlash of "prescriptive literature" exhorting women to be meek, respectful, virtuous, and obedient—an indication, as Dr. Offen observes, of male anxiety arising from the fact that tradition alone could no longer suffice.[7]

As for the Quakers, the American Revolution temporarily severed their strong transatlantic alliance and weakened the Society of Friends in the United States, where some pacifist Quakers were incarcerated in prisoner camps. Still, Quaker women took a prominent role, as Rebecca Larson puts it, in "abolition, temperance, prison reform, and women's rights."[8]

Moreover, the ideals and disruption of the American Revolution certainly raised the expectations of some women. Thus in 1777 Lucy Knox wrote a letter expressing her love for her husband General Henry Knox ("My dearest friend"), who had long been absent while fighting the British. After then telling him of her fear that "being long accustomed to command" might make him "too haughty for mercantile matters," Lucy concluded with the hope "you will not consider yourself as commander in chief of your own house, but be convinced that there is such a thing as equal command."[9]

The French Revolution inspired more explicit demands for gender equality, such as Condorcet's *Plea for the Citizenship of Women* (1790) and Olympe de Gouges's 1791 *Declaration of the Rights of Woman*. But Condorcet died in prison and Gouges was guillotined as a royalist; in October 1793 the French government outlawed all female participation. The best know feminist achievement of that revolutionary era was Mary Wollstonecraft's *Vindication of the Rights of Woman*, a work of 1792 that would inspire later generations—the great American Quaker feminist leader, Lucretia Coffin Mott, who surely equaled her friends Elizabeth Cady Stanton and Susan B. Anthony in historical importance—always kept a copy of Wollstonecraft's *Vindication* on the central table of her house.[10] But the fact that Wollstonecraft had had an illegitimate daughter and known affairs with various men defiled the book in the eyes of most Victorian Anglo-Americans.

From the mid-1790s to the 1820s relatively few writings questioned the status of women. As American states widened suffrage to include virtually all white males, they began denying the vote to free blacks and, in New Jersey, to women, who had briefly won this privilege following the Revolution. In the 1820s and for decades to come married women could not own property, make contracts, bring suits, or sit on juries. They could be legally beaten by their husbands and were required to submit to their husbands' sexual demands. Even the aristocratic Alexis de Tocqueville, who toured America in 1831, was shocked by the immobility and restrictions placed on an American married woman, whose independence was "irrecoverably lost in the bonds of matrimony," who "lives in the home of her husband as if it were a cloister," and who was forbidden to step beyond "the narrow circle of domestic interests."[11] For later feminists these invisible chains would confirm Mary Wollstonecraft's remark in her last novel, *Maria, or the Wrongs of Women* (1797), "Was not the world a vast prison, and women born slaves?"[12]

That said, Bonnie S. Anderson, Linda Kerber, Nancy Cott, and numerous other historians of nineteenth-century American women have shown that the constraints on the virtuous mother and housewife were cushioned by a republican "cult of domesticity" that encouraged education and the highest female literacy rate in the world—to say nothing of parlor literature and friendly groups like Cincinnati's Semi-Colon Club, where young Harriet Beecher mingled socially with New England professors, ministers, doctors, their wives, and single women who listened to and discussed one another's "papers," before dancing, consuming sandwiches, and coffee, and a fine brand of madeira.[13] If such mixed-couple social groups were rare, there was a broad consensus that the virtue and stability of a republic would depend on the kind of mothers who could raise presidents like Washington. Like their French predecessors, many American women came to feel they had a supreme republican mission. Several historical changes made this possible, among them progressive mother-centered theories of child-rearing; the disappearance of the home as a household of industry; and the emergence of the middle-class home as a "haven in a heartless world" that would provide refuge and serenity for exhausted husbands while also training sons for competition and upward mobility.

As it happened, this "cult of domesticity" proved to be an invincible barrier to nineteenth-century feminists even if they borrowed the notion that women were morally superior to men, less dominated by sexual and violent impulses, and thus better prepared to use politics as a way of purifying and reforming society. By emphasizing motherhood, the ideal of domesticity widened the gendered differences symbolized by pregnancy, birthing, breast feeding, child care, and menstruation, pointing to women's relative incapacities outside the home. And in the long era before effective birth control, some of the boldest feminists such as Angelina Grimké Weld and Elizabeth Cady Stanton were incapacitated for long periods by motherhood, a fact that deeply troubled the younger Susan B. Anthony, who was single and often hostile to "baby-making."[14]

Ironically, even Stanton expressed anguish after her second daughter and sixth child, Harriot, was born in 1856, and at age forty-one longed to burst free from mothering chores and join Anthony traveling and canvassing on the open road.[15] The two women established a famously close friendship and working relationship that lasted until 1902 when Stanton died. But as the Civil War approached there was little that feminists could accomplish in the short run, and as Harriot grew up and became Harriot Stanton Blatch, she would be the one who would actually achieve American woman suffrage in 1920, long after her mother and Anthony had passed away. As we have seen in our own era, full gender equality is a revolution that requires many generations.[16]

Bonnie S. Anderson's *Joyous Greetings* is the only work I know of that puts the first crucial stage of the American woman's movement—1824 to 1860—within the complex transatlantic context required for any full or even adequate understanding.[17] From Eleanor Flexner's classic 1959 *Century of Struggle: The Woman's Rights Movement in the United States*[18] to Ken Burns and Paul Barnes's 1999 documentary film *Not for Ourselves Alone: The Story of Elizabeth Cady Stanton and Susan B. Anthony*, historians have emphasized the isolation of the United States, seemingly cut off from Europe and even from the Revolutions of 1848 (not mentioned by Flexner). The book and film versions of *Not for Ourselves Alone* refer to revolutionary events in nine

European cities in 1848 but far from seeing any influential connections, stress that the Seneca Falls Convention "signaled the start of a revolution that would have more lasting consequences than any of the others."[19]

Yet, as Anderson shows, it was the news that revolutionary France had outlawed colonial slavery that heartened American abolitionists and that "energized Mott, who had been silent on women's rights for much of the 1840s," to make the European revolutions a theme of her lecture of May 9, 1848, to the American Anti-Slavery Association in New York ("When we look abroad and see what is now being done in other lands, when we see human freedom engaging the attention of the nations of the earth, we may take courage"). And it was this optimism generated by revolutionary Europe that inspired Mott on July 13 to renew contact after eight years with the depressed Elizabeth Cady Stanton in Seneca Falls, New York, and immediately plan with her, with Mott's sister, and with two other Quaker women the famous women's rights convention of the following week. Nor does that convention seem quite so highly exceptional when we learn that in the previous month Joseph Hume had moved in Parliament that all women householders be given the vote, a motion supported by Benjamin Disraeli but nevertheless defeated. In 1848 American attention was so glued to Europe's "springtime of nations" that New York City held a festival on March 25, featuring fourteen addresses in four languages as well as a day-long parade down Broadway. The *New York Herald* arranged in April for special shipments by steamship of copies of *La Presse* from Paris. Only slowly did the news of the bloody "June Days" and later repression begin to set in.

Bonnie Anderson, a professor of history at Brooklyn College and the Graduate Center of the City University of New York, has done extensive research in French, German, English, and American sources that show that by 1847 there were hundreds of feminists in both Europe and America. By "feminists" she means women who knew they were not innately inferior to men and believed they should not be subordinate to them in any way. Anderson has chosen twenty "core women" and twenty-one others "on the periphery of the core group," including women born in France, England, the United States, German states, Poland, Hungary, Finland, Ireland, and Scotland. What is truly remarkable is the way these individuals interacted as editors, public speakers, founders of magazines, letter-writers, and immigrants. Anne Knight, for example, the English Quaker founder of the Sheffield Female Political Association, worked closely in Paris with Jeanne Deroin, one of the radical heroines of Anderson's book, who appears on the first page in 1851 with Pauline Roland in the stone cell of a medieval prison for women, writing letters to their "sisters" abroad.

Many of the women on Anderson's list dealt with Ernestine Rose, the Polish-born daughter of a rabbi who renounced Judaism as she moved from Berlin, Paris, and London to the United States, where among other activities she translated feminist works written in French and German. Unlike the later suffragists, Rose envisioned a "radical and universal" reformation: "It is not the mere perfecting of a progress already in motion, a detail of some established plan, but it is an epochal movement—the emancipation of a class, the redemption of half the world, and a conforming re-organization of all social, political, and industrial interests and institutions."

＊

Unfortunately, perhaps, feminism increasingly became "a detail of some established plan." In Europe it became attached in the 1820s to Owenite and then Saint-Simonian socialism (named after the Englishman Robert Owen and the Frenchman Comte de Saint-Simon). In the United States feminism emerged in a far more religious form from the temperance and antislavery movements, though such figures as Lydia Maria Child, the Grimké sisters, Abby Kelley, and Elizabeth Cady Stanton became increasingly secular in their outlook. Following the Seneca Falls Convention of 1848 Elizabeth Cady Stanton and Elizabeth W. McClintock wrote a long letter to the *Seneca Falls Courier* in response to a hostile sermon they had heard that invoked the Bible:

> No reform has ever been started but the Bible, falsely interpreted, has opposed it. Wine-drinking was proved to be right by the Bible. Slavery was proved to be an institution of the Bible. . . . Capital punishment is taught in the Bible. . . . Why, the self-styled christians of our day have fought in and supported the unjust and cruel Mexican war, and have long held men, women, and children in bondage. Oft-times, when no conclusive arguments can be brought to bear upon a subject, a cry of "infidelity" is raised, that the mind of the public may be prejudiced against it. . . . The wicked Jews made God the author of all their wars and calamities. They claimed for themselves His peculiar guidance.[20]

Radical women began changing the nature of Anglo-American reforms in the mid-1820s, when Elizabeth Cady was nine and Susan B. Anthony four. In 1824 Elizabeth Coltman Heyrick, an English Quaker, published an explosive pamphlet, *Immediate, Not Gradual Abolition; or, An Inquiry into the Shortest, Safest, and Most Effectual Means of Getting Rid of West Indian Slavery.* In America the Quaker abolitionist Benjamin Lundy reprinted this pamphlet in his newspaper, *The Genius of Universal Emancipation,* and by the early 1830s "immediatism" had become the ideal and slogan for most British and American abolitionists.[21]

In 1824 an Irish socialist named Anna Wheeler, who had joined a Saint-Simonian commune in Normandy, persuaded another socialist, William Thompson, to write *Appeal to One Half of the Human Race, Women, Against the Pretensions of the Other Half, Men, To Retain Them in Political, and Thence in Civil and Domestic Slavery,* which was published the next year.[22] Attacking the arguments of James Mill, the father of John Stuart Mill, for excluding women from political rights, Wheeler and Thompson maintained that marriage converted a woman into "the literal unequivocal *slave* of the man who may be styled her husband." Indeed, this tract insisted that married white women were worse off than West Indian slaves since in addition to being owned outright, they were "forced to feign love for masters." Only socialism, it appeared, could liberate women from being forced to submit to men's "caprice of command." Almost identical arguments had been advanced in revolutionary France in the early 1790s, but not connected with socialism, only to revolutionary change in general (Anna and William would have been shocked if they could have seen the sexual powers exercised by the autocratic socialist John Humphrey Noyes in his later and famous Oneida Community).

It was also in 1824 that the wealthy Scot and Owenite socialist Frances Wright began traveling with General Lafayette on his triumphal tour of the United States, visiting the elderly Jefferson and Madison and advocating the emancipation of women as well as slaves. With the aid of Andrew Jackson, Wright bought a tract of land in the western Tennessee wilderness, named it Nashoba, and then purchased a group of slaves with the bold intent of showing by experiment that the blacks could earn the cost of their freedom in five years while also "amalgamating" with white settlers. This sexual freedom, coupled with public whippings of alleged criminals and Wright's long absence and later "infidel" lectures and writings, contributed to a popular image of "that Jezebel beast of a woman." After Nashoba expired in 1830, "Fanny Wright," as she was known, succeeded in "colonizing" about thirty of the blacks in Haiti, but her bold radicalism provided the enemies of feminism with much ammunition.[23]

*

If there were hazards for feminism in becoming an adjunct of socialism or English Chartism—and when the chips were down, P.-J. Proudhon and the Chartists discarded woman's rights as a juvenile, bourgeois, or irrelevant cause—there were similar dangers in relying on male abolitionists. Yet in America hundreds of female abolitionists made the discovery well-summarized by Mary Kelley: "In striving to strike [the slave's] irons off, we found most surely that we were manacled *ourselves*." As we have seen, Wollstonecraft and earlier Continental feminists made use of the slave analogy, which is rooted in the Bible, the *Iliad*, the *Odyssey*, and other ancient literature and law.

The Anglo-American abolitionist movements gave women an unprecedented opportunity to gather and sign petitions; to found their own essentially political and often interracial organizations; to collect funds; to write tracts, pamphlets, and novels; and to engage in public lecturing.[24] The African-American Maria W. Stewart was apparently the first woman of any color to address mixed, or what were called "promiscuous," audiences of men and women.[25] To a Boston audience she stressed in 1832 that the condition of free black women, who were kept by racial prejudice from rising above the rank of servants, was "but little better" than that of southern slaves.[26]

The first American white women to follow Stewart's example were the famous Grimké sisters, Sarah and Angelina, who were born and brought up on a large South Carolina plantation before they moved north to Philadelphia and became Quaker converts. What made them famous, or infamous in the eyes of most northern clergy, was their willingness to challenge even the radical Hicksite Quaker restrictions by lecturing to sexually and racially mixed audiences on the sinfulness of slavery, which they knew firsthand, as well as the need to recognize women's equal rights. Angelina, who would later marry the great abolitionist Theodore Weld, inflamed the South in 1836 with her book *An Appeal to the Christian Women of the South* and two years later became the first woman to speak to an American legislative body as she urged a committee of the Massachusetts legislature to accept the right of women to petition. In the same year her sister published a pioneering feminist work, *Letters on the Equality of Sexes and the Condition of Women*.

But this mixing of races and genders, which became public at the 1838 Second Anti-Slavery Convention of American Women in Philadelphia, provoked a government-sanctioned riot. As the Philadelphia police and fire department remained in willed paralysis, a mob of thousands burned the recently constructed Pennsylvania Hall to the ground and threw piles of abolitionist papers into the Delaware River in a claimed reenactment of the Boston Tea Party.

There were many reasons for the tragic division of the American antislavery movement in 1840. Arthur and Lewis Tappan, wealthy partners in the largest silk-jobbing firm in the country, had during the early 1830s moved from supporting various religious philanthropies, such as the distribution of tracts and campaigning for the strict observance of the Sabbath, as in their native New England, to organized abolitionism. It was Arthur Tappan who paid for William Lloyd Garrison's release from a Baltimore jail in 1830, who then helped finance Garrison's *Liberator* and his first trip to England to forge ties with the triumphant English abolitionists, and who helped to launch the American Anti-Slavery Society late in 1833, becoming its first president.

But the fervently religious Tappan brothers also harbored doubts over Garrison's vague religious beliefs and commitments, doubts that turned into alarm when Garrison denounced America's churches and clergy, attacked the authenticity of the Sabbath, and even repudiated government and all politics, including the duty to vote, on the grounds that government, like slavery, relied ultimately on physical force. Lewis Tappan and other abolitionists who had mobilized an impressive antislavery petition campaign to Congress insisted that "the woman question" was merely the precipitating occasion, not the underlying cause, of the great division of the American Anti-Slavery Society in May 1840. Lewis Tappan told Theodore Weld that the real issue was Garrison's desire "'to make an experiment upon the public' by foisting a host of radical issues upon the Society."[27]

But if Garrison weakened the potential appeal of abolitionism by adopting the perfectionist views of such radical thinkers as John Humphrey Noyes and Henry Clarke Wright, thus challenging the central beliefs and values of the vast majority of Northerners, he also favored gender equality and, unlike the Tappans, had no misgivings about allying himself with Unitarians and Hicksite Quakers. He was thus able to bring from Boston to New York a large boatload of women as well as men for the May 1840 meeting of the American Anti-Slavery Society. Even at the 1839 meeting the Tappans and the separate political abolitionists, who were founding the Liberty party, were disillusioned by the victory of "Boston heresies" when James G. Birney called for a condemnation of the "No-Government" and "Non-Resistance" philosophies and was defeated.

By 1840 plans supported by the Tappans were already afoot to found a rival American and Foreign Anti-Slavery Society, on the British model, barring women from the vote. The crucial test in the May 1840 meeting came when the Garrisonians elected the radical feminist Abby Kelley to the business committee by a vote of 557 to 451. In the eyes of Lewis Tappan, who thereupon resigned, it was highly immoral for a lady to sit behind closed doors with miscellaneous gentlemen. Moreover, Abby Kelley's movement for woman's rights would inevitably alienate many potential supporters of slave emancipation. The veteran Quaker abolitionist and poet John Greenleaf Whittier seemed to agree, as he wrote in a half-humorous vein after the meeting: "I am getting rather off from woman's rights. . . . This last exploit of my good friend Abby in blowing up the Amer.A.Slavery Society is too much for me. Abolition women. . . . Think of the conduct of Mrs. Adam— how Delilah shaved Samson—how Helen got up the Trojan War—and last but not least this affair of Abby's and the society."[28]

＊

In an influential book of 1976, the historian Ronald G. Walters presented strong arguments against the view, endorsed even by Garrison, that this schism seriously weakened the antislavery cause.[29] After years of reflection, I have changed my mind and have concluded that Walters was wrong. Without becoming immersed in details, I'm impressed by the fact that it was a united if diverse movement in Britain, including thousands of women, that achieved the abolition of colonial slavery and ex-slave "apprenticeship" at remarkably early dates. A united movement in America might have done much more to build on the Supreme Court's *Amistad* decision of 1841—which set free the rebels on a Spanish-owned slave ship—to prevent or delay the annexation of Texas as a slave state, and perhaps even to curb or modify some of the proslavery actions that followed. Besides, the linkage of American abolitionism and feminism also led in 1840 to what Anderson calls "a decisive defeat for the supporters of women's rights" at the World Anti-Slavery Convention in London.[30]

American abolitionists elected seven female delegates to the Convention, including Lucretia Mott and the young bride Elizabeth Cady Stanton, who accompanied her delegate husband, Henry. The British leaders of the eminent British and Foreign Anti-Slavery Society refused to accept the American women's credentials and consigned them to the role of nonvoting spectators in a roped-off chamber of Freemasons Hall. Although the occasion allowed

British and American feminists to fraternize, and the outraged Mott and Stanton talked about holding a woman's rights convention sometime in the future, Anderson compares the setback to the one suffered by French feminists with the collapse of Saint-Simonianism in 1834. It is surely significant that after 1840 the American *antislavery* women never held a fourth convention of their own.

Despite the "joyous" revival of international feminism from 1848 to the mid-1850s, one can see in the tensions of 1840 a conflict over priorities, or the relative unimportance of feminism compared to abolitionism, which would much later lead Stanton and Anthony to adopt shockingly racist language, arguments, and even form coalitions with racists when they felt betrayed by male abolitionists who failed to fight for the inclusion of female rights in the Fourteenth and Fifteenth Amendments. Wendell Phillips expressed the male abolitionists' position when he insisted, "'One question at a time.' This is the negro's hour." In response, Stanton and Anthony denounced the Fifteenth Amendment for establishing "an aristocracy of sex on this continent." Stanton wrote: "Think of Patrick and Sambo and Hans and Yung Tung who do not know the difference between a Monarchy and a Republic, who never read the Declaration of Independence or Webster's spelling book, making laws for Lydia Maria Child, Lucretia Mott, or Fanny Kemble."[31]

Stanton and Anthony further alienated themselves from Charles Sumner, Phillips, Garrison, Horace Greeley, and Frederick Douglass and other blacks by allying themselves with George Francis Train, a wartime copperhead, racist, and millionaire who financed their newspaper *The Revolution*, and who took joy in crying out "nigger, nigger, nigger" as he tried to help Stanton and Anthony win woman's suffrage in Kansas by opposing the enfranchisement of blacks. This development was especially painful to Frederick Douglass, who had attended the Seneca Falls Convention of 1848 and whose eloquent support had helped gain passage of the controversial demand for woman's suffrage.

As if in imitation of the 1840 abolitionists, the post–Civil War feminists divided into two hostile groups, pitting Stanton and Anthony against Lucy Stone and such figures as Julia Ward Howe. According to Anderson, the vision of *full* equality and international cooperation gave way to more isolated and nationalistic efforts to win suffrage state by state. Before 1900, Wyoming, Utah, Colorado, and Idaho had granted women full suffrage, and in 1911 the new Progressive device of public initiative—conferring the right to change legislation by demand—brought triumph to the cause in Oregon.[32] In 1915, however, New York defeated the measure after a major feminist campaign.

The documentary film by Ken Burns and Paul Barnes aired on PBS in 1999 and the accompanying book by Geoffrey C. Ward and Burns are much-needed efforts to inform the general public about the early stages of the American feminist movement, encapsulated in the long lives and remarkable partnership of Stanton and Anthony.[33] The authors are well known for their documentary films and books on the Civil War and baseball. Clearly the background sounds of a guitar, violin, chirping birds, and a piano playing "Rally Round the Flag" cannot match the roll of Civil War drums, the crunch of marching troops, and the rumble of cannons as the viewer moves from Bull Run to Appomattox. But despite some petty criticisms and complaints of boredom I have heard from a few historians and editors, Burns and Barnes are masters at bringing still photos to life on a television screen and having significant passages from letters, diaries, and proclamations read aloud in a moving way. I can well empathize with their frustration in not being able to find a single photograph in which the incredibly grim-faced Susan B. Anthony smiles or even shows a trace of happiness.[34]

For a documentary on the feminist revolution, whether in print or film, the key document is the "Declaration of Sentiments," written by Stanton and her four colleagues, and followed by eleven resolutions that were also adopted by the Seneca Falls Convention of 1848. While the film conveys accurately the nature of the "Declaration" and resolutions, there can be no substitute for reading the full texts, which are included in the book and which should be required reading for all high school students in America, especially males.

Previous reform groups had used Jefferson's Declaration of Independence as a model for expressing their rights and grievances, but Stanton (who seems to have been the principal author) could not have been more imaginative and eloquent in moving from the "self-evident" truth "that all men and women are created equal" to the "long train of abuses" illustrating the fact that "the history of mankind is a history of repeated injuries and usurpations on the part of man toward woman, having in direct object the establishment of an absolute tyranny over her." And in truth Jefferson's indictments of George III for extending southwestward the laws and jurisdiction of Quebec, for exciting "domestic insurrection among us" (i.e., Lord Dunmore's proclamation in Virginia that he would free any slaves who joined his ranks), and for imperiling "our frontiers" with "the merciless Indian savages," pale when compared with the women's indictments of male rule. For example:

He has compelled her to submit to laws, in the formation of which she had no voice. . . .

He has made her, if married, in the eye of the law, civilly dead.

He has taken from her all right in property, even to the wages she earns. . . .

He has monopolized nearly all the profitable employments, and from those she is permitted to follow, she receives but a scanty remuneration. . . .

He has denied her the facilities for obtaining a thorough education, all colleges being closed against her. . . .

He has endeavored, in every way that he could, to destroy her confidence in her own powers, to lessen her self-respect, and to make her willing to lead a dependent and abject life.

Similar indictments had been made in Europe in the eighteenth century, but they had been attacked, mocked, and largely forgotten. The American feminists of 1848 acknowledged that "we anticipate no small amount of misconception, misrepresentation, and ridicule," but vowed to "use every instrumentality within our power to effect our object," from tracts, agents, and petitions to "a series of Conventions embracing every part of the country."

The Euro-American feminist movement, from the 1820s through the 1850s, presented a direct challenge to the most deeply rooted and ancient form of human inequality and exploitation. Subordinating one-half of the world's population, this inequality was so deep, from the domestic to the state level, that it seemed invisible and "natural" to most women as well as men. Thus while all the essential feminist demands and arguments had been made by the 1840s if not earlier, and while hundreds of activists in America, Britain, France, and the Germanic states shared a cheering sense of like-mindedness and what Bonnie Anderson calls "joyous greetings," they failed to provide any institutional continuity of the kind achieved, for example, by the British and Foreign Anti-Slavery Society. Feminism suffered in Europe from the failure of various forms of socialism and in the United States from the Civil War and continuing racial divide. Probably because it attacked male privileges that seemed so "natural," no other revolutionary cause has been so subject to ridicule and mockery. Yet as feminists continued to emphasize that it was manmade privileges and inequalities that violated nature, the opposition became more alarmed and serious.[35] As Carrie Chapman Catt told the International Woman's Suffrage Association meeting in Budapest in 1913:

> When movements are new and weak, Parliaments laugh at them; when they are in their educational stages, Parliaments meet them with silent contempt; when they are ripe and ready to become law, Parliaments evade responsibility. Our movement has reached the last stage. . . . Parliaments have stopped laughing at woman suffrage, and politicians have begun to dodge! it is the inevitable premonition of coming victory.[36]

Because feminism challenges our very understanding of "nature," then, it is a revolution with many stages. The Declaration of 1848 stood halfway between 1776 and the winning of woman's suffrage in America in 1920.[37] Another seventy-two years brings us to 1992, by which time women had made enormous gains in higher education, the professions, and the labor force in general thanks to the renewal of feminist demands in the late 1960s and 1970s, accompanied by affirmative action and laws prohibiting discrimination based on sex and race. By 2064, after another seventy-two years, one hopes that something approaching full equality will be spreading from the United States and the most "developed" nations to much of the rest of the world, perhaps even Afghanistan.

Notes

This is a revised version of an essay printed in the *New York Review of Books*, October 5, 2000, pp. 42–47. I am much indebted to Dr. Karen Offen, Historian and Senior Scholar at the Stanford Institute for Research on Women and Gender, for sending me several essays that helped me revise one part of the essay. Unfortunately, Dr. Offen's *European Feminisms, 1700–1950: A Political History* (Stanford University Press, 2000), appeared too late to be included in this review essay.

1. Andrew Hacker, "The Unmaking of Men," *The New York Review*, October 21, 1999, p. 26, table A.

2. William T. Vollmann, "Across the Divide: What do the Afghan people think of the Taliban?" *The New Yorker*, May 15, 2000, pp. 58–73.

3. Gerda Lerner, *The Creation of Patriarchy* (Oxford University Press, 1986). I won't try to speculate on the origins of female subordination or women's apparent complicity in accepting and transmitting such a patriarchal system from generation to generation. "There is not a single society known," Lerner observes, "where women-as-a-group have decision-making power *over* men or where they define the rules of sexual conduct or control marriage exchanges" (p. 30). I think Lerner is right in linking prehistoric patri-archal power over women with the enslavement of war captives, but this is necessarily speculative. The modern achievements of women from the Olympics to physics clearly disprove all theories of innate inferiority. What now seems so striking, especially in view of hundreds of years of female protest, is the lateness of effective feminism and the continuing depth and power of male resistance.

4. See my essay "At the Heart of Slavery" in this volume.

5. Linda K. Kerber, *Toward an Intellectual History of Women: Essays by Linda K. Kerber* (University of North Carolina Press, 1977), p. 48.

6. For the nineteenth-century French origins of the word "feminism" and justification for using it historically, see Karen Offen, "Sur les origines des mots 'féminisme' et féministe,'" *Revue d'histoire moderne et contemporaine* (Paris) volume 34, number 23 (July–September 1987), pp. 492–496, and Offen, "Defining Feminism: A Comparative Historical Approach," *Signs: Journal of Women in Culture and Society*, volume 14, num-ber 1, pp. 119–157.

7. Karen Offen, "Reclaiming the European Enlightenment for Feminism: Or Prologomena to any future history of eighteenth-century Europe," in *Perspectives on Feminist Political Thought in European History: From the Middle Ages to the Present*, edited by Tjitske Ak-kerman and Siep Stuurmann (Routledge: London, 1998), pp. 85–103; Offen, "Women's Memory, Women's History, Women's Political Action: The French Revolu-tion in Retrospect, 1789–1889–1989," *Journal of Women's History*, Vol. 1, Number 3 (Winter 1990), pp. 211–230.

8. Rebecca Larson, *Daughters of Light: Quaker Preaching and Prophesying in the Colonies and Abroad, 1700–1775* (Knopf, 1999), pp. 94, 182, 185, 292–295, 302–303; David Brion Davis, *The Problem of Slavery in the Age of Revolution, 1770–1823* (Oxford Uni-versity Press, 1999; originally published 1975), pp. 213–254. Unfortunately, in the nineteenth century Quaker leaders became more conservative and often rebuked Friends who joined with outsiders in radical antislavery activities. The "Hicksite Quak-ers," following the schism led by Elias Hicks in the late 1820s, were more active in the struggles for women's rights and slave emancipation.

9. *The Boisterous Sea of Liberty: A Documentary History of America from Discovery to the Civil War*, edited by David Brion Davis and Steven Mintz (Oxford University Press, 1998), pp. 195–196.

10. For a comparative analysis of Wollstonecraft's work, see Karen Offen, "Was Mary Wollstonecraft a Feminist? A Contextual Re-reading of *A Vindication of the Rights of Woman, 1792–1992*," in *Quilting a New Canon: Stitching Women's Words*, edited by Uma Parameswaran (Sister Vision: Black Women and Women of Color Press, 1996), pp. 3–24. Offen concludes that Wollstonecraft *was* a feminist.

11. Alexis de Tocqueville, *Democracy in America*, edited by Phillips Bradley, translated by Henry Reeve (2 vols., Vintage Books, 1945), II, p. 212.

12. Bonnie S. Anderson, *Joyous Greetings: The First International Women's Movement, 1830–1860* (Oxford University Press, 2000) p. 70.

13. Joan D. Hedrick, *Harriet Beecher Stowe: A Life* (Oxford University Press, 1994), pp. 82–85.

14. Neither Stanton nor Anthony favored abortion.

15. To Susan B. Anthony's dismay, Stanton actually had one more son in 1859, at age forty-three.

16. See Ellen Carol DuBois's biography of Elizabeth Cady Stanton's remarkable daughter, *Harriot Stanton Blatch and the Winning of Woman Suffrage* (Yale University Press, 1997). When editing her mother's papers, Harriot made no effort to hide her mother's anguish over Harriot's apparently unplanned and unwanted birth.

17. Like Bonnie Anderson, I generally use "woman's movement" and "woman's rights," the phrases used in the nineteenth century, instead of the plural "women's."

18. Harvard University Press, 1959.

19. The few sentences in Ward's book on the Revolutions of 1848 (pp. 38–39) are used simply as a buildup to the Seneca Falls Convention. An uninformed reader would think that it was purely coincidental that the Seneca Falls Convention occurred in 1848. Because Ward and Burns present Stanton and Anthony as the initiators of the feminist revolution, they ignore many crucial people and events preceding 1848—in America as well as Europe, though the book does include a short and helpful essay by Martha Saxton that deals with Abigail Adams, Mary Wollstonecraft, Lydia Maria Child, and Frances Wright). France, unfortunately, they ignore.

20. *The Selected Papers of Elizabeth Cady Stanton and Susan B. Anthony*, Volume I: *In the School of Anti-Slavery, 1840–1866*, edited by Ann D. Gordon (Rutgers University Press, 1998), pp. 89–90. This collection, coupled with Ann Gordon's Volume II: *Against an Aristocracy of Sex, 1866–1873* (Rutgers University Press, 2000), will be indispensable for future studies of American feminism.

21. See my essay, "The Emergence of Immediatism in British and American Antislavery Thought," in Davis, *From Homicide to Slavery: Studies in American Culture* (Oxford University Press, 1986), pp. 238–257. Heyrick's influential pamphlet was first published anonymously.

22. Although Thompson was presented as the author, since in 1825 works by males were taken far more seriously, Anderson stresses that Wheeler inspired Thompson to write down what she had "so often and so well stated in conversation, and under feigned names in such of the periodical publications of the day as would tolerate such a theme."

23. Nevertheless, Elizabeth Cady Stanton and Susan B. Anthony read Wright's last book in

1848 and used her attractive portrait for the frontispiece of their 1881 *History of Woman Suffrage* (Anderson, *Joyous Greetings*, pp. 79–80, 164). Since Owen attacked the degradation and exploitation of women, his socialist journal, the *Crisis*, had considerable influence on such central figures as Harriet Martineau, Ernestine Rose and her husband, William, and John Stuart Mill and his wife, Harriet Taylor.

24. For the crucial role of women in the antislavery movement, see Julie Roy Jeffrey, *The Great Silent Army of Abolitionism: Ordinary Women in the Antislavery Movement* (University of North Carolina Press, 1998), which was the runner-up for the Frederick Douglass Book Prize in 1999. For a new and extremely useful collection of documents, coupled with a long and authoritative introduction, see Kathryn Kish Sklar, *Women's Rights Emerges Within the Antislavery Movement, 1830–1870* (Bedford/St. Martin's, 2000).

25. Maria W. Stewart is not listed in Ward and Burns's index, but she is well known to historians, and two of her lectures appear in *The Norton Anthology of African American Literature*, edited by Henry Louis Gates, Jr., and Nellie Y. McKay (Norton, 1997), pp. 201–207.

26. Anderson, *Joyous Greetings*, p. 117.

27. Henry Mayer, *All on Fire: William Lloyd Garrison and the Abolition of Slavery* (St. Martin's Press, 1998), p. 282.

28. Anderson, *Joyous Greetings*, p. 126.

29. Walters, *The Antislavery Appeal: American Abolitionism after 1830* (Johns Hopkins University Press, 1976). Walters even contends that the movement was strengthened by division and a greater range of choices.

30. Anderson, *Joyous Greetings*, p. 128.

31. Elizabeth Cady Stanton, "Manhood Suffrage," in Ann D. Gordon, ed., *The Selected Papers of Elizabeth Cady Stanton and Susan B. Anthony*, volume II: *Against an Aristocracy of Sex* (New Brunswick, N.J.), p. 196.

32. For an extremely insightful and up-to-date account of the long struggle that led to the Nineteenth Amendment of 1920, which extended universal suffrage to women in America one year after Great Britain had enfranchised a privileged group of women, a step toward full suffrage in 1928, see DuBois, *Harriot Stanton Blatch*.

33. As a historian, and more-or-less familiar with school textbooks, I found it amazing to hear Burns say that he and Barnes had never heard of Elizabeth Cady Stanton until Barnes read a biography shortly before they decided to make this film.

34. Anthony's letters in Ann D. Gordon's first two published volumes of a planned six-volume set, *Selected Papers of Elizabeth Cady Stanton and Susan B. Anthony* (Rutgers University Press, 2000) portray a personality entirely different from the stiff, grim, and almost frightening photographs. Anthony either hated cameras or could not adjust to them.

35. In 1867 Stanton and Anthony kept appealing to Frederick Douglass and Sojourner Truth as well as to the racist millionaire George F. Train ("God bless you. . . . Yes, with your help we shall triumph"). *Selected Papers*, II, pp. 11–12, 47, 95.

36. Quoted by Karen Offen in a letter to me of October 2, 2000.

37. As already indicated, some states, beginning with Wyoming and Utah Territories in the 1860s, had adopted woman's suffrage before 1920.

Credits

The following essays are reprinted with the permission of their publishers and/or copyright holders.

"Martin Luther King, Jr." (originally titled "Pride and Prejudice"), *The New Republic*, 5 January 1987, 34–38.

"Religion and American Culture" (originally titled "Review Essay, *Encyclopedia of the American Religious Experience*"), *Religion and American Culture* 1, no. 1 (February 1991). Copyright © 1991 Center for the Study of Religion and American Culture.

"The Other Zion: American Jews and the Meritocratic Experiment," *The New Republic*, 12 April 1993, 29–36.

"The Significance of the Northwest Ordinance of 1787" (originally titled "The Significance of Excluding Slavery from the Old Northwest Ordinance in 1787"), *Indiana Magazine of History* (March 1988), 75–89.

"Capitalism, Abolitionism, and Hegemony," in *British Capitalism and the Caribbean Slavery: The Legacy of Eric Williams,* ed. Barbara Solow and Stanley L. Engerman (Cambridge: Cambridge University Press, 1987). A slightly different version of this essay appeared in *The American Historical Review* 92, no. 4 (October 1987), 747–812.

Index

'abd, as black slave, 141, 339n17
abolitionism: British, and Cuban slave trade,
    183; economic costs of, 193, 211; and femi-
    nism, 367, 369–71; and ideological hegem-
    ony, 218, 227–31 passim; and Protestant
    Christianity, 143; in the United States, 231
abolitionists: and Abraham Lincoln, 304n8; and
    Amistad affair, 186, 187–88; and Anglo-
    American slavery, 157; black, 291–92, 295,
    299; and black dehumanization, 347–48; and
    consequences of emancipation, 332–33; and
    free wage labor, 220–21; and labor discipline,
    157; and sexual abuse of female slaves, 253
"abroad marriages," 286
Adams, John, 152, 163n3, 172, 173
Adams, John Quincy, 186, 187, 188
affirmative action: and African-American fami-
    lies, 281, 283; and ethnic quotas, 85; and the
    quota ideal, 59
Africa: and Atlantic slave trade, 63–65; as Dark
    Continent, 143; emigration to, by American
    blacks, 81–82; and Islamic slave market, 147–
    48; tribal distinctions in, 64–65, 155
African Americans: and colonization, 81, 336,
    338, 344, 348; and emigration to Northern
    cities, 353–54; family and social relationships
    of, in antebellum Virginia, 277–89; genetic
    diversity of, 335–36; and inner-city crisis, 345;
    and intermarriage, 87–88, 335–36; and Jewish
    history of liberation, 77–80; and mutual-
    protection organizations, 256; and other im-
    migrant groups, 59; and relationship with

American Jews, 73–91; as sharecroppers, 353;
    as slaveowners, 71; upward mobility of, and
    racism, 333–38
Africans: and "black" classification, 141; com-
    pared to Native Americans, 315–17; as inden-
    tured workers, 210; as innocent children of
    nature, 133, 134; as Muslims, 148; as partici-
    pants in slave trade, 64–65, 152, 155, 316
Agrarians, Southern, 117, 118
Ahlstrom, Sydney E., 37, 38
American Colonization Society, 81
American Revolution, 170; black participation
    in, 274n1; and British capitalism, 206; and
    change in moral vision, 133–35; and Country
    mentality, 170; and gender equality, 361; and
    human slavery, 195; as model of liberation, 79;
    and principle of emancipation, 346–47; and
    Quakers, 361
Amistad mutiny, 184–88, 369
Anderson, Bonnie S., Joyous Greetings: The First
    International Women's Movement, 359, 363–
    71
Angola, as source for slaves, 68, 316
animalization: of Africans, 310–11, 316–17; and
    emergence of antislavery thought, 131; of
    peasants and "lower orders," 314–15; and
    slavery, 126–30
Anstey, Roger, 217, 229
Anthony, Susan B., 362, 363, 365, 370
anti-Semitism: and Atlantic slave trade, 63–71;
    of blacks, 58–59; and immigration policy, 53–
    54; and the Inquisition, 65, 68, 160; and

anti-Semitism (continued)
Jewish achievement, 51, 52; and Jewish support for African Americans, 75; and Marcus Garvey, 82–83; and quotas, 57–58
antislavery ideology: and global capitalist economy, 192–202; moral concepts of, 198; origins of, 131–32, 218–20
antislavery movement: in Britain, 175, 212–15, 231, 269–71; divisions within, 365–68; in France, 213, 232; religious character of, 63–64, 131–32; and eighteenth-century change in moral vision, 133–35; and woman's rights schism, 369–71
antislavery policy, economic costs of, 210–12
antislavery societies, 230, 231, 368, 369
antislavery thought, emergence of, 131–32
Antwerp, as center for sugar refining, 160, 180
Aptheker, Herbert, 111, 167, 291
Arab merchants, and African slave trading, 64, 141, 146–48
Aristotle, on slavery, 123, 126, 128–29, 150n10, 326, 328, 360
Asian textiles, and Atlantic slave trade, 152, 181
Asian workers, indentured, 193, 210
asiento contracts, and slave trading, 69, 160
assimilation: and identity, 87–88, 89–90n16; and Jewish achievement, 59–60
Atlantic slave system, 130–32; creation of, 309, 310, 316; and Federalist policies, 174–76; participants in, 63–64
Atlantic slave trade, 151–64; as "Black Holocaust," 77; and Constitutional Convention, 196; effect of, on family and social authority, 282; and European industrialization, 208–12; and industrial capitalism, 193–96; Jewish participation in, 63–72; and number of Africans exported, eighteenth century, 178; and number of slaves imported, 1811–60, 194
Auld family, and Frederick Douglass, 242–44
Axe Laid to the Root (periodical), 225, 331

Bahia, sugar production in, 179–80
Baldwin, James, 347
Baldwin, Roger, 186–88
Barbados: declining profitability of, 207–8; Jewish population of, 70; slave uprising in, 271, 302; and sugar industry, 69
Barnes, Paul, Not for Ourselves Alone (documentary film), 359, 363–64, 371–73
Barrett, Leonard E., 43–44
Bartels, Emily C., 308, 313, 316, 329

Belmonte, Manuel de, 69–70
benevolence, ethic of, and British Protestantism, 133
Benjamin, Jacob, 77, 91n31
Bensch, Stephen P., 158, 320
Berbers: army of, and black slaves, 318, 329; caravan trade of, 158; and trans-Saharan slave trade, 63, 64, 319
Berbice, slave revolt in, 261
Berlin, Ira, 292, 293, 329
bestialization: of Africans, 310; and Islamic enslavement, 328; of "lower orders," 313–14; and slavery, 126–30
Bible: and color prejudice, 144; and curse of Canaan (Ham and Cain), 309–14 passim, 328–29, 347; interpretations of, and reform, 365; slave analogies in, and feminism, 367; and themes of bondage and liberation, 79–80
Birney, James G., 200, 368
Biruni, Muslim scholar, 313
black, as term: for classification, 141; and lower orders, 314; for peasants or serfs, 326–27; religious meanings of, 77, 318; and skin color, 145
Black Abolitionist Papers project, 291–92
Blackburn, Robin, 309, 313, 320; The Making of New World Slavery: From the Baroque to the Modern, 1492–1800, 151–64; The Overthrow of Colonial Slavery, 1776–1848, 260, 267–72
blackface performance, 74, 78
black nationalism, 74, 82, 83
blacks: emigration and colonization of, 81, 82, 239, 336, 338, 344, 348; expulsion of, from Europe, 77; and Jews, 58–59, 63–72, 73–91; and sexuality, 287, 288n7, 301–2; as soldiers in Union army, 240, 299, 302–3; upward mobility of, 333–38. See also free blacks
Black Sea area, slave trade in, 147, 158, 159, 320
Blake, William, 262, 264
Blatch, Harriot Stanton, 363, 375n16
Blyden, Edward, 82
B'nai B'rith, 56, 83
bondage, human, 143–44; and chattel property, 131; and New World slavery, 157
Bondi, August, 77, 91n31
Bowden, Henry Warner, 39, 43
Brackman, Harold, 88n3, 325
Bradford, M. E., 117, 118
Braude, Benjamin, 309–10, 312–13, 318, 319, 329